ARCHAEOLOGY, HISTORY, AND CUSTER'S LAST BATTLE

ARCHAEOLOGY, HISTORY, AND CUSTER'S LAST BATTLE

The Little Big Horn Reexamined

By Richard Allan Fox, Jr.
Foreword by W. Raymond Wood

UNIVERSITY OF OKLAHOMA PRESS : NORMAN AND LONDON

By Richard Allan Fox, Jr.

Grass, Tipis, and Black Gold (coauthor) (Billings, Mont., 1976)
Archaeological Insights into the Custer Battle: An Assessment of the 1984 Field Season (coauthor) (Norman, 1987)
Archaeological Perspectives on the Battle of the Little Big Horn (coauthor) (Norman, 1989)
Archaeology, History, and Custer's Last Battle: The Little Big Horn Reexamined (Norman, 1993)

Library of Congress Cataloging-in-Publication Data

Fox, Richard A.
　　Archaeology, history, and Custer's last battle : the Little Big Horn reexamined / by Richard Allan Fox, Jr. ; foreword by W. Raymond Wood. — 1st ed.
　　　　p.　cm.
　　Revision of thesis (Ph. D.)—University of Calgary, 1988.
　　Includes bibliographical references (p.　　) and index.
　　ISBN 0-8061-2496-2 (alk. paper)
　　1. Little Big Horn, Battle of the, 1876. 2. Little Big Horn Battlefield National Monument (Mont.)—Antiquities. 3. United States. Army. Cavalry, 7th. 4. Indians of North America—Montana—Antiquities. 5. Montana—Antiquities. I. Title.
E83.876.F6　1993　　　　　　　　　　　　　　　　　　　　　　92-31269
973.8′2—dc20　　　　　　　　　　　　　　　　　　　　　　　　　　CIP

The paper in this book meets the guidelines for permanence and durability of the Committee on Production Guidelines for Book Longevity of the Council on Library Resources, Inc. ∞

Published by the University of Oklahoma Press, Norman, Publishing Division of the University. Copyright © 1993 by Richard Allan Fox, Jr. All rights reserved. Manufactured in the U.S.A.

2　　　3　　　4　　　5　　　6　　　7　　　8　　　9　　　10

With respect and admiration, this volume
is dedicated to the memory of
WALTER MASON CAMP

CONTENTS

Part Six. Closing

FIGURES

FOREWORD

By W. Raymond Wood

The battle of the Little Big Horn has aroused controversy from its conclusion on June 26, 1876, to the present day. This one battle has perhaps generated more scholarship (good, bad, and indifferent) than any comparable clash of arms in history. It holds a fascination for both amateur and professional historians that many find enigmatic, and a parade of books and articles chronicling both sides of the conflict continues to appear year after year. Unlike so many rewrites of this confrontation, however, the present study adds significantly to that literature. No single source can hope to resolve all the problems that worry historians of this event, but the present synthesis departs from the traditional dependence on conventional documents and oral accounts by providing fresh archaeological data from a previously untapped source: the material remains left by George Armstrong Custer's men and their Sioux and Cheyenne Indian antagonists.

Archaeology is commonly thought of as investigating the prehistory of humankind. In truth, however, the discipline has been concerned with historical events from its inception: Heinrich Schliemann's late-nineteenth-century investigations at Troy launched serious classical and historical archaeological research. Today the techniques of excavation and analysis developed by past generations of archaeologists are finding applications outside the usual confines of the profession. Refining our understanding of recent warfare is not in the mainstream of modern archaeology, but it does fall within the definition of archaeology as the study of artifacts in relation to human behavior, prehistoric or historic. Techniques and approaches devised for clarifying prehistoric problems have been applied successfully to recent events as disparate as the industrial revolution and World War II. Fox also has devised new analytical strategies for getting at behavior that is restricted in space *and* time—an unusual circumstance for archaeology—including tracking combatants across the landscape using cartridge-case-signature analyses.

In this study Fox attempts to deduce human behavior from the material remains found on the Custer battlefield, recognizing and describing battle events principally from archaeological evidence. He views these data from the perspective of combat modeling, then correlates this information with documentary and oral historical records. He goes further, claiming that whenever an historical event has left physical traces, its history is not complete until archaeology has been done. This is a conclusion many historians will reject, but archaeologists will find it consistent with both their theory and past findings. In this book physical evidence, in the form of battlefield by-products, takes precedence over and guides the interpretation of documentary data. "The ground itself [and, we might add, what it contains] is a document which the scholar must not neglect," as the historian Robin W. Winks once said.

Archaeologists and historians agree that history is a construction of past events, never a reconstruction. Such constructions more closely approximate past actuality, however, when the approach used to derive them is holistic, and when it begins without an emotional bias. Fox's construction is based on his knowledge of battlefield behavior theory in general, the physical remains at the Custer battle site, the insights provided by combat modeling, and the documentary and oral-history base. This approach, in his words, "forces the fair investigator to recognize and shed preconceived notions," and it is obvious to even the most novice reader on Custer and the Little Big Horn battle that preconceptions about that engagement are almost as common as are undisputed facts.

Indeed, the Custer battle of today is mostly a romantic story of fate, of doomed soldiers forced on the defensive by an overwhelming force, and of a futile but stalwart resistance—sometimes to the last man and last bullet. But Fox argues that the artifacts record a sudden, unexpected, and irreversible collapse in the tactical capabilities of Custer's force. Fox sees little evidence of a determined struggle, let alone a defensive posture ordained by fate. When the documents are analyzed in the light of archaeology, there emerges an offensive strategy, one which, in vivid scenes of panic and flight, suddenly sputters and rapidly fades away.

This is an important book. It will be warmly debated by Custer aficionados for a very long time, especially those who prefer the fatalistic theme and the romantic image of a "glorious defiance," of a last stand. The latter will reject Fox's construction of the troops' loss of tactical stability in proximity to the enemy and will spurn the notion that jammed carbines, ammunition depletion, poor training, inadequate unit pride, and fatigue contributed nothing to the disintegration of Custer's battalion. Fox presents an integrated story of what happened that day, not without some ambiguities, but certainly within the hard boundaries of the evidence. The resulting narrative is every bit as interesting as any of those based on whimsy, intuition, or fantasy.

The real significance of this study, however, perhaps lies more in what it tries to say and do than in what it has done. Battlefield archaeology is a new area of study. Fox has shown that it is as important to understanding combat in general as it is crucial to this one battle, popular and overestimated as that confrontation may be. Many past interpretations of this and other bygone battles are more often based on intuition than on knowledge of military tactics particular to the time of the conflict. There are the many studies "on war," by, for example, Clausewitz, Du Picq, Jomini, and Liddell Hart. But such studies of strategy do not affect the common soldier in the heat of battle. It is in the latter area that modern studies by J. Baynes, S. L. A. Marshall, and others, prove important on combat effectiveness as a function of morale, combat cohesion, and stress, for they reinforce an alternative view of how Custer's battalion acted in the face of enemy action on the Little Big Horn. This study demonstrates that the integration of archaeology, combat modeling, and history inevitably will bring us closer to the truth of past events. Scholars of military history will be as intrigued with this book as Custer fans will be, because it provides a model for the study of other confrontations.

PREFACE

This book about the Custer battle has been some time in the making. The first version appeared in 1988 as my Ph.D. dissertation ("Discerning History through Archaeology: The Custer Battle," University of Calgary). Since then, others have reviewed my work and offered considerable input, and I have had the time to hone my ideas. The result is this volume, which, like the dissertation, paints a Custer battle quite unlike all versions that have come before. My story is unique because it uses archaeology as an interpretive foundation, just as in the dissertation. But here more historical data are added, and I have revamped my conception of how the strategic environment fueled this affair. But that comes later. For now I should like to pay my debts in the currency of recognition, for no work springs wholly from an author in isolation.

The whole thing began in 1983 when a range fire swept across the Custer battlefield. James V. Court, then the superintendent of this National Park Service facility, invited me to look the ground over, rid as it was of obscuring vegetation. He wondered what, in terms of an archaeological record of the battle, might be left that would aid in his public interpretive mission. So I checked out the field and prepared two reports in which I argued that the physical traces of Custer's last battle exhibited significant interpretive potential. This led to more investigations. Much has already come of Superintendent Court's well-informed curiosity, and this work is the latest chapter. In a sea of indifference, he understood the value of archaeology. His foresight, dedication, and assistance have produced information of immeasurable value.

Douglas D. Scott, Chief of the Rocky Mountain Division, Midwest Archeological Center (National Park Service), reviewed my initial reports. He too saw great potential and subsequently organized a two-year archeological project (1984–85). He and I participated as coprincipal investigators, and in fact, the data base used here resulted from that work. Working with him has been a great experience, and I wish to acknowledge his considerable input. Hats off, too, to the other project principals: Melissa Connors, Dick Harmon, Vance Haynes, Clyde Snow, and Neil Mangum, then Chief Historian at Custer Battlefield National Monument. (I refer to the Custer Battlefield National Monument throughout the book. When I submitted this manuscript to my publisher, that was the name. Now it is officially, and aptly, the Little Bighorn Battlefield National Monument.)

During 1984–85, other talented folks came to us from around the nation (and beyond) as volunteers expert in Custer battle matters and in the use of metal detectors. From them I learned that a metal detector in any hands does not a metal-detecting machine make. Our project could not have succeeded without these volunteers, and I am more than grateful for their help.

Our volunteers' names appear in two books on Custer archaeology that Douglas Scott and I helped author (see References Cited under "Scott, D. D."). Those two volumes are mostly descriptive. This one is very different; it is a synthesis based on both archaeology and history. Apparent inconsistencies between this and the earlier works might be a function of authorship (the other books are products of multiple writers) or of the modifications that ideas and details usually undergo in the process of synthesis—the logical outcome of descriptive analysis. In fact, I have changed my thinking in some ways. This is normal, and I hope whatever differences crop up do not lead to confusion.

Funding came from the Custer Battlefield Historical and Museum Association, a nonprofit friends-of-the-battlefield organization headquartered at the national monument (Custer Battlefield, Crow Agency, MT 59022). Guided by the association officers, plus Shirley Coates and LeAnn Simpson (Executive Directors), the association made the financial arrangements that supported our work. However I said thank you, it would end up a colossal understatement. In addition, the Midwest Archeological Center furnished research and laboratory facilities, and so did the Nebraska State Highway Patrol Criminalistic Laboratory. F. A. Calabrese and his staff at the center supported us all the way. Esley Kotschwar and Mark Bohaty of the patrol introduced us to firearm identification analysis.

I might add that there is a helpful staff at the national monument as well. They go out of their way to accommodate my inquiries. During fieldwork we kept them busy with all kinds of requests. Can I borrow the Cushman? Do you have some shovels? Can I use the archives? Will you fill in that trench? Can we stay in the apartments? Yes you can, yes we do, and sure, we'll do that—every time. We had fun. Thanks!

Much of what you find herein is the result of urging and direction from my dissertation committee. Thanks go to them—Drs. James Deetz, Jane Kelley, B. O. K. Reeves, and Donald Smith—and especially to my supervisor and friend Dr. Richard Forbis. I had the good fortune to conduct much of my research at the University of Calgary while supported by an Izaak Walton Killam Memorial Scholarship. I am grateful for the generous stipend provided and the honor bestowed. Thanks also for the research stipend awarded by the University of Calgary Graduate School.

Two individuals especially stand out because they helped me in every phase of my writings, from the very beginning until now. They are Michael Moore and

Brian Pohanka. I cannot tell you how knowledgeable they are—and not just on the Custer affair. Both believe in my approach and have supported me to the hilt. Many times they have borne the expense of two-hour-plus telephone conversations. A great deal of what you see here is the result of their ideas. Whatever credits might accrue I shall quickly share with them. At about the time I started on this volume, I ran into Douglas C. McChristian and Thomas Buecker. Doug is now Chief Historian at the National Monument. Tom is Curator at the Fort Robinson Museum (Nebraska). Both had a hand in compiling the information contained in this document. Please step forward, Douglas and Thomas.

There is yet another fellow, Dr. Don Rickey. He also was a Custer Battlefield historian, and during that time (when I was a kid), he was my next-door neighbor in Hardin, Montana. Don is an accomplished, highly regarded western frontier historian, particularly in military matters. Right away I sent him a copy of my dissertation, and back came a lengthy list of constructive comments. Most of these are reflected in what you will find here. I respect and thank him. Brian and Michael sent their comments as well, as did two others who reviewed the manuscript for my publisher. One of these was an anonymous historian; the other was Stanley South, who furnished, by virtue of his profession, an archaeological critique. Their comments have been helpful; I am indebted to them. Thanks are also due to manuscript editor, Teddy Diggs, and the Press editors, Sarah Morrison and John Drayton. The book is better because of their work.

There were some information banks involved in this project. Institutions also played a large role, as did many people: staff and professional folk at the Griffith Library (Sheridan College), the National Archives, the Montana Historical Society, the University of Calgary Library, the Chester Fritz Library (University of North Dakota), the Billings (Montana) Parmly Library, the Custer Battlefield National Monument archives, the City of Calgary Library, the State Historical Society of North Dakota, the Big Horn County Library (Hardin, Montana), the Armed Forces Institute of Pathology, the Lilly Library (Indiana University), the Braun Research Library (Southwest Museum, Los Angeles), the Sheridan Public Library, and the Library of Congress.

People also shared with me, sometimes indirectly, the fruits of their archival research at these institutions and at others (Smithsonian Institution, Hearst Library [Lead, South Dakota], University of Oklahoma Libraries, Nebraska State Historical Society). In no particular order, many thanks go to John Gray, Jerome Greene, Kenneth Hammer, Michael Donahue, Tim Fox, Francis Taunton, and Wayne Wells. I hope I have not forgotten anyone. If I did, I owe you. Sharon Hanna programmed the computerized figures in this volume.

Acknowledgments customarily have a disclaimer, and rightly so. So here it is: any mistakes in the book are mine. Before ending this, I must proclaim an indebtedness to the many "Custer battle" students who have preceded me. Some of these people—such as Walter Mason Camp—spent what seems a lifetime searching out the facts. Others have contributed significantly to an enormous corpus of interpretive literature. At times I am critical of their conclusions, but it is more than appropriate to emphasize that if I have seen anything at all, it is because I was able to stand on their shoulders.

Finally, if I may be permitted some devotion, let me thank my mother. She tells me I took an interest in things bygone at about the age of six or seven. I don't recall that, but I do remember she always nurtured my interest in the past. Someday, I used to dream, I will be an archaeologist.

PART ONE.
OPENING

1
INTRODUCTION

The derivation of the word archaeology *gives little evidence of its present use.*

—Carl Russell Fish[1]

Battles are the laboratories of war. Military theoreticians have long drawn on experiences of battle to heighten preparedness for future conflict. S. L. A. Marshall,[2] for example, analyzing the conduct of U.S. Army combat units in World War II, concluded that inadequate training techniques and too little attention to the psychological well-being of the common soldier severely hampered combat effectiveness. His ideas eventually led to reforms in the U.S. Army, which in turn produced demonstrated improvements in its effectiveness during the Korean conflict. J. Keegan's[3] historical analyses of past battles, including the French and English conflicts at Agincourt (A.D. 1415) and Waterloo (A.D. 1815), as well as the World War I Battle of the Somme, led to important insights into conflict between various branches of the military (e.g., cavalry and infantry), into the individual soldier's will to combat, and into other trends in battle.

Marshall's analyses proceeded from actual combat studies; Keegan's came purely from historical studies of past battles. But there exist additional fertile and largely untapped venues relevant to the analyses of processes in warfare. In recent years, interest has surfaced in the archaeology of war. L. G. Ferguson, for example, excavated at Fort Watson, once a British outpost in South Carolina. Attacked in 1781 by American forces, the king's forces soon surrendered. The battle left a peculiar patterning in musket balls, which Ferguson revealed and recorded. From these patterns, and by locating the principal American position, he neatly deduced the strategy and tactics used to force the British to capitulate.[4]

S. South and R. A. Gould have also highlighted the value and versatility of archaeology in warfare studies. Their works illustrate how patterns in artifacts of war can reveal much about behavior during wartime. South, in examining Ferguson's Fort Watson research, felt the contextual relationships of arms-related artifacts there perhaps represented a "Revolutionary War Military Battle Pattern" applicable to other Revolutionary War battle sites.[5] Though he did not pursue the matter further, South intimated that such a battle pattern might be explained either in terms of a battle or within the context of "supply lines, logistic bases, military supply, types of arms available, etc."[6] Each of these analytical domains is interconnected, and indeed, one might expect analyses at one level to assist in explanations at another.

Gould's interest in the archaeology of war seems to stem from his investigation of World War II aircraft wrecks.[7] Drawing on differences in craftsmanship—differences recognized archaeologically—between aircraft engines made in the United States and Britain, Gould[8] suggested that aviation archaeology might provide a material basis for inferring nonmaterial aspects of national behavior during wartime. In this case, he noted that compared with U.S.-manufactured Merlin aircraft engines, British-made Merlins preserved much better in an archaeological context. From that, Gould tentatively concluded that requirements of mass production in the United States superseded quality requirements and thus the engines reflected differences in wartime manufacturing standards, conscious or unconscious, between the two countries.

Building on this theme, Gould later argued that British recycling of both Spanish (Armada) and German (Battle of Britain) war materials provided an "archaeological signature" of defensive stress suffered by the British during both wars.[9] The salvage and reuse, for example, of cannon and shot from Spanish Armada shipwrecks revealed an urgency experienced by the British in their defensive role. So too did the recycling of aluminum from German aircraft wrecks during World War II. Using the British experience, Gould proposed that the greater the defensive isolation of a combatant, the more adversary war materials, where available, will be salvaged and reused or recycled.[10]

Gould further noted that defensive recycling, from an archaeological perspective, "will tend to produce a skewed sample of wreck remains," an archaeological signature of defensive stress, leaving only those wrecks in inaccessible or hidden locations and those too badly damaged for efficient reuse.[11] In the case of defensive recycling, his general proposition is perhaps premature, for one can envision a number of variables, including inadequate wreck site inventories, that might skew analyses. Similarly, in his discussion of aircraft engines, Gould could not control for numerous depositional variables, including variations in soil chemistry, that might lead to differential preservation of aircraft wrecks.

Although aware of the limitations and the preliminary natures of their work, Gould, South and Ferguson recognized the value of archaeological resources in studying the scourge of humankind—warfare. These pioneering steps stand in opposition to Noël Hume's observation that through archaeology, "little can be said about battlefield sites."[12] Such pessimism is rejected here. Archaeology *is* a useful tool for studying battlefield sites, and much *can* be said about battles in particular and warfare in general. This book is about history, but not history in the traditional vein. It relies heavily on archaeology, a unique and wondrous discipline that shares a common goal with history—understanding the past.

The fundamental tenet on which archaeology rests is straightforward enough. Human behavior is mostly patterned. People generally get the job done in a finite number of ways, each of which is more or less fixed by cultural constraints that channel and mold behavior. It therefore follows that the residue of human activities should also be patterned and should reflect the actions and events that produced the physical remains. Archaeologists exploit these links between behavior and artifacts in explicating the past.

War, though hardly a credit to humanity, is a distinctly human enterprise. Combat behavior is, from the archaeological perspective, no more and no less susceptible to analyses than any other form of human endeavor. Battlefields, the theaters for war, represent the sites at which armed adversaries engaged in combat. Armaments—weapons and equipment—are the implements of war, and few battles have been fought without them. It is thus not asking too much to expect that battlefields are replete with the remains of armament. These are the residues of warring behavior, the records of tactics and strategies, of decisions and responses, of successes and failures. Is it, then, not possible to investigate battlefield events using the remnants of armed conflict? Is it not possible to seek in the archaeological record processes that led to the results of a particular contest?

It is. Historical archaeology is a legitimate, even necessary, approach to the study of past battles. As the name implies, historical archaeology manipulates data from two sources—the written word and material remains. Historical archaeologists turn pages, not just the ground. The discipline, sometimes called historic sites archaeology, has been around for some time, but its application to battlefield studies is original.

Blending archaeology with history is analogous to criminal investigations. The analogy between detectives and historical archaeologists, developed by my colleague Douglas Scott,[13] is instructive. Witnesses are important but so are clues provided by physical evidence of a crime. Detectives interview witnesses while others gather blood samples, fingerprints, and perhaps even the "smoking gun." This evidentiary partnership enhances the likelihood of obtaining a conviction.

In similar fashion, historical records and documents are tantamount to eyewitness testimony; the archaeological record contains related clues in the form of physical remains—artifacts. Checks and balances between the two data sets allow a more complete understanding of the nature of historical events. It is hard to imagine a police force that would not assemble all available evidence, or at least try to do so. So it should be with history, and that is what historical archaeologists do.

Battles throughout history span a time period measured in millennia—from remote times to Egyptian, Greek, and Roman wars, and to modern battles of the twentieth century. Although the face of warfare in human terms has remained constant, warring technology has changed dramatically through time. G. Dyer,[14] and J. Keegan and R. Holmes,[15] present excellent summaries of the technological developments in warfare over the ages, from bludgeons and lances to automatic rifles. Though the practice of historical archaeology is not restricted in time, so long as written sources are available, it is necessary here to limit study to the era of modern conventional warfare.

The modern era is set off in time by the transition from musketry to rifled, breech-loading firearms and their projectiles—self-contained, metallic ammunition. Widespread use of the new, improved weapons began during the American Civil War and can be dated roughly to the mid-1860s. This transition in firearm technology and its effects on the nature of battle are treated in more detail in part 2. It is sufficient here to note that in future references to *battlefields,* I mean those battle sites that date from the inception of modern conventional warfare.

One such site is the Custer battlefield in Montana, the scene of archaeological investigations in 1984–85. Events occurring there over a century ago are the centerpiece of this book, but the showcase here is historical archaeology. Some of the physical traces of battle unearthed during the mid-1980s expedition, of which I was a part, are put to work in an analytical role. What really happened during the Custer battle? The answer to that question has been more elusive than the wind. Now, archaeology helps capture that moment from the past.

2

ARCHAEOLOGY AND OBJECTIVES

Reports of soldiers in battle are often deficient.
—*Jan Vansina*[1]

Although archaeology is often perceived, in practice or utility, as limited to prehistory, it is not. Human behavior produces material remains, the domain of archaeology, no matter what the age. Today, archaeologists study garbage from Tucson suburbs, technology among Eskimos, slavery in the antebellum South, and the origins of agriculture and they explore even dimmer recesses of time—cultural developments of our prehuman ancestors. In no way is the practice of archaeology restricted temporally. But history, by definition, is. It is limited to a study of the past recorded principally in documentary form. So long as there are material remains available for study, archaeology is a legitimate partner in historical endeavors.

This study addresses three broadly conceived objectives predicated on this belief: (1) to propose an analytical framework designed to extract past behavior from material remains at battle sites; (2) to demonstrate the utility of this framework in practice; and (3) using the results to show that history and archaeology, when applied together, furnish sturdy bridges to the past—much sturdier than either discipline alone.

The analytical framework proposed here is unique, for it relies foremost on the archaeological record. Indeed, Gould, examining the potential in the archaeology of war, noted that archaeologists, on purely archaeological grounds and within the parameters of archaeological reasoning without reliance on non-archaeological evidence, should be able to discern the combat behaviors that produced certain residues.[2] As in any endeavor, this potential can be realized in varying degrees of resolution. In this book I show that differences in behavior under a variety of combat circumstances can be distinguished in the archaeological residues of battle.

To do so, I develop a theoretical model of combat, called the stability/disintegration model, that casts combat behavior within an archaeological framework. I design innovative methods to link the model with patterns in the material remains of battle. In this way, combat behaviors in time and space can be exposed, and battle events can be explicated and explained. Application of the analytical framework—the theory and the method—provides a solid archaeological foundation for studying battlefield events at battlefield sites dating to the era of modern warfare.

My laboratory is the Custer battlefield, now part of the National Park Service system. Custer Battlefield National Monument is located next to Little Big Horn River in what is now south-central Montana (near Crow Agency and Hardin). This site marks the scene of the Little Big Horn fight, which comprised several related but separate engagements. The fight took place in June 1876, during the American Indian wars period, an era of strife spanning the years between 1846 and 1890 that saw the eventual subjugation of the American West's Indian peoples.[3] The Little Big Horn fight resulted in defeat for the U.S. 7th Cavalry regiment, including the deaths of over 260 soldiers, scouts, and civilians, and a monumental, if fleeting, victory for the Sioux and Cheyenne Indian nations. Some members of the regiment died on a field some four miles from the Custer battle site, but most fatalities, about 210, occurred at the Custer battle. In this confrontation, warriors rubbed out to the man a battalion of five companies led by George Armstrong Custer, then the 7th Cavalry acting regimental commander. Lieutenant Colonel Custer by this time had gained fame, not to mention a meteoric rise to the rank of brevet major general, during the American Civil War. Entirely because of his presence at the Little Big Horn, the Custer battle— the subject of this book—is today etched indelibly on the American consciousness.

In applying the analytical framework to the Custer battle material record, I set out to deduce behaviors—behaviors of the type defined by Gould[4]—from material remains alone. Thus battle events are recognized and described principally on archaeological grounds. The sequence used in developing this approach to understanding Custer's last battle is of methodological interest. From the beginning, I knew certain historical data regarding the site location and the participants, and I had read other descriptions and explanations of the battle. I augmented this "common" knowledge with extensive research into late-nineteenth-century military tactics, as well as more general background information about the composition of military units and armament. Such data provided the basis for formulating and then applying the stability/disintegration model to the Custer battlefield archaeological record. In applying the model, and in assessing its implications, I proceeded with my basic data analyses along research lines customarily used by archaeologists.

My archaeological results provided the comparative base by which I evaluated and then incorporated the historical record into a historical-archaeological explanation of battle events. The process of weighing the archaeological knowledge against the documentary record led to a rather detailed construction of this famous episode in western history. Although Custer's final contest has entered the realm of American folklore—indeed mythology—there is to this day no real understanding of its exact course. Historical archaeology, I believe, succeeds in placing the events of June 25, 1876, in much clearer focus. This, I anticipate, will be of substantial interest to the many people enchanted by the events of that day.

But just as important, historical-archaeological analysis of the fight provides the opportunity to probe relationships between history and archaeology as vehicles to discover the past. Elucidation of these relationships constitutes the last objective of this book. Wherever a historical event has left physical traces, the full story of its history has not been told until archaeology has had its say. Under these circumstances, history and its methods alone are not sufficient to provide the most satisfying explanations of the past.

Of course, these are bold pronouncements, and if I were a historian, they would be heretical. A disturbing reaction to archaeological investigations at the Custer battlefield (and to other historical archaeology endeavors) has been the use of archaeological data as mere appendages to history. Some Custer battle historians, taking the documentary base for their interpretive foundation, have attempted to find reflections of the historical record in archaeological findings.[5] In doing so, they have tended to use the material record selectively. This seems to be an unproductive endeavor, for it guarantees that archaeology will serve merely as endorsement to one's favorite interpretation over another's. Furthermore, such an approach is inherently faulty because it misuses archaeological data by failing to consider the contextual significance of material remains. In archaeology, context is paramount; the meaning of one fact, one artifact, cannot be fully understood without reference to all others. Without doubt, the whole is significantly greater than its parts.

There is, then, a substantially more prominent role for archaeology in the analysis of armed conflicts played out at historic battlefields. This is evident insofar as archaeological reasoning is thought to provide a sound basis for interpreting documentary sources. Yet archaeology is more than an exercise in historiography. Archaeologists seem to grasp this concept well. James Deetz, for example, has argued for complementarity between archaeology and history by using the material record as an analytical point of departure.[6] But how can this complementarity be achieved in battlefield studies?

Battle events and their causes cannot be adequately delineated without reference to modeled behavior. Models of combat set the parameters in which the historical-archaeological analysis of battles can be undertaken. Certain behaviors attend to men in combat, and these seem to prevail consistently through time and space, the level of technological sophistication available notwithstanding.

For standing armies, battle is undertaken in accordance with codified tactical prescriptions. On the battlefield, tactics dictate the maneuvers of soldiers in quest of strategic goals, and they standardize individual actions for the common good. Tactics among standing armies, then, are the codified manners in which strategy is carried out.

In battle there is never a guarantee of success. Though an army engaged in combat, or its constituent military units, may maintain tactical stability and still be defeated, defeat comes far more commonly through disintegration of the unity imposed by tactics.[7] Above all, commanders fear disintegration in combat. When tactical stability disintegrates, commanders lose the power to maneuver subordinates and maintain control. Fearful and panicky, soldiers fend for themselves, and usually not by resisting. Defeat is almost certain; success is impossible. This view of behavior in combat provides a model of tactical stability and disintegration.

The factors at work in maintaining stability and preventing disintegration in a combat environment are of intense concern to military theoreticians. They consequently go to great lengths in studying such processes. The stability/disintegration model, explicated in detail in part 2, is derived from military studies of this type. The model, however, is unique in that it renders combat behavior amenable to archaeological analyses. As such, it represents an important initial step in the archaeological approach to battlefield studies. How is this accomplished, and why is such modeling an important tool in archaeological analyses?

These concepts provide the structural basis for generating predictions about human behavior under specified battle conditions. Thus, for example, under the constraints of tactical stability, conduct in combat can be expected, at least ideally, to be uniform, ordered, and standardized. Accepting the proposition that material remains reflect the human actions that produced them, we would expect the residues of combat undertaken in stable conditions to be similarly patterned. Conversely, disordered, unstructured battle remains should reflect various states of tactical disintegration.

Combat modeling is not the exclusive domain of archaeology; models can also be applied to the historical record. But by its very nature archaeological interpretation is wholly unrelated to history, its methods, and its results. Thus archaeology, compared with history, serves up not only a unique data base (facts) but also an epistemology, a way of knowing independent of historical method. This new way of knowing ensures that the facts of archaeology do not emerge as mere appendages to history. The archaeological perspective provides an entirely fresh approach to our studies of past events.

What, in reference to battlefield studies, are the insights available from archaeology? This issue is most profitably explored in terms of time-space systematics. A battle consists of a series of episodes interrelated in time and space. It is necessary to understand the nature of these relationships. The stability/disintegration combat model, by virtue of its emphasis on individual behaviors, requires an ability to understand the temporal and spatial relationships between individual actions.

Of course, documents also record the actions of individuals, great and small. But historians have tended to write their histories in broad sweeps across the stage, focusing on the prominent actors. Typically this is the emphasis for written histories in general, but for battle histories, the exclusion is glaring. The lesser actors participated too; indeed the sweeping events of history are not possible without them. Yet they tend to disappear in our great schemes of things past. Archaeology provides a way out. Physical records at battlefield sites contain information about the individual stripped of historical visibility.

Discerning the actions of individuals from the material remains of battle imposes special methodological requirements. Such methods allow the tracing of individual positions and movements about the battlefield. Since individuals are involved in events, the delineation of their movements provides, with varying degrees of detail, temporal linkages between episodes distributed in space. These relationships help to tell us about the internal chronology, or development, of a battle. At a more inclusive level, the interrelationships of individual patterns, when interpreted in light of combat models, reveal the behavioral natures of battle events.

Such analyses result in a purely archaeological construction of a battle. But Deetz has noted, "No amount of excavation can ever provide the kind of data used by historians to create a coherent, highly detailed construction of the past."[8] So history cannot be given short shrift. Certainly the detail provided by the historical record is superior to that given by archaeology. Using the analytical framework described herein for archaeological constructions of battles, we can trace military units across the battlefield, but without history, we cannot know individual identities, unit affiliations, composition, leaders, and other detailed data. Archaeology reveals the skeleton, which history then clothes.

For armed engagements, however, Deetz's reference to coherence in construction is another matter altogether. Battles are extremely confusing events, and in history they are recorded through eyewitness accounts. For an eyewitness to be reliable, he or she should have been (1) able to see, (2) able to understand what was seen, and (3) free of preconceived opinions that could distort what was seen and reported.[9] Vansina has noted that accounts given by battle combatants are virtually always deficient in the last two criteria.[10] This is not surprising. Individuals in battle can see only a fraction of what is happening. They can never mentally record the battle in its entirety, much less report all that is witnessed.

Moreover, the confusion and stress of battle—the fog of war—tend to blur their understanding of what they see. Because of these limitations, eyewitness accounts of battle are necessarily incomplete and typically contradictory, the same event being perceived differently from one witness to the next. Such problems are exacerbated in the Custer battle documentary record by cultural and language differences (only Indians survived to tell the story), as well as by—and I emphasize this—researcher biases in soliciting testimonies. Thus for this fight it has been impossible, using primary manuscript evidence (i.e., eyewitness testimony), to formulate a coherent behavioral and chronological framework.

Obviously, difficulties in the primary record of the Custer battle do not render history useless. They are similar to problems inherent in all documents. But archaeological constructions of battle can provide frameworks—temporal, spatial, and behavioral—that are vitally useful in evaluating manuscript evidence. The process of amalgamating archaeology and history into a complementary whole is not a simple matter of matching archaeological observations with historical accounts. Records from both history and archaeology are expected to be incomplete and, to some extent, mutually exclusive. Thus the procedure is more a process of culling spurious data, interpreting relevant happenings, and in some cases, filling historical gaps on the basis of archaeological evidence. This interplay between archaeological and historical records will usually require modifications in the interpretation of both sets of data, providing the complementarity necessary in the study of battlefield sites.

The archaeological methods developed herein for discerning combat behavior at battlefield sites constitute an unusual precision in archaeological analysis. The business of archaeology is to make reasonable inferences about the past. It is the task of archaeologists to link evidence with inference. But typically in archaeology there is considerable variation in the nature and completeness of evidence. Archaeology usually deals with time, space, and artifact assemblages. The level of confidence in archaeological inference is directly related to the methodological precision available in analyzing these and other variables. In reference to time, precision is often limited. Resolution is seldom available beyond a few scores of years. Occasionally, attempts are made to identify artifact makers, such as tracing pottery artisans through fingerprint analysis. Far more commonly, artifact assemblages are classified in general categories to infer various temporal, spatial, and/or functional relationships. Similarly, spatial problems are resolved by discerning activity areas, living floors, or other phenomena.

These are useful analytical criteria, but for the most part they do not approach the precision that archaeologists desire in their interpretations of the past. The methods developed here for battlefield studies help alleviate these limitations and inspire heightened levels of confidence in inferences derived from the material remains of battle. There are several reasons for this. First, battles are often measured temporally in weeks, days, or even minutes. Custer's final engagement probably unfolded in no more than two hours, with the decisive fighting, as I shall show, taking much less than an hour. Archaeological methods devised here allow perceptions of events (with some exceptions) that transpired within this short period of time. Second, analyses of artifacts in a single class (specifically, expended cartridges) help to reveal the behaviors of individuals. For this, there is no need to rely on gross classification schemes. Finally, in many instances, it is possible to trace the positions and movements of individuals in battle. These capabilities offer a resolution to problems of time, space, and form seldom achieved in archaeology. Moreover, refinements in these critical conceptual areas provide a solid factual foundation to complement documentary evidence of George Custer's final engagement.

3

ABOUT THIS BOOK

Sometimes, after reading some of the stories of that affair, I am inclined to doubt if I was out there at all and that I only dreamed that I was.

—*W. O. Taylor*[1]

Plenty of people have written about the Custer battle. There is, as a result, no shortage of ideas about what happened—some thoroughly inane, others quite scholarly and provocative. Those ideas in the latter class have influenced my thinking considerably. They are worthy of repeated consideration, for this famous battle cannot be comprehended without reference to its historical legacy. Thus I regularly draw on and refer to that legacy. In doing so, I have developed two broad themes, inextricably intertwined, which run throughout this book: (1) the Custer battle as myth, and (2) the Custer battle as fate—or what I call the fatalistic theme. The first will be treated in this chapter; the second must await some familiarity with the historical background, which is presented in the following chapter.

Once introduced to these themes, the reader may then anticipate the direction, import, and relevance of combat modeling and analytical methods, particularly with reference to the Custer fight. Models and methods are examined in chapter 5, which begins by formulating in detail the stability/disintegration combat model. The model provides the basis for predicting combat behaviors reflected in patterns of material remains at historic battle sites. These patterns, and the methods for discerning them, conclude the chapter. Chapter 6 presents the archaeological record, mainly burial and artifact distributions.

Modeling and methods are brought to bear on the archaeological record of the Custer battle in chapter 7. This application provides the basis for examining the engagement principally on archaeological grounds. The resulting construction, devoid as it is of historical detail, provides the key for opening the documentary record to analyses. History and archaeology are amalgamated in the chapters composing part 3. It is here that the particulars—the events, the nature, and the course of the battle as recalled in history—are analyzed in light of archaeological results.

Archaeological deductions reveal that defeat of the battalion led by General Custer arose directly from a frequent though dysfunctional process in warfare, the transition from tactical stability to disintegration. Except at the beginning of battle, the soldiers were in disarray, without much semblance of unified purpose. Although Custer's battalion entered the fray in good tactical order, after the Indians attacked in earnest, that order, that cohesion, quickly dissipated. Indeed, tactical stability broke down early; panic and fear, the prime ingredients in collapse during combat, spread throughout the tactical units. The battalion quickly lost its ability to fight. This scene is also found, in vivid detail, in many documentary sources describing the action.

Archaeology and history together paint a picture substantially different from those composed from historical data alone. This disparity points up the imperfections, which I have alluded to, in the historical record. But in some cases the differences run deeper. Many misconceptions about this struggle have developed from the mythological aura that surrounds the event, then and now. It has long been popular to perceive of Custer's soldiers as disciplined and unwavering, even in the face of certain death. Indeed, it is this heroic status that is an essential part of myth.

Authors of the works I am familiar with have, in one degree or another, uncritically accepted this perception in their stories of Custer's last battle. As a consequence, the tendency has been to portray tactical stability in the ranks, which in fact did not exist throughout much of the fight. After all, it is difficult to imagine brave soldiers fighting to the end while maintaining anything other than discipline, with or without tactical order. These models, those that ignore or downplay disintegration processes, have a dual fallibility. They obscure the nature of events (temporal, spatial, and behavioral) of a particular battle, which in turn prohibits identification of causal processes operative in warfare. But popular images of cavalrymen valiantly fighting to the end can no longer be entertained.

Among those works that portray the popular image are Edgar Stewart's *Custer's Luck* and Charles Kuhlman's *Legend into History*. There is much good in Stewart's work, and in the efforts of other authors mentioned herein. But in addressing the Custer affair, Stewart wholeheartedly subscribed to the idea of unfailing tactical stability among the general's battalion. He envisioned cavalrymen who sold "their lives as dearly as possible"[2] and who sustained the brunt of the Indian attack unflinchingly, with determined resistance, dying "to the last man in the positions where they had been placed."[3] All cavalry movements on the battlefield, he believed, had been organized and undertaken with a tactical purpose. Apparently aware of the potential for the development of chaos in combat, Stewart could not accept it for the Custer battle.[4] Unaware of or ignoring the numerous Indian accounts that express disorder, panic, and flight in metaphor (in the sense that such behavior represented actions so foreign to

Plains Indian warfare that warriors had to draw on experiences more familiar to them), Stewart relied heavily on the accounts of military men who viewed the aftermath of the fight. These eyewitnesses tended to interpret body positions and other associated data, such as expended cartridges, as evidence for disciplined fighting within the constraints of prescribed tactics. But interpretations of this type can be expected from military men—soldiers conditioned by tactics and discipline—men loathe, in the tradition of honor, to criticize fallen comrades.

Stewart's model of tactical stability offers a gratifying, even aggrandizing, basis for interpreting battles to a bewildered general audience and is consistent with the heroic ingredient of myth, but it lacks objectivity. Such confusion in the historical dissection of the Custer fight stems from the failure to recognize the volatile nature of battle. Perhaps most representative in this regard is Kuhlman. Unlike Stewart, he failed altogether to recognize the potential for the erosion of tactical order within and among military units. Instead, Kuhlman contended that a knowledge of tactics alone was sufficient to reconstruct the battle events.[5] As a consequence, he ignored, or at least eliminated, a considerable body of historical data that did not suit his preconceived notions, thereby grossly misinterpreting events during the Custer engagement. Indeed, Kuhlman insisted that the fight proceeded from north to south when, in fact, the battle progressed in the exact opposite direction. This error alone, not to mention his emphasis on tactical stability (laced with an abundance of conjecture), provides sufficient grounds for rejecting his interpretation outright.

W. A. Graham, in 1926, rendered one of the earliest lengthy discourses on Custer's defeat in *The Story of the Little Big Horn*. Though he incorrectly thought every soldier and officer "sold his life as dearly as he might," Graham at least recognized that aside from the initial fighting, "all was confusion."[6] The problem with his narrative is that he gives absolutely no details. In the main, his is a romantic story of gallantry, with little in the way of substantive information on the battle.

Information, however, is not lacking in Graham's *Custer Myth,* written in 1953. Chock-full of primary accounts, it is an important source book on the subject.[7] But Graham attempts neither analysis nor synthesis. The volume reflects his chronic inability to resolve the many contradictions that plague Indian eyewitness accounts of the fighting. This is unfortunate, for there is an inverse relationship operating here. The strength of the Custer myth diminishes the more thoroughly one contemplates the Indian eyewitness stories. Fortunately, some researchers have not been so overwhelmingly impeded. Not every story about Custer's last fight is influenced by mythic propensities.

Jerome Greene, for example, conceded that "disorganization" developed in the ill-fated battalion, but only in the very late stages of fighting—after cavalry manpower had been considerably depleted.[8] The weight of the Indian attack on tactically deployed soldiers produced attrition. Only when all was lost did a company of soldiers attempt to flee in panic. Greene's construction relegates disruptive processes of disintegration to a minor role and fails to consider them as a causal mechanism in defeat. It is in the latter role that loss of tactical stability is most apt to operate.

Greene's account, like Clifford Nelson's, was among the first to recognize the potential of physical remains for analyzing the Custer battle.[9] But the work, intended mostly for public consumption, is not definitive. Even more general are the Custer Battlefield handbooks, the official National Park Service publications prepared by Robert Utley. In the original version, Utley thought that Custer's battalion "swiftly disintegrated," but he confounded the issue and obscured his meaning by contending that each of the five companies made "individual stands."[10] A "stand," either in the popular image conjured by the word or by definition, is quite different from tactical disunity produced by shock. Utley meant to convey an image of firm resistance, however disorganized, an image that does not at all properly characterize this day on the Little Big Horn. Swift collapse is more appropriate. The recently revised handbook, sticking to the popular image, eliminates all reference to disintegration.[11]

Utley's latest work, a biography of George Custer published in 1988, also deals with the legendary battle. Here Utley endorses the popular image without the equivocation found in the original handbook. Again, each of the five companies made a "last stand"; the soldiers fought bravely. Admitting some "confusion [and] scattered pockets of panic," Utley says that stories of "mass hysteria" simply cannot be believed. Such stories came from "a few self-serving" Indians, or possibly from interpreters.[12] But accounts of hysteria, which in its nonclinical meaning is virtually synonymous with panic, are hardly few in number. They occur frequently in eyewitness accounts, often as metaphor, and more frequently than those accounts describing what might be called "mass bravery." Aside from this, the "self-serving" argument might be turned on end. As we will learn through the aid of archaeology, the warriors who told of collective bravery most often harbored ulterior motives.

Several years ago, Michael Moore wrote an account of the Custer battle based largely on Indian eyewitness testimonies.[13] Much of this Indian testimony described panic and fear among the troopers. Moore correctly placed the panic in the early stages of fighting, describing wavering morale, troops "melting away,"[14] and "disorganized and demoralized remnants."[15] But in concluding, he retained the notion of a determined resistance, however disorganized.[16] Moore has since changed his view completely on this matter. But this preconception of gallantry—the mythical foundation—inhibited his earlier ability to internalize the impact of a massive erosion in battalion unity. Most notable in Moore's work cited above, however, is his commendable attention to Indian eyewitness accounts. Custer battle interpretations of every kind, with but a few exceptions, have altogether or substantially ignored these indispensable resources on the grounds that the many Indian stories cannot be reconciled.

Graham personified this approach.[17] But his frustrated dismissal of Indian accounts is, if not acceptable, at least understandable: Indian sources are often devoid of any temporal clues and thus are difficult to arrange chronologically. Though not always the case, this is a substantial limitation. A common interpretive error in using Indian testimonies is to muddle the actual sequence of Custer battle events. Another frequent tendency is to attribute a story to the wrong part of the battlefield. D. H. Miller's interpretation, which attempted to tell the story from Indian perspectives, is culpable; a number of the combat events described by his informants are chronologically and spatially out of place.[18]

A more recent attempt at interpreting the well-known battle, by Charles du Bois, also occasionally falls victim, at least partially, to the temporal and spatial inadequacies in Indian testimonies.[19] Yet Indian testimonies, despite inconsistencies, contradictions, and vagaries, are not irreconcilable. In the main, Indian eyewitness accounts are descriptions of combat behavior during the fight—soldier and Indian alike. Given a construction derived from material remains rendered intelligible through combat modeling and methods, it is in many cases possible to match behaviors recognized archaeologically with those described by Indians. Temporal, spatial, and behavioral problems that are posed by vagaries in Indian accounts and that confound historical research are substantially reduced.

One other research avenue closely related to the disintegration issue—and hence the myth—is worthy of mention here. This involves the configuration of the Custer battalion—five companies plus the regimental headquarters staff—as it entered battle. Researchers bent on unraveling the enigmatic affair do not dismiss battalion makeup as incidental. It is important. But my feeling is that in configuring the battalion, authors start from the wrong end. Custer battlefield is unique in that the locations of soldiers' bodies are fairly well known. Many individuals, whose company affiliations are known, can be located through historical records. Once this is done, however, problems arise. Some men are not in the "right" place—they are not with their companies. Here elements of the myth intervene. If each man died in the position he had been placed, or if each company made a discrete, individual stand, then the battalion, as it entered battle, was not organized in accordance with tactical prescriptions. Imbued with such preconceptions, body patterning, to the extent it is known, tends to reflect a variety of possible battalion configurations. Consequently, configuration "theories" proliferate in many forms,[20] resulting in widespread disagreement over company locations and movements and, ultimately, the nature and progression of battle events.

It thus seems to me more productive to start at the other end, at the onset of fighting. Among standing armies, preparations for battle, like execution, are prescribed by tactics, and battalions can be expected to be configured accordingly. Accepting this for the moment, we can view differently the problem of cavalry troopers in the "wrong" places. One of the products of the loss of cohesion in stable fighting units is exactly this disorder. When soldiers, initially organized into tactical bodies, become terrified, they tend to scatter willy-nilly. This is what happened during the Custer battle, and this, for the most part, is why the out-of-place bodies are out of place.

Although any military configuration, even in the heat of combat, might be possible in theory, the determinant is most likely to be tactical prescription. Armies strive to maintain order, and that is the underlying function of tactics. Indiscriminate picking and choosing, and conjuring configurations that suit biases, lack the methodological rigor available through an appeal to tactical prescriptions. Contrived Custer battle configuration theories fail to accommodate the facts, facts that must include the specter of the evaporation of unity in battle. Cavalry deployment theories using erroneous alignments suffer the same fate. In the end, they do not offer an adequate foundation for comprehending the nature and sequence of events during the fight. They are somewhat akin to Newton's physical laws, which explain some motions but not all. On the other hand, as Utley's[21] latest Custer battle interpretation indicates, choosing a satisfactory configuration does not automatically guarantee success. That path winds through the maze of historical fact rendered intelligible by archaeological reality.

The issue of battalion configuration, and other issues raised here, are worked out in later chapters, including those in which I evaluate the written evidence in light of archaeological knowledge. Examination of the documentary record results in a detailed construction of the chronological, behavioral, and spatial aspects of the battle. It also results in refutations of historical analyses of specific aspects of the confrontation. The historical-archaeological construction provides the basis by which the causes for a fatal breakup in the Custer battalion can be examined. Causes are examined not only on the local level but also where necessary in light of military policies of the day. This task is accomplished in the first of the two chapters composing part 4. Here it is shown that traditional explanations for defeat, which shift the onus from the soldiers to factors entirely beyond their control, cannot be accepted. Nevertheless, some of these arguments, when modified in light of historical and archaeological knowledge, assume relevance with respect to processes that erode stability and produce collapse.

Ability in combat to resist the ever present pressures of disintegration is dependent on the degree of moral fortitude possessed by soldiers. *Moral fortitude* is synonymous with *morale*—the more familiar term—in that it conveys a mental condition of courage, discipline, confidence, and enthusiasm under fire. *Moral* is a standard term employed by military analysts to suggest this concept, and it is used here. In concluding part 4, chapter 15 deals with the moral preparedness of the 7th Cavalry soldiers. Here it is argued that training deficiencies and fatigue factors rendered the troopers susceptible to disintegration processes. Given the nature of this battle, one that developed from a sudden and unexpected Indian attack, it is not surprising that the five-company battalion fell apart.

In the previous chapter, I mentioned that by using the material record as a point of departure, we can derive insights that are not always available from documentary sources. For instance, I have already proposed that for the struggle on Custer's field, denouement was the result of disintegration. But the analysis of physical traces found at this site bears enormously on events and decisions that precipitated actual battle, that is, on developments beyond the Custer battlefield in areas untouched by the archaeologist's tools. Discussions in part 5 illustrate this potential. The historical-archaeological construction of the Custer battle (part 3), plus the analyses of immediate and contributing factors in disintegration (part 4), provides considerable insight into the broad sweep of events beginning early on June 25 and ending later that day on the killing field. In general, part 5 shows that (1) Indian warriors did not drive Custer's men to the ground on which they died (as is typically supposed); (2) the battalion was on the offensive when its cohesion evaporated; and (3) each of the principal players, contrary to partisan arguments, shares responsibility in defeat. Further, the end came at a time when the offensive strategy mirrored that undertaken just earlier in a coulee just south of the killing field, and the Indian village situated along Little Big Horn River fueled neither phase of operation.

This glimpse of the book should raise the eyebrows of experienced Custer battle researchers, for it is far afield from conventional ideas. And since archaeology launched the new synthesis, we should contemplate its value as a historical tool. The book concludes (part 6) by offering the Custer battle as it is constructed here as an example of the important role of archaeology in historical studies. Success in achieving the stated objectives within these parameters is evaluated. In conclusion, I argue that history and archaeology are two methods of investigating the past. When used in a complementary fashion, they provide more complete and satisfying constructions of our past. Furthermore, the historical-archaeological approach developed here is relevant to future battlefield studies at various analytical levels.

The Indian in the Custer Battle

The stability/disintegration model derives from the behavior of line soldiers in organized armies. This approach to modeling combat behavior is not meant to slight participation by the Indians. After all, they won. Sioux and Cheyenne Indians, of course, immersed themselves in battle—a way of life depended on it—but the nature of their conduct in warfare, indeed that of most Plains Indians, hardly compares to the standardization imposed on combatants by prescribed tactics. Indian warriors saw battle as a vehicle to gain individual status—even in extraordinarily critical situations. When the opportunity arose to gain personal honors, they generally felt free to engage as they saw fit, without adherence to the white man's codes and rules of battle. Leaders with sufficient influence might attract followers but could not command them (in the tactical sense). In no way did Indians feel impelled to maintain battle lines, establish combat intervals, fire on command, or perform other tactical maneuvers typical of prescribed tactics.

Thus the modeling approach I use, one that depends on prescribed tactics for its analytical and predictive powers, cannot be applied to the physical traces left by Indian combatants. Nonetheless, such residues exist at the Custer battlefield, in abundance. The analytical methods (as opposed to the theory of combat modeling) developed in chapter 5 are applicable to these remains. Analyses provide some important insights into the nature of Indian warfare, at least as it was carried out during the Custer battle. The individualistic view of Indian participation in battle noted above to an extent seems to hold true at the Custer battlefield. Dispersed and random distributions of residues from Indian firearms, shown in chapter 7, suggest that many warriors acted on their own. This type of behavior, as I show elsewhere, can also be discerned in the documentary base.

On the other hand, a clear pattern in tactics employed by the Indians emerges in residues left by their firearms. Cartridge cases, primarily from repeating rifles, suggest that warriors at least took advantage of the shock effects of rapid fire massed against enemy positions. Moreover, in some places we find these cases tightly clustered. It becomes apparent, then, that shock tactics, whether by design or not, played an important role in the defeat of Custer's cavalrymen. This aspect of what appears to be cooperative tactical behavior, as opposed to idiosyncratic, is illustrated in part 4.

The patterns in Indian artifact residues are evaluated in the archaeological analyses section (chapter 7), as is the relationship between these patterns and the military patterns left by U.S. soldiers. Another important aspect of Indian tactics is that of infiltration. Archaeological analyses indicate that warriors attained positions very close to the troopers. Subsequent historical analyses, particularly in part 3, reveal that they did so exercising considerable stealth. For most of the time infiltration was passive, with only a small portion of the warriors actively engaging in skirmishing. Only when provoked did the Indians attack in force, and then in response to the confusion and panic generated by the onset of terror among the cavalrymen.

Clearly, Indian tactics used in the fight do not seem to have been guided by an overall, premeditated, purposeful strategy—one formulated before the start of hostilities. There is virtually nothing in the Indian testimony to suggest otherwise. Indeed, Iron Dog, a participant, said that the Indians had no strategy, no trap, no plan.[22] The fact that most Indian accounts lack chronological continuity and describe events in restricted space shows that the warriors implemented no preconceived strategy. If they had, one might expect to encounter in primary Indian accounts at least some testimony on what others were doing at different times and places during the battle. Such testimony is lacking, except now and then in native oral histories and traditions about the battle—stories that developed and circulated years after the event.

Historical evidence does, however, make it clear that once Custer's column attracted their attention, Indians here and there implemented several hastily developed but apparently unrelated strategies of sorts. Evidently included among these were instructions to capture or stampede the cavalry horses. As I shall show, the warriors acquitted themselves quite successfully in this endeavor, and their prowess aided in defeating the troopers. In addition, the Indians, first attacked at the southern edge of their encampment along the Little Big Horn, eventually determined that another body of troopers—Custer's battalion—was moving to strike the village, or so it seemed to some, farther to the north. Principally concerned for the women and children, many warriors rushed downstream hoping to prevent this. As a movement with purpose, the northerly surge minimally qualifies as strategy, but it is not the grand scheme of entrapment—the sandwich effect, with warriors at the column's rear (south) and at its front (north)—that conventional wisdom so often portrays.[23] Indeed, as S. L. A. Marshall noted and as I shall develop, this and other strategies bore fruit largely through circumstance rather than by design.[24]

4

GLANCES FORWARD AND BACK

In sorrow I am sending a feeble voice, O Six Powers of the World. Hear me in my sorrow, for I may never call again. O make my people live.

—Black Elk's lament, ca. 1931[1]

Some sort of backdrop is necessary to understand Custer's final engagement in context. The historical narration provided here, brief as it is, consists of views commonly held about the military preparations for, the broad strategies of, and the role of the 7th Cavalry in the 1876 Indian campaign. It was during this campaign, sometimes called the Centennial Campaign, that Custer's cavalry met its fate. But looking backward, we see that fate took root in earlier white-Indian relationships. These circumstances led the 7th Cavalry to the Little Big Horn.

Whereas the 1876 campaign can easily be portrayed in broad sweep, it is a different story for Custer battle events. Even summaries, however broad and with the most benign intent, invite criticisms, for the subject is so controversial. As part of this chapter, though, I find it worthwhile to preview, in summary form, the findings of historical archaeology. The forward glimpse is intended not so much as a statement but as a vehicle to introduce prevailing themes, the conventional analytical approaches to the Custer battle. Virtually every explanation of the battle, along with the myth, is somehow wrought from these themes. Since my views, derived from historical archaeology, contrast markedly with those molded from documents alone, an awareness of the latter views helps focus all that follows in this book.

A Historical Narrative

During the 1850s, increasing contact with the western Indian tribes led to the formulation of official U.S. government policies designed to confine Indians to fixed tracts of land called reservations. One of the western reserves was the Great Sioux Reservation, which encompassed much of what is now western South Dakota. The Black Hills, considered to be sacred lands by Sioux people, lay in the heart of the vast reserve. Treaty obligations of 1851 and 1868 guaranteed the Sioux that the reservation would not pass from their possession. But in the summer of 1874, the 7th Cavalry Regiment of the U.S. Army, led by Lt. Col. George Custer (breveted a major general during the Civil War), mounted an expedition into the Black Hills (in South Dakota and Wyoming). Under orders to locate a site for a military post (to be used to prevent Indian raids), the expedition included scientific investigations among its goals.

The nation learned, as a result of the "scientific" findings, that the Black Hills contained substantial gold deposits. Despite attempts to suppress word of the discovery, the news quickly leaked, precipitating an influx of white entrepreneurs. Within a year the white populace in the region had grown significantly, and political pressures to open the Black Hills to permanent white settlement magnified. Eventually the Great Sioux Reservation was drastically reduced in size, and the Sioux lost their sacred lands entirely.[2] During this process of change, reservation Sioux grew disenchanted with continuing treaty violations. In the period between 1874 and 1876, many left the reservation to return to their old way of life. They moved west, often to join nontreaty brethren roaming unceded lands in Montana and Wyoming territories. Others—the "summer roamers"—regularly left agencies during the summer months but returned to spend the winter. The summer of 1876 was no different. Reservation and non-reservation Sioux alike, allied with the Northern Cheyenne, were soon to meet the 7th Cavalry and engage in battle on Little Big Horn River.[3]

Government officials perceived the Sioux wanderings as threats, not only to Indian policies but also to the security of settlers pushing ever westward. Thus in late 1875 and early 1876, the U.S. Army devised plans to intercept the Indians and return them to the reservation. According to the loosely formulated strategy, three army columns would converge on the Indians in pincer-like fashion. One column fell under the command of Gen. Alfred Terry. Terry's command included the 7th U.S. Cavalry Regiment led, of course, by General Custer. This column left Fort Abraham Lincoln (on Missouri River near Bismarck, North Dakota) on May 17, 1876, and marched westward, expecting to find the Indians in what is now southeastern Montana.

Gen. George Crook and Col. John Gibbon commanded the other columns participating in the 1876 campaign. Crook's responsibility was to prevent the Indians from escaping to the south. Thus he left Wyoming Territory with over 1,000 men and moved north into southeastern Montana Territory. Gibbon departed Fort Ellis, near Bozeman, Montana Territory, and marched east down Yellowstone River. In mid-June, Gibbon joined with Terry on the Yellowstone near where Rosebud, Montana, is now located. From here, the 7th Cavalry soon would set out in pursuit of the Sioux and Cheyenne. But a few days before this, on June 17, Indians had checked Crook on Rosebud Creek in a battle that took place about 36 miles southeast of the Custer battlefield. Crook's column, though hardly damaged, temporarily retired from the field. Eight days after the Rosebud battle—on June 25, 1876—Sioux and Cheyenne warriors, many of whom had helped stalemate Crook, decimated the 7th Cavalry on Little Big Horn River. Eventually the three columns linked, but not until after July 12—when Terry's messengers reached Crook.

The 7th Cavalry Regiment, some 600 men strong, departed General Terry's command on June 22 and struck out on a journey that would end disastrously at the Little Big Horn. Earlier intelligence reports had indicated that the Indians might be found somewhere in this area. Terry and Gibbon, it was agreed, would arrive in the Little Big Horn vicinity around June 27. Custer had orders to scout the country and locate the Indians. Much of the controversy surrounding the Little Big Horn battle centers on these orders and whether or not Custer had received authorization to attack. This issue will be outlined in more detail later.

The prelude to the Little Big Horn battle began late on June 24 (regiment movements leading to the battle are represented in figure 4-1). The 7th Cavalry, after leaving the Yellowstone and moving south up Rosebud Creek, camped near the present-day town of Busby, Montana. Late on the night of June 24, Custer's soldiers broke camp, and the command moved to the divide between Little Big Horn River and Rosebud Creek. The divide, high atop rugged hills, afforded an opportunity to survey the Little Big Horn Valley lying to the west. There, in the early morning hours of June 25, at a place called Crow's Nest, scouts spied a large Indian gathering. Though no one knew exactly at the time, the encampment stretched for quite a distance along the west bank of Little Big Horn River. Custer, betting on the element of surprise and fearing that he had been detected, now determined to attack.

As the twelve companies of the 7th Cavalry descended through broken country westward toward Little Big Horn River, the commander split his regiment into three battalions, plus an additional force. The latter consisted of one company, a few men from others, and some civilians (about 130 men in all) to escort the packtrain—mules bearing various supplies, including ammunition. Capt. Thomas McDougall commanded the packtrain (not shown on figure 4-1), which for most of the day lagged well behind the main force. Capt. Frederick Benteen's battalion consisted of three companies (approximately 125 men). Benteen received orders to march southwestward, ostensibly to block a possible escape route. After his departure, the remaining eight companies proceeded west toward the valley (where they would ultimately find a substantial Indian village). The column, led by Custer, headed west down a small tributary (now known as Reno Creek) of Little Big Horn River.

At a point several miles above the river valley, the command again split up.

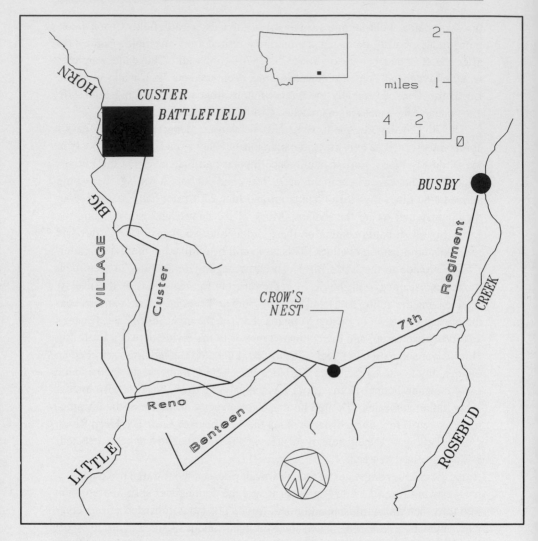

Fig. 4-1. General representation of the 7th Cavalry Regiment movements on June 24–25 leading to battle (scale approximate).

Maj. Marcus Reno, second-in-command of the regiment, led one battalion consisting of three companies (roughly 130 men); Custer personally commanded the other battalion of five companies (about 210 men). About this time, Custer instructed Reno to attack and charge into the valley. The major spurred his command ahead, continuing down Reno Creek into the Little Big Horn Valley. The next phases may be followed on figure 4-2. Reno crossed Little Big Horn River at the mouth of Reno Creek (extreme lower right, fig. 4-2) and—headed

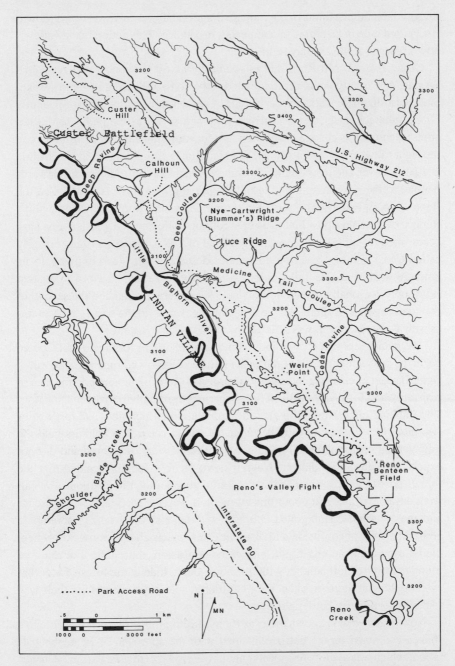

Fig. 4-2. Map of the battlefield area including the Custer battlefield, the Reno-Benteen battlefield, and some topographic features mentioned in the text.

toward the southern limits of the Indian village—charged northwestward (down-river) for a mile or so before encountering resistance. This action in the valley is now known as Reno's valley fight.

Custer had advised Reno that he would be along in support of the major's assault. Apparently the general intended to do so by following in Reno's wake, or at least the major thought so. Instead, Custer veered to the north, evidently intent on attacking farther downriver, although so far as we know he did not advise Reno of this change. After Reno's departure, the Custer battalion bore to the right (downriver) and ascended the high bluffs along the east bank of Little Big Horn River and overlooking the valley. The battalion rode northwestward, parallel to the river and along the bluffs, passing over what is now called the Reno-Benteen battlefield. Later, Sioux and Cheyenne would lay siege against Reno's men at this position. Custer's column followed the present-day park access road (roughly) until reaching the head of Cedar Ravine, more commonly called Cedar Coulee. The five companies descended the steep drainage to its juncture with Medicine Tail Coulee, a tributary of Little Big Horn River that flows only seasonally. At about this time, the general dispatched the second of two messengers to Captain Benteen. Still maneuvering to the south, the captain, as well as the packtrain, was ordered to rejoin Custer's battalion.

The maneuvers that Custer and his men undertook in Medicine Tail Coulee occurred at roughly the same time as the failure of Reno's command in the valley fight. Instead of charging the enemy, as ordered, Reno dismounted in the face of resistance and formed a skirmish line. Warriors eventually flanked his position. The flanking maneuvers soon caused the battalion, which now had lost one or two men, to withdraw into timber adjacent to the river. The soldiers held the timber position for about 30 minutes. During this time, the command did not experience substantial danger. Nevertheless, Reno evidently decided that the threats posed by infiltrating Indians required abandoning the position. The call went out to evacuate. At about this moment, a warrior party attacked closeup, and the battalion disintegrated. Pursued by Indians, the troopers scrambled across the river in confusion and disorder to the bluffs above. Some 30 soldiers died during the headlong flight, and in the confusion, more than a dozen men found themselves left behind, with no choice but to hide in the forest. Later that evening these stragglers joined their comrades, miraculously making their way to the Reno-Benteen battlefield.

Now began what is known today as Reno's hilltop fight. The arrival of Reno's shaken command on the bluffs coincided with the approach of Benteen's battalion, which was at the time proceeding, as ordered, northward to rejoin Custer. Reno's predicament, however, caused Benteen to halt and provide assistance. When the two forces joined, Indian pressure diminished, allowing a respite—for as much as an hour. Reno's battalion, aided by Benteen, began to reorganize. Eventually McDougall and the packtrain straggled in. During this time, it is generally agreed, the Indians disengaged to move downriver and meet the new danger now posed by Custer's battalion. This threat had developed in Medicine Tail Coulee, where Custer's men had begun light exchanges with warriors. Skirmishing in Medicine Tail Coulee represents the earliest stages of the fight known as the Custer battle. Eventually the battalion left the coulee and continued northward (farther downriver) to the area now designated as the Custer battlefield. Here, fighting ultimately intensified, and it is here that Sioux and Cheyenne wiped out Custer's battalion.

The Custer engagement, in its entirety, took place in something short of two hours. Hostilities at the Custer battlefield, lasting an hour or a little longer, represented the final stages of the affair. These stages, the final fighting at Custer battlefield, are the ones I address through archaeology. Archaeological investigations at other Custer battle sectors (e.g., Medicine Tail Coulee) have yet to be undertaken. So unless otherwise stated, references to Custer battle archaeology are restricted to the final stages of fighting—at the Custer battlefield. I present a less scanty, yet still brief, historical overview of the Medicine Tail Coulee events later, in chapter 8. Discussions there are intended as an orientation to the final stage of fighting. Still later, in part 5, I delve much more thoroughly into these and other events. In these chapters (16 through 19), I offer a detailed look at battle events beyond the Custer battlefield, interpretations made possible by insights derived from archaeological investigations on Custer battlefield.

The final moments of Custer's battle are the most celebrated. The combined Reno-Benteen command may have witnessed from afar some of this struggle. Reno's battalion reorganized and attended to the wounded for about an hour after arriving on the bluffs. With order somewhat restored, the command, which now consisted of Reno, Benteen, and the packtrain and its escort, began to move slowly northwest along the river bluffs, following Custer's trail. In doing so, the officers hoped to join with their commander's battalion. The leading troopers soon reached Weir Point (fig. 4-2), an elevation high above Medicine Tail Coulee. Some officers later reported that on reaching the point, they could hear shooting and see figures riding around the field below. What anyone really saw is murky, since distance, gunsmoke, and dust prevented all but a hazy view; in any case, their written recollections are none too clear. In a short time, however, a considerable number of Indians gathered in front of the column and started firing. This the soldiers saw clearly. The warriors mounted enough pressure to prevent further progress, and the column soon found it necessary to retreat. The troopers retraced their route and eventually consolidated at the Reno-Benteen battlefield. By now the Custer battle had concluded.

As Indians surrounded the combined Reno-Benteen command, they confronted a hastily established defense perimeter. As it turned out, the troopers had chosen a defensible position, but much of the perimeter lay rather badly exposed to enemy fire. Some soldiers eventually scraped out shallow rifle pits for protection. Others fronted their positions with various wood boxes, and some took cover behind dead horses and mules. After a roughly 36-hour siege spanning two days, the Indians, on the afternoon of June 26, suddenly ended the engagement, broke camp, and moved south up Little Big Horn River. The hilltop fight had ended. The next day, Terry and Gibbon rode in with their commands. Their arrival signaled the end of the battle at the Little Big Horn. Eighteen more men had met their deaths during the hilltop siege. In all, some 268 men from the regiment died. Indian casualties, which are difficult to estimate, numbered perhaps 30 to 100 warriors.

Stunned by these events, and neither prepared nor inclined to give chase, the survivors spent the next few days burying fallen comrades and treating their wounded. On June 30, the entire outfit, stung by defeat, moved down to Big Horn River, where the steamboat *Far West*, captained by the intrepid river pilot Grant Marsh, lay moored near the mouth of the Little Big Horn. Able-bodied men transferred the wounded to the steamer, which took them down the Big Horn, then the Yellowstone, and finally the Missouri to Fort Abraham Lincoln, Dakota Territory. Several soldiers died en route. At Bismarck, telegraphers wired details and confirmation of the defeat to an astonished and disbelieving public in the midst of celebrating America's centennial. Thus began the Custer epic, which has not abated in intensity to this day.

After the fight on Little Big Horn River, Crook and Terry again took up the Indian trails in pursuits that proved largely fruitless. Only once would the soldiers, this time commanded by Crook, and the Indians meet again in the summer of 1876, at Slim Buttes in what is now western South Dakota. Stung by his failure on the Rosebud, Crook claimed a great victory at Slim Buttes, but the battle can hardly be considered a victory.[4] The 1876 campaign ended in complete failure; many Indians remained free, whereas others eventually returned to various reservations on their own volition. Months after the battle, the Sioux spiritual leader, Sitting Bull, took his followers to Canada. Here they remained for four years before agreeing to return to reservation life in the United States. Black Elk was at the Custer battle. Only 13 years old then, he was sufficiently wise in his old age to lament (see the chapter epigraph) the tragedy endured by his people.[5]

A Historical Archaeology Preview

I have previously claimed that historical archaeology reveals an account of the Custer battle considerably different from those explanations proffered from history alone. Nowhere is this more evident than in the Custer battalion movements and deployments. A fundamental advantage of cavalry is mobility. Current Custer battle historical themes, for reasons introduced throughout this book, tend to severely restrict battalion mobility before annihilation. According to historical archaeology, the battalion not only enjoyed mobility for some time before denouement but also exercised that advantage. By outlining these movements and deployments, I am able to introduce historical themes—themes that I find unsatisfactory and that underpin conventional wisdom. Again I emphasize that the subject is the Custer battle, which we have just seen to be one of several composing the Little Big Horn fight.

Figure 4-2 may be used to track movements. Events began with the arrival of Custer's battalion around Calhoun Hill. Recall that earlier phases took place in Medicine Tail Coulee. Also, before reaching Calhoun Hill, the battalion had split into two wings (see note 20, chap. 3). The battalion consisted of a three-company right wing (Capt. Myles Keogh, commanding) and a two-company left wing (Capt. George Yates, commanding). The two wings separated at or near Luce Ridge. The left wing followed Medicine Tail Coulee to its mouth. Subsequently it ascended Deep Coulee en route to Calhoun Hill (Deep Coulee is also called North Medicine Tail Coulee). During this ascent, Keogh's right wing proceeded overland via Nye-Cartwright Ridge (also known as Blummer's Ridge). The wings rejoined at Calhoun Hill. The rendezvous set the stage for the final stages of Custer's last battle.

After delaying briefly on Calhoun Hill, the left wing alone struck out in search of an advantageous point of attack. The northern sojourn took the wing along the ridge—known today as Custer Ridge—between Calhoun and Custer hills, then westward into the valley, and finally to the banks of Little Big Horn River. There, it seems, officers found a suitable place to press an attack. Rather than attacking immediately, however, the wing returned to take up positions below and to the west of Custer Hill.

While the left wing maneuvered to the north, its counterpart maintained a position around Calhoun Hill. This slight elevation is so named because it is here that Lt. James Calhoun's right-wing company skirmished with infiltrators. Although during this time many warriors had arrived, with some infiltrating very close to right-wing positions, fighting remained quite light. This allowed the remaining two right-wing companies to hold in reserve, behind Calhoun's line. Thus when the Custer battle began in earnest, only one of the three right-wing companies had deployed in battle formation. At the same time, the left wing remained on a long, low ridge that slopes gently westward from Custer Hill. About a mile separated the wings. The battalion waited, expecting Benteen's arrival. Later, the left wing moved up to positions nearer Custer Hill. Then, one of the two companies in Yates's wing deployed in skirmish order. The battalion continued to wait.

For some time the soldiers kept warriors at bay, mostly because the latter chose to creep about, improving their positions, rather than launch an assault. As time passed, the right wing became vulnerable. Warriors east and south of Keogh's companies had found it necessary to remain at a distance. Relatively open terrain in these directions prevented them from attaining closeup positions. But to the west and northwest, toward the river, broken terrain provided cover. Indian infiltration in one of the coulees there, and along a nearby ridge, began to pose a threat as warriors moved near.

Responding to this threat, the right-wing commander dispatched C Company. This deployment signaled the beginning of the end for the Custer battalion. Warriors initially gave way but then mounted a counterattack. Their assault broke the company and sent it reeling in disorder back toward Calhoun Hill. Many troopers died along the way. Confusion sparked by the rout spread to the two remaining right-wing companies, and they too eventually succumbed to panic. The surviving soldiers scurried north, seeking safety with the distant left wing. The Indians, sensing vulnerability, seized the advantage and pressed their attack. Only about 20 of the 120 men (approximately) in the right wing made it to Custer Hill. The rest died en route, their bodies later found strewn along Custer Ridge.

This predicament compelled the left wing, consisting of a little more than 80 men, to assist their comrades by taking up positions on Custer Hill. The enemy quickly surrounded the embattled group. The famous "last stand" had begun. At some point during this episode, a body of troopers charged down Custer Hill, apparently to drive away Indians. This was E Company, but like C Company earlier, it too fell apart. Warriors drove the panicky soldiers to Deep Ravine. The knot of cavalrymen on Custer Hill dwindled as pressure took its toll. Finally, the few remaining alive fled toward their comrades in the ravine, where the last men died. The Custer battle had ended.

This is the Custer battle that I shall develop. It is one wholly at odds with exclusively historiographical interpretations, which are virtually always built on the fatalistic theme. The result of these accounts is a Custer battle that invariably falls into line with the myth, whether intended or not. Indeed, interpretations built on fatalistic notions are largely responsible for perpetuating the myth, and some have been formulated precisely with that intent. Subsumed under the fatalistic theme are two other aspects. One involves action at the so-called South

Skirmish Line, and the last, as I shall explain, is not so much a historical theme as it is in practice a nontheme. All three are intricately interrelated.

According to the fatalistic theme, warriors drove Custer's battalion to the final battlefield, a poor position but the best available given the predicament.[6] There, without any chance for survival, the battalion attempted to fight off the warrior masses, which decisively and quickly (or nearly so) overwhelmed the soldiers. All this began at the mouth of Medicine Tail Coulee, where Indians en masse first confronted Custer's five companies. Warrior hordes, it is said, pre-empted a cavalry attack here, and the battalion found itself, desperate, on the defensive. The offensive, so clearly evident in Reno's attack and Custer's northern move, sputtered and faded out.

Fatalistic versions vary. Some, in one way or another, implicate Reno in Custer's demise. In its most virulent form, this variation is purposely designed to roundly condemn Reno. His failure in the valley fight, it is said, released hordes of Indians, all of whom rose mightily as a body at Custer's front. Reno's failure thwarted the plan and sent Custer and his men to their doom. This version surfaced soon after the fight; in fact, the fatalistic theme has a long history. Faced with severe criticism not long after the Little Big Horn battle, Reno demanded and got a military inquiry, the findings of which officially exonerated him.

Other versions implicate the regimental commander. Anti-Custer proponents point out that Reno himself met a superior force and had no choice but to terminate his attack. Such variations do not deny that Reno's predicament allowed warriors to overrun Custer. But in these instances, blame is shifted to the general for making the decisions that led to these circumstances. Though pro- and anti-Custer biases persist to this day, recent works, albeit a scant few, tend to approach the Custer battle on more objective footings. Still the confusing and contradictory historical record intervenes. I will show how this happens, but in the end, the results are the same. Warriors leave the valley fight and quickly confront Custer, perhaps driving him from Medicine Tail. The general's offensive falters on Custer Ridge.

Such explanations that are available in fatalistic form are in some ways symptomatic of Custer battle studies—horrendous results must have suspicious origins. Yet it cannot be denied that Sioux and Cheyenne Indians earlier busy with Reno's outfit later helped to destroy Custer and his men. But I shall show that various factors, some of which can be attributed to the Custer battalion even after engaging the Indians, also figured in the debacle.

Ideas about the South Skirmish Line mesh nicely with the fatalistic theme. By the time of this episode, the battalion is irrevocably committed to the defensive and is in desperate straits. In a last-ditch effort to improve the situation, E Company is deployed (often C Company is included). There are two variations. Either frenzied warriors cut E Company to pieces as it desperately tries to reach Custer Hill (in order to secure a defensive position). Or the company first establishes a defensive hold (usually on Custer Hill but I have also seen Calhoun Hill), then deploys from there, only to be dispatched, though not without determined resistance, however short. In both cases, the end came on a low ridge extending from Custer Hill to Deep Ravine. And, in either instance, it is noted that Lame White Man, a Cheyenne, led the onslaught. Virtually every author, then and now, subscribes to this theme in one form or another. But all the various interpretations derive from erroneous readings of the documentary base.[7] Once again, confusing documentary sources prominently figure in this error, but so too do preconceptions fueled by fatalistic biases.

I will show that archaeological evidence forces a reevaluation of historical data. In fact, the sources that describe Lame White Man's attack refer to the C Company deployment and its subsequent rout. This, as I alluded to above, sparked the disintegration process, which ultimately proved to be the downfall of Custer's battalion. Refuting the popular South Skirmish Line theme (also referred to herein as the E Company/South Skirmish Line hypothesis) illustrates the role of disintegration in the celebrated defeat, something long unrecognized. Quite clearly, subscription to the South Skirmish Line theme has obscured this role. As much as anything else, obscuration has precluded any satisfactory explanation of the nature of this battle.

Finally there is the historical nontheme: certain historical evidence is (and has always been) virtually ignored in constructing Custer battle events. One is the left-wing action on and beyond the long, low ridge that gently slopes westward toward the river from Custer Hill. I call this event the Cemetery Ridge episode (because the Custer Battlefield National Cemetery is now located there). Why has the Cemetery Ridge episode remained a nontheme through all these years? Quite simply, it does not fit, in any way whatsoever, with fatalistic versions of embattled soldiers on Custer Ridge hopelessly outmanned and overwhelmed in a blaze of glory. Battalion elements supposedly got no farther than Custer Hill. Hordes of Indians either drove the battalion to the ridge or caught it there, stopping it in its tracks. Therefore, nothing could have happened on Cemetery Ridge or beyond, and any historical evidence to the contrary is bogus. But insights derived from archaeology suggest otherwise. Viewed from this perspective, pertinent historical accounts demand attention, and when so approached, they are not as confusing or suspect as might be thought (or desired).

Research results guided by ulterior motives, the worst of bias, are suspect. But preconceptions and biases can, and usually do, quite subtly influence research (I expect to hear about mine). Faced with conflicts and vagaries in the historical record, Custer battle historiographers tend to construct scenarios that fit the established mold. Although other possibilities exist in the malleable documentary base, the most satisfying ones are chosen. The most palatable more or less conform to the myth, which in its extreme form portrays doomed but stalwart and defiant soldiers resisting to the last. In other scenarios, some confusion among the troopers is allowed, but never disintegration. To be fair, some later-generation researchers work to slip the myth. Gallantry and defiance take a back seat. But the old solution persists. Doomed, Custer's soldiers are driven and overwhelmed (the fatalistic theme), but not before they launch a desperate gamble (the South Skirmish Line theme), while all the time nothing more is possible (the nontheme). Here again, the specter of disintegration fades as soldiers do their best against overwhelming odds.

I propose now to show that, in light of historical archaeology, the old line—conventional wisdom whatever its trappings—should be abandoned. Challenging the venerable Custer battle historical themes no doubt seems presumptuous. Is not persistence and popularity a strong measure of validity? But here is the rub: these ideas, for the most part, originated in an atmosphere filled with ulterior motives and not-so-subtle biases. The historical record itself is permeated with bias (including Indian testimonies). That atmosphere, in spite of the best of efforts, has yet to be purged. Archaeology provides a new data base, a new atmosphere in which the historical record can be sifted. Recognizing, as did one writer, that "the mystery and legend of the [Custer battle] will endure, defying logic and scholarship,"[8] I shall continue on.

PART TWO.
ARCHAEOLOGY

5

MODELS, METHODS, AND PATTERNS

Decisive battles almost always lead first to the psychological and then, as a result the physical collapse of one side.
— *Stephen D. Wesbrook*[1]

Artifacts as the residues of battle are the product of combat behavior. Contextual relationships—those spatial, temporal, and formal attributes of an artifact connecting it to all other artifacts at a site—are the keys to discerning behavior in combat. Theoretical models allow contextual relationships to be manipulated. They supply the analytical power to turn the key. From this emerges archaeological explanation. In historical archaeology, explanation derived from material traces must eventually be weighed in concert with the historical record. The act of uniting the two disparate information sources establishes complementarity. In terms of explanatory results, complementarity is some measure more than either discipline alone can offer. The result is a more complete and satisfying look at the past.

In this part of the book, I shall focus intently on archaeology, looking not only at the Custer field but also at what it takes to render intelligible the data expected at historic battlefield sites. In this chapter, my intent is to (1) develop a theoretical model of combat behavior; (2) devise analytical methods applicable to the artifacts of combat; and (3) propose archaeological patterns that can be expected under various combat conditions.

The success of modeling in discerning combat behavior is somewhat dependent on the proposition that there will be no two distinctly different sets of actions responsible for the same archaeological patterning. Whereas tactics and technology have changed dramatically over the centuries, behavior in war has remained remarkably predictable in fundamental ways. Either men fight or they do not.[2] When armies fight, their actions are predictable. Tactics govern their behavior. The will to fight, prompted by leadership, sustains men in battle. When this will is lost, unity disintegrates, and defeat invariably ensues. Behavior resulting from collapse is also predictable. Shaped by this dichotomy, then, combat can be modeled on the basis of tactical stability and tactical disintegration, or stability/disintegration. Certain expectations in behavior attend each of these conditions of warfare. The archaeological record should reflect these conditions.

Of course, commanders go to great lengths to prevent loss of stability in combat. While actively engaged in combat, they often have a number of preemptive options at their disposal. Such options might include the capability to reinforce troop strength, the logistical networks to maintain critical supplies such as ammunition, and the possibility of support from other units. Although not limited to these options, variables such as these may affect applications of the stability/disintegration model to the archaeological record. Some ramifications of resupply and reinforcements are discussed in this chapter. At the Custer battle, however, options of this type were either unavailable or not forthcoming as stability within the battalion broke down. Thus it is possible to model the transition from stability to disintegration as a continuum, and I do so here without regard to variables that might impede or prevent the process. Although archaeological manifestations of this transition at the Custer battlefield are relatively straightforward, investigations at other battlefield sites may require consideration of additional variables, like those mentioned above, which increase the complexity in assessing material remains within the parameters of combat modeling.

Tactical Prescriptions

Modern military theorists are engaged in modeling factors that enhance the will to fight, and they study the results of battle under conditions of either tactical stability or tactical disintegration. They need to understand the tactical prescriptions, or tactics, that produce the stability from which disintegration develops. Before examining the stability/disintegration model, then, let us review the tactics that governed U.S. Cavalry operations in 1876.

Tactics define the framework within which military units are expected to operate, from drill and ceremony to combat, the actual prosecution of war. Combat tactics are the concern here. Tactics are distinct from strategy. Strategy broadly directs the goals of war, whereas tactics define the roles of men and women in battle. In battle, soldiers ideally conform to prescribed tactics, but tactics cannot ensure that soldiers will fight. The 7th Cavalry, in 1876, operated under cavalry tactics newly formulated for the U.S. Army.

Historical Background

The new cavalry tactics, adopted in 1874, had achieved widespread use at the time of the Custer battle. Emory Upton's manual[3] codified these tactics, in part, to accommodate the use of improved firearms. Breech-loading rifles with self-contained, metallic ammunition enhanced accuracy, range, and firepower. The new breechloaders could deliver at least five times the firepower of muskets (measured by rate of fire), and barrel rifling increased accuracy. These technological advances required the dispersal of forces on the battlefield.

Improved firearms and modified tactics ushered in the era of modern warfare. Firearm technology advanced rapidly during and immediately after the Civil War and rendered existing tactics obsolete. Previously, mass formations, with unwieldy maneuverability, had proved practical because of the limited accuracy available from musketry, even among trained troops (and even after attempts to improve musketry by rifling barrels). Massed troops, elbow-to-elbow in many instances, could be thrown at the enemy with some confidence that relatively few musket balls would find targets. Musketry limitations, in fact, prompted one German field marshal, in 1803, to issue orders that forbade aiming while firing.[4] Taking aim, which wasted time, reduced firepower rates.

The new firearm technology—rifled arms using self-contained, metallic cartridges—dramatically increased the ability to select, aim, fire, and hit a target. In response, the adoption of dispersed formations diminished the pressure induced by the new weapons. Dispersed formations placed men on the firing lines at intervals, most often with yards between them, certainly not shoulder to shoulder. Although the improved rifle could accurately deliver bullets, accuracy when confronting single targets in dispersed lines depended on proficiency. Errant bullets fell not into a group but harmlessly beyond the individual. As noted by the French strategist Ardant du Picq, commenting around 1870 on the advantage of dispersed over mass formations, it was better to have bullets fall between soldiers than among them.[5]

New tactics afforded maneuverability and dispersal of forces, but they were slow to be adopted. While firearm technology advanced significantly, tactical improvements lagged. For nearly 10 years before 1874, field commanders in the U.S. Army experimented wildly with personal, outdated, and sometimes makeshift tactical procedures. The army tactics eventually disintegrated into such a disorderly condition that an outraged observer complained, in 1872, that no two regiments had a common system of drill. Upton's 1874 manual established a uniform system.

A distinctive change incorporated by Upton affected tactical maneuverability. He introduced, and the army adopted, a "set of fours" as the basic, or smallest, unit—four men. The "set of fours," or squad, simplified operations, increased speed, and eliminated cumbersome maneuvers. The squad concept in practice functioned primarily as a mechanical improvement in maneuvering. The army of the day did not consider, nor did it employ, the squad as a fundamental tactical unit capable of initiating and sustaining independent operations. Today, modern armies utilize the squad in this capacity; essentially it is the smallest tactical unit available to infantry commanders. In the U.S. Army of 1876, however, that distinction—the primary tactical unit—belonged to the platoon.

Upton's tactics, except for the squad, utilized previous concepts of a hierarchal tactical organization. The unit configurations that applied to the 7th Cavalry Regiment at the Little Big Horn were, in ascending order of size and composition, the squad (four men), platoon (squads), company (platoons), wing (companies), battalion (wings), and regiment (battalions). Nominally a cavalry regiment consisted of 12 companies. The hierarchy proceeded upward to include the brigade (regiments) and so on, but we need not continue with that here. Companies played conspicuous roles in the Custer battle, and as the occasions arise, I shall reveal strengths and other details about the companies.

Regardless of organization level, the primary mode of engaging the enemy was skirmishing; thus, skirmish tactics assume relevance in the following discussion. Skirmish tactics are presented in great detail by Upton in his complicated and highly technical chapter "Instructions for Skirmishers."[6] I have tried here to reduce the instructions to elements amenable to archaeological applications. The bottom line, then, is that certain tactics are more likely to be exhibited in this context than others, specifically, prescribed intervals between skirmishers and formation structures. Other, less significant tactics, from my perspective, include deployment procedures and the composition of military units. The latter tactical elements are not expected to appear in the physical remains of battle, but they are valuable historically in comparing eyewitness accounts in light of the archaeological evidence.

Skirmish Tactics

Upton tailored his skirmish tactics for cavalry to provide for the dispersal of men on a combat or firing line. Skirmishers could deploy on the march or at the halt. On the march, they served to clear the way for the main body, which did not exchange fire. Skirmishing on the march could be undertaken either mounted or on foot. In practice, cavalrymen did not often use mounted skirmishing in the later nineteenth century; they operated more as mounted infantrymen. At the halt, skirmishers served as protection for stationary forces. In such instances it became advantageous to dismount to reduce visibility.

The preparatory command "To fight on foot," followed by "As skirmishers," told the soldiers how to deploy. Tactics prescribed a normal interval of five yards between skirmishers on the line, with intervals of 15 yards between squads. Here it becomes evident that the large intervals provided for the dispersal that was necessary with the new weapons technology. At the commander's discretion, however, intervals might be greater or lesser. He could close or extend intervals on one or both flanks at will. Whatever the stations, pedestrian skirmishers ideally assembled in linear fashion.

Dismounted men on a skirmish line fired exactly as did mounted skirmishers. Cavalrymen in 1876 used a single-shot carbine. Odd-numbered skirmishers in each squad fired a round on command and then reloaded as even-numbered skirmishers fired on order. Each skirmisher then continued to fire without regard to the others until receiving the cease-fire command, though the initial procedure tended roughly to maintain an even-odd sequence. Dismounted skirmishers knelt to get better aim, and they could seek cover when available but not at the expense of firepower. Firing procedures allowed direct and oblique fire. Skirmishers delivered direct fire forward from the line and oblique firing to the right and/or left.

Skirmish tactics could be utilized by the platoon, company, battalion, and even at the regimental level. The 7th Cavalry Regiment, however, operated as battalions of companies, so my discussion here is restricted to these levels of organization.

The Battalion

The battalion consisted of at least two but not more than seven companies, with four the normal complement. Custer's three battalions (Benteen, Custer, Reno) approximated the normal distribution within a regiment. Ideally, a cavalry company in 1876 consisted of about 60 officers and men. But for various reasons, actual strengths of companies, including those of the 7th Cavalry, usually hovered at considerably lower figures.[7]

Battalions formed in line or in column. The column is familiar to moviegoers—a long, sinewy formation trailing along, at its head the battalion commander with battle flags fluttering. When in line, battalions formed abreast. The position of a company in either formation depended on its commander's rank or seniority within rank. A five-company battalion (such as Custer's) in line formed right to left as follows (visualize line formation as moving toward the top of the page):

2nd—4th	3rd—5th—1st
left wing	right wing

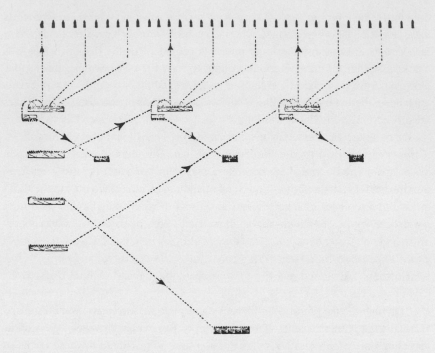

Fig. 5-1. Page 261 from Upton's 1874 *Cavalry Tactics* (1876 edition). A column of four companies in line (left) deploys as skirmishers, one company acting as reserve (bottom center; note also the three company reserve positions below and to right of respective companies). Paragraph 671 allowed the commander to deploy one or more companies as skirmishers.

Here the 1st through 5th designations represent companies by each commander's rank. Companies in column formation (moving toward the right of the page) maintained the same order, with the first company, commanded by the senior company officer, leading. The junior officer (5th) in the battalion followed with his company, trailed by the companies commanded by the third-, fourth-, and second-ranking officers. A battalion consisted of two wings, right and left, with odd-numbered companies assigned to the right wing.

Near an enemy, the battalion or wing commander deployed one or more companies as skirmishers, either mounted or on foot. In accordance with tactics, skirmish deployments required the establishment of company and battalion reserves as in figure 5-1. The size of reserve forces rested with the commander but usually consisted of one or two companies per wing. In mounted skirmishing, the battalion reserves retired to positions approximately 300 yards to the rear of the respective skirmish lines. The reserve force aided the skirmish lines by sending men to support the lines or by "timely" charges. The reserve deployment, especially timely charges, deserves emphasis here; later I shall show the relevance to the Custer battle.

Skirmishing on foot required the protection and control of the riderless horses. One man from each squad, designated as the horse holder, stayed mounted and controlled the riderless horses of the three other squad members. The horse holder tended the *led horses,* a term that I use often in this book. With the led horses secured, the remaining three men deployed on foot to the skirmish line. Horse holders retired to safe positions in the rear of their respective companies or, at the commander's discretion, to the rear of the battalion reserve. Dismounted reserves were posted in the same positions (i.e., 300 yards to the rear) as mounted reserves. When deployed as skirmishers, the battalion executed its movements by the commands and means prescribed for a company of skirmishers.

The Company of Skirmishers

A company consisted of two parts, ideally equal in number, called platoons. One or the other platoon could be utilized separately as a tactical unit, in which case its tactics nearly mimicked those of the larger company. Platoons were usually omitted in an understaffed company. The five companies in the Custer battalion were small compared with authorized strength, and I have seen no evidence they operated at the platoon level. Not only was Custer's battalion below strength, but some men had been assigned to Reno's and Benteen's battalions just before the battle. Thus company strength in the battalion ranged, approximately, from 38 to 44 men, including officers.

Obviously, tactics presumed a normal complement of soldiers per organizational unit. Nonetheless, each company commander on the skirmish line designated one or more squads to act as reserves. The squad(s) initially moved a few yards to the rear of the line to be established. On deployment of the skirmish line, the reserve commander conducted his men to a position about 150 yards to the rear, at the center of the skirmish line, as in figure 5-1. Dismounted skirmishers executed all the movements of mounted skirmishers. The company commander remained 80 yards behind his skirmish line. A mounted guard kept the led horses under cover and safe from enemy fire. Mounts could also be positioned with the company reserve if desired.

This brief overview provides the historical background for incorporating tactics into my investigations. In sum, tactical manuals prescribed the manner in which tacticians expected combat to be carried out. They provided the framework within which tactical stability might be maintained. Through rigid codes of behavior, tactics brought unity and cohesion to fighting individuals. Yet, as I have stressed, this is but one part of the equation in a combat environment.

Breakdowns in codified behavior can occur, and without rectification, they lead to disintegration. Unity dissipates, and the tactical unit, whatever its organization, ceases to exist as a fighting force. With this synopsis, it is possible to present a model of combat behavior relevant to archaeological investigations.

Modeling Combat Behavior

The study of battle is about "solidarity and usually also of disintegration—for it is toward the disintegration of human groups that battle is directed."[8] Military scholars debate the factors that make men fight and those that guard against disintegration. Ancient armies offered the prospect of compensation through plunder and ransom as an incentive for risk taking. In contemporary armies, normative forces are exploited. Tactical stability springs from the psychological conditions that induce men to face life, conditions such as loyalty, friendship, confidence, and responsibility to others.[9] Inculcation of these values encourages the individual to recognize that his welfare and that of the group are intertwined.[10] Today, normative forces strengthened through training hone the individual's willingness to fight.

The will to fight, the moral involvement at the moment of combat, is fixed and can seldom be elevated during battle. In combat it thus falls on leadership to wring the utmost from the moral commitment available. Behavior in combat is the product of moral intensity and of leadership choreographed by tactics. A military unit can remain tactically stable and enjoy victory or suffer defeat. Clearly, behavior responsible for tactical stability is likely to approximate tactical prescriptions; behavior leading to disintegration results from debilitating deviations from prescribed tactics. It is therefore prudent to model combat on a range from disciplined to disordered behavior.

Tactical Stability

Battles are extremely confusing experiences.[11] Order is paramount but difficult to maintain. Events are often shaped by accident.[12] G. Dyer argues that tactics, drill, and responses usually reduce the uncertainties of battle but are never an absolute guide to success.[13] Tactics are prescriptions against confusion and disorder. Nevertheless, some disorganization attends every stage of an advance.[14] Despite tactical prescription, intervals cannot be precisely maintained.[15] Some lines advance slower or faster than others. Terrain may influence movements of the skirmish line. Enemy fire affects order.[16] Some soldiers may malinger to avoid the impending clash.

Further, many soldiers in modern battle simply refuse to fire, although recognition of this phenomenon has come about slowly.[17] As early as 1870, du Picq observed that firepower on the battle lines does not equate with manpower; not every soldier will fight.[18] S. L. A. Marshall's World War II battle studies concluded that up to 85 percent, but more commonly 70 percent, of men in a company dispersed along a battle line will not fire. The root of this problem lies in the dispersal of troops on the line. Supervision among dispersed troops is more difficult than among massed troops.[19] During the Korean War, the percentage of soldiers who used their weapons increased to 55 percent, primarily as a result of improved training.[20] Though the Korean experience suggests that fire efficiency is variable, it remains clear that firepower on the line will not equal manpower.

Another prevalent behavior is the tendency for individuals on the line to draw closer together. Du Picq referred to this as "crowding".[21] Men tend to narrow the skirmish intervals, unconsciously closing together. The entire skirmish line begins to compress. The crowding tendency grows stronger as the distance from the enemy narrows. Crowding on the skirmish line increases exposure by lessening dispersal. Good leadership on the line is most important to keep men properly spaced and effectively fighting. But it is in the near presence of the enemy that tactical integrity is most shaky. As du Picq put it, "In these moments, everything hangs by a thread."[22]

If leadership deteriorates, or is poor at the onset, crowding escalates as enemy contact increases. Marshall described this phenomenon as "bunching": men "will always bunch unless they are insistently told by voice to stop."[23] J. Keegan believes that men press together for protection as extreme fear develops.[24] This is the essence of bunching, and it is what du Picq alluded to—everything hangs by a thread. During World War II, when casualties mounted, survivors tended to bunch around their most effective firearm, in that case the Browning automatic rifle.[25] Protection or safety, whatever the form, tends to draw men together in tight situations.

Du Picq seems also to have recognized bunching behavior, though he attributed it to confusion. According to him, "Men will gather into small groups and become confused."[26] He therefore argued for the adoption of a dispersed, single-rank formation in infantry operations, concluding that increased space between soldiers would increase order. But Du Picq apparently failed to realize that bunching of men is not specific to certain formations. The urge to bunch can, even at the slightest provocation, infect men spread over the widest of lines. And even though it is a normal psychological reaction, bunching is very much a debilitating urge.

An instance of bunching occurred in the 1st U.S. Cavalry less than a year after the Little Big Horn battle. The place was White Bird Canyon in Idaho. The tenacious and elusive Nez Percé Indians were the foe.[27] The first few shots had reverberated through White Bird Canyon without much cause for alarm. H Company soon formed front into line at five-yard intervals, whereupon a small Nez Percé party skirted its right flank. At a distance of 100 yards, and beyond a ravine, the Indian dash posed no immediate threat. Yet soldiers stationed on the right quickly abandoned their positions and huddled together at the center of their company line, rather than contest the movement. Fear had set in. As it turned out, failure to resist the flanking action enabled the Nez Percé to press the attack from the rear. Capt. David Perry rushed to provide aid with his company, but without success. Now at an advantage, the warriors eventually sent the entire cavalry column reeling back in confusion.

Crowding and bunching phenomena resulting from stress are not, however, irreversible. An infusion of leadership, or sometimes reinforcements, can correct either problem, but not always. Captain Perry failed at White Bird Canyon for several reasons. Having lost all of his trumpets, he had earlier forfeited timely communication. When he reached H Company with instructions, the fear prevalent there spread to his men, causing them to either bunch up or break from the ranks. Meanwhile, an inability to control the horses—a factor in Custer's defeat—exacerbated the developing predicament.

Quite the contrary occurred at the Little Big Horn when the Reno battalion left Weir Point. This incident is a testimony to effective leadership in times of peril. Lt. Edward Godfrey commanded the company that protected Reno's retreat. Godfrey had thrown out a skirmish line to protect the rear of the battalion as it moved back. He observed that in the initial stages of the retreat, his company displayed "a semblance of conformity" to tactics. But later, "the tendency was to close into groups." Godfrey, with the able assistance of Lt. Luther Hare, halted his men and made them take proper intervals until within reach of the Reno-Benteen battlefield.[28] Only one soldier among the hundreds lost his life.

Rectification, such as Godfrey instituted, is not always available no matter how brilliant the officer. But without it, the bunching phenomenon, as at White Bird Canyon, is likely to result in tactical disintegration. Perhaps the most dramatic example occurred in 1866 during an engagement near Fort Phil Kearny (near present-day Sheridan, Wyoming, some 80 miles south of the Custer battlefield). On December 21, Capt. William Fetterman led a contingent of about 80 soldiers after some warriors who were harassing a wood-gathering detail. The Indians lured Fetterman and his party some distance beyond the fort, then attacked. Every soldier died. Later, a special investigating commission reported that the bodies of Fetterman, another officer, and about 65 soldiers lay bunched "in a space not exceeding thirty-five feet in diameter." The commission report noted that within this space, "there were no indications of a severe struggle. . . . No empty cartridge shells were about."[29]

The Fetterman episode highlights an effect of bunching behavior in most grim fashion. Fetterman and his men, trapped well beyond the fort and in rough terrain, found they could not flee to safety. At the last moments the men, it seems, bunched around their leader, a normal behavior much like gathering around the most effective weapon. Then the huddled group, under extreme pressure, disintegrated (i.e., they did not resist), all men dying bunched up. But the collapse of tactical unity can also result in flight, especially with the prospect of safety, real or perceived. Later I will illustrate how disintegration during the Custer battle resulted principally in flight. Though it did not end in safety, flight did proceed toward units that initially maintained stability.

Disintegration

Disintegration usually develops with lightning quickness.[30] It can develop from what Keegan has called "collective indiscipline."[31] R. A. Gabriel's "combat fatigue" is a similar concept.[32] Collective indiscipline usually builds gradually; it results in disintegration when soldiers simply refuse to enter battle. This happened to the French army in World War I when 54 of 110 divisions would not engage the enemy.[33]

Another type of disintegration is brought about by the shock of an enemy attack. Sudden and acute, combat shock is most debilitating.[34] Soldiers engaged with the enemy may quit fighting and die on the spot (as at the Fetterman fight) or, perhaps, surrender. Or they may break and flee in panic and disorder, occasionally with—but usually without—any significant resistance. With or without individual resistance, flight is perceived as a means of survival.[35] If flight is not possible, soldiers are usually consigned to death—especially when surrender is not acceptable to either victor or vanquished[36] (again, as at the Fetterman fight).

The latter type of disintegration—combat shock—is emphasized here because it is the type that befell the Custer battalion. Behavior, such as bunching, that results from shock disintegration can be extraordinarily extreme. At the battle of Waterloo, in 1815, panic-stricken French soldiers died in masses exceeding a meter in depth.[37] Four hundred years earlier, victorious English soldiers at Agincourt sorted through "heaps [of bodies] . . . higher than a man" to find live Frenchmen for ransom.[38] Piles of humanity underscore the extent to which men will cling to one another at the moment of death. Similar behavior, if not nearly as extreme, occurred at the Custer battle, most notably during the "last stand" and in a rugged ravine not far away.

Armies may flee by retreating in perfect tactical order. Or individuals may flee in terror while others remain in position. It is the mass flight following disintegration, however, that is the most dangerous. Once men take to flight, they do not stop until overcome by some obstacle or exhaustion.[39] Marshall has described instances of mass flight precipitated simply by the authorized but rapid movements of a few men to the rear. Nearby soldiers, hardly under duress at the moment, became confused and fled in complete disorder when they saw their comrades running.[40]

Obviously, flight developing from confusion, such as that described by Marshall, can be disastrous if the enemy seizes the advantage. However, when remaining in place is certain to result in death, flight is legitimate. At this point, all men in battle reserve the right to flee.[41] Flight under this condition is generated by extreme terror and is driven by panic.

But the legitimate breaking point is seldom reached, since perceptions induced by combat stress usually overwhelm reality. Thus the "right" to flee becomes a major factor in prompting disintegration, even under the most ludicrous situations (viewed in retrospect). For example, the breaking point was not reached at Wounded Knee (in southwest South Dakota on the Pine Ridge Reservation), though some cavalrymen from the 7th Regiment behaved as if it was. With a Sioux village virtually surrounded by troops, gunfire unexpectedly rattled the crisp December morning in 1890. The army at this moment, not to mention throughout the day, enjoyed complete control. Yet, shaken by the first shots from the village, by gunfire they could not even see, men from two of the surrounding companies "dropped, ran—did anything they could to get away."[42] Officers regained control, but not before surprise had bested the edgy troopers. The results of this tragic episode, which spared neither woman nor child, aged nor infirm, are well known. The incident shows that even in the most secure situations, the unexpected can sometimes instigate collapse. Surprise on the battlefield is an effective way to generate panic.

In warfare, the enemy strives to instill fear. If the enemy is perceived as superior, then moral commitment can erode and eventually disintegrate. Losing the will to fight through moral disintegration differs from losing the capacity to fight. Although army defeats have resulted from inferior or depleted material and manpower, moral disintegration is usually at the core of defeat.[43] Indeed, victory through moral disintegration is the objective of most armies because it is less taxing on the resources of war. The recent war in the Persian Gulf provides no better example. Military men thus find it expedient to use perceptions of power to induce shock and generate fear in the enemy. One way of accomplishing this, which happened at the Custer battle, is to mass firepower at the enemy from close positions.

Disintegration is complete at the moment of surrender or death. Soldiers who escape can, of course, be reorganized, but that option is not of concern here. Experience has shown that fleeing soldiers can be regrouped only with the aid of fresh, newly deployed units,[44] which were not available during the Custer battle.

Keegan illustrated the uncertainties of surrender, calling it "one of the most obscure of all battlefield transactions."[45] There is simply no guarantee of acceptance, and the more the uncertainties the greater the chance that disintegration will result in flight. The Custer battle seems to have unfolded under these circumstances. Soldiers on the western plains during the latter half of the nineteenth century, expecting a torturous death by Indians, loathed the prospect of capture. Their expectations seem to have developed from rumor as much as reality.[46] Nevertheless, it is doubtful that any who died in the Custer battle entertained thoughts of surrender, preferring instead to flee.

Flight, like any other condition of disintegration, is usually undertaken in virtual disorder. Soldiers die in the largest numbers when they run.[47] Resistance on an individual basis is ineffective, and in the near presence of the enemy, it is predictably fatal. The enemy, themselves suddenly released from danger, can inflict a terrible toll. "Pitiless blood-lust" is typical of pursuers.[48] This blood lust so infected Russian troops while sacking a city in 1704 that the commander, Peter the Great, tried to restore control by killing a crazed officer.[49]

The bloody carnage resulting from disintegration and flight can develop at any time during an engagement. At the Custer battle, soldiers sparred with warriors for some time before tactical stability disappeared. But in a clash during the 1873 Modoc Indian wars in California, disintegration enveloped infantrymen at the opening fusillade. Modoc warriors, secreted in a labyrinth of lava beds, suddenly and surprisingly opened fire. Lt. Harry Moore later remembered that the troops instantly became demoralized. He wrote that the men deserted and "fled like a pack of sheep."[50] Quickly the Modocs responded, and the slaughter began. Later the grim results of the panicky flight became apparent. Four of the five officers involved and 24 enlisted men lay dead, as Rickey described it, in "one confused heap." Don Rickey[51] drew a lesson from this debacle—soldiers trained in parade-ground drill prove no match for furtive opponents—a lesson that will later merit attention in analyzing the Custer defeat.

Fear did not result in such mayhem at White Bird Canyon. Nonetheless, the two companies did disintegrate and run, thereby rendering the entire cavalry force sorely ineffective. Officers now and then attempted to rally the men and at one point even mounted a charge. This too ended in confusion as the chargers became hopelessly scattered. Ultimately, Perry's column fled in disarray, leaving behind 33 dead. Some survivors scurried directly to the town of Grangeville. Others, including Captain Perry, retreated haphazardly to a nearby ranch house, with the Nez Percé in dogged pursuit. Only when an armed party of civilians arrived from a nearby town did the Indians retreat.

This farcical ending to the White Bird Canyon affair must have provided some comic relief, at least to townsfolk who, worried about an Indian threat, had enlisted aid from the army. But much less comical is one other White Bird Canyon incident. Early in the fray, when Perry's company fled, some men became so rattled that they simply left their weapons behind.[52] Indeed, decades earlier, frightened French infantrymen at Waterloo threw down their arms and huddled together as death approached.[53] Such seemingly odd behavior is entirely possible, even probable, under extreme combat duress—real or perceived—and it happened at the Custer battle.

Flight and its attendant behaviors are predictable consequences of disintegration. Like other aspects of battle, flight should produce peculiar patterns in the archaeological record. It remains, then, to develop the process by which archaeological residues of combat may be evaluated within the parameters of the model presented here. This chapter concludes by formulating methods for discerning battle behavior and by postulating archaeological patterns—making predictions—which can be expected from various circumstances of engagement.

Discerning Combat Behavior

Conventional battle, by its nature, requires coordinated, collective behavior. Tactical units enter battle coordinated by tactics, with each individual, each unit, acting as part of the whole. Unit actions constitute "episodes" that are undertaken in time and space. During battle, episodes may occur simultaneously at different locations on the battlefield, at different times, or sequentially at the same place. Episodes may be exceedingly brief, perhaps measured in minutes, or may take much longer. The tactical unit may be of any size as long as it is capable of initiating and sustaining tactical operations. I noted that in contemporary armies, the smallest tactical unit is often the squad; at the Custer battle, it was nominally the company.

Each episode develops from individuals performing in the aggregate. Under tactically stable conditions, individuals act on behalf of the military unit to achieve a common goal, and their behavior is decidedly standardized. Under conditions of disintegration, combatants act alone, and the common group goal is subordinated. Because individuals compose episodes, individual actions form the basis for determining the nature of a battle. Individual actions, therefore, must be recognized and tied to episodes. From an archaeological perspective, a battle is best evaluated in this manner. The archaeological application of firearm identification analysis, a procedure proposed by R. A. Fox[54] and developed in D. D. Scott and R. A. Fox,[55] is instrumental in determining individual behavior on the battlefield.

Firearm Identification Analysis

From an archaeological perspective, it is rarely possible to recover the intimacy of personal behavior, and in any case, that is not the goal here. Instead I speak of individual behavior. By this I mean behavior that is represented in the positions and movements of individuals on the battlefield. Firearm identification procedures provide the method for determining this type of combat behavior. These procedures involve the comparative analysis of distinctive attributes imparted to ammunition components during the process of firearm discharge and reloading. Firearm identification analysis is routinely conducted in police laboratories to help solve crimes in which firearms were discharged.[56] It is, for example, often possible to trace a bullet, lodged in the deceased, to a particular gun. Details of the archaeological application of firearm identification analysis at the Custer battlefield are contained in two earlier books that I coauthored.[57]

What are ammunition components? They make up the object we often call a cartridge or shell. Self-contained, metallic ammunition components include the cartridge case and the bullet (and often a primer). These assembled components, plus the powder charge, constitute the cartridge. When a cartridge is discharged, the firing-pin mechanism in a weapon is activated, leaving firing-pin marks on the cartridge case base. In this sequence, pulling the trigger causes the firing pin to release and to strike the cartridge at its primer. The primer ignites and explodes the charge, which in turn sends the bullet on its way. The expended, or spent, cartridge is then removed from the chamber by any number of extractor mechanisms, which also leave distinct marks on the cartridge case. When a firearm is discharged, bullets are sent down the barrel. The rifling of the barrel leaves land-and-groove marks on the bullets. All these marks—firing pin, extractor and land-groove—represent "signatures" useful in assessing individual actions on the battlefield.

As a reminder, these types of firearm signatures can be expected at battlefield sites that postdate the widespread adoption of improved firearms and metallic, self-contained cartridges (ca. 1865). Before the introduction of these cartridges, and compatible weapons, percussion firearms were commonplace. Handlers loaded percussion arms through the barrel using gunpowder, wad, ball, and ramrod (muzzle-loaders). Trigger activation released the hammer, which struck an explosive cap. The cap charge ignited the powder, which in turn fired the bullet. It may be that percussion cap signatures exist (and perhaps land-groove signatures on bullets fired from rifled muskets), but such potentials are not explored here.

The soft lead bullets used in nineteenth-century muzzle-loaders and breech-loaders tend to oxidize in time, notably in archaeological context, thus generally obscuring land-and-groove signatures. As a result, oxidized bullets are typically not useful beyond assessing firearm types. For example, a certain bullet type (caliber, weight, shape) might represent one firearm type. Cartridge cases can also be manipulated in this way, as discussed below. But cartridge cases are most useful in assessing individual behaviors of the kind defined earlier—positions and movements.

Copper and brass cases tend to preserve well, and firing-pin and extractor signatures remain prominent. The utility of cartridge case signature analysis lies in the ability to distinguish between individual weapons, even in the absence of firearms (as was the case at the Custer battle site). All extractor and firing-pin mechanisms exhibit minute variations that, from an archaeological perspective, render each individual firearm unique. Variation is caused by specification tolerances in, and wear on, the tooling machinery used to manufacture firearm mechanism components. Assembled firearm mechanisms amplify these variations. The result is a firearm that leaves, when discharged, a unique set of firing-pin and extractor mechanism marks on the cartridge case. Put another way, no two firearms impart identical signatures. Thus, comparative analyses of unique signature variations allows a sorting of cartridge cases representative of individual weapons.

Signature analysis is visualized in the photomicrographs of figures 5-2 and 5-3. The former shows two cartridge cases (light and dark areas) with nearly identical firing-pin signatures (overlapped for comparative purposes). These two cartridge cases were fired from the same weapon. Figure 5-3 depicts extractor signatures on two cartridge cases. The marks, which exhibit short tails angling downward at the left, appear somewhat different due to lighting variations. But distinct similarities indicate that they too were discharged from the same weapon. The two sets of cartridge cases in the figures are in fact the same specimens. The two signature sets corroborate the "fired from the same weapon" identification.

Signatures representative of individual weapons are "unique" signatures. Unique signatures are distinguished from "type" signatures. Firearm identification usually begins with the analysis of firearm types. Types may be established by recovering firearms, or firearm parts, but these are rarely found on historic battlefields (we found several parts at the Custer battle site, but no guns). Unlike firearms, however, spent cartridges—the cases—are, as a matter of course, discarded. In comparison, then, they are relatively ubiquitous at battle sites, and they aid in establishing types. Firing-pin and extractor mechanism designs typically differ between firearm types. Thus, cartridge case signatures are also distinctive of types.

Type signatures are very useful because firearm type cannot always be established on the basis of ammunition component characteristics alone (e.g., caliber, weight, shape). Many ammunition calibers can, for example, be fired in a vari-

Fig. 5-2. Comparison photomicrograph of firing-pin signatures on two overlapping .44-caliber cartridge cases fired from the same weapon (Henry or Model 1866 repeating rifle). Courtesy Nebraska State Highway Patrol.

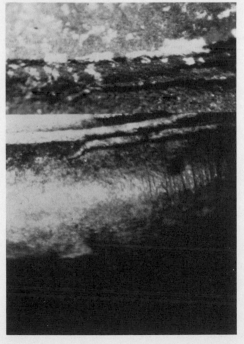

Fig. 5-3. Comparison photomicrograph of extractor mechanism signatures on two .44-caliber cartridge cases fired from the same weapon. Courtesy Nebraska State Highway Patrol.

ety of firearms. The .44-caliber Henry cartridge, a popular nineteenth-century ammunition, could be fired not only in the Henry repeating rifle (for which it was designed) but also in the Winchester rifle, the .44-caliber rimfire Colt pistol, and the .44-caliber rimfire Remington revolver. Firing pins or extractors in each of these types of firearms differ, making it possible to discern weapon type on the basis of cartridge case signatures. In figure 5-3, for example, the extractor signatures are peculiar to the Henry repeating rifle. The firing pins in figure 5-2 represent either the Henry or the Model 1866 Winchester. But because of the extractor signatures, the firearm type can be narrowed to the Henry. Bullet land-and-groove marks, by the way, might also vary between firearm types, but they are far less reliable even when preserved.

Like unique signatures, firearm type signatures are important in battlefield studies. Once weapon capabilities are understood, the role of firearms can be assessed, particularly in evaluating the arms types used by each side and the firepower differences between the two. Such assessments might provide insights into the results of a battle, and I shall do so for the Custer battle. Firearm type analysis typically aids in distinguishing between adversary positions on the field. A certain position may exhibit type-diagnostic cartridge cases and/or adversary bullets. Further, type analyses can provide insights into the nature of an episode. A preponderance of bullets at one location may suggest a brief, and perhaps unsuccessful, occupation by the defenders, especially in the absence of spent casings among the bullets. Type studies can also help differentiate between multiple episodes at the same location. A defensive position might have been abandoned and subsequently occupied by the foe, thereby leaving evidence of firearms used by both sides.

Firearm typing is obviously critical where supporting archaeological data, such as equipage (often different between adversaries), are equivocal or lacking. This is not the case for the Custer battle, except for Indian items. Soldier positions reveal all manner of nonfirearm-related artifacts, from personal items to horse equipment. These certainly provide position clues, but they are not emphasized in this study because ammunition components serve well enough. Readers interested in the variety and detail of 7th Cavalry equipage may consult, among others, two books that describe the Custer battlefield archaeology.[58]

Individual Behavior

Signature analyses provide the ability to identify firearm types and to distinguish between individual weapons within each of the several types. The latter capability is important in determining individual behaviors. Most notable is the use of cartridge cases, which, unlike bullets, tend to fall very near the weapon when ejected and are assumed to approximate a weapon's position. In this way, unique firearm signatures can be used to trace firearms throughout the battlefield. A tight cluster of cases from the same weapon, for example, most likely indicates a single firing position. Casings from several discrete locations, but with identical signatures, would indicate movement across the battlefield. Signature patterns, then, at the least represent the positions and movements of weapons.

Obviously, each firearm is carried and operated by an individual. It follows, then, that the spatial distributions of firearm signatures can be correlated with the positions and movements of individual combatants. Earlier I proposed that different actions should not result in similar archaeological patterns. But site formation processes may skew patterns. Minor soil disturbances are likely to be insignificant, but severe ground displacements can affect artifact provenances. The use of captured weapons may also bias interpretations of the military identity of individuals. Also, cartridge case locations may not necessarily signal exact firing positions because spent casings can be carried in the chamber for some time. And relic collection over time may erase, either wholly or partially, records of one or more firearms. Such biases are considered in the following chapter and others when I examine individual positions and movements on the Custer battlefield.

Individual behaviors taken alone are poor measures of the specific nature of a battle, for two reasons. The first is behavioral and the second is temporal. I have argued that individuals wage battle as part of a group; military units perform as a whole under tactical prescriptions, or they disintegrate in predictable ways. Thus, battles are episodic, and individual behaviors must be evaluated under these circumstances. Second, combat is undertaken in time and space. Until now I have considered only spatial aspects. But movement of individuals also implies elapsed time. Individual movements are represented by two or more identical firearm signatures, each at a different location, this set of locations forming a pattern that resulted over time.[59] Directionality, however, is not always reflected in the pattern. Nevertheless, the nature of episodes can help alleviate the temporal limitation because individuals in combat tend to behave in predictable ways. Predictability imparts directionality to individual behaviors and thus adds the time element to pattern. Patterning reveals the behaviors constituting episodes and can assist in unraveling the temporal relationships between episodes.

Episodic Behavior

In practice, unique signatures are compared and grouped as individual weapons within types. Signatures representative of individual weapons are mapped in order to recognize contextual relationships among individual positions and

movements. Contextual relationships reveal patterns that provide the data necessary for hypothesizing episodic behavior. Theoretically, the maintenance of stable tactical behavior during an episode should result in patterning reminiscent of
tactical deployments, such as skirmish lines or, under conditions of severe pressure, the tendency to crowd or bunch. Conditions that bring about disintegration
ought to be reflected in haphazard patterning or in the absence of evidence for
resistance with firearms. Each of these combat behavior characteristics is examined in detail in reference to the archaeological patterns that might be expected
to develop.

Tactical Stability

Tactics evolve; my discussion is restricted to the 1874 cavalry tactics and, in
particular, skirmish deployments. It is clear that skirmish behavior should leave
recognizable patterns on the ground. Ideally, a skirmish line would be revealed
in the linear dispersion of unique weapon signatures at specified intervals. The
intervals should reflect deployment by squads. Signatures of squad members
should be spaced at five-yard intervals, with 15-yard intervals between the signatures representing squads. Theoretically, the number of unique signatures per
squad should vary between mounted and dismounted skirmishing, the latter
reflecting the loss of one soldier to horse-holding duties.

In practice, however, ideal conditions cannot always be expected. The nature
of battle is such that prescribed intervals can seldom be maintained. Some soldiers are apt not to fire their weapons. Also, tactics allowed commanders to
lengthen or shorten intervals between soldiers and squads. Site formation processes may also disturb patterning. And practical limitations often prevent the
complete recovery of archaeological data. Thus, in an archaeological context,
intervals between unique firearm signatures may not be regularly spaced. These
limitations, however, should not diminish the ability to recognize skirmish lines.
It is expected that regardless of intervals, unique signatures should be dispersed
in a more or less linear fashion. Linearity should be more pronounced for stationary forces than for moving skirmish lines.

Provided that tactical integrity is maintained, discrete military units (such as
a company) skirmishing independently of others should produce discrete sets of
unique signatures. This set is representative of the tactical unit. Thus, the potential exists for identifying a unit involved in a series of episodes at various locations. Theoretically, discrete sets of unique signatures can exhibit directionality.
Continuing manpower attrition at each location would produce a corresponding
reduction in unique signatures within the set. The location with a greater number
of unique signatures would represent the initial engagement, and locations with
fewer and fewer signatures in the set would show the latter engagements. Since

attrition on the skirmish line may require replacement with reserves, an increase in new unique signatures from spot to spot might also signal the direction in which the skirmish line moved.

Other archaeological data may also aid in determining unit directionality. Ideally, locations with a low artifact density and/or few artifact classes may represent an initial clash, with increases at other locations representing subsequent episodes. This, like reduction in unique signatures, is a matter of attrition. There is, however, no guarantee that attrition will occur during battle, and it may be that loss of men and equipment is negligible. In such cases, it is difficult to determine the movements of military units. Thus, under tactically stable conditions, temporal relationships between episodes may be difficult to discern archaeologically. This limitation may require a dependence, in part, on the historical record to determine the movements of units across the battlefield.

Crowding behavior will modify the integrity of skirmish lines. When individuals crowd closer to each other, they shift positions. On a stationary skirmish line, assuming that each skirmisher continues to fire, crowding should produce unique signatures at intervals narrower than prescribed. In contrast, skirmishers who hold their original positions will leave tightly clustered patterns of unique signatures at or near prescribed intervals. Under ideal conditions, crowding may not be discernible from skirmishing undertaken at closed intervals. Other limitations, such as data recovery, site formation processes, and fire behavior, may also affect the ability to recognize crowding on the skirmish line. Nevertheless, the skirmish line, though somewhat compressed, should retain a semblance of linearity quite unlike the pattern expected for the bunching phenomenon.

Instances of bunching behavior can be expected to produce a number of unique signatures clustered within a restricted area. Signature patterning for bunching should not resemble the linear skirmish line. Rather, a typical pattern might result from men massed in circular fashion. Distances between unique signatures should be short and irregular. Because bunching develops from deterioration in leadership, there should be some indiscriminate movement among the individuals. Thus, signatures from the same weapon might tend to be dispersed throughout the area of bunching.

Without restoration of order, bunching behavior will very likely result in disintegration of the military unit. Indeed, unconstrained bunching may be considered tantamount to disintegration. Disintegration, however, can proceed from any deployment. Even well-ordered skirmish lines can quickly disintegrate. Disintegration, it may be expected, should produce a patterning quite unlike that indicative of tactical stability.

Disintegration

Men gathered in armies enter actual combat under some sort of tactical control. Given sufficient moral fortitude, victory may ensue. Similarly, the dreaded prospect of defeat always lurks nearby. Men may fight to the end, never wavering, and still maintain tactical stability. But under stress and in the face of extreme pressure, soldiers will more likely lose stability. From an archaeological perspective, therefore, an episode may reflect the gamut of combat behaviors, beginning with solidarity and ending in disintegration.

Transformation from tactical stability to disintegration can provide directionality, or chronology, to the episode. A useful analogy is that of the second law of thermodynamics: disorder proceeds from order. (Under actual combat conditions, the reverse may sometimes occur, as when disintegrated units reorganize, but only after original failure of tactical stability. Extending the thermodynamics comparison, we can view reorganization as analogous to an open system. The Custer battle, as I shall show, approximated a closed system, one with no additional energy source available.) It is virtually inconceivable that a military unit would enter battle disordered and then organize. Disintegration preserved in the archaeological record should therefore provide directional clues, which in turn measure temporal sequencing. Under circumstances of disintegration, the individual assumes prominence, since actions on behalf of the group cease. Chronology might be indicated by the helter-skelter distribution, signifying flight, of individual movements that originate on a known battle line—that is, a line detected archaeologically. Similar patterning could be expected in movements originating from bunching behavior or, as I have indicated, at any stage of deployment. In these instances one might imagine a multitude of lines splayed every which way from the location where stability evaporated. Strictly speaking, such a distribution is not a pattern, except as it represents a chance configuration (unlike the skirmish line). Chance patterning produced by disintegration is much like the snowflake crystal: no two are thought to be exactly alike.

Whereas disintegration is likely to result in splayed patterning, individuals may flee in attempts to join other units positioned elsewhere on the battlefield, resulting in somewhat more coherent signature patterns—though still far from anything resembling a stable combat unit. Many may flee without turning about to shoot. But if some individuals in flight continue to discharge weapons, their movements will be recorded in unique signature patterning. Such patterns should reflect the sporadic resistance typical of terrified men resisting on their own. This distinction should be fairly obvious when evaluated with reference to behavior governed by prescribed tactics. But these haphazard movements should also display some common directionality in patterning—toward presumed safety with comrades. In the end, these patterns, or nonpatterns if you prefer, should, with some degree of resolve, link spatially discrete units, and thus temporally discrete episodes, and should help to sort the battle chronology.

Archaeologically, behavior in combat can also be recorded through dearth. Quite often during disintegration, men overcome with fear do not stop to fire weapons. They are, indeed, even prone to abandon arms in panic. When men offer no firearm resistance during flight, signature analyses obviously are of little use. But absence of firearm-related evidence for resistance may or may not be a sign of disintegration during an episode. Brevity of action might preclude reloading (and thus on-the-spot ejection of spent cartridges) before an orderly withdrawal, though the episode may be clearly defined by enemy bullets. Or an encroaching enemy might initiate hand-to-hand combat before any significant firearm discharge. Events of this nature are rare in modern combat, though they occurred during the Custer battle.

Whatever the alternatives, and doubtless others can be entertained, supporting data seem to be necessary to deduce disintegration, instead of other options, from a lack of evidence for resistance—notably firearm discharge. Supporting data from the Custer battlefield, in episodes soon to be detailed, include concentrations of Indian-delivered bullets at soldier positions marked principally, in the absence (or nearly so) of government cartridge cases, by equipage, human remains, and burial locations. These episodes are also highlighted, as we shall see in examining the historical record, by graphic descriptions of behavior tantamount to tactical disintegration.

Fire Behavior

The differences in fire behavior under conditions of tactical stability and disintegration are largely qualitative. Each will produce a different pattern in the archaeological record. Quantitative measurements are not as readily informative, and this is especially the case in reference to fire behavior during an episode. Intermittent firing, for example, over a lengthy period might produce residues quantitatively equivalent to heavy firing for a brief time. Thus the duration and the intensity of fire behavior during an episode cannot be accurately measured archaeologically. This constraint limits the utility of absolute comparisons of combat intensity between episodes as well. Nevertheless, quantitative measurements do provide relative data useful in positing hypotheses, which can be checked against available historical accounts that address combat intensity. Absolute fire behavior comparisons between individuals on the same line are possible assuming that each man endures equally and the entire line faces similar opposition.

Summary

Combat behavior, in various forms, is predictable. Behavior under tactical stability is expected to conform, by varying degrees, to prescribed combat tactics. Behavior during disintegration deviates completely from tactical prescription. This dichotomy enhances the probability that a range of combat behaviors can be recognized in the physical traces of battle.

Archaeological analysis as it is conceived here is predicated on the ability to discern individual behaviors. These behaviors are delineated through the archaeological application of firearm identification analysis. Unique signatures, which represent the positions and movements of individual combatants, provide the basis for recognizing individual behavior. Individual actions are undertaken on behalf of the unit, and therefore the unit assumes importance in discerning combat behavior. Military units participate in episodes, and it is the relationships between episodes that largely define the nature of a particular battle.

Analyses in chapter 7 utilize the model and methods proposed here, with specific reference to the Custer battle site. My intent is to discern behavior embedded in archaeological patterning by using the stability/disintegration model, identify episodes and determine the nature of combat at each, and link the episodes, where possible, in chronological order. This exercise provides the analytical framework—one derived foremost from the ground—within which documentary evidence can be incorporated into the analyses. First, however, some other matters must be taken up in chapter 6. Since context is so important, data collection procedures ought to be reviewed. And we should develop an acquaintance with another class of archaeological remains—soldier burials. Finally, the artifact record will be exposed by mapping firearm component distributions across the battlefield.

6

FIELDWORK, BURIALS, AND DISTRIBUTIONS

Hitherto [American historians] have depended too much on manuscript evidences.
—T. J. Wertenbaker, American historian[1]

Working out the most intricate details of past battles is a trying experience. History has a time of it, and Custer's last is probably the best proof. Sorting battles chronologically, linking events, and getting at the how and why questions are difficult propositions for the Custer battle historian. In the end, recollections of the event seldom jibe. Consequently, various explanations by numerous analysts have surfaced. Archaeology helps surmount such dilemmas if only because material remains and their patterns are not produced by someone's imperfect recall, not to mention biased recollections. I do not propose that archaeology serves up all the answers to various questions unanswerable through historiography. But perspectives from the ground prove indispensable when poring through the documents.

Here and in the next chapter, material remains as a behavioral record of the Custer fight assume center stage. Of course, I did not go into this endeavor unaware of the various ideas about the battle. Certainly I did not labor in a historical vacuum. If anything, I entered more or less numbed by the fatalistic tradition. That has changed. In any case, I have worked assiduously to avoid shaping or tailoring analyses to fit or reject one or another of the diverse Custer battle theories. Conclusions at times may resemble those derived from historical research, and there is no reason why this should not be. History and archaeology can reach similar judgments. But I think you will find that any coincidences are restricted to elements of a whole. What emerges as unique is a unified account— the whole—that rids the bogus (plenty of that), exposes the legitimate (not too soothing), accommodates the contradictions (in the end more apparent than real), explains the mysteries (not so intractable), and importantly, an account capable of receiving new facts.

Battles consist of interrelated events—episodes—undertaken in space. I refer to the spatial aspects of episodes as sectors. My primary objective is to illuminate the nature of combat behaviors at each sector and link the behavioral episodes, where possible, in a chronological framework. This is a straightforward task. In developing the archaeological view of Custer's fight, I rely heavily on the theoretical framework and analytical procedures formulated in my approach to combat modeling. Behavioral aspects are derived from patterning—contextual relationships between the various types of artifacts that form the material record. The temporal solution relies on the expectation that certain combat behaviors follow from others. I have already mentioned one example: disintegration is expected to proceed from tactical stability.

Confidence in archaeological interpretation is always tied directly to strategies, methods, and techniques used to extract data. In the final analysis, sloppy methods and ill-conceived planning diminish trust. It is appropriate, then, to outline the ways in which archaeological data were extracted and analyzed. The nonhistoriographical analysis of the Custer battle begins here, with a definition of the study area plus an overview of the methods used in data recovery.

Fieldwork and Procedure

Congress established what is informally known today as the Custer battlefield as a U.S. National Cemetery in 1879. The War Department administered the property, land set aside not only to commemorate the famous event but also to provide the final resting place for hundreds of American veterans from many wars. Today the national cemetery is a prominent feature, one that is confusing to many interested in the battle. "Did all these men die with Custer?" is a question often asked. The answer is no, but a few of Custer's soldiers have been reinterred there, and the plot contains remains of some who survived the campaign. Mostly, those buried here are veterans (and family members of veterans) who served in wars ranging from the Indian war period to the Vietnam era.

Legislation redesignated the national cemetery as Custer Battlefield National Monument in 1946, six years after jurisdictional transfer to the National Park Service. Since then, park facilities have expanded to include a housing complex, a maintenance area, and a visitor center. Today the Custer battlefield portion of the national monument encompasses 667 acres, including the land where the final stages of conflict took place. The remaining acres include much of the Reno-Benteen battlefield on a hilltop some four miles distant.

Of the 667 Custer battlefield acres 121 lie in heavily timbered river bottoms next to Little Big Horn River. The remaining 546 acres consist of broken upland terrain east of the Little Big Horn. Except for parts of one episode, the final actions of Custer's last battle occurred on the these uplands. During 1984 and

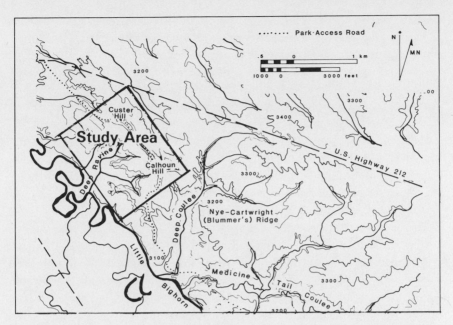

Fig. 6-1.   Location of the study area relative to the Custer battlefield boundaries.

1985, Douglas Scott, of the National Park Service Midwest Archeological Center, and I directed a study that produced an abundance of battle-related artifacts from the uplands. Certain classes of these specimens are treated here. The study area is depicted, relative to the Custer Battlefield National Monument boundaries, in figure 6-1. The study area topography is illustrated in computerized form on the project base map (fig. 6-2). Throughout this book, unless noted otherwise, terms such as *Custer (Custer's) battlefield* or *field* or *battle site* are synonymous with *study area*. There is also, however, much to say about events beyond the study area.

Archaeologists' business is artifacts, and they set out equipped to find artifacts. But in archaeology, it is equally important to know where things are not. Thus, the initial planning included a strategy that would cover, or survey, the entire upland area of Custer's field. The survey strategy included three phases: (1) orientation, (2) inventory, and (3) inventory evaluation. Details of these operations are available in the initial publication on the Custer battlefield archaeology.[2]

The orientation phase established spatial control. For meaningful analyses, it is necessary to know precisely the location of every find. To this end, professional land surveyors, led by Walt Egged, of Hardin, Montana, laid a grid system over the entire study area, placing permanent control points at 100-meter

Fig. 6-2. The study-area topography (15-foot contour intervals, elevation MSL). Tick marks along the border represent 100-meter (109-yard) intervals; grid north is to the top of the page.

(ca. 109-yard) intervals. The grid is illustrated in figure 6-2 and is oriented at right angles to the eastern and southern boundaries of the Custer battlefield. For archaeological purposes, reference is to grid north. Grid north is oriented 39 degrees west of or, looking at the figure 6-2 map, to the left of magnetic north.

Three sequential operations made up the inventory phase: survey, artifact recovery, and artifact recording. The primary objective during survey operations was to recover artifacts useful in evaluating the nature of the Custer battle. Based on the assumption that most battle artifacts would be metallic, or associated with metal objects, the survey methods emphasized the use of modern, hand-held metal detectors. The controlled, systematic use of metal detectors represents an advanced method for locating and illuminating artifact distributions at battlefield sites. Although visual inspection of the ground surface played a role, we learned that over 99 percent of the battle-related artifacts lay buried. Depths rarely exceeded six inches, with the average ranging between two and four inches. Thus, buried materials reposed at depths well within the detection capabilities (up to two feet) provided by state-of-the-art detectors. Furthermore, the plan called for the use of only highly experienced operators, and we found them in metal-detector clubs across the nation. The contribution of these operators cannot be overstated; I discovered—up close and personal—that a detector in the hands of just anyone does not make a metal-detecting unit.

From an archaeological perspective, the Custer battlefield is a vast expanse. Its great size precluded metal-detector coverage of every square inch of land (cubic inch would probably be more appropriate). Thus we devised a survey strategy that would produce a representative sample of artifacts contained within the study area. Metal-detector operators aligned themselves side by side at roughly 15-foot (five-yard) intervals. Fewer than four operators in a detecting crew proved inefficient, and more than six resulted in management problems. Operators walked transects oriented to grid cardinal directions while holding, as closely as possible, the prescribed interval. A crew chief assisted in maintaining orientation and proper spacing. Detector personnel operated their machines in a side-to-side sweeping motion as they walked. We estimated that each operator covered a sweep of 5 to 6.5 feet.

On detecting a metallic object, the operator stopped to pinpoint the spot and then marked it with a flag. After identifying a find spot in this way, the surveyor continued along the designated transect. Although areas between crew members were not detected, operators covered the entire study area in this manner. Results of this procedure constitute a systematic sample of artifacts extant on the battlefield when investigations began.

An artifact-recovery crew assumed responsibility for exposing the flagged find spots. Each crew consisted of excavators and metal-detector operators. The operator further refined location and provided depth information, thereby allowing a careful and accurate approach to the buried specimen. The excavator conducted digging with hand tools, taking care to unearth the artifact without disturbing its position. Recovery personnel then moved on to the next find location, leaving the newly exposed artifact in place.

Once an artifact was exposed, a recording crew located it in reference to a known grid coordinate, measured depth below ground surface, and determined orientation as it lay undisturbed in the soil. Modern surveying instruments provided distance and azimuth reckoned from nearby grid coordinates—distance parameters within four inches and azimuth to the nearest half minute. Crew members recorded provenance data (distance, azimuth, depth, orientation), provided a preliminary description, and assigned each artifact a unique catalog number.

Inventory phase activities resulted in the recovery of over 1,000 artifacts deposited, discarded, or otherwise abandoned during the battle. I want to reiterate that we found no guns, only several parts. Artifact distributions allowed the identification of various sectors in which battle actions took place. These sectors are identified in figure 6-3, and they provide the basis for defining and evaluating Custer battle episodes in archaeological and historical contexts. Battle sectors and topographic features identified in figure 6-3 are also illustrated in figure 6-4, an aerial view of the battlefield. This view shows the terrain detail—especially its rugged, broken character—which is lost in computer mapping. In figure 6-4, note the deeply incised draws, including Calhoun Coulee and Deep Ravine. The meandering Little Big Horn River is at the left of the photo. As I shall mention later, modern construction at the national monument has hampered archaeology, with Cemetery Ridge bearing the brunt of improvements. These constructions, including the national cemetery and park facilities, are evident in figure 6-4.

I should point out that whereas battle sectors are identified on the basis of the total artifact assemblage, only ammunition-component artifacts are considered in this study. Cavalry sectors yielded an abundance of other artifact classes, including personal accoutrements, horse trappings, military hardware, and the like. Readers interested in these artifacts should consult either of two descriptive works on the battlefield archaeology.[3]

Sampling investigations recovered an unknown fraction of the artifacts present when the project began. Realizing this, we incorporated an inventory evaluation phase into the survey strategy to determine the effectiveness of five-yard transect interval sampling. This phase included the selection and resurvey, again using metal detectors, of five 100-meter-square grid units (fig. 6-5). This time, the transect spacing between operators was two yards rather than the original

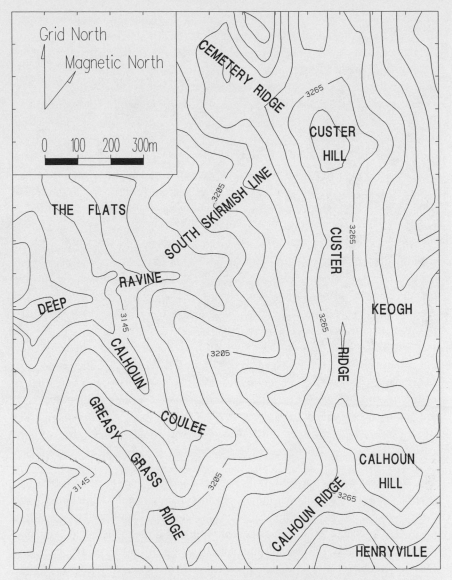

Fig. 6-3. The Custer battlefield sectors and topographic features referred to in the text.

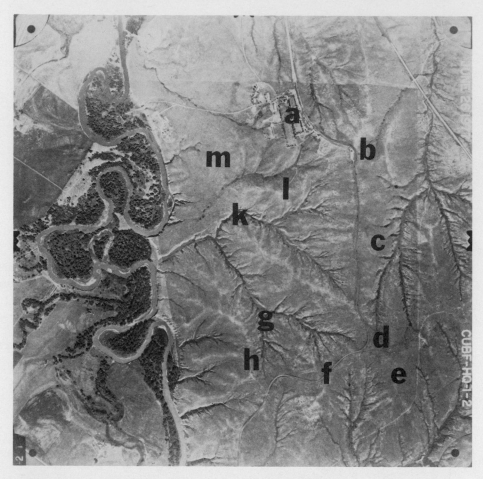

Fig. 6-4. Aerial photograph of the Custer battlefield showing sectors, topographic features, and national monument facilities referred to in the text. Grid north is to the top of the page. Facilities on Cemetery Ridge (right to left from Custer Hill) include the visitor center, parking facilities, the national cemetery, and the maintenance and housing complexes. Key: a, Cemetery Ridge; b, Custer Hill; c, Keogh sector; d, Calhoun Hill; e, Henryville; f, Calhoun Ridge; g, Calhoun Coulee; h, Greasy Grass Ridge; k, Deep Ravine; l, South Skirmish Line; m, The Flats. Little Big Horn River is at left. Photograph taken June 26, 1977. Courtesy Custer Battlefield National Monument.

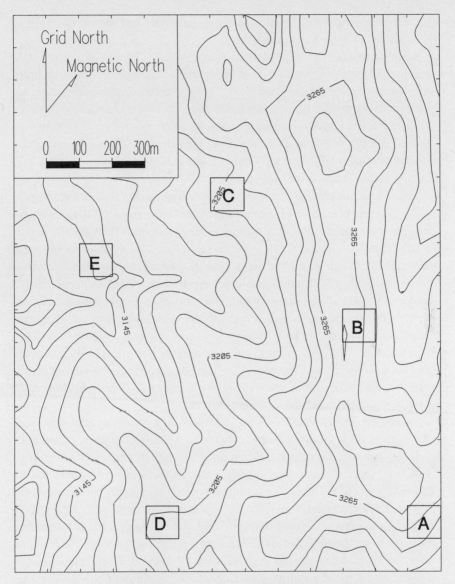

Fig. 6-5. Location of 100-meter-square grid units resurveyed using 2-meter-interval metal-detector sweeps during the inventory evaluation phase.

five. Close interval transects allowed somewhere near 100 percent coverage of the surface area of each sample unit.

Sample unit selection depended on a subjective evaluation of artifact yield obtained during larger-interval (five-yard) transect sampling. These samples included one high-yield unit (unit A, fig. 6-5), two 100-meter squares that produced moderate artifact quantities (units B and C), and two low-yield units (units D and E). Each reinventoried unit produced about twice ($\pm$ 10 percent) the number of artifacts recovered during the initial detector sweeps.[4] This suggests that the large-interval procedure yielded about a 33 percent sample of the total artifacts at the Custer battlefield.

This sample percentage, however, is misleading. Most metal detectors operate on the cone principle. Electronic signals emanate from a circular detector coil, penetrate the earth, and converge at the cone apex. The detector signals metal objects that lie within this cone. In any given sweep, only half the earth below the coil (to the maximum depth capability of the detector) is subjected to electronic coverage. Thus, the close-interval procedure covered 100 percent of a sample unit surface area but only half the subsurface below. Given this, it is probable that detecting at two-yard intervals failed to detect about half the metallic artifacts remaining in each 100-meter-square grid unit. Had these artifacts been recovered, the close-spacing yield would have been four times that of the large-interval sampling. Therefore, the sample percentage obtained with the latter strategy, that used to cover the entire study area, is probably nearer 20 percent of the total number of artifacts present.

This percentage is of necessity an approximation. Sampling strategists usually begin with a known universe, that is, a specified quantity. Then they typically sample a percentage of that quantity, say 10 percent of a specified land area. Here, though, the universe—all artifacts present—could not be known a priori without digging up and counting every item. Nonetheless, the projected sample size (20 percent) is, by statistical standards, valid. Technically, then, data recovered through large-interval surveying are representative of the sampling universe—in this case, the artifact patterns and distributions from which the sample derived. In fact, inventory evaluation results, though adding to the quantity of artifacts at each sample unit, did not alter patterns recognized using the large-interval strategy. Such patterns included clustering of cartridge cases at sample units A and D, a widely scattered distribution of bullets at unit E, and a quantitative disparity between bullets and cartridge cases at units B and C (bullets predominating by approximately a 10:1 ratio). Moreover, inventory evaluation results indicate that the large-interval sample is representative of the variety of battle-related artifact types present throughout the field.[5] These assurances make it possible to confidently draw, from sample data, inferences about the battle without completely digging up the site.

The Custer Battlefield Burials

The survivors of the Reno-Benteen fight, assisted somewhat by the rest of Terry's command, buried the Custer dead where (for the most part) each man lay when found. Most interments took place on June 28—the third day after the battle. When the soldiers departed on June 29, they left fragile wooden stakes to mark the hastily prepared graves—in most cases very shallow interments covered by a thin blanket of soil and/or brush. For several years thereafter, the media and other observers roundly criticized the insubstantial nature of these burials. (Look at it, however, from the perspective of a whipped command anxious to help their wounded but first charged with burying bloated, malodorous corpses.) The army responded by dispatching two details with orders to improve the grave sites. The first, in 1877, also exhumed officer remains for reburial according to family wishes. Another detail occurred in 1879. These attempts did not silence critics. In 1881, with the army still suffering censure, an official party of troopers collected what skeletal remains could be located and placed them in a mass grave atop Custer Hill. These men again marked the original grave sites with stakes (as best they could). They also replaced a cordwood memorial, set up a few years earlier, with a massive granite obelisk at the mass grave. That monument, standing today, is visible in figure 6-6. The photograph also illustrates the extent of modification to Custer Hill and Cemetery Ridge. Shown are the Custer Hill parking area, the access road, the visitor center, and beyond that, portions of the national cemetery (see also fig. 6-4).

Nine years after authorities installed the obelisk, Capt. Owen Sweet appeared on the scene. Sweet's mission was to further honor the fallen cavalrymen. He brought 246 marble markers to the battlefield, determined the original individual grave sites as best he could, and placed the stones at these locations. The headstones were similar in size and shape to a tablet. Some of those on the western slope of Custer Hill are depicted in figure 6-7. Below the stones—on Cemetery Ridge—the visitor center and the tree-lined national cemetery are also visible in this photograph (see also fig. 6-4).

In the years since 1890, and for reasons that are either spurious or not entirely clear, battlefield caretakers set an additional six stones. The 252 markers dotting the battlefield today exceed by 42 the number of men who died (that figure varies, but I shall use 210, a good estimate). This disparity can be traced, in largest degree, to the fact that Sweet incorrectly placed on Custer's battlefield 44 markers intended to memorialize Reno's dead.[6] At the time, he thought 202 stones were meant for Custer's dead. So from this perspective he placed 44 extra.

Fig. 6-6. View of Custer Hill and granite obelisk from above. Beyond (west-ward) on Cemetery Ridge are the visitor center and portions of the national cemetery. The conical structure in the foreground is a water reservoir which no longer exists. Photographer unknown, July 1954. Courtesy Custer Battlefield National Monument (#15410).

Using a 210 estimate, Sweet erected 36 too many. However it is computed, Sweet's total, plus the six added later, account for the 42 extra memorials.

Sweet accomplished his task 14 years after the event, and after the three previous interment efforts (1877, 1879, 1881). Such circumstances left ample room for error. But used with caution, the markers are a valuable archaeological resource. They purport to denote where the men of the 7th Cavalry fell, and most are inscribed with words to that effect. Obviously, with too many stones on the field, these mute claims—a trooper fell here—must, until determined other-wise, be regarded suspiciously. Thus, the extra memorials somewhat detract from the archaeological value.

Sweet[7] did leave a clue regarding locations of spurious stones. In his report, the officer noted that all parts of the field exhibited evidence of men who had fallen in pairs. There are, indeed, 43 pairs of markers (i.e., stones placed within a yard or two of each other) scattered across the field. Following Sweet's lead, students of the battle, in the heroic tradition, sometimes interpret paired stones

Fig. 6-7. Some of the memorial stones on the western slope of Custer Hill. Beyond (westward) on Cemetery Ridge are the visitor center and the tree-lined national cemetery. Further west are the housing and maintenance complexes which are obscured by the national cemetery. Photograph by Tom Garry, 1965. Courtesy Custer Battlefield National Monument (#15444).

as locations where close friends fell while slugging it out together. An alternate explanation, however, is that each brace represents only one interment. The original burial detail in many instances simply scooped earth from either side of the deceased and threw it over his body. This left shallow depressions on both sides of the corpse. Sweet's report indicates that he set markers not only at staked locations but at depressions as well. So remote in time from the event, he likely assumed that depressions represented two inhumations and placed stones accordingly.[8]

The archaeological plan included controlled test excavations at double markers to assess this hypothesis. Working under practical constraints, the crew could not investigate all 43 paired sites. Crew members ultimately dug at 11, each site determined by using random selection procedures. Ten of the 11 test units contained the partial skeleton of a single individual; the other excavation lacked any evidence of human skeletal parts. In most instances, remains present at the 10 positive units consisted of small bones, such as from the hand, overlooked by the 1881 reinterment party. At several, though, excavators unearthed more substan-

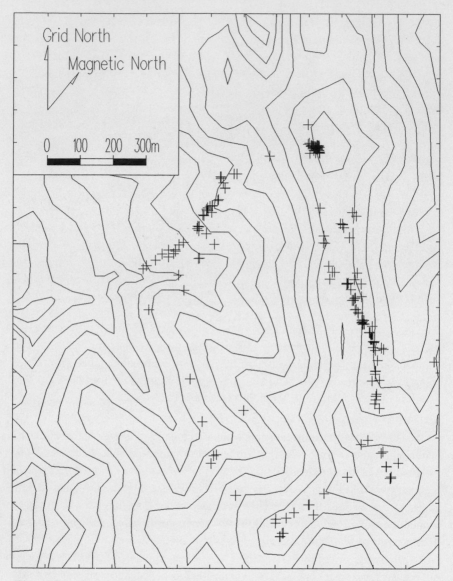

Fig. 6-8. The distribution of marble markers on the Custer battlefield, corrected for pairing errors.

tial body elements, such as long bones. I will talk about some of the larger finds later. But under either circumstance, remains proved sufficient for the type of analysis necessary to quantify individuals present. (If no bone element at a burial site is duplicated, then all bones there came from the same individual. In cases of symmetry, right and left bones from an individual are easily distinguished.) Sampling results (10 in every 11) indicate that 91 percent (n=39) of the 43 paired memorial stones do indeed represent the burial location of one individual. The results are very close to the extra markers set by Sweet. Thus, it is probable that most locations with two stones set close together exhibit a spurious marker.

Figure 6-8 depicts the distribution of battlefield markers less one stone at each of the 43 paired sites. The distribution shows 209 markers, a figure that very closely approximates the number of army men who, by best estimates, died on Custer's field. And, as it turns out, elimination does not at all upset gross patterns displayed by all 252 memorial stones standing today. But from sector to sector, the pairing corrections can be important. Where occasions dictate, corrected distributions are used in this way. Mostly they are used in conjunction with patterns of conflict revealed by firearm data, or scarcity thereof as it sometimes happens. This evaluation—the residues of firing—begins with a synthesis of weapon data based on firearm identification analyses. Readers may obtain a more detailed map of marker locations in a 1987 book on the Custer battle archaeology.[9]

Firearm Component Distributions

Table 6-1 lists the minimum numbers of individual Custer battle firearms within each type. Future investigations at and surrounding the Custer battlefield will almost certainly add to the type list, not to mention individual weapons within types. Thus, the number of types must be regarded as a minimum figure as well. Details on firearm identification analyses of the Custer battle guns are available in *Archaeological Insights into the Custer Battle* and *Archaeological Perspectives on the Battle of the Little Bighorn.*[10]

Government troops possessed the .45-caliber Springfield carbine (single-shot) and the six-shot, .45-caliber Colt single-action pistol. A few warriors had acquired carbines during earlier encounters, including Reno's valley fight, and they captured carbines and Colt pistols during the Custer battle. Thus, Indian armament ultimately included all 29 firearm types listed in table 6-1.

The variety in Indian armament is astonishing considering the U.S. policies designed to restrict Indian access to firearms. Some insight into the breadth of the Indian trade networks responsible for firearm and ammunition procurement is given in works by G. B. Grinnell and D. Brown.[11] It is unfortunately not

Table 6-1. Minimum Numbers of Individual Custer Battle Firearms
Listed by Weapon Type.

Firearm Type (n=29)	Number of Firearms
Forehand and Wadsworth .32-caliber	1
Colt .36-caliber	1
Sharps .40-caliber	1
Unknown .40-caliber	4
.44-Caliber	
Smith and Wesson	3
Evans	1
Henry	62
Winchester Model 1873	7
Colt conversion	1
Colt Model 1860	1
Colt Model 1871	1
Remington Model 1858	1
Remington Model 1858 conversion	1
Ballard	1
.45-Caliber	
Colt Model 1873 pistol	12
Springfield Model 1873 carbine	69
Sharps	1
Unknown	1
.50-Caliber	
Maynard	1
Sharps	27
Springfield	6
Unidentified	1
Unknown .50-caliber balls	1
Others	
Starr .54-caliber	1
Spencer .56/56	2
Spencer .56/50	3
Enfield .577-caliber	1
Unknown .44 or .45-caliber balls	2
Unknown shotgun	1
Total	215

NOTE: Where cartridge cases were absent, balls and shot were assumed to represent one firearm for that type (unknown). Data extracted from Scott et al. 1989.

practical to explore this fascinating issue here. Nevertheless, Indian armament at the Custer battle ranged from obsolete muzzle-loaders to the then modern repeating rifles such as Winchesters and the Henry rifle, both .44-caliber pieces. The perceived ease with which Indians procured firearms prompted an 1876 tongue-in-cheek *Army and Navy Journal* editorial.[12] The editor first noted that government agents at Indian reservations, and traders too, had sworn that they were not responsible for firearm procurement by the Indians. Therefore, quipped the writer, Indians themselves must be manufacturing the arms. The wry commentary continued by urging the Winchester firearm company to sue the natives for patent infringement.

The procurement issue aside, bullet and cartridge case patterns provide the starting point for archaeologically examining the behavioral nature of Custer's battle. It is therefore essential to map distributions of these ammunition components about the battlefield. By the way, we also found quite a number of loaded cartridges, mainly government and in cavalry positions, but since these lack the necessary signatures, there is no point in mapping them here.

Ammunition Component Distributions

Distributions presented in the following figures derive from raw data contained in earlier volumes on the Custer battle archaeology.[13] Considered first are bullet distributions, which are useful in identifying combatant positions. Cartridge case distributions then lay the groundwork for determining individual positions and movements of soldiers and Indians. Below I will treat cartridge cases and bullets separately, but the two may be considered jointly in assessing the Custer battle events, as is done in the next chapter.

Bullet Distributions

All bullets are made of lead. Though I use the term *bullets,* Indian-delivered projectiles also included balls and shot. Bullets from government firearms represent only one caliber (45) but two firearm types, the carbine and the Colt pistol. The distinction between these types is important because the effectiveness of each differed according to fighting conditions. The Springfield carbine, because of its single-shot limitation, functioned effectively in longer-range encounters. More distant exchanges made for a less stressful combat environment, and in turn, the shooter enjoyed plenty of time to reload. Yet even the most relaxed riflemen could rarely discharge more than four rounds a minute.

The repeating capability of the Colt pistol made it more useful in close-up fighting, and in any case its range, measured in accuracy, did not exceed 50 or so yards. This dichotomy becomes evident in later chapters. It is therefore useful to map government bullets according to firearm type. Whereas bullets identified here as Indian came, without much doubt, from firearms in the hands of warriors, not all government bullets were delivered by soldiers. This distinction is considered, when examining battle events, by invoking supporting data where possible to determine whether soldiers or Indians delivered government-issue bullets.

As for Indian bullets (fig. 6-9), they are represented by .50-caliber bullets and balls, .44-caliber bullets, and miscellaneous specimens including .32- and .40-caliber projectiles, .44/45-caliber balls, Sharps .45-caliber bullets, and a few shot. Deformed bullets cannot, on the basis of caliber, be assigned to either Indian or soldier, but they are included in figure 6-9 because most were found at soldier positions. Some weapons known to be present on the basis of cartridge case types, such as caliber .56, are not represented in the bullet inventory.

Figure 6-10 illustrates the distribution of .45-caliber government bullets delivered from Springfield carbines. The carbine is distinguished from the rifle, which was a heavier, longer arm carried by infantrymen but which used the same size cartridge case. Colt .45 projectiles, which are not too plentiful, are depicted in figure 6-11. Hereafter, and for convenience only, .45-caliber bullets manufactured for use in the carbine are referred to as .45/55 bullets, the designation denoting the caliber (.45—caliber is the diameter of a casing in hundredths of an inch) and powder charge (55 grains) of the cartridge case that contained the projectile.

Cartridge Case Distributions

All calibers of Indian cartridge case distributions are mapped in figure 6-12. I should note that here and in other figures, cases at certain locations are sometimes so thick that they show up as a solid, darkened mass. Computer mapping restricted to page size unfortunately cannot avoid this. The .45-caliber Springfield carbine cartridge case distribution is depicted in figure 6-13. These specimens are henceforth referred to as .45/55 cases, with the designation, like .45/55 bullets, referring to caliber and powder measure. Figure 6-14 illustrates the distribution of Colt .45 cartridge cases, which number even fewer than the corresponding bullets.

Cartridge cases, by virtue of unique signature data, represent individual combatant positions and movements. Movements in the distributions are depicted by connecting individual positions by means of identical cartridge case signatures. Connecting lines do not necessarily represent actual routes. The purpose of the lines is to link those cartridge cases fired from the same weapon. Linkages show that the combatant fired from various positions during the battle. These linkages are called "pathways." Direction of movement in pathways cannot be deduced until episodes and their temporal relationships are examined.

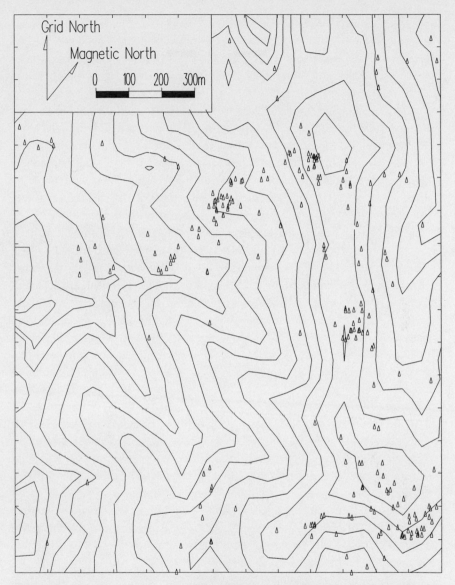

Fig. 6-9. The distribution of Indian bullets (all calibers) in the Custer battle-field study area.

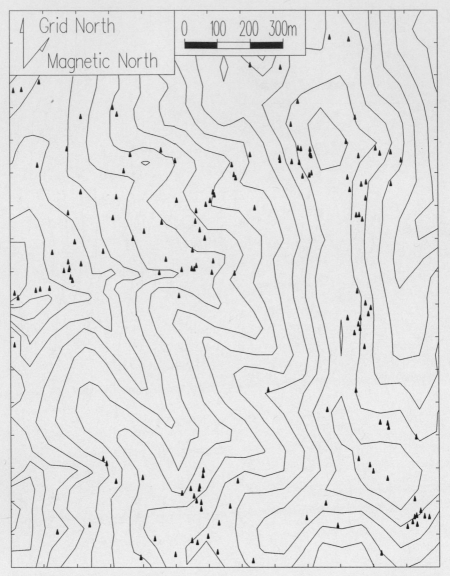

Fig. 6-10. The distribution of .45-caliber Springfield carbine bullets in the Custer battlefield study area.

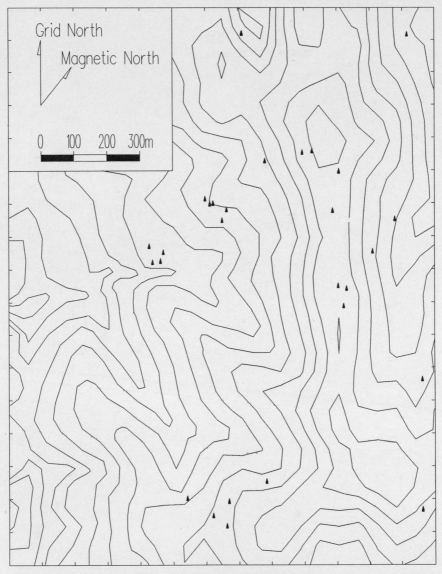

Fig. 6-11. The distribution of .45-caliber Colt bullets in the Custer battlefield study area.

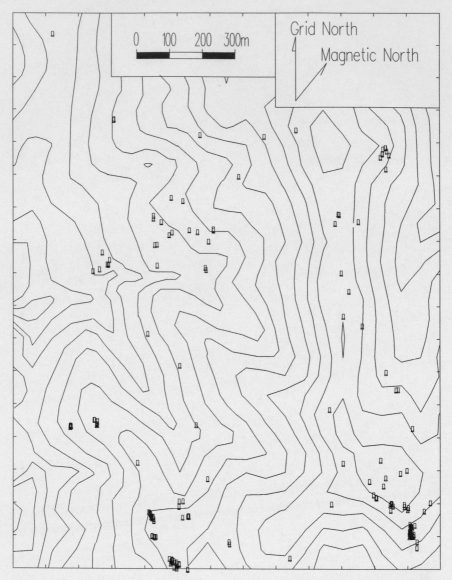

Fig. 6-12. The distribution of Indian cartridge cases (all calibers) in the Custer battlefield study area.

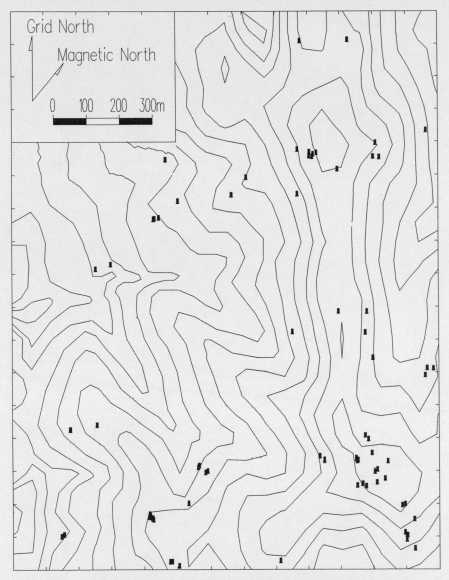

Fig. 6-13. The distribution of .45/55 cartridge cases in the Custer battlefield study area.

Fig. 6-14. The distribution of Colt .45 cartridge cases in the Custer battlefield study area.

Individual Positions and Pathways

Positions and pathways are marked by spent casings. Individual Indian positions and pathways are mapped according to caliber in order to reduce cluttering on the small-size maps. Indians used .44-caliber Henry repeating rifles and .50-caliber weapons. Individual positions and pathways represented by cartridge cases fired from these firearm types are depicted in figures 6-15 and 6-16. Miscellaneous Indian firearm types and calibers include the Spencer .56/56 and .56/50, Smith and Wesson American .44, Winchester Model 1873, Evans Old Model .44, Forehand and Wadsworth .32, and .44-caliber Colts. Individual positions and movements represented by cartridge cases from these weapons are illustrated in figure 6-17.

Figure 6-18 depicts individual positions and pathways represented by .45-caliber Springfield carbine cartridge cases. All .45-caliber Colt cartridge case signatures are unique. Thus individual pathways are not present in this weapon type. Except for certain miscellaneous Indian armament, this is the only weapon type in which this situation applies.

I have already raised the issue of captured weapons. Obviously, given the outcome of this battle, soldiers found themselves in poor positions to capture opponents' weapons. But not the warriors. Government cartridge cases, then, ought to be expected at both Indian positions and troop positions. This raises two possibilities: sequent occupations by the two adversaries, one after another, or the use of captured firearms by Indians. These options, like directions of movements represented in unique signature data, are examined later when events in battle sectors are discussed.

Summary of Ammunition Components

Bullet distributions provide a means for identifying adversary positions. Indian bullets from nongovernment-issue firearms are expected to mark troop positions. Indian cartridge cases should mark only Indian positions. The distributions of government bullets nominally reflect Indian positions but are subject, as are .45/55 and Colt pistol cartridge case distributions, to the issue of captured weapons.

Positions of individual combatants are denoted by the locations of cartridge cases on the battlefield. Individual combatant movements are represented by identical cartridge case signatures at various positions. The lines that connect such positions are called pathways. Determining the directions of movement in pathways and, in some instances (i.e., captured weapons), the identities of the combatants is subject to relationships within and between episodes.

Custer battle episodes occurred in various areas. Cavalry sectors include Calhoun Coulee, Calhoun Ridge, and Calhoun Hill, as well as the Keogh sector,

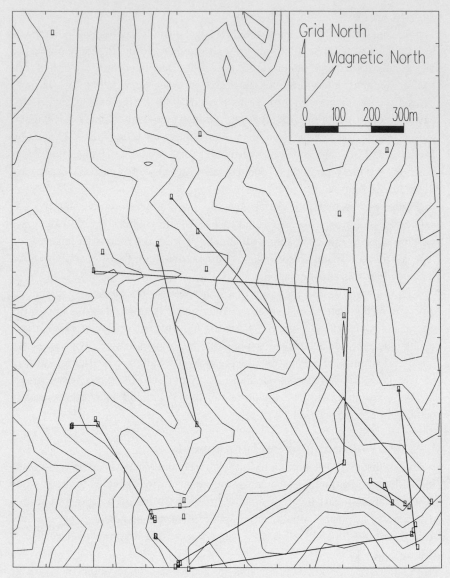

Fig. 6-15. Individual Indian positions and pathways represented by .50-caliber cartridge cases.

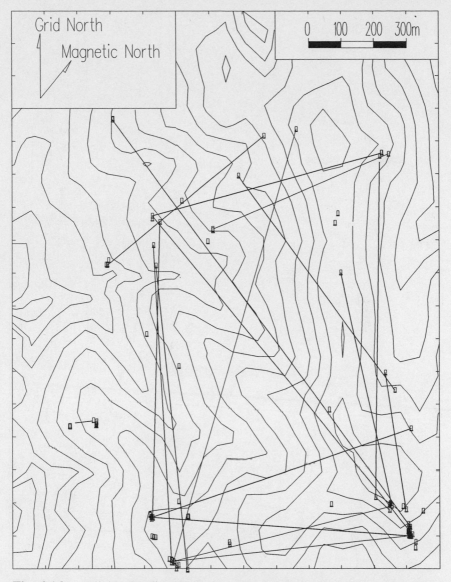

Fig. 6-16. Individual Indian positions and pathways represented by .44-caliber cartridge cases.

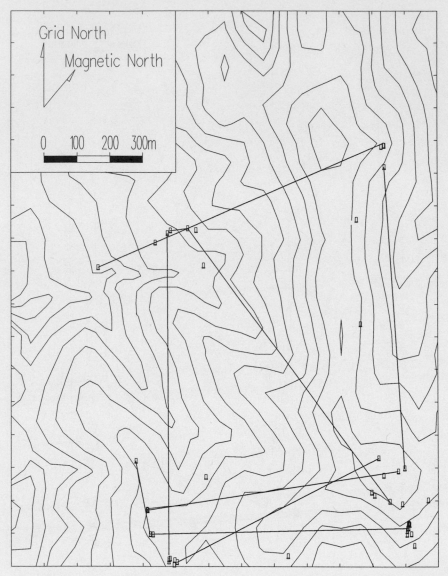

Fig. 6-17. Individual Indian positions and pathways represented by cartridge cases of miscellaneous calibers.

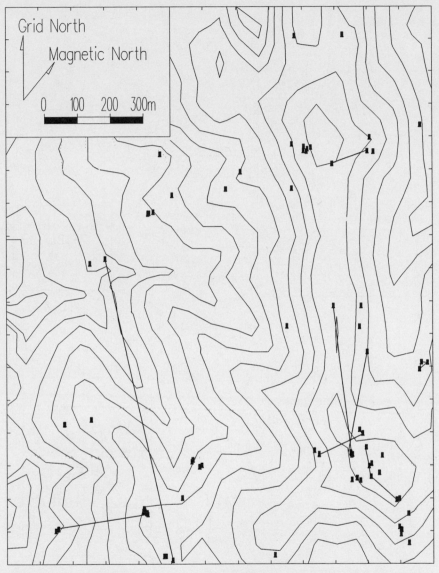

Fig. 6-18. Individual positions and pathways represented by Springfield cartridge cases (.45/55).

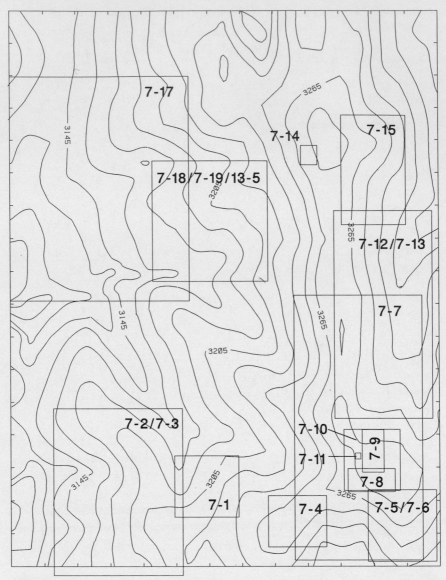

Fig. 6-19. Locations in the study area of the following enlarged computerized figures. The computerized figures are identified here by figure number.

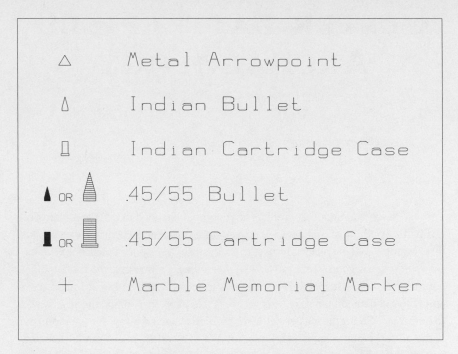

△   Metal Arrowpoint

◊   Indian Bullet

▯   Indian Cartridge Case

▲ OR 🔺   .45/55 Bullet

▮ OR ▮▮   .45/55 Cartridge Case

+   Marble Memorial Marker

Fig. 6-20.   Key to symbols used in computerized figures throughout the text.

Custer Hill, and the South Skirmish Line. Indians also occupied some of these areas, as well as Henryville, Greasy Grass Ridge, The Flats, and Deep Ravine. Chapter 7 addresses archaeological findings at these various areas. In many cases during the following discussions, mapped areas of the battlefield are enlarged to show relevant detail. Figure 6-19 shows the battle sectors and may be used to locate enlarged figures within their overall spatial context. Figure 6-20 defines symbols used in computerized figure blowups.

One final thought: we are dealing with a model of combat that represents behavior in transitional form—from stability to chaos. Under conditions of chaos, or disintegration, individuals exhibit certain behaviors, particularly the tendency to offer little resistance or none at all. Certainly, without any firearm resistance, cartridge cases—and hence signature data—will be absent. Notice, though, that absence—or dearth—is just as much a part of patterning as presence and is thus equally informative under parameters established by the stability/ disintegration model. This is about to become apparent, particularly when evidence from certain battle sectors is evaluated in conjunction with stone memorial markers.

7

CUSTER BATTLEFIELD ARCHAEOLOGY

And the rest is history. And archaeology.

—*Richard Fox*

Combat modeling predicts how combatants tend to behave under various battle conditions; archaeology serves up a physical record of those behaviors. Manipulated in concert, both furnish a sort of bare-bones picture of events. Inherently this is good, since most often it is not easy to mistake the fundamental nature of an event stripped of its outer layers. As much as history supplies a colorful and detailed tapestry, it is this very richness that, maddeningly, serves to obfuscate. So for the Custer battle that which is peeled away, for the moment, is the all too pliant documentary record. We can call it, in colloquial fashion, getting at the heart of the matter. That is what I will try to do in this chapter—reveal the archaeological skeleton, and an articulated one at that. With this aid, the convoluted historical weave is rendered far more intelligible than before.

Events take place in battle sectors; spread over time, these events constitute episodes. So battle episodes are interrelated in space and time. Episodes are generally discussed here by sector. As a reminder, Custer battle sectors are marked in figures 6-3 and 6-4, with these sectors identified using all artifact classes turned up during archaeological work. But also as a reminder, emphases here are placed on ammunition components because of their analytical potential. Memorial markers are used as well. After all, the stones are as much an archaeological resource as anything else on the field, not because of their age but because of their physical links with the event.

The Calhoun Coulee Episode

The story begins with those sectors making up the Calhoun Coulee episode. The starting point is discernible in material remains insofar as the stability/ disintegration model predicts entropy in combat. Stability can be demonstrated archaeologically during this episode—at Calhoun Hill—thus establishing at least a rough measure of the flow of battle. And in the end, numerous eyewitness testimonies make it clear that the final stages of Custer's last battle began about the folds, knolls, and ridges that form the southern terminus of Custer Ridge.

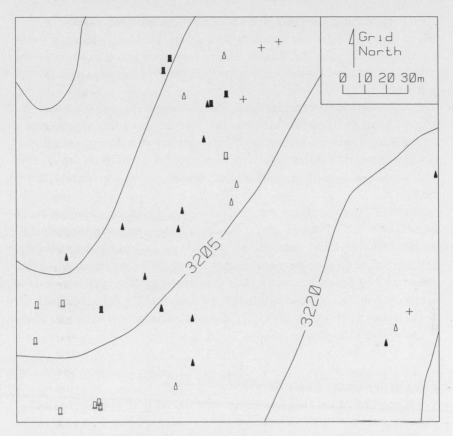

Fig. 7-1. Enlargement of the Calhoun Coulee sector depicting artifact distributions and marker locations.

The Calhoun Coulee Sector

Calhoun Coulee, you will notice (particularly in fig. 6-4), joins Deep Ravine. One of the two upper branches of Calhoun Coulee heads toward Calhoun Hill; the other, which begins near the park access road, parallels Greasy Grass Ridge. The Calhoun Coulee sector is located on a low, sloping ridge in the upper reaches of the gully between its two branches (at about 3,175 feet above mean sea level [MSL]). This sector is conspicuous because of the presence of four markers memorializing the deaths of cavalrymen. Test excavations undertaken at one stone produced the nearly complete skeletal remains of a single soldier.[1] Excavation results suggest that these four markers represent a troop position.

This interpretation is confirmed by the presence of ammunition components at the sector. These are fairly widespread, much more so than the marble markers. Figure 7-1 presents a close-up of memorial stones and artifacts in Calhoun

Coulee (the excavated marker is at lower right). Among other types, .45/55-caliber cartridge cases and Indian bullet calibers are located near the markers. We can assume the .45/55 cases resulted from army firing, but the presence of Indian bullets and trooper remains provide the strongest case for a cavalry position.

Government .45/55 cartridge cases seem too dispersed, and too few, to indicate a linear skirmish line. Also the few markers in no way approximate a tactical battle formation. Lack of evidence for orderly skirmishing, and the paucity of government cartridge cases, indicate only brief activity during the cavalry occupation. Nevertheless, the markers suggest at least four soldiers died in the fighting.

Evidence clearly indicates that Indians also occupied the Calhoun Coulee sector. Figure 7-1 illustrates several Indian cartridge cases, representing individual warrior positions. Soldiers, as indicated by the nearby .45/55 bullets, apparently fired on these positions. Sequencing of the Indian and army occupations cannot be determined on the basis of archaeology. The important point to note is that both foes occupied and fought in this sector. The Indian occupation is not surprising given the proximity of Calhoun Coulee to the warrior stronghold at Greasy Grass Ridge.

The Greasy Grass Ridge Sector

This portion of the field is situated west of and next to Calhoun Coulee. Indian positions at Greasy Grass Ridge are illustrated in figure 7-2 by substantial numbers of spent Indian cartridges. Here, at its highest point (3,225 feet MSL), Greasy Grass Ridge rises some 80 feet above the nearby coulee bottom. The Indian casings are located slightly below the ridge crest and opposite the smaller coulee branch. Clearly, warriors here used the crest for protection. Firearm identification analysis shows that the spent casings came from eight firearm types, which included at least 15 repeating rifles. That the cavalrymen's antagonists occupied these positions is substantiated by the presence of numerous government .45/55 bullets on and near the ridge (fig. 7-2).

Government .45/55 cartridge cases are also present at Indian positions on Greasy Grass Ridge (fig. 7-3). One recent observer, Richard Hardorff, suggested that the carbine casings indicate a government position overrun by Indians.[2] More than 80 years ago, Walter Camp had a similar idea, proposing that some unknown part of Custer's command occupied the Greasy Grass sector.[3] The same suggestion has been made on the basis of an 1891 U.S. Geological Survey (USGS) topographic map (Custer Battlefield), which depicts three of the four markers in the Calhoun Coulee sector but which places them on Greasy

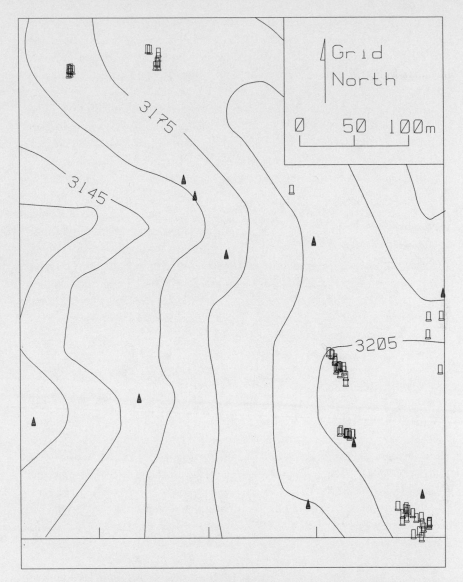

Fig. 7-2. Enlargement of the Greasy Grass Ridge sector depicting Indian cartridge cases and .45/55 bullets.

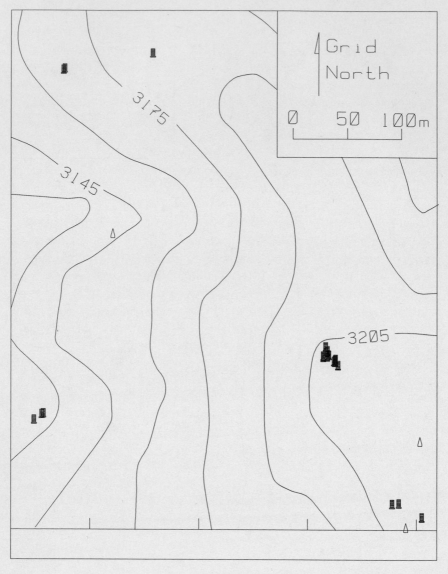

Fig. 7-3. Enlargement of the Greasy Grass Ridge sector depicting .45/55 cartridge cases and Indian bullets.

Grass Ridge rather than below in the draw, where today we know they are located. The three markers, however, are inaccurately located on this early map, and details of this have been presented elsewhere.[4]

Despite inaccuracies on the USGS map, Hardorff's interpretation may have some credibility. An Indian bullet is associated with the three .45/55 casings at the extreme lower right of figure 7-3. The presence of this bullet suggests that these .45/55 casings represent a cavalry position, and some of the .45/55 bullets (fig. 7-2) found on the west slope of Greasy Grass Ridge could have been fired from this position.

Mitigating against this interpretation, however, is the fact that the three .45/55 casings are located amid a large cluster of nongovernment cartridge cases (compare figs. 7-2 and 7-3). In fact, all .45/55 casings on Greasy Grass Ridge, with the exception of one location (fig. 7-3, lower left), are coincidental with clusters of what cannot be anything other than Indian cartridge cases (compare figs. 7-2 and 7-3). Coincidence in patterning strongly suggests that all .45/55 cases in the sector resulted from Indian firing. Thus, if a cavalry element did stop here, there is no record that anything of import happened. This seems a more reasonable conclusion, given the sparse evidence for Indian bullets in the sector, and it is the interpretation favored here. Indians acquired government carbines after Reno's valley fight and likely used them, as did comrades armed with other weapon types, at Greasy Grass Ridge. Importantly, however, there is nothing in this patterning to suggest *when* warriors used the captured carbines on Custer's battalion. I will address this matter later, in conjunction with testimonies.

Indian and .45/55 cartridge case clusters are, for the most part, located just below the ridge crest on its western slope. Apparently the ridgetop offered protection. In tactical terms, then, these positions lie at the military crest. This distribution suggests that riflemen, positioned on the western slope and using the crest as a natural breastwork, directed their fire primarily to the east of Greasy Grass Ridge. Judging from proximity, warriors very likely targeted troop positions to the east in Calhoun Coulee. They may have also directed their fire toward Calhoun Ridge, which lies 400 to 550 yards east of the crest of Greasy Grass Ridge.

The Calhoun Ridge Episode

Calhoun Ridge winds its way down from Calhoun Hill to join, near the southern boundary of the national monument, with Greasy Grass Ridge. This elevated landform, which slopes in elevation from about 3,270 feet to 3,230 feet MSL, extends from Custer Ridge roughly at a right angle. The episode at this sector is revealed, notably, by the virtual absence of expended government cartridges and, primarily, by spatial associations between Indian bullets and memo-

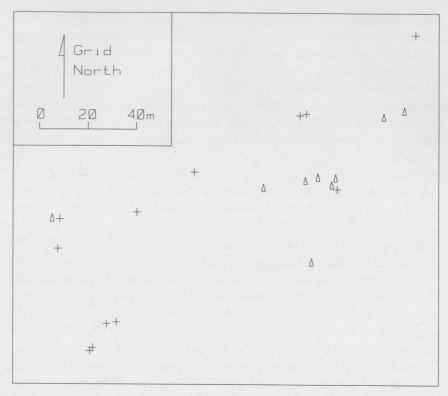

Fig. 7-4. Enlargement of the Calhoun Ridge sector depicting Indian bullets and marker locations.

rial stones (fig. 7-4). Spent .45/55-caliber cartridges are lacking (fig. 6-13), and investigations in the sector turned up only two Colt pistol casings (fig. 6-14). The Indian bullets, associated as they are with stone markers, indicate that Calhoun Ridge was the site of a government troop position. Note as well that spent Indian cartridges are also virtually absent (fig. 6-12) and that there are only a few (n=3) .45/55 bullets at the sector (fig. 6-10).

Indian bullet orientations, exposed in the ground during recovery operations, suggest that warriors shooting toward Calhoun Ridge delivered their fire from positions to the east, south, and west. J. Greene's review of relic collecting near the Custer battlefield indicates, based on cartridge case finds, that several warriors fired from positions located below and south of Calhoun Ridge but outside the federal boundary line.[5] Some Indian fire at troops on the ridge probably derived from these southern positions. The cavalry presence here undoubtedly drew other fire from Greasy Grass Ridge (west) and Henryville (east). The Henryville warrior position is discussed in the context of activities at the Calhoun Hill sector.

Markers on Calhoun Ridge are portrayed in figure 7-4. Though documentation is not available, it is rumored that nearby road construction perhaps required the removal of some stones in the right-of-way to the ridge crest. Figure 6-4 shows that the park access lane traverses the ridge. Thus, this rumor may be true to some extent. Excavations at one memorial, for example, produced no skeletal remains or artifacts at all. This marker is very likely spurious. Nevertheless, Indian bullets at the sector tend to verify Calhoun Ridge as an army position. Indeed, the second of two marker excavations at the sector produced human hand bones, a broken tooth, and a cluster of river cobbles.[6] The bones almost certainly represent soldier remains, since historical records make it clear that burial details did not find Indian bodies on the field. This observation seems consistent with the Plains Indian practice of removing their dead, sometimes even as a battle raged, for burial rites. Also, as soldiers prepared the original interments, they placed small stone mounds at the burial sites.[7] These findings bolster the interpretation of troopers present on Calhoun Ridge.

The paucity of government cartridge cases on Calhoun Ridge suggests relatively little firing by soldiers there. The roughly linear distribution of grave markers along the elevation has prompted widespread speculation that a skirmish line was deployed. If so, the formation apparently did not endure long. But in light of the archaeology, there is an alternative explanation. The few government cartridge cases could reasonably suggest that the soldiers did not stop but moved along the ridge, without firing much. At the same time, bullets delivered by warriors hit around them (and, so it appears, in them). Material evidence clearly indicates troops under duress. If the markers are near correct in number, up to a dozen soldiers died along this ridge (adjusted for pairing error). Thus, this line of stone memorials, if in the aggregate generally valid, may represent not a skirmish line but men who died as they traversed the ridge. In either case— very brief skirmishing or moving men—the important aspect of Calhoun Ridge archaeology is that cavalrymen there apparently offered little resistance to an Indian attack.

The Calhoun Hill Episode

Calhoun Hill is equal in elevation (3,300 feet MSL) to its counterpart at the other (northern) end of Custer Ridge—Custer Hill. The Calhoun prominence overlooks and commands considerably lower terrain—Deep Coulee to the east and Calhoun Coulee to the west. Physical evidence for an episode in this region includes combat action at both Calhoun Hill and Henryville. At the latter, a concentration of Indian bullets indicates that government forces came under an undetermined volume of fire (fig. 7-5). The linear patterning of unique cartridge case signatures (on .45/55 casings) suggests that some soldiers in the sector

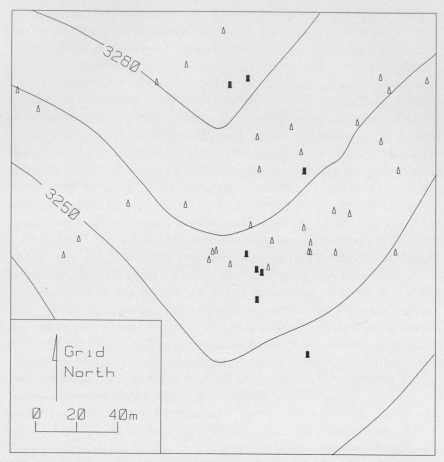

Fig. 7-5. Enlargement of the Henryville sector depicting .45/55 cartridge cases and Indian bullets.

deployed in skirmish formation (fig. 7-5; there are no stone markers at Henryville). Four individual trooper positions are spaced at nearly regular intervals, but beyond the habitual five yards. A fifth position is some distance to the south. The line, judging from extant evidence, may have been as much as 60 yards in length. Adhering to prescribed tactical intervals, it seems to represent something less than company strength. (A 40-man company, with horse holders absent, ought to be dispersed over a minimum of about 150 yards.)

Quite clearly, warriors at some time also occupied the Henryville position, where there are numerous expended Indian cartridges of various calibers (fig. 7-6). Like the cartridge cases at Greasy Grass Ridge, these are found, in many instances, tightly clustered. Many are .44 Henry casings, representing 20

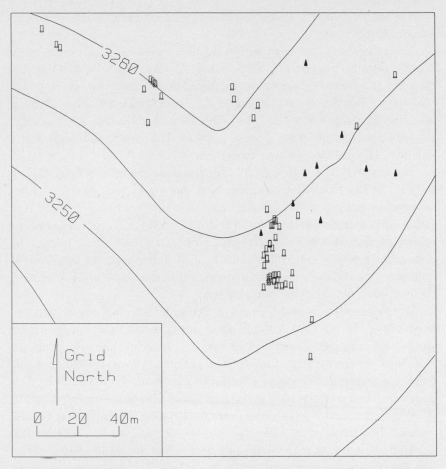

Fig. 7-6. Enlargement of the Henryville sector depicting Indian cartridge cases and .45/55 bullets.

repeating rifles. Figure 7-6 also depicts .45/55 bullets, presumably fired at the Henryville Indian positions.

The co-occurrence of Indian and government artifacts demonstrates occupations at Henryville by each opponent. In what sequence did this occur? One possibility is multiple occupations by warriors and troopers, but it seems impossible to discern this theory through archaeological evidence. Yet it is at least likely that the Indian combatants occupied the sector last. This hypothesis is based on the Henryville skirmish line location. The line (fig. 7-5) is situated just below the crest, on the east side of a low ridge that slopes gently south from Calhoun Hill. The ridge is in fact part of the southern flank of the hill. This positioning suggests that army personnel, using the military crest for cover, fired to the west. Indian bullets distributed near the crest on the west slope support this possibility.

On the other hand, Indian projectiles are also arrayed on the east slope, many near the skirmish line position. Very possibly, the rear or left flank of the skirmish line at some time came under fire from Indians ensconced outside of the study area.[8] Whether or not this caused skirmishers at Henryville to abandon their position, pathway F, which links identical signatures on two .45/55 casings, suggests a movement up the slope to Calhoun Hill, where additional action unfolded. This pathway is illustrated in figure 7-7.

On Calhoun Hill, archaeological patterns relating to soldier activity suggest tactical stability followed by disintegration and flight. Such patterns are reflected principally in .45/55 cartridge case distributions. Between A and B in figure 7-7 is a linear pattern of .45/55 casings, denoting a number of individual soldier positions. Linearity is interpreted as evidence for a skirmish line. The distribution is approximately 100 yards long. A dispersal of this magnitude is sufficient to accommodate an under-strength company of 40 or so, excluding one or two reserve squads and horse holders.

Given a roughly east-west orientation, skirmishers deployed in the A-B formation logically faced either to the north or the south. Evidence for nearby warrior positions to the north and northwest is minimal, not only within the study area (see fig. 6-12) but also in reports, admittedly not too reliable, of relic collecting beyond the monument boundary.[9] But substantial Indian firing residues were found at Henryville and, to some extent, beyond the area of study.[10] It is therefore reasonable to conclude, with the evidence available, that the A-B skirmish line faced south. Moreover, pathway F in figure 7-7 indicates that skirmish line A-B included a soldier once deployed at Henryville. This observation supports the hypothesis that the Henryville skirmish line moved up to Calhoun Hill, where it redeployed to face whatever southern threats existed at the time. Figure 7-8 depicts line A-B cartridge cases and Indian bullets, which tend to confirm the presence of this skirmish line.

A second skirmish line, also based on a linear distribution of .45/55 casings denoting individual troop positions, seems to have existed at Calhoun Hill (line C-D, fig. 7-7). The line of cartridge cases is similar to line A-B but, based on sampling data, is about 20 yards longer. Interpretation of this pattern (C-D) as a skirmish line is bolstered somewhat by the presence of several Indian bullets, including two .45/55 projectiles (fig. 7-9).

The orientation of line C-D—approximately north-south—indicates that the soldiers faced Indians located either to the west or the east. The formation, however, is situated close to the western edge of Calhoun Hill. Effective firing toward low-lying eastern locations would have been difficult because slightly

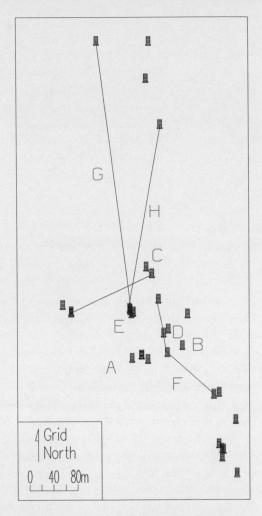

Fig. 7-7. Enlargement of the individual trooper positions and pathways in the Henryville, Calhoun Hill, and Keogh sectors.

higher elevations intervene. In any event, Indian positions in the study area east of Calhoun Hill are absent. In addition, relic finds in that direction, but beyond the boundary line, are few in number.[11] This, plus the line position relative to topography, suggests that skirmishers aimed at western targets. Indeed, line of sight from formation C-D west toward Greasy Grass Ridge is unimpeded by topographic features. Thus it is probable that skirmishers reformed to face threats posed by antagonists on or once near Greasy Grass Ridge. Government

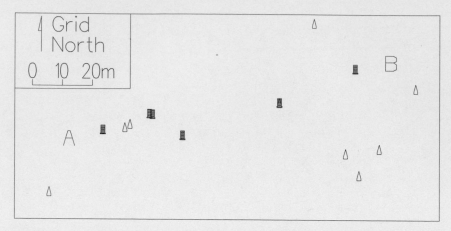

Fig. 7-8. Enlargement of skirmish line A-B and associated bullets at Calhoun Hill.

.45/55 bullets at the skirmish line, though few, would suggest that enemies to the west, including those Greasy Grass warriors who possessed the Springfield, fired at the second skirmish line. Warriors at Henryville probably can be eliminated from consideration because they do not seem to have had carbines.

Dual skirmish lines on the hilltop raise the issue of temporal relationships between the two. One option is that the deployments existed simultaneously, but this seems altogether remote. Pathway F indicates that one soldier occupied a position in both lines. It is not likely that soldiers would shift from one tactical unit to another during skirmish operations. A more reasonable explanation is that personnel in one line redeployed to form the other. This option can account for the various individual soldier positions included in pathway F. The issue, then, appears to center on which line deployed first on the knoll. I have argued that Henryville skirmishers moved up to Calhoun Hill and redeployed into line A-B, doing so to face whatever threats existed when they left the Henryville position. Immediate redeployment into line C-D, which is improperly oriented to deal with threats to the south, would not have accomplished this purpose. It is therefore probable that line A-B deployed first and subsequently shifted to form the second skirmish line (C-D). The realignment, then, must have been in response to new developments in the Greasy Grass Ridge/Calhoun Coulee regions.

Skirmish line developments, as proposed, are consistent with later occurrences on Calhoun Hill. In part, these events are depicted by memorial markers about the hillock. Collectively, the stones are arranged in no apparent order, although several could represent men who fell on or near the skirmish lines.

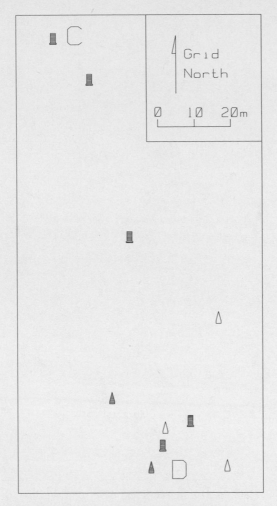

Fig. 7-9. Enlargement of skirmish line C-D and associated bullets at Calhoun Hill.

Figure 7-10 depicts the markers and their relationships to lines A-B and C-D. These memorials suggest that as many as 11 men died in the fighting. More important in discerning later events is the evidence for bunching behavior. Point E in figure 7-7 depicts a tight cluster of expended .45/55 cartridges. A close-up of this cluster shows that signatures on seven cartridge cases represent six individuals (fig. 7-11). Two individual pathways (G and H, fig. 7-7) project from the cluster in a northern direction. Applying the maxim that in battle, disorder proceeds from order, we can surmise that tactical stability at Calhoun Hill, so

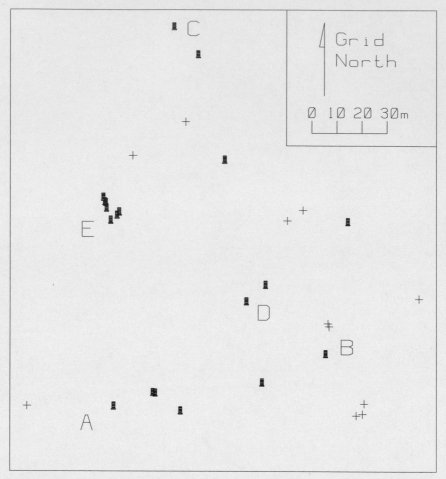

Fig. 7-10. The Calhoun Hill markers and their relationships to skirmish lines A-B and C-D.

evident in the skirmish lines, broke down, causing some troopers to bunch and eventually flee. Under these circumstances, individual pathways G and H show that huddled men—not necessarily only six—proceeded northward into the Keogh sector. Given the tendency for distressed men to move toward safety, movement in this direction strongly suggests that relief, apparent or real, existed to the north.

It is difficult to ascertain prior positions of the clustered men. Individual pathways linking either skirmish line with point E are absent, though this does not eliminate the possibility that men drifted from the battle line to bunch there. Or perhaps bunching originated among reserve skirmish squads. Despite uncer-

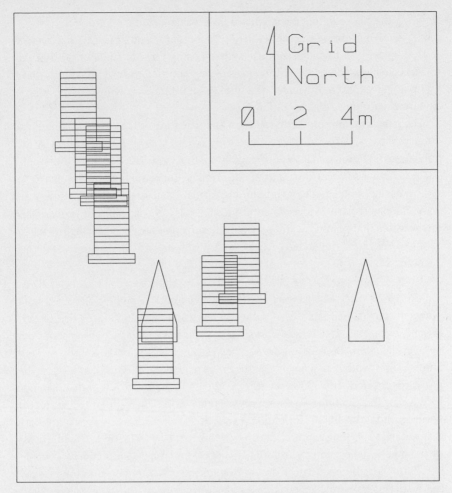

Fig. 7-11. Close-up of the cluster of .45/55 cartridge cases represented by item E in figure 7-7.

tainties as to just how this developed, it seems reasonable, under the conditions of combat modeling, to infer that men forsook tactical rigor and drew close together as pressures mounted. Men gathered in a knot; some continued to fire their weapons. Others by now had died. Those still alive moved, as pathways G and H attest, toward the Keogh sector.

Archaeological evidence for an orderly, well-implemented retirement is absent. Sampling survey procedures, of course, cannot recover everything, but statistically valid samples do indicate trends. The apparent absence of government cartridge cases between Calhoun Hill and the Keogh sector (see fig. 7-7) suggests that those falling back offered little or no coordinated, effective resistance. Viewing episode activities in the aggregate, and referring to combat modeling, we can hypothesize that tactical formations on Calhoun Hill broke down, causing soldiers to cluster. Thereafter, men fled toward apparent safety, but in doing so failed to counter pressures. All of this is indicative of the transition from stability to disintegration.

The bunching interpretation relies on identification of the .45/55 casing cluster at point E as firing residues created by soldiers. Two Indian bullets at the point (fig. 7-11) add tentative confirmation to this view. But clustered individual positions can also be attributed to Indian combat. Indeed, clustering seems to be typical of the Indian mode of fighting, as is clear from some known positions of warriors, particularly, and as noted, those at Greasy Grass and Henryville. Thus it is possible that point E resulted from Indian firing. A bunch of warriors using captured carbines might have fired from Calhoun Hill at cavalry positions elsewhere.

There is, however, little physical evidence in support of this option. At Greasy Grass warrior positions, .45/55 cases are found tightly clustered with others of varying calibers. This pattern is not found on Calhoun Hill. Instead, expended carbine and Indian cases are segregated spatially. Though quite a number of Indian cases lie on the southern slope of Calhoun Hill, only a small number (six), widely dispersed, dot the area vacated by soldiers (fig. 6-12). The nearest is located some 200 feet from point E. Indeed, the few Indian casings here, compared with the proliferation at Henryville, suggest that Calhoun Hill never served as an important Indian position. In light of this, it seems unlikely that warriors carrying captured carbines would occupy Calhoun Hill while most of the others, using nongovernment firearms—obviously the majority—would not. A further inference can be drawn from the dearth of Indian positions. Many more warriors are represented archaeologically at Henryville than Calhoun Hill. Evidently not many, no matter the firearm in hand, stopped to shoot as soldiers progressed north. I suggest, then, that the troopers' northern movement constituted flight, a predictable consequence of disintegration.

Developments at Calhoun Hill apparently followed the establishment of the second skirmish line. This formation probably confronted threats mounted by Indians farther west. If so, events at the Calhoun Coulee and Calhoun Ridge vicinities must be directly related to developments on Calhoun Hill. The soldiers in these sectors probably had deployed to blunt threats emanating from the western ridge (Greasy Grass) or nearby. There are no soldier pathways leading to Calhoun Hill. It appears, then, that the unit(s) involved differed from the Calhoun Hill contingent. What appears to be failure in the western sectors, however, must have allowed warriors there to move closer to Calhoun Hill.

Indian pathways, which imply movement between Greasy Grass and Calhoun Hill (figs. 6-15, 6-16, 6-17), support this interpretation. Evidently, the new concern prompted skirmishers on Calhoun Hill to adjust their original line, implying that Indian movements between Greasy Grass and the hill proceeded from west to east. Presumably, troopers in Calhoun Coulee and those on Calhoun Ridge moved the same way, toward Calhoun Hill.

Evidence indicates that an entire skirmish line relocated. An adjustment of this sort probably could not have been made had the original line been experiencing much pressure. Such circumstances raise two implications. Pressure is often caused by proximity of and volume fire from the enemy. Quite likely, skirmishers in the first deployment had, for some unknown period of time, experienced rather subdued fighting from distant adversaries to the south. The tactical environment allowed them to adjust their line. But any shift of this sort would have exposed the new line's left flank to southern warriors. No longer directly opposed, the Indians, it appears, decided to seize an advantage by moving closer. Much, if not all, of the Indian firing from Henryville probably occurred at this time. Here warriors with all manner of firearms did get close, and as archaeology shows, at least 20 possessed repeaters capable of volume fire. It seems that at this point, with the second skirmish line fronted and flanked, stability began to erode.

The Keogh Episode

The Keogh sector is located on the eastern slope of Custer Ridge, the side away from Little Big Horn River. Here the ground grades from the crest (roughly 3,280 feet MSL) into a coulee (about 3,200 feet MSL) just beyond the battlefield boundary. Trooper pathways (G and H, fig. 7-7) clearly link episodes in the Calhoun Hill and Keogh sectors. The proposed transitional nature of the tactical environment—stability to instability—indicates the Keogh episode followed action on the hill. A south-to-north flow is also evident in individual Indian pathways (figs. 6-15, 6-16), which show that Sioux and Cheyenne involved in the Calhoun episode also fought at the Keogh sector. As soldiers left Calhoun Hill, warriors followed. Unlike the Calhoun knoll, however, the Keogh sector lacks any physical evidence that might argue for even minimal fighting by cavalrymen—at least with firearms. This is astounding considering that stone memorials, even corrected for pairing errors, suggest that up to 70 soldiers died during the episode. Spent Colt pistol cartridges number three (fig. 6-14), and there are only seven .45/55 cases at the sector. These residues do not necessarily mean that only 10 or so troopers discharged their weapons, but they do exemplify very low-level responses to whatever resulted in wholesale destruction. Figure 7-12 illustrates the few .45/55 cases with respect to Keogh sector markers. Many

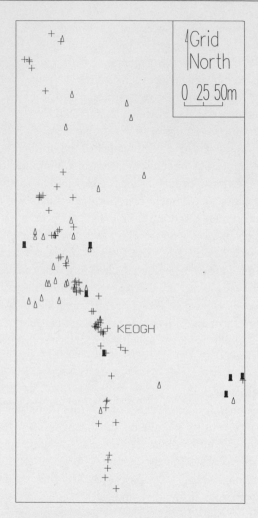

Fig. 7-12. Enlargement of the Keogh sector depicting .45/55 cartridge cases, Indian bullets, and marker locations.

Indian bullets, mapped in figure 7-12, tend to confirm the sector as a cavalry position.

The soldiers' northern move off Calhoun Hill implies, by virtue of a tendency to seek safety during extreme anxiety, that other battalion elements may have been somewhere in the Keogh sector. There is another indicator—the proliferation of markers here, more than at any other part of the field. Presumably this (or these) element(s) arrived as a stable unit; stability, after all, is reflected at Calhoun Hill. The precise whereabouts of sector troopers, however, are difficult to narrow. A concentration of Indian bullets is evident in figure 7-12, left center. But this is a product of more intensive survey at square B during the inventory evaluation phase (see fig. 6-5); it does not necessarily signal a discrete cavalry position. There is, however, a rough line of clustered stones here. The small clusters begin at Captain Keogh's marker (after whom the sector is named) and run grid north-by-northwest for some 220 yards. Perhaps these mark a cavalry position.

Despite the likelihood of cavalry here and considering the many deaths at the Keogh sector, there is little physical evidence for battle deployments. The few stone clusters, though arranged somewhat linearly, do not reflect prescribed formations. On the basis of extant archaeology, then, the best explanation is that the decampment from Calhoun Hill caught up Keogh sector men, and both groups continued north. Flight, as combat modeling predicts, can account for the archaeological implications that soldiers in the sector did little firing. And, in fact, sector markers are distributed from Calhoun Hill nearly to the Custer prominence. Indian pathways impart images of warriors chasing soldiers, now and then shooting at the soldiers as they continued north. Some paths lead to positions about Custer Hill (figs. 6-16, 6-17).

Figure 7-13 illustrates, on the basis of expended Indian rounds, known individual Indian positions in the Keogh sector. There is no evidence for intense, or even moderate, Indian firing. Since casings are underrepresented, it would appear that warriors fired at this position from a distance. Recorded relic finds beyond the eastern boundary fence of the monument include about 60 spent Indian cartridges.[12] Aside from this, however, Indian bullets and cartridge cases are hardly numerous, especially in light of the many and widely spread soldier deaths that occurred here. Indeed, this relative scarcity is curious given the fact that Indians relied heavily on firearms around Calhoun Hill and elsewhere to the west. This quite noticeable transition, available only from archaeology, suggests that many warriors involved in the Keogh episode abandoned, or rather quit using, their guns in favor of close-in fighting. All of this would suggest behavior attendant to an absence of tactical unity.

In sum, the episode seems permeated with the behavioral characteristics of disintegration generated at Calhoun Hill. Certainly, there is no evidence for sustained, tactical resistance on the part of the cavalry. And the paucity of bullets and cartridge cases, plus the many dead, is consistent with such behavior. Inference suggests that close-in fighting developed as a northern flight continued. Scrambling soldiers, judging from the general direction of movement, headed toward Custer Hill, though not without many deaths en route. This movement might suggest that perceived safety (and we know in retrospect that it could only have been perceived) lay with cavalry elements in that direction.

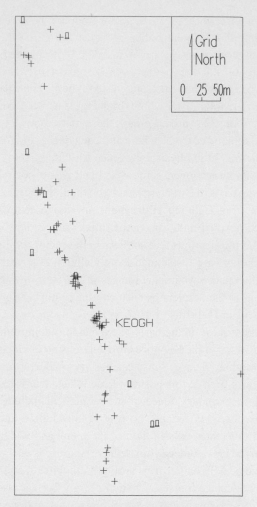

Fig. 7-13. Enlargement of the Keogh sector depicting Indian cartridge cases and marker locations.

The Custer Hill Episode

One of the most famous elevations in the annals of armed conflict is the north end of Custer Ridge—Custer Hill. I can think of others—Masada, Pork Chop, San Juan—and surely Custer Hill ranks with these. Although archaeology at this sector reveals that a number of men gathered on the hill, there is no evidence for stable, tactical formations such as skirmish lines. Rather, evidence hints that troopers huddled together on the rise, a place where many died. Physical clues

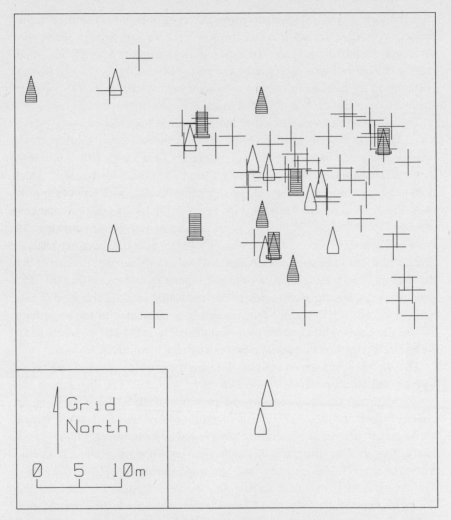

Fig. 7-14. Enlargement of the western slope of Custer Hill depicting .45/55 cartridge cases, bullets, and marker locations.

for this theory come from the western slope of the knoll. Bunching behavior is depicted by the clustering of a few .45/55 cartridge cases at this location, by associated Indian bullets, and most conspicuously, by some 43 tightly knotted memorial markers (corrected for pairing error). Figure 7-14 depicts the contextual relationships among these three artifact classes.

Indian bullets, though not numerous, clearly define the cavalry position. There are, however, several .45/55 government bullets interspersed with those of calibers indisputably fired by warriors. These seemingly aberrant bullets were probably delivered by Indians using government carbines captured during previous episodes. Certainly, on the basis of what we have seen in sectors just discussed, the Indians had plenty of opportunities to capture Springfields. Also, there are no indications—spent Indian casings are absent (fig. 6-12)—for warrior positions on the hillside. Without contradictory evidence, I assign the western slope of Custer Hill exclusively to the cavalry.

The only known concentration of Indian positions in the vicinity is located some 250 yards directly east of Custer Hill. There is a small knoll here; the warriors' vantage points are on the back side, away from Custer Hill. Apparently they tried to use the knoll crest for cover. But .45/55 bullets on the knoll, which is 20 to 50 feet lower than Custer Hill, suggest that soldiers detected their presence. Figure 7-15 portrays relationships between the Indian positions and government .45/55 bullets. Warrior locations are denoted by varied cartridge case types and several expended carbine rounds (.45/55 cases). Laboratory analysis revealed that the latter are split longitudinally along the casing, indicating that the Indians fired captured .45 Springfield rounds in larger-caliber guns. It is generally recognized that .50-caliber firearms would produce this kind of rupture. Thus, the .45/55 casings can reasonably be attributed to Indian activity. During the Custer Hill episode, then, and probably at the end of events in the Keogh sector, the knoll area clearly belonged to the Sioux and Cheyenne.

The .45/55 bullets shown in figure 7-15 are distributed such that they extend well beyond Indian positions denoted by cartridge cases. The disparity in area between the two classes argues for the presence of many other warriors. Of course, these "invisible" antagonists might have used muzzle-loaders, which, unlike breech-loading arms, tend not to leave conspicuous traces. But it is just as likely, if not more so, that many did not possess guns. Indeed, metal arrowpoints found at Custer Hill indicate bow-and-arrow use during the episode (fig. 7-16). The nearness of government bullets (fig. 7-15) to Custer Hill indicates that during the episode, the Sioux and Cheyenne got very close to the clustered men. In fact, judging from the distribution of .45/55 bullets around the elevation, it appears that Indians nearly surrounded the troopers, a minor exception being directly to the south along Custer Ridge (fig. 6-10).

Soldiers on the western hillside and Indians to the east could not possibly have exchanged gunfire because of intervening higher terrain (although arrows could have been lobbed in). The Custer Hill apex prevented this. Warriors on the east, then, must have confronted troopers stationed on or near the hill crest, not those on the west side. Unfortunately, construction projects (figs. 6-4, 6-6, 6-7) have completely erased any evidence that might have remained from this activity. It is thus impossible archaeologically to determine the nature of soldier deployments atop the prominence.

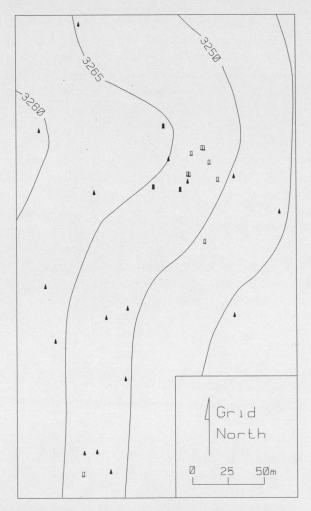

Fig. 7-15. Enlargement of the area east of Custer Hill depicting Indian cartridge cases, .45/55 cartridge cases, and .45/55 bullets.

Nonetheless, that warriors nearly encompassed Custer Hill indicates that the entire army contingent, regardless of its various positions, suffered extreme duress. There is thus no reason to suspect that men near the apex effected any better organization than those below on the western slope. Indeed, the picture emerges of embattled soldiers, grouped closely together, fighting without benefit of tactically prescribed deployments. That is clearly the case on the western slope of Custer Hill. Fighting all about the elevation, as it appears in the extant

Fig. 7-16. Distribution of metal arrowpoints in the Custer battlefield study area.

material record, could not have amounted to anything more than a defensive resistance.

The few .45/55 cases found on Custer Hill are not sufficient for postulating bunching on Custer Hill. The disordered, clustered markers on the western slope, however, do provide images of tactical instability during the episode.

Hardorff suspects that up to 15 of the 54 stones are spurious.[13] Calculations derived from pairing errors hint at 10 or 11 extras. Whatever the case, the disorderly patterning has never been questioned and need not be. Excavations at four of five randomly selected memorials produced soldier skeletal remains (four individuals) and associated artifacts.[14] The results of these excavations are informative on two counts. A one-in-five ratio suggests that 11 of the 54 markers should not be there, a figure comparable to that obtained through pairing-error assessment. More important, the high percentage (projected) of valid head-stones adds conviction to the impression of disorder imparted visually by patterning.

Derivation of those soldiers who occupied the hill cannot be conclusively demonstrated on archaeological grounds alone. One possibility arises from pathways, which indicate that warriors near the Calhoun sectors also operated around Custer Hill. The paths are depicted in figures 6-16 and 6-17, which show Indians moving north. An opposite flow seems unlikely in light of southern events, which, from the archaeological view, resulted in collapse. Probably, then, warriors followed soldiers north with both groups (or at least some troopers) ending up at Custer Hill. But the situation on this prominence could also have derived, in part, from tactically stable units elsewhere. This hypothesis fits the combat model in two ways. The first I have already proposed: soldiers moved from south to north toward perceived safety (i.e., stable units). The other is also behavioral in nature: bunching (observed on Custer Hill) can be expected to stem from organized elements. There is a problem with this, however. Clear and unmistakable archaeological clues for stable tactical deployments about the field are absent except on Calhoun Hill. But there are less direct lines of evidence, and these relate to Cemetery Ridge.

The Cemetery Ridge Episode

The national cemetery site lies in this sector, hence the name. Cemetery Ridge is generally a broad, flat landform that slopes west from Custer Hill to Little Big Horn Valley. Just short of a mile long, the ridge widens considerably as elevation decreases (a 100-foot drop at the terminus). The upper ridge is included in the study area, but the lower reaches extend beyond to the valley. Unfortunately, hard data about this episode are unavailable through archaeology. Post-battle disturbances, including installation of the national cemetery, landscaping, roads and parking lots, walkways, maintenance shops, residences, and a visitor center, have all but destroyed the original scene here. But even though only indirect evidences are available, some are sufficient to posit the presence of cavalry units on Cemetery Ridge.

Figures 6-6 and 6-7 provide a glimpse of Cemetery Ridge looking west from

Custer Hill. In these you can see some disturbances. Most noticeable are the visitor center and the national cemetery. Not visible—but farther west—are the maintenance and housing areas, best viewed in Figure 6-4, an aerial photograph that shows the magnitude of construction on the upper ridge. As a consequence of this development, the nature of combat activities in the sector can, on the basis of archaeology, only be inferred from evidence elsewhere.

Government .45/55 bullets occur frequently and are widely dispersed on the area identified here as "The Flats." Figure 7-17 depicts this distribution—from the South Skirmish Line to the western limits of the study area. The orientation of 60 percent of these bullets indicates Cemetery Ridge origins. Many are arrayed along the northern bank of Deep Ravine, with some near Indian positions, as denoted by spent cartridges. Others are distributed on flat land to the north and west. This patterning suggests that Sioux and Cheyenne emerged from the ravine to occupy The Flats, a warrior presence that would surely have drawn fire from soldiers. It is posited, then, that some fire did come from cavalrymen on Cemetery Ridge.

The bullet orientation concept is a tentative measure of origin points. Some bullets can be expected to lodge in the earth consistent with the origin direction. On the other hand, tumbling on impact can also occur. But it may be that of all bullets fired from a given location, a statistical constant (i.e., percentage) or narrow orientation range can be expected. Such measures may indicate points of origin. Experimental firings, which have not been conducted, ought to confirm, deny, or modify the idea. Nevertheless, it is at least plausible that many of the .45/55 bullets came from undetermined Cemetery Ridge locations.

But what about the idea of stable units? Note that government bullets about The Flats are widely spread (fig. 7-17). Such dispersal, it seems, could not have been achieved by anything other than organized, tactical deployments. Indeed, this very effect is one predictable outcome of manpower dispersion in a skirmish line. Bunched men cannot, as a result of eroded discipline within restricted space, easily achieve widespread coverage. Firepower and coverage can be expected to decrease wherever disintegration ensues. Considering the characteristics of bunching, then, I would suggest that the western slope of Custer Hill as an exclusive point of origin can be ruled out. And soon I shall argue against the nearby South Skirmish Line sector on grounds that the record there is suggestive of total collapse.

In addition, assessing this matter of a cavalry presence on Cemetery Ridge is aided by battle-related relic finds made over the years beyond the battlefield boundaries (the study area). Greene recorded several expended Indian cartridges low on Cemetery Ridge.[15] One Indian position is within 350 yards of Little Big Horn River (one .50/70 casing). Another position farther from the river yielded

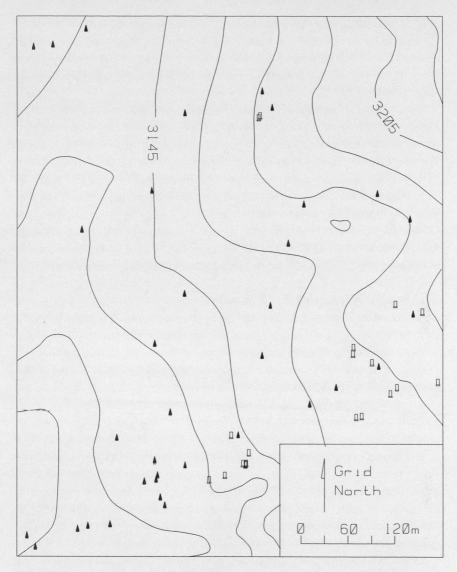

Fig. 7-17. Enlargement of The Flats sector depicting the distributions of .45/55 bullets and Indian cartridge cases.

six Spencer and Henry casings. Not far away, to the east, there is another find consisting of 35 Henry and Spencer casings in a small area.[16]

Relic collectors found these casings in locations that, because of intervening terrain, clearly prohibited firing at targets anywhere other than on Cemetery Ridge. Moore also reported spent Indian cartridges in similar spatial contexts.[17]

And, incidentally, one collector turned up a cavalry spur at the foot of Cemetery Ridge near the river. Finally, five Indian bullets on The Flats are located within about 125 yards of the western boundary of the study area (extreme upper left, fig. 6-9). Presumably soldiers, who evidently had progressed quite far down the ridge, drew this fire.

Finds by relic hunters, discoveries of individual Indian positions on The Flats, orientations of government bullets there, and five seemingly isolated Indian bullets circumstantially increase the likelihood of action on or about Cemetery Ridge. Thanks to modern disturbances, however, the specific nature of tactics undertaken from the ridge is now beyond an archaeological determination. Nonetheless, dispersion observed in .45/55 bullet patterning over The Flats very likely came from organized, cohesive deployments. In addition, the Custer Hill episode as revealed above cannot be strongly considered as a source for carbine bullets about The Flats. I have suggested that, as a point of origin, the South Skirmish Line can also be eliminated, and I shall now turn to that record.

The South Skirmish Line Episode

Archaeology disputes images conjured by the name given this sector, demonstrating that the South Skirmish Line is inaptly labeled—and ineptly too. There is, here, not a shred of ammunition evidence for any type of organized cavalry formation. Today, as in the past, claims for a skirmish deployment during this episode derive from the mostly linear distribution of stone markers at the sector (fig. 6-8). Viewed from Custer Hill, and with a serene and beautiful river valley beyond, these memorials captivate the observer. All kinds of historical data are juggled and rejuggled to explain why they are there. Most are spread along a ridge. Actually nothing more than a low-lying, elongated rise, the ridge slopes gently from Custer Hill (3,300 feet MSL), running almost due south for some 2,000 feet to its end near Deep Ravine (3,130 feet MSL). In marked contrast to the ridge, this gully is rugged and deeply cut, hence its name. (Later, in historical discussions, Deep Ravine figures prominently in the South Skirmish Line episode, but not so much here.) The several upper tributaries of Deep Ravine reach all the way to Custer Ridge (fig. 6-4). Here—just below the ridge—the drainage pattern forms an expansive but shallow basin, and here too are a number of memorial stones. Deep Ravine, as it runs west by southwest, eventually discharges its seasonal flow into Little Big Horn River.

Many of the marble stones dotting the scene are misplaced, although excavations at each of six memorial sites did yield human remains. The markers (53) do, however, portray the approximate number of troopers who died during the episode. Resolving the issue of misplaced stones and showing that they are a rough barometer of soldier deaths are chiefly historical problems. Nevertheless,

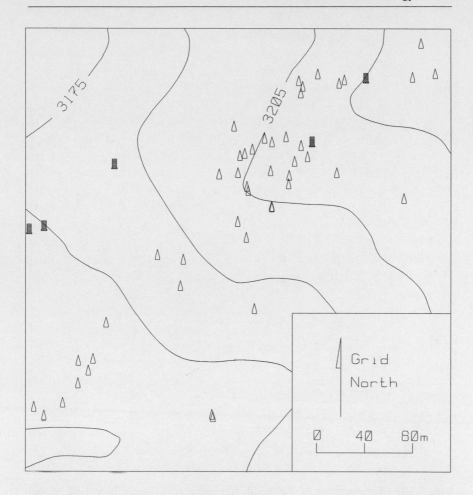

Fig. 7-18. Enlargement of the South Skirmish Line sector depicting Indian bullets and .45/55 cartridge cases.

the value of other archaeological data is not diminished by this misplacement, provided one accepts, for the moment, that some 50 cavalrymen died in and around the ravine, the basin, and the ridge.

A cavalry presence on the South Skirmish Line is amply demonstrated by numerous Indian bullets there—along nearly the entire length of the ridge. Figure 7-18 depicts this distribution as well as expended government cartridges, which number only five. Note also the evidence for the use of arrows against soldiers here (fig. 7-16). The great numerical disparity between government cases and Indian bullets is provocative. It immediately raises the prospect that troops suffered considerably while on the ridge and were ill-prepared, unable, or

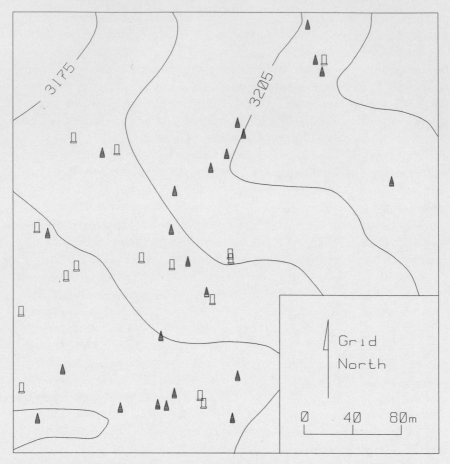

Fig. 7-19. Enlargement of the South Skirmish Line sector depicting Indian cartridge cases and .45/55 bullets.

unwilling to react tactically. Certainly there is nothing at all in the .45/55 casings suggestive of a skirmish line, and Colt .45 cases are entirely absent (fig. 6-14).

There is clear evidence in the sector for the presence of first one opponent and then the other. Figure 7-19 locates numerous empty Indian cartridges, each representing a warrior position, and .45/55 bullets fired by cavalrymen. So striking are the sequent occupations that the impact of captured weapons, if used at all here, is effectively dampened. The question then surfaces: in what order did these events occur? No firm answer can be obtained, but we can make several inferences. Perhaps troopers first occupied the sector. If so, they put up little fight, and many deaths occurred. Then warriors moved in, only to come under fire from enemy riflemen stationed elsewhere.

Alternatively, Sioux and Cheyenne initially took up positions in this sector and experienced enemy fire. Numerous spent Indian cartridges indicate a sizable force here. Carbine bullets also occur in quantity. Somewhat widely dispersed, they are coincidental with the casing distribution. Quantity and coincidence imply that soldiers somewhere nearby paid considerable attention to this group of Indians. Warriors at the sector may have posed threats sufficient to provoke a relief deployment. This could account for the soldier presence here, a maneuver that, by all physical clues, proved unsuccessful.

In either option, archaeology says the troopers failed. Which, though, seems more reasonable? Assuming cavalrymen first occupied the sector implies tactical intent, plus a chance for success. It also requires the prior absence of Indians firing from the ridge proper. Presumably, then, tactical deployments could be implemented after reaching the destination. Yet there is no inkling of such, specifically a battle line, which might be expected if troopers occupied the ridge before Indians began to move in on them.

The cavalry-first option may also be viewed within the archaeological context already developed—the flow of battle. That is, some parts of the battalion farther south collapsed, and remnants subsequently moved north (remnants because it is clear many died along the way). These episodes seem to have occurred before much action in the South Skirmish Line sector. Why is that? Certain pathways show that warriors involved in southern events, notably in the Greasy Grass Ridge and Calhoun Hill vicinities, advanced to take part in the northern episodes (figs. 6-15, 6-16, 6-17). I have deduced also that they followed troops who were seeking safety farther north. If, during this time, the South Skirmish Line sector supported a tactical deployment—a skirmish line—presumably it would have received comrades and met the enemy influx, very likely leaving in the process some physical traces of its activities. Once again, none exist.

Reiterating, archaeology places soldiers at the South Skirmish Line sector, disallows battle lines, and in fact, portrays a rather hapless cavalry there. Many men died, evidently without offering much resistance. The scene is reminiscent of the disintegration process. What factors might promote this? Proximity and firepower are two. The warrior-first option provides both of these and is seemingly more consistent with the hard evidence. For example, judging from statistical projections based on firearm identifications, slightly less than half the Indians in the sector area used Henry repeating rifles. Thus, under this scenario, army riflemen fired into the sector as warriors, some from the southern sectors, gathered in the South Skirmish Line vicinity. Sometime thereafter, soldiers deployed to counter the Indians. A combination of considerable firepower and closeup antagonists, both evident in the archaeological record, prevented realization of the tactical mission, including establishment of a battle line.

From Indian bullet distributions (fig. 7-18), it is evident that whatever happened during the episode took place along nearly the entire ridge. These bullets are arrayed over some 500 yards, from somewhat below Custer Hill to Deep Ravine. It is not hard to imagine that cavalrymen drew this fire. Under normal tactics, it would take about 100 soldiers to form a 500-yard-long skirmish line. Surely more than two of these would have discharged their weapons (the two carbine casings in fig. 7-18). Some alternative is demanded. More likely, Indians fired at targets moving along the ridge. Under the degree of pressure implied archaeologically, movement would have been rapid. Throw in 50 or so deaths, plus sparse evidence for resistance, and one can envision a quite chaotic situation. If soldiers here did deploy tactically, it was not for long, and the line dissolved before skirmishers could issue anything in the way of effective fire.

Organizational derivation of the South Skirmish Line troops cannot be deduced archaeologically. Nonetheless, they came from somewhere. In a scene of chaos and disorganization, such as revealed in physical remains, that origin might have been Custer Hill. This is only inference, for there are no soldier pathways connecting the two sectors (see fig. 6-18). The hilltop, though, is close by and only 200 yards from the nearest of the Indian bullets that hit along the low ridge. It is also interesting to note that the tactical environment on the hill, so far as it can be painted archaeologically, appears as something less than stable. Sioux and Cheyenne nearly surrounded the elevation and included warriors occupying the South Skirmish Line sector. The result for the soldiers was a more or less desperate situation, one that can account not only for the derivation of men on the so-called skirmish line but for results of that deployment as well. It is hypothesized, then, that troops in this sector, hoping to relieve pressures, came from Custer Hill and that the two episodes are related.

This conclusion, hypothetical as it is, begs the possibility of a Cemetery Ridge derivation. I have argued that a stable element, or elements, of the battalion occupied portions of this ridge at some time. These troopers could be the same men who died at the South Skirmish Line sector. But given the park improvements at the battlefield, there seems little chance for assessing this alternative using trowel and spade. Whatever the option, heavy Indian fire and the lack of clear evidence for tactical stability are compelling measures of tactical disintegration at the South Skirmish Line sector. Indeed, the episode seems to parallel events at the Keogh sector insofar as clues from the ground—the history beneath our feet—tell of many men dying without offering much resistance. Whether soldiers came from Custer Hill or Cemetery Ridge, whether cavalry or Indian first occupied the area, there is not much to support a clash between organized cavalrymen and warriors in this sector. This simple observation diminishes any likelihood of assigning remains on The Flats to soldiers at the South Skirmish Line sector.

Considerations of Site Taphonomy

Confidence in analytical results, I noted earlier, is strengthened by sound methods. Understandings of site taphonomy, or how the ravages of time have affected the archaeological record, also promote trust. In this context, cultural and natural processes active at a site usually need to be assessed. I have already mentioned some cultural disturbances. Most notable are the various types of improvements, so to speak, at Custer Hill and those along Cemetery Ridge. These projects have completely obliterated portions of the material record, if any existed. Less certain is the role of road building on the battlefield. The narrow access road, shifted slightly from its original course, today runs along three named ridges: first up Cemetery, then along Custer, and finally down Calhoun, where it exits the battlefield at the southern boundary. As noted before, road construction at the least might have affected marker locations in several sectors. Otherwise, most of the field has escaped serious perturbation by human agency.

Natural agents also pose problems. Sites with many levels representing different time periods are most seriously affected by these processes, which can mix artifacts, causing problems in analysis. The Custer battlefield is not such a property. It is, for the most part, a single-episode site. Except for minor soil movement, disturbances on the uplands can be ruled out on the basis of geomorphological observations.[18] Thus, artifact provenances and the contextual significance of extant material remains have not been compromised by natural processes.

Postbattle cartridge cases can be found at the battlefield site. Reenactments and ceremonies over the years have left spent Springfield casings lying about. These can be identified, however. The army, in 1877, began stamping carbine cartridges with month, year, and place of manufacture. This fortunate change has allowed archaeologists to discriminate between battle-related casings and later ones.

However, one author learned of an early-day park superintendent who allegedly scattered nonstamped carbine casings about the field so that visitors might be able to find a souvenir.[19] This information came to the author third hand—at the least—so it hardly inspires confidence. But what if that had occurred? How might that affect archaeology at the Custer battlefield? The author cautioned that it casts doubt on the authenticity of "some finds"—which finds he did not say.[20] To me, the alleged "salting," if it happened, suggests that there was never much in the way of government casings to collect. And that, of course, is exactly what archaeological results at most sectors show.

Relic collecting can compromise the material record. The archaeological deductions in this chapter are predicated on patterns observed in ammunition components. Much of the analysis is quantitative and distributional in nature. Analytical results—which portray stability, disintegration, flight, and at many cavalry sectors, minimal resistance—deviate substantially, indeed entirely, from the heroic tradition. Consequently, detractors will argue that relic collecting, particularly at those sectors where the disintegration phenomenon is so vivid archaeologically, has badly skewed the analysis.

That relic hunting at the battlefield has occurred cannot be denied. I have found four references to indiscriminate collecting, principally of unidentified cartridge cases, or shells as they are often called.[21] Though bullets could be collected too, those found archaeologically generally outnumber cartridge cases. Tracking spent carbine cases seems most important, for they are the basic indicators of how much and how well the soldiers fought. Carbine ammunition components in the artifact inventory total 87 cartridge cases and 143 bullets. This discrepancy might signal selection by relic hunters. But more parsimonious factors can be found, including the distinct probability that areas disturbed by construction contained expended Springfield cartridges. Another likelihood is that some carbine bullets came from Indians who fired captured Springfields from locations outside the study area. Casings beyond the monument boundaries and in disturbed areas can no longer be accounted for. Thus the numerical disparity between carbine bullets and casings is doubtless somewhat deceiving.

Further, it is hard to imagine that relic hunters carried away nearly every .45/55 shell, particularly if troopers putting up a stiff fight discarded great numbers. In any case, there are substantial numbers of Indian casings remaining. Knowing this, one who favors a skewed analysis must suggest that relic hunters tended to select one type over another. I find that degree of sophistication extremely doubtful. Arguments against extensive collecting are all the more compelling in light of relative distributions between cavalry sectors. Compared with other sectors, Calhoun Hill exhibits abundant spent carbine shells. Did collectors nearly pick clean all troop positions except this one? This seems unlikely, since indiscriminate collecting over the long run is always random, not only between artifact types but throughout space as well. A logical answer, then, is that varying behavioral circumstances between episodes produced qualitative and quantitative differences in physical remains across the battlefield and that these differences remain informative, regardless of relic collecting.

This is the fundamental premise, one available only through archaeology, with which I approach the written record of the Custer battle. Among many other things, I will show, in sifting through the documents, that descriptions by some military men who observed the battle aftermath are harmonious with distributional patterns of spent government cases as noted above. Moreover, many Indian accounts describe actions that could only have resulted in observed artifact patterns, not of just one type or one area but of all. Native and white eyewitness testimonies that do not match archaeological results are thus dubious at best. Additional archaeological and historical observations presented in part 4 are also relevant. They provide data that support the contention that there was never much in the way of government ammunition residues to collect.

Summation

It might be wise, before turning to the historical record, to quickly summarize the archaeology. Material remains from sector to sector differ in fundamental ways. Despite effects of taphonomic processes, differences reflect a gamut of combat behaviors illustrative of a transition from tactical stability to disintegration. That process, which peaked at Calhoun Hill, seems to have signaled the beginning of the end. Bunching and flight evidently developed from tactical failures at the Calhoun Coulee and Calhoun Ridge sectors. Developments there caused the original skirmish line at Calhoun Hill to redeploy facing west. The adjustment implies that the first battle line had, until the western threats materialized, encountered nothing too serious in the way of enemy action. Redeployment, however, allowed the Indians to the south to seize advantages and move closer to the hilltop cavalry position. Much of the Indian firing at Henryville probably occurred at this time. The second skirmish line, now faced with attacks at the front (from the Greasy Grass Ridge vicinity) and the left flank (from Henryville), started to waver. Ultimately, command discipline eroded, men tended to bunch together, and flight ensued.

Decampment from Calhoun Hill proceeded northward into the Keogh sector. Why a northward flight instead of elsewhere? Fugitives probably sought safety with Keogh-sector soldiers. If there, presumably they reacted to help their fleeing comrades, but clearly not from a standard battle formation. Anything even remotely resembling a skirmish line is lacking, an absence that suggests a troop element caught unaware by a rather sudden change in the tactical environment. How can this be? It is consistent with observations of less than vigorous fighting before collapse in the Calhoun sectors. Remembering tactical prescriptions of the time, we can infer that a Keogh sector cavalry element, seeing no need to immediately deploy and fight, functioned as a reserve group.

Of course, a badly besieged force would not assume such a posture. But then where are the five skirmish lines? Should not five companies under duress equal five battle lines? There is nothing at the Keogh sector. By any measure of extant physical data, flight continued unabated through this area. No soldier pathways link Custer Hill with the sector, but Indian paths do indirectly. Marker stones also point to this elevation as a destination, or at least the direction of movement. The hill shows an army presence but no evidence of stable tactical units. Conse-

quently, it is tempting to view the occupation there as stemming from the breakdown in cohesion during southern episodes. In part this may be true; some
fleeing men perhaps reached Custer Hill. But why rush toward that prominence?
Again, safety in the form of comrades probably existed there or nearby. Keeping
this in mind, and taking into account behaviors of men in combat, we can view
the Custer Hill episode, at least in part, as the product of erosion in the military
unity of cavalry located elsewhere.

This possibility requires proof of cohesive units at positions other than Calhoun Hill, proof that is nonexistent archaeologically. There are, however, some
indicators of tactical cavalry operations on Cemetery Ridge. If so, possibly
these cavalrymen, or some, ended up at Custer Hill. The surmise is predicated,
in the absence of hard data, on modeling combat behavior. Beyond this, individual troop positions about the hill, so far as artifacts and markers show, are
devoid of plan and order, all of which is indicative of a defense posture taken up
under dire circumstances. Clustered together, men there found themselves virtually surrounded by Indians, many apparently close at hand. Under terms of the
model, this posture, plus the flow of battle, rather clearly suggests that the
Custer Hill episode unfolded during the latter stages of the confrontation.

We find, using the same reasoning, that the South Skirmish Line episode also
occurred after confusion enveloped cavalrymen at the Calhoun and Keogh sectors. As pathways show, warriors around Greasy Grass Ridge and Calhoun Hill
followed a northern flight. Some made their way to the low ridge below Custer
Hill, where they confronted soldiers, who left no physical trace of fighting by
the book. Indeed, the South Skirmish Line episode seems to have paralleled, in
terms of combat behavior, events at the Keogh sector. In both places, archaeological evidence for soldier resistance, tactical or otherwise, is virtually absent—
but disaster is not. Although the derivation of South Skirmish Line soldiers is
inconclusive, it is important to note, contrary to the name given this sector, that
there is no evidence for skirmishing. Rather, physical data suggest that troopers
only briefly occupied the sector and, indeed, probably passed rapidly over the
ridge. This, it would seem from a historical perspective, is the important point to
keep in mind when studying the documents.

Archaeological analyses do not support conventional views of the Custer
battle—images of disciplined, organized cavalrymen engaged in a stubborn but
futile defense—canonical tales as Stephen Jay Gould might class them.[22]
Instead, the picture emerges of a far more typical process in warfare, that of
psychological debilitation followed by physical collapse. The enemy seems to
have induced disintegration. Thereafter, troops evidently struggled against their
foe in confusion and disorganization. There is little in the archaeological record
to indicate organized skirmishing before disintegration. The clear exception,

of course, is at Calhoun Hill. But why only there? Should not one expect a beleaguered command—a battalion on the defense—to throw out as many battle lines as possible after reaching Custer Ridge, five companies/five lines? I should think so, yet none exist at other sectors, except possibly Cemetery Ridge, a landform fully—and curiously—a mile from skirmishers at Calhoun Hill. Why such a distant separation if not for reasons other than defense? One might even see in the record at Calhoun Hill something less than a dangerous combat environment before collapse. All of this points toward two things: first, a battalion that experienced not attrition but collapse, which strategists typically find to be sudden and rapid. And if this is the case then, second, there is considerably more room for supposing, contrary to fatalistic bents, that an offensive mode existed at the time disaster set in.

So went the Custer battle, or so it seems from the archaeological perch. But by some measures the fight continues. Many argue today, as others have for 100-plus years, over the course of events at the Little Big Horn. It is worth noting again that controversies stem largely from the usually contradictory, sometimes vague, and often ambiguous nature of the documentary base. Contending theorists, however objective, can at times offer virtually the same historical data as proof of their schemes. Throw in biases and preconceptions, and the whole business is muddled further. Archaeology provides an analytical framework grounded in physical remains, one capable of resolving many of the historical dilemmas. So now it is time to interpret the written legacy using archaeological reasoning. Aside from furnishing new data and new ideas, the process includes searching for parallels while culling inconsistent historical data. In this effort, archaeology often forces a fresh interpretation of familiar stories. Next, by amalgamating archaeology and history, I attempt to achieve a holistic, unified picture of the Custer battle—the final stages first and then the broader sweep.

Part Three.
History and
Archaeology

8

PRELUDE

*These white men [in Custer's battalion] wanted it, they called
for it and I let them have it.*
                              —*Iron Hawk, a Hunkpapa Sioux*[1]

Archaeological reasoning has furnished an elementary view of the
Custer battle. Patterns, which vary across sectors, reflect the disintegration
process and also argue for an offensive mode at the time of collapse. Working
from the ground up, and trusting this foundation, we should see a similar picture
in the written evidence. That picture begins here with a look at the historical
record, which consists of various testimonies and relations. Though hardly
exhaustive, this purview does place in perspective the difficult interpretive
nature of the written record. The last section sets the stage for the event on
Custer Ridge.

The Written Record

Needless to say, the jumble of recollections about Custer's last fight is complex. There are Indian eyewitness accounts and reminiscences recorded by
white chroniclers. Mostly these are accounts of personal deeds or descriptions of
cavalry actions, but there are also several versions of Cheyenne oral tradition. It
is clear that much of what the Sioux and Cheyenne related years after the fight in
part derives from orally transmitted histories. Also available is a substantial
literature compiled by non-Indian informants, such as survivors of the Reno-
Benteen battle. These men mostly commented on what they saw in the death
scene, though many, based on such observations, unhesitatingly offered their
ideas on how it all happened. In addition, this famous battle has seduced count-
less others. Its mysteries have provoked an enormous interpretive literature that
purports, with varying degrees of success, to "explain" the Custer battle. In
combining history with archaeology, I concentrate largely on primary accounts,
incorporating the interpretive literature where useful.

Seldom do participants witness a complex event in its entirety. Yet individuals
come together and relate their experiences. If the event is important enough,
these relations usually find their way into oral history. A major function of oral
history is to make use of many personal accounts by organizing them mean-
ingfully into a coherent portrayal of what happened—a standardized account.

Nonliterate societies depend on this type of device to preserve the past. Stories of the Custer battle given by the Cheyenne woman Kate Bighead are oral histories.[2] Her renditions are, as it turns out, fairly consistent chronologically. Thus, when properly understood, they provide a good overview of the nature and progress of the battle.

So also does the Wooden Leg compilation.[3] Wooden Leg, a Cheyenne warrior, apparently engaged the soldiers midway through the battle. Consequently, his story relies partly on Cheyenne oral history (before he arrived at the scene) and partly on his own experiences. The Bighead and Wooden Leg accounts are remarkably similar in content, and in some instances descriptions of events are nearly identical. This coincidence of similar wording is no doubt partly due to the fact that Thomas Marquis, an early physician at the Cheyenne agency, rendered both. But the internal consistencies stem from the standardizing nature of oral history.

Curley, and several other Crow Indians, served with the 7th Cavalry as a scout. He was dismissed immediately before the Custer engagement because scouts, employed only as pathfinders, were not required to do battle. Curley on several occasions admitted as much.[4] Yet white recorders regularly sought him out, and Curley had many stories to tell. Typically, students of the battle tend to discredit his accounts because he did not participate in the actual fighting, but this is a mistake. Curley, though a Crow, clearly shared in Cheyenne and Sioux oral histories (and Crow oral history, which evidently incorporated Sioux and Cheyenne stories). Thus he could comment in various detail on the battle, though at times his versions are garbled.[5] Most of the confusion rises from Curley's propensity to include himself in his narrations, which sometimes paint a detailed picture of the battle. He evidently did so either to add validity to the story or to inflate his role. But the addition has had the opposite effect: numerous researchers have rejected Curley entirely on the grounds that he lied. Nonetheless, as oral history, his accounts provide valuable information about the fight.

A peculiar aspect of Cheyenne oral history lies in references—by Big Head and Wooden Leg in particular—to mass suicide among the soldiers in the Custer battle.[6] This is not the place to refute the claim in detail, although it still surfaces in such "authoritative" media as the *National Enquirer*.[7] Quite simply, the contention is nonsense. A few troopers undoubtedly took their own lives,[8] but it is hard to know what factors fostered the idea of wholesale suicide. Perhaps the claim stemmed from the well-known occurrence of accidental killings during combat.[9] The nature of this battle, soon to become evident in detail, might also have figured insofar as failing to resist death is similar to suicide. In any case, Wooden Leg in later years retracted his claim.[10] Further, absolutely no mention of such behavior occurs in Sioux accounts.[11]

Oral histories relate events that occurred within the lifetimes of the participants. When the last participant is gone (technically), oral history ceases to exist. Histories are then maintained as oral traditions. The latter are also included in the Custer battle documentary record. Interpreting oral tradition as history is subject to various checks and balances.[12] Traditions passed orally from generation to generation are historically relevant when it can be shown they rest on original, valid events.[13] I employ Cheyenne traditions in this way. Traditional stories of the Custer battle passed down by Cheyenne people even today are largely ignored for two reasons: they are not eyewitness accounts, and they do not square with the myth. Yet archaeology provides the link between these traditions and historical reality, most notably concerning the Cemetery Ridge episode. Moreover, other materials, white and Indian, help confirm this battle episode. And elements of Cheyenne oral tradition have been validated, at least in principle, through artifacts (mostly soldier and Indian cartridge cases) unearthed by relic hunters in areas south of the Custer battlefield.[14]

Many Indian accounts of the Custer battle are by an eyewitness relating personal experiences and deeds. Emphasis on self is not surprising, since prowess in battle helped promote social status. The Indian view of conflict as a social vehicle might be compared to the esteem conferred in modern times on soldiers returning from war, at least during "popular" strife. In this respect, the institution of war can place unreasonable demands on veterans, who at least occasionally feel compelled to embellish their experiences. After the Custer battle, White Bull apparently found it necessary to enhance his role by belittling other native combatants. But this does not render his and similar testimonies invalid, provided one can penetrate the ornamentation.

With few exceptions, warrior testimonies describe only portions of the battle, and unlike oral history and traditions, such testimonies are generally incomplete accounts. Consequently, it is often difficult to place Indian descriptions in the proper temporal and spatial contexts. This limitation is compounded by various other factors hindering the use of native eyewitness testimony. Chroniclers transcribed many accounts years after the battle. Memories by then had often dimmed. Interpreters made mistakes in rendering a foreign tongue. A tendency to fear implication is sometimes evident, which might also help explain the stories of mass suicide.

Indian informants, sometimes fearing retribution or hoping to curry favors, often tailored their stories to conform with what they thought their white audience wanted to hear. Elements of the testimony provided by Gall, a Sioux leader, are notorious in this regard, particularly concerning the soldiers' combat behavior—behavior that he described in near heroic terms. Similarly, the Indian perspective of war probably compelled a few warriors to portray unwavering soldiers (rather than passive foes gripped with fear and unable to resist effectively) so that they might wring the maximum social value from their deeds. And straightforward accounts were subject to errors, ambiguities, and misrepresentations imparted by the interpretive biases of white interviewers. Predisposition and bias spawned leading questions and, more seriously, precluded certain avenues of inquiry. Finally, interviewers solicited testimony within the frameworks of concepts wholly unfamiliar to Plains Indians. White man's time is one example. And Indians could not possibly know about cavalry tactics, formations, and deployments from the technical viewpoint. As a result, *Custer* (and other terms frequently used to describe soldier actions) can mean most anything, from the entire battalion to an element thereof (but not the man, for the Indians had no idea who they fought until later).

Non-Indian accounts of the battle, particularly those of military personnel, tend to be fraught with inconsistencies as well. The Reno court of inquiry transcripts,[15] for example, are full of reticence and hedging on the part of 7th Cavalry officers and men. This military court convened in January 1879 to examine charges against Major Reno. Sentiment at the time demanded a scapegoat, and Reno found himself the candidate. To blunt the criticism, he requested an inquiry (not a court-martial). Basically, detractors charged that Reno had been derelict in his duties, leading to the demise of Custer. In this atmosphere, the court listened to testimony pro and con, deliberated, and eventually found that although the major had hardly distinguished himself, his actions did not merit condemnation.

Edgar Stewart has called the inquiry a gigantic farce and concluded that Reno-Benteen battle survivors collaborated in testifying, either to protect the 7th Cavalry image or, themselves vulnerable to criticism, to prevent retaliation by Major Reno and his friends.[16] In some respects, Stewart's evaluation is defensible, particularly concerning the actions of the Reno-Benteen officers. But court transcripts also deal in part with the Custer battle, providing a great deal of primary data untainted by ulterior motives. Useful sources, these still must be examined in light of predispositions. Many accounts by military men, for example, are colored by the tendency to see, in the physical remains of Custer's battle, examples of stability, deployments, and order that did not always exist.

Archaeology helps to overcome the deficiencies in and limitations of the written record. Although historical details of the Custer battle presented here are subject to revision, the overall conclusions, I believe, cannot be seriously disputed. The Custer battalion suffered enormously from the effects of tactical disintegration. Once unity dissipated, the command offered little effective resistance.

The Beginnings of Battle

Any story of Custer's last battle necessarily begins with an introductory orientation of some nature. The same is true here. This manuscript deals principally with the final stages of a confrontation that began some distance south of Custer Ridge. Denouement, of course, came on this elevation. But in the early stages, the two adversaries initiated contact in Medicine Tail Coulee (fig. 4-2). In the formative years of study of the Custer battle—during the nineteenth century—two schools of thought arose. One argued that Custer's battalion crossed the coulee but never got anywhere near Little Big Horn River and instead marched from the high bluffs (where Reno held out) directly to Custer Ridge. Contenders said no—the column went down Medicine Tail to its mouth before riding onto the ridge. This impasse persists in some circles.

In light of current knowledge, both sides may claim a measure of validity. Today, three facts seem incontestable. First, Custer's five 7th Cavalry companies operated as a battalion consisting of two wings. Second, the wings separated during the early skirmishing in Medicine Tail Coulee. One went to the river; the other did not—movements that are examined in more detail later when dealing with strategy (part 5). Third, and finally, the wings subsequently left the Medicine Tail area and reunited, if only briefly, at or near Calhoun Hill,[17] thus setting the stage for the much celebrated climax.

Artifact finds by relic hunters south of the Custer battlefield[18] tend to support the dual-wing, separate-operation interpretation. Collected without design and reported haphazardly, these discoveries reveal little but do establish presence. Battle-related items are scattered from near the mouth of Medicine Tail Coulee north to Calhoun Hill via Deep Coulee (not to be confused with Deep Ravine; Deep Coulee is also known as North Medicine Tail Coulee). Similarly, material remains are found north by northwest from Luce Ridge across Nye-Cartwright Ridge to Calhoun Hill. Relics in both instances primarily consist of expended government cartridge cases and corresponding evidence for Indian firing. Such evidence does not eliminate the possibility that the same unit (i.e., the battalion) traversed these localities at different times, but Indian accounts suggest otherwise. Two Eagles[19] said that some troopers left the upland ridges and proceeded down Medicine Tail to the river. Then this group moved up Deep Coulee to Calhoun Ridge. Meanwhile, he remembered, other soldiers stayed on the eastern ridges (i.e., Luce) before going northward to Calhoun Hill (or nearby).

One unit that approached the river was clearly E Company. Joseph White Cow Bull, a Sioux, confronted it there. He reported that men on gray horses rode to the mouth of Medicine Tail.[20] The Cheyenne warrior White Shield, there at the time, remembered that troops who came down to the coulee mouth rode horses that "were pretty white" (i.e., gray horses).[21] E Company rode grays, these clearly distinguishable from the bays and sorrels of the other four troops. Though this much can be established, the composition of each wing—the wing affiliation of each company—is, in an understatement, a source of debate.

E. I. Stewart and J. A. Greene[22] identified the two independent units as battalions, one consisting of Companies I and L, the other of Companies C, E, and F. Their ideas are likely based in whole or in part on Edward Godfrey's interpretation of Gall's Custer battle account.[23] But there are two errors evident. One is in terminology, the other in wing makeup.

The division of the regiment into battalions came very early in the day—just after leaving the divide between Rosebud Creek and the Little Big Horn. This left Custer's five companies operating as a single battalion. This much the officers sitting in judgment on the Reno Court determined,[24] although occasionally court witnesses loosely referred to two battalions.[25] It then is not likely, at least from the military perspective, that this discrete unit (Custer's battalion) subsequently organized into two battalions. Tactical prescription dictated, when appropriate, organization of a battalion into two wings. Though seeming to be terminological nit-picking, prescriptions thus do not accommodate the wing configurations of battalions as offered by Stewart and Greene.

In addition, C. G. du Bois's[26] organization of the Custer battalion is also at odds with prescriptive expectations of the period. He too called each of the wings "battalions," assigning Companies I and L to one and the cavalrymen of E and F to the other. According to du Bois, C Company at some point divided into two platoons, with one assigned to each "battalion" in order to equalize unit strengths. Tactical prescription, however, did not require equal-strength wings in a battalion. Indeed, in a five-company battalion, one wing could be expected by design to have an additional company. And platoons could be eliminated altogether in understrength companies such as those in the Custer battalion.[27] All in all, there is simply no evidence for tactical divisions smaller than the company. In any event, Capt. Myles Moylan remembered that three companies operated in one wing and two in the other.[28] The du Bois speculation, then, is extremely difficult to justify.

Misunderstandings of the battalion concept allow any combination of companies within battalion units and invariably reflect an author's preconceptions of how the Custer battle unfolded. Unfortunately, errors of this sort flaw analyses. Stewart,[29] for example, placed C Company near Custer Hill, whereas Greene[30] located this troop at the South Skirmish Line. Neither interpretation is correct, as I will show, and both theories eliminate the role of Company C in the most critical stages of Custer's battle—the Calhoun episode.

Cavalry tactics instituted in 1874, as I have shown, prescribed wing composition on the basis of company commander seniority. The five companies that entered the Custer battle were C, E, F, I, and L. Their respective commanders, with dates of rank and seniority,[31] were Capt. Thomas Custer (December 2, 1875, third in rank), 1st Lt. Algernon Smith (December 5, 1868, fourth in rank), Capt. George Yates (August 19, 1867, second in rank), Capt. Myles Keogh (July 28, 1866, first in rank) and 1st Lt. James Calhoun (January 9, 1871, fifth or last in rank). According to the tactical manual, therefore, the battalion should have been apportioned with Companies I, C, and L in the right wing, Captain Keogh (I Company) commanding, and Companies F and E in a left wing commanded by Captain Yates (F Company): F, E, C, L, I, with wing division between E and C.

There are reasonable suggestions that Captain Custer temporarily served headquarters staff as aide-de-camp to brother George, leaving 2d Lt. Henry Harrington as C Company commander (and the only officer with the company).[32] Thus, possibly, the battalion consisted of a right wing with Companies I (Keogh, first in rank), E (Smith, third in rank), and C (Harrington, fifth in rank) and a left wing of F (Yates, second in rank) and L (Calhoun, fourth in rank). This apportionment is not likely, however, for tactics allowed a company to maintain its prescribed battalion position in the absence, usually brief, of its commander.[33] Captain Custer, if with the command staff, was technically not absent. A headquarters staff (regiment), by the way, consisted of the regimental commander, his aide, an adjutant officer, the sergeant major, a trumpeter, and others. In the strictest sense, the battalion consisted of five companies and the staff.

Sometimes, contrary to the prescribed tactical configuration, assignments might be established in accordance with the order in which company commanders reported to headquarters. Evidently that practice did not occur on June 25. In an 1879 lecture delivered at West Point, Edward Godfrey commented: "We moved out and crossed the [Rosebud/Little Big Horn] divide about noon. Here the command was divided without reference to the order in which they had reported."[34]

Godfrey's recollection, of course, does not refer specifically to the Custer battalion, but it does seem to rule out organization by reporting order on that day. In any case, Daniel Kanipe, a C Company sergeant dispatched as a messenger by General Custer just before the ill-fated engagement, recalled a battalion composition that clearly reflects two wings apportioned by company commander seniority.[35] Lt. Winfield Edgerly, a 7th Cavalry officer with Reno, did not exactly confirm this, but, clearly drawing on tactical knowledge, he did say that Kanipe's division "was quite possible."[36] Archaeological evidence and other historical data indicate that Kanipe's recall and Edgerly's surmise are accurate.

This, then, puts F Company with the gray horse troop, the two together composing the left wing. Thus it is this wing (E and F) that approached the mouth of Medicine Tail Coulee, finally making its way up Deep Coulee to the Calhoun sectors. The right wing (companies C, I, and L) remained on the ridges to the east, ultimately converging with its counterpart at or near Calhoun Hill (fig. 2-1). Brave Wolf remembered, through his interpreter, that the left wing (some soldiers, according to him) moved up Deep Coulee in battle lines,[37] an observation confirmed by Two Moons, who described the movement of dismounted soldiers in two "wings," or companies.[38] Concurrently the right wing proceeded northward in "two lines."[39] Apparently both wings reached the Calhoun Hill vicinity in good tactical order. The left wing then departed, moving northward, and eventually occupied Cemetery Ridge.

Such was the prelude to disaster. The remaining chapters in part 3 unravel the last stages of the battle events that began in the Calhoun sectors. These final episodes are typically regarded by many as irretrievably lost in veils of secrecy. It is often here that Custer battle chroniclers, frustrated by limitations in the historical record, are most likely to throw up their hands, lamenting that "no one shall ever know for sure"—or something to this effect. But things are not at all so dismal if one is privy to the archaeological record. Filtered through a stability/disintegration model, archaeology suggests that actions around Calhoun Hill signaled the beginning of the end. Suddenly routed, demoralized soldiers spilled into the Keogh sector, joining others in panicky flight toward Custer Hill. Then came the end, swift and deadly in the confusion. In short, there occurred that day an irrevocable erosion in military structure.

This view, understandably, is hardly palatable. After all, myths of steadfastness in battle against all odds are soothing. And George Custer's captivating aura remains larger than life. Yet in substance, the stability/disintegration thesis, when clothed in historical detail, emerges as much closer to the truth. Consider body identifications (not all men were recognized). Postbattle identifications included corpses from only a single company (C) at Calhoun Ridge, one only at Calhoun Hill (L), three companies (C, I, and L) at the Keogh sector, and some from all five units at Custer Hill. This is not a pattern indicative of protracted tactical stability. Rather it is, if short of unerring proof, at least entirely compatible with the model of stability followed by disintegration.

The transition in military posture during the Custer battle is demonstrable in much more detail and persuasion than by simple body identifications. Indeed, it is the rich detail available in history that ultimately carries the day. So now it is time to render history more intelligible using the discriminating eye of archaeology, an eye previously focused by the stability/disintegration model. The best place to start is at the "beginning of the end"—the Calhoun episode.

9

THE CALHOUN EPISODE

It looked like a stampede of buffalo.

—Runs the Enemy[1]

Archaeological analyses indicate that actions at the three Calhoun sectors—the coulee, the ridge, and the hill—are linked. Thus, they may be considered within the context of a single episode. Historical data must be evaluated accordingly, and that is my intent here. We begin with the left and right wings now in the Calhoun Hill area.

Like many other warriors, Two Moons crossed Little Big Horn River at Medicine Tail and approached the southern extremities of Calhoun Hill, more a knoll than anything else. The prominent Cheyenne leader apparently ascended the long, sloping ridge that is now traversed by the Custer Battlefield road.[2] This put him in a position to observe the initial soldier deployment in the Calhoun sectors. He remembered that the Sioux and Cheyenne then moved in, leaving an impression of quick envelopment. Actually, the Indians' movement took time, but the sequence is correct—starting with the initial deployment. The dispersal, from a tactical perspective, seems to have been orderly, according to Two Moons: "A bugle sounded, and they all got off horses [*sic*], and some soldiers led the horses back over the hill. Then the Sioux rode up the ridge on all sides, riding very fast. The Cheyennes went up the left way."[3]

One element of the Sioux attack that unfolded during the Calhoun episode is associated with the Sioux leader Gall. Although he, like other prominent Indians, did not command warriors, many did accompany Gall. Some of these warriors apparently had initiated minor skirmishing in the Medicine Tail Coulee area, and now, around Calhoun Hill, they continued to harass the cavalrymen. Gall's observations accord well with the archaeological evidence for skirmishing at Henryville and the trooper pathway leading to Calhoun Hill. Gall, while at the battlefield in 1886, indicated to General Godfrey (a lieutenant during the Reno fight) that dismounted soldiers worked their way to the Calhoun area via Henryville.[4]

Two Moons's description of mounted soldiers is at odds with the dismounted troopers observed by Gall.[5] (Two Moons possibly also saw the dismounted soldiers, but this is not clear.)[6] This discrepancy is best explained by the convergence of the two battalion wings. It is clear that the left wing ascended Deep Coulee on foot, and this is probably what Gall reported. Red Feather, an Oglala Sioux, also saw troopers stop, dismount, and then get on a hill (i.e., Calhoun).[7] The mounted men that arrived in this sector were probably those in Captain Keogh's right wing. In any case, Two Moons watched those on horseback dismount, evidently following the dismount trumpet call,[8] and then saw them (i.e., the horse holders) lead their animals behind the hill.[9] Apparently the right wing followed tactical prescription by placing the led horses under cover. The Crow scout Curley[10] may have witnessed this maneuver from a distance, though his description of dismounted men flanking horse holders also fits the left-wing formation described by Two Moons.[11]

Joseph White Cow Bull, a Sioux, apparently accompanied Gall's contingent. He probably witnessed the right-wing deployment on this hill—at the southern end of Custer Ridge. White Cow Bull remembered that before getting off to fight on foot, mounted soldiers delivered an intense fire that drove back Indians in his area.[12] There appears to be no archaeological evidence for such firing in the Calhoun sectors. This action seems best explained instead by the evidence for soldiers firing near and on Nye-Cartwright Ridge—that is, before reaching the south end of Custer Ridge. Mike Moore reports that relic collectors have found up to 800 carbine casings (caliber .45/55) on the southern ridges traversed by Keogh's wing.[13] Finally, as White Cow Bull neared Custer Ridge, he saw some of the soldiers at Calhoun Hill dismount and hide behind their horses to fire.[14]

White Cow Bull reported that none of the pedestrian soldiers proceeded any farther north along Custer Ridge.[15] This implies that the mounted troopers did move north, and these could only have been soldiers in the left wing. Apparently the left wing remounted after reaching Calhoun Hill. The role of this wing—Companies E and F—is discussed later in part 3. But the implication is, and I shall draw on corroborating evidence, that only Companies C, I, and L stayed in the Calhoun vicinity. The left wing had departed. Of course, archaeological evidence shows that some soldiers in the Calhoun sectors did eventually proceed north along Custer Ridge, but under extreme duress. White Cow Bull's statement is thus taken to mean that the right-wing positioning was permanent, insofar as he understood the situation.

The intense fire described by White Cow Bull probably constituted the celebrated "volleys" heard by some in the Reno contingent[16] and interpreted by others as Custer's distress signal.[17] There is no need for this romantic interpretation, however. Tactics allowed volley firing on command, an option equally as viable as firing at will. Indeed, the left wing too, as it moved from the Medicine

Tail Coulee mouth, probably delivered volleys at approaching warriors. Standing Bear reported that these men, dismounted and holding their horses by the bridle, "rained" bullets upon his comrades.[18] This incident occurred before Captain Yates's wing reached Calhoun Hill.

History is essentially mute regarding the precise nature of right wing placements on the knoll. Some deductions can be advanced, however, largely on the strength of archaeological knowledge. It is reasonably clear that the skirmish lines at this sector are too small for more than one company. Since personnel apparently did not occupy the lines simultaneously, it follows that only one company in the right wing deployed to skirmish on the hillock. This seems consistent with prescription, since procedure did not necessarily commit the entire tactical unit, in this case Keogh's wing, to battle lines. It is also consistent with the tactical environment at the time. Runs the Enemy noted from his position south of the soldiers that neither side fired as warriors began to reach the hill environs. Only after some Sioux made a "charge," in his words, did the troopers become provoked.[19]

Nothing critical resulted from this provocation. As Runs the Enemy implied, no sense of urgency pervaded the command after arriving at the hill, notwithstanding the earlier skirmishing around Medicine Tail Coulee. It is thus likely that the remaining two companies of the right wing were not immediately involved in the action. The led horses that Two Moons saw probably accompanied the main body to the rear (north) of the skirmishers.[20] Indeed, Two Moons's description of soldiers organized into "three branches with a little ways between" almost certainly refers to the right wing.[21] One of these "branches," by the elimination process, had to be I Company, captained by Keogh, and the other C Company, led most likely by Harrington. Both units doubtless acted as the wing reserve. This can be deduced from three lines of evidence. First, there is nothing in the archaeology to suggest that more than one unit deployed to skirmish. Also, these two companies are, until they surface during disintegration, virtually invisible in the documentary record. Finally, Indian accounts, except those that compress time, report only casual exchanges.

I make these assignments knowing, as do all other Custer battle researchers, that Company L skirmished on Calhoun Hill. In the aftermath of the fight, Lieutenant Edgerly,[22] like several other survivors from Reno's engagement,[23] noted that the Company L officers, Lieutenants Calhoun and John Crittenden, were found dead near the bodies of their charges, these corpses forming, by some opinions, "a very regular skirmish line." Clearly, these men fell while dismounted.[24]

No other companies had formed on Calhoun Hill, as we learned from archaeology. This rather modest commitment of cavalry firepower from the hilltop belies popular accounts of beleaguered soldiers suffering a savage onslaught[25] and belies Curley's estimation of troopers being driven from Medicine Tail Coulee as well.[26] Some warrior testimonies describe heavy assaults—which did occur later—but these convey false impressions by compressing time. Indeed, most Indian descriptions of early-stage fighting around the Calhoun sectors suggest nothing other than desultory activity. These testimonies parallel the archaeological evidence for relatively restrained fighting. Initial fusillades evidently checked the Indian threat. Thereafter, warriors contented themselves with infiltration, while soldiers used one company on a skirmish line for sniping.

Runs the Enemy, as noted above, witnessed the initial provocation at Calhoun Hill, one that resulted in the warriors' hasty retreat.[27] As Standing Bear and others neared the hillock, soldiers atop immediately started to shoot.[28] White Cow Bull also described the initial firing, but in general terms.[29] Curley told Walter Camp of a firing episode consisting of two controlled volleys.[30] Though the Crow scout made it clear that soldiers directed the shots at the enemy, Camp wanted very much to see the volleys as distress signals.[31] Curley probably drew on his knowledge of oral history in relating this story. Nevertheless, the description is consistent with other accounts.

Certainly, it is clear that Company L skirmishers discharged their weapons while operating within tactical guidelines. Volley firing, it would appear, is simply not possible among confused and disordered men. Indian accounts of the firing line, though, are vague. Wooden Leg noted soldiers "spreading themselves into lines along a ridge."[32] Sometime after the cavalrymen ascended Calhoun Hill, Two Moons observed men standing while others kneeled.[33] This is consistent with the alternative postures available in skirmish tactics, or it might reflect skirmishers (on knees) with file closers (standing) directing the fire. Standing Bear observed soldiers "sitting" on the hill.[34] Tactics did not prescribe firing in the sitting position, though there is no reason to suspect that this did not happen.

One clear indication of tactical stability is provided by White Cow Bull. Each company of Custer's battalion carried a miniature U.S. flag—a guidon.[35] When a company established its position, the guidon bearer generally planted the flagstaff either right or left of the line. White Cow Bull observed Yellow Nose, a Ute Indian captured and raised by the Cheyenne, dash near soldiers (the L Company line) and snatch the guidon.[36] Grinnell[37] and Stands in Timber[38] reported Yellow Nose's action also, though the latter account misplaces the event chronologically. In fact, this incident, as shall become clear, occurred near the end of the episode on Calhoun Hill. Aside from when it happened, the event does indicate that at least one company established an orderly, fixed position.

Though the deployment successfully marshaled firepower early in the episode, it is abundantly clear that fighting soon became opportunistic, with little initiative on either side. Red Feather remembered that if either side showed a head, an adversary would shoot at it.[39] Gall told Godfrey that Indians crept up the hill slope far enough to remain hidden while prone but in a position to fire while erect.[40] Indians exposed themselves only long enough to shoot. Much of this activity undoubtedly occurred on the slope at Henryville. The initial skirmish line at Calhoun Hill clearly formed in response to furtive warrior tactics, with the soldiers firing only when the foe presented a target.

A number of Indians described their own tactics. Runs the Enemy saw "hundreds and hundreds of Indians in the coulees all around."[41] One Sioux woman, Mrs. Spotted Horn Bull, either witnessed or later heard of this infiltration.[42] Red Feather watched Indians sneaking along in the ravines; some darted from sagebrush to sagebrush.[43] Crow King joined others and crept up a gully (Calhoun Coulee) that brought him very close to the soldiers.[44]

The lull in fighting and the Indian tactics are best described in Cheyenne oral history accounts, specifically those of Wooden Leg[45] and Kate Bighead.[46] Some Indians dashed about on horseback.[47] The action, though, was predominantly slow, long-distance harassment. Other Indians crawled through the gullies and sagebrush. The cavalrymen could not see them, except when a warrior would suddenly jump up and shoot.[48] According to Bighead, the Indians—after a while, hundreds of them—used gullies, crevices, ridges, and knolls for cover. "The Indians all around were gradually creeping closer to the soldiers."[49] And "at this stage, the fighting was slow and few were killed as both sides remained hidden."[50]

Bighead claimed to have witnessed these events firsthand while searching for her nephew. Her account implies she viewed all this from near Greasy Grass Ridge. Runs the Enemy did observe a woman among the Cheyennes darting about the Calhoun sectors but did not specify her ethnicity.[51] This might have been Bighead, since she too was a Cheyenne. At least one Oglala woman, however, participated in the fray, and several Sioux women apparently accompanied Gall's contingent.[52] Moving Robe, a young Sioux woman, might also have watched from safety.[53] On the other hand, Bighead may have included herself in the oral account to add eyewitness validity to what she had to say. Whatever the case, it is clear the infiltration tactics that she described occurred around the Calhoun sectors. Wooden Leg's account is similar.

Apparently, warriors attempted to stampede or capture led cavalry horses.[54] Gall's instructions, to the extent they are known, urged his brethren to frighten the mounts and kill horse holders.[55] Many steeds did, indeed, end up in the hands of Indians. This interest, of course, was normal; Plains Indian societies placed great economic and social value on horse ownership. The Wooden Leg account describes horses, pierced with arrows, plunging about and knocking soldiers down.[56] Moving Robe remembered seeing one man holding 8 or 10 horses.[57] Tactics prescribed four animals to a holder. Perhaps this individual held the mounts of an incapacitated comrade or managed more than the normal complement to free another man for skirmish duty. Whichever, Moving Robe said the steeds finally got away.

Such descriptions tend to leave the impression that led horses died or bolted shortly after the right wing deployed.[58] Lone Bear, Two Eagles, and Hollow Horn Bear said that animals got loose at the very first of the fight.[59] But these statements must be assessed with reference to other happenings at the time, notably left-wing activities, which constituted the Cemetery Ridge episode. Yates's wing had ridden far beyond their stationary comrades. In doing so, the wing consumed considerable time, and not until much later did the situation turn about—when lull turned to frenzy. In the eyes of some warriors, like those mentioned above, this transition represented the beginning of fighting—the frenzied fighting. It was at about this time that horse management problems reached critical proportions, not earlier. Wayne Wells, in agreement, has recently noted that many horses lay dead in this vicinity, indicating that troopers retained mounts for a lengthy period.[60]

According to Two Eagles, mounted horse holders had to dismount when the riderless steeds became unmanageable. Cavalry tactics required led horses to be placed under cover, and that probably happened. Runs the Enemy noticed frightened mounts that "rushed upon the ridge," implying that horses holders retired to small draws below ridges.[61] Wooden Leg's story suggests that the wing sequestered at least some horses just west of Calhoun Hill, probably in a branch gully of Calhoun Coulee that leads to the knoll. Infiltration of the channel recesses doubtless placed these mounts in jeopardy. Now, after some time had passed, safety of the horses suddenly loomed as a prime concern.

The archaeological record of the coulee sector does not reflect this magnitude of infiltration. Though Bighead and Wooden Leg make it clear that many Indians at this time were equipped with bows and arrows, certainly a number at Greasy Grass Ridge possessed firearms, including carbines captured from Reno's command.[62] Steadily increasing threats such as these could not have been tolerated long by the right-wing soldiers, even during light fighting. As it turned out, they were not. Soon, related Bighead, "some impatient soldiers mounted an attack off the ridge, galloping on their horses."[63] The troopers charged "down the broad coulee toward the river, toward where were the Cheyennes and Ogallalas."[64] Bighead's reference to "impatient soldiers" indicates the low-key action before the mounted excursion.

In Wooden Leg's description of this development, the party consisted of "about forty" soldiers.[65] Another estimate, provided by Cheyenne informants, is from 30 to 40 men.[66] Such figures should be viewed critically, but 40 was the average size of a Custer battalion company. It is certainly reasonable to consider that a maneuver of this nature would require a company-size force. Runs the Enemy noticed, just before this activity, that "some" of the men around the Calhoun elevation were near their horses.[67] He probably saw the soldiers as they organized for their excursion into the gully. In any case, it is quite evident that only part of the right wing became involved. As the soldier body rode down, nearby Indians fled across small ridges and into the deeper recesses of the coulee.[68] The advance flushed White Bull from his vantage point.[69]

Thomas Marquis, who must have accompanied his Cheyenne informants to the site, estimated that the charge proceeded about 500 yards down a draw.[70] The soldiers pulled up and dismounted "at a low ridge where the Indians had been."[71] Bighead also related the abrupt stop-and-dismount procedure. "The soldiers who had come galloping stopped and got off their horses along another ridge [other than the ridge they came from], a low one just north of the deep gulch."[72]

Bighead's description, in particular her reference to a low ridge "just north of the deep gulch," has led to an immense amount of confusion regarding the timing of this action. In turn, the confusion has eliminated any chance of properly assessing the critical role the event played in the demise of Custer's two battalion wings. Virtually every historian and enthusiast places this action in the latter stages of battle, attributing it to some kind of a company-size force—usually E Company and sometimes including C—along the so-called South Skirmish Line.[73] It is widely thought the movement took place under duress and originated from Custer Hill. On other occasions, E Company is cut to pieces moving toward the hill. Yet no such notion can be possible, and there are compelling arguments to the contrary. Archaeological evidence provides the key for properly interpreting the cavalry deployment.

But first, it is important to reiterate that the Wooden Leg and Bighead narratives are consistent chronologically. These accounts, like that of Runs the Enemy,[74] place the incident well before intermediate (Keogh) and subsequent (Custer Hill) episodes. Second, the mounted, orderly event, as R. G. Hardorff recognized, was a unit action (i.e., a company), with a specific purpose.[75] It could not have been undertaken during latter episodes, by which time, as archaeology shows, tactical integrity had largely eroded. Indeed, Hardorff understood this (from documents, not archaeology), but clinging to the E Company/South Skirmish Line interpretation, he finally doubted Wooden Leg's veracity regarding the tactical nature of this maneuver.[76]

Third, it is clear that the varied popular interpretations are based largely on Bighead's reference to a low ridge "north of the deep gulch." This deep gulch is interpreted as Deep Ravine. The South Skirmish Line is on a low ridge north of Deep Ravine. And "north," in this and other Indian accounts, is invariably interpreted in the customary directional scheme. But Bighead's reference to "north" can be understood only within the context of the Cheyenne way of reckoning direction (Sioux informants also used this scheme).

Custer Ridge, defined at either end by Calhoun and Custer hills, is the primary directional reference point for most descriptions of the battle. The ridge is oriented northwest-southeast in relation to magnetic north. White descriptions of the fight customarily refer to the Custer Hill end as north, whereas the Calhoun prominence is viewed as the southern extremity. The Keogh sector is east, and west is commonly assigned to the river side of Custer Ridge. (Unless otherwise noted, I use the customary scheme throughout.) But in many Indian accounts (not all, and this further adds to the interpretive confusion), including Bighead's, north is equivalent to customary east, south is customary west, east is customary south, and west is customary north. Since the ridge is oriented magnetic northwest-southeast, either usage is acceptable. The duality may be visualized as shown in figure 9-1.

Thus, Bighead's low ridge "north of the deep gulch" becomes, in the customary scheme, a low ridge "east" of this gully. Deep Ravine at the South Skirmish Line runs roughly east-west (magnetic); thus, it is impossible, given battlefield topography, to find a low ridge east (customary usage) of this ravine. The

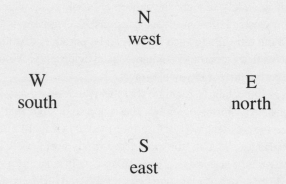

Fig. 9-1. Indian-versus-white directional reference points for the Custer battle (N=customary north, *north*=Indian reckoning, etc.). Custer Ridge runs on a diagonal from the customary NW to the SE.

only other deep gulch is Calhoun Coulee, and there is a low ridge east (customary) of this drainage. In fact, and this is the fourth point, archaeological evidence for sequent occupations in the Calhoun Coulee sector is on a low, sloping ridge, east of the upper reaches of the gulch. This is the low ridge described by the Cheyennes as first occupied by Indians, then soldiers, and finally Indians again. The archaeological evidence begins about 440 yards down the ridge, a distance quite similar to the 500-yard estimate of Marquis.[77]

Bighead's description of massive Indian infiltration via the gully bearing Calhoun's name is intelligible in light of the Cheyenne directional concept. She told Marquis, "Almost all of the Cheyenne and Ogallala Sioux had crawled across a deep gulch at the bottom of a broad coulee south of the ridge where were the soldiers, and about halfway between them and the river."[78]

Adjusting directions, her "south" becomes customary west. Deep Ravine and Calhoun Coulee are, in the more familiar customary usage, west of Custer Ridge ("where were the soldiers"), but only the coulee is "halfway" between the ridge and Little Big Horn River. Deep Ravine, in fact, heads at Custer Ridge and empties into the river, running roughly perpendicular to both, and thus cannot be midway between the two. Moreover, the Calhoun waterway is a broad coulee above, entrenched only in the lower half. Deep Ravine is not anywhere along its reach a broad channel. I should also point out that Wooden Leg's description of 40 or so soldiers who came from the "east part of the ridge" (Custer Ridge) and the account of his ride to the "eastern end" of Custer Ridge[79] are best explained this way as well. Here east becomes south, or Calhoun Hill. Grinnell's reference to "southeast" also is intelligible only in this directional scheme.[80]

Finally, there are other testimonies, largely ignored or misinterpreted, that support this view. Before discussing these, I should review the rationale behind this argument. Clearly, the left and right wings reached the Custer battlefield with some Indians trailing in the rear. The left wing soon departed to the north. Company L quite reasonably deployed on the Calhoun hilltop to check the potential threat. With little danger, the remaining two right-wing companies held in reserve. Some, if not all, led horses were placed under cover in a draw or draws west of Calhoun Hill. Thus deployed, the right wing confronted warriors during a period of subdued fighting.

During this time, other Indians infiltrated the Calhoun Coulee sector west of the soldiers.[81] These warriors eventually jeopardized the safety of the horses. Here is the last provocation, the beginning of the end; Bighead's soldiers came "galloping" down to the low ridge "just north of the deep gulch." Red Horse, a Sioux, said that a soldier "band" charged, and the "Sioux fell back." Then, while facing the soldiers, the Sioux counterattacked.[82] Waterman, an Arapahoe by birth, called it one of the first Indian attacks, but he did not make clear just

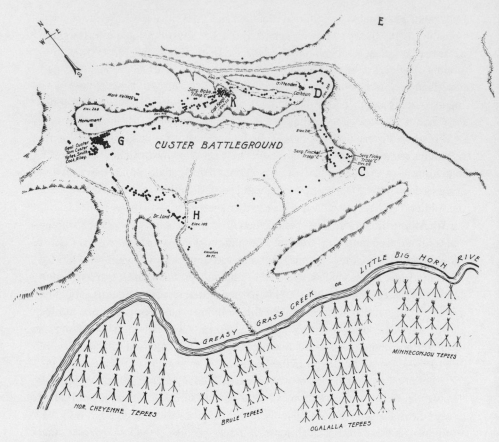

Fig. 9-2. Reproduction of the Custer battlefield portion of Walter Mason Camp's map compiled from various eyewitness testimonies taken in the first two decades of the 1900s. Here C to D is Calhoun Ridge, D is Calhoun Hill, K is the Keogh sector, G is the Custer Hill locality, and H is Deep Ravine. Greasy Grass Ridge is the feature drawn just below C. Point E is an elevation east of Custer Ridge. Some identified men are located in death (most are correct); the dots represent stone memorial sites. Reproduction from Custer Battlefield National Monument.

where it came.[83] Red Horse's recollections lack spatial and temporal clues altogether; they are unintelligible without reference to independent sources such as those available from archaeology.

Another relevant account is that of Red Bird (also known as Little Wolf), recorded by Walter Camp in 1918. Using Camp's map, a portion of which is reproduced as figure 9-2,[84] Red Bird pointed out that Lame White Man, a

Cheyenne leader, and others charged the soldiers on Calhoun Ridge.[85] In this assault, Lame White Man apparently received mortal wounds.[86] The Lame White Man affair is typically, and erroneously, associated with the E Company/ South Skirmish Line interpretation. Though this prominent Cheyenne eventually died near the South Skirmish Line, Red Bird's testimony indicates that his death came, ostensibly as a result of the earlier wounds, during the Keogh episode (which, as the next chapter demonstrates, evolved from events in the Calhoun sectors).

In an interview with Stanley Vestal, Two Moons's nephew (known as young Two Moons) also described Lame White Man's decisive action.[87] In this account, accompanied by a sketch, the leader is called Walking White. Wells shows that Walking White is Lame White Man.[88] Yellow Nose either accompanied the Lame White Man party or charged nearby. According to young Two Moons, their actions, the "first [Indian] charge," drove soldiers up the "side of a hill" to its "top." The developments put Yellow Nose in position to grab the L Company guidon. The young nephew's account is numerically keyed to Vestal's obviously hurriedly sketched map.[89] The sketch seems to pick up Lame White Man's action at Calhoun Hill rather than earlier around the Calhoun Coulee or Calhoun Ridge sectors. The drawing also shows that the Lame White Man party pursued soldiers north through the Keogh sector, ultimately meeting other warriors below (west of) Custer Hill.

Wooden Leg and Bighead also described Lame White Man's involvement. Shortly after the soldiers "came galloping from the east [south] part of [Custer] ridge down toward the river" (via Calhoun Coulee), Lame White Man rallied the warriors recently hidden in gulches and behind folds.[90] Included among these were Contrary Belly and Comes in Sight, both of whom are sometimes credited with instigating an assault.[91] The Indians then counterattacked.[92] Though Bighead's and Wooden Leg's stories claim that all of these soldiers committed suicide, Runs the Enemy related other events. Runs the Enemy's account of his movements—first in the Calhoun sectors, then near Custer Hill, and finally on return—indisputably places the action in and around the coulee below and west of Calhoun Hill. "Some of the soldiers made a rush down the ravine toward the river, and a great roll of smoke seemed to go down the ravine. The retreat of the soldiers was met by the Indian advance from the river, and all who were not killed came back again to the hill."[93]

This account is revealing. Only "some of the soldiers" rushed from Calhoun Hill. The reference to "some" is consistent with accounts of 30 to 40 men. Though Runs the Enemy (or his interviewer) called the action a retreat, clearly it is an error in perception (made in light of the grisly outcome; we shall see much more of this tendency). This body of troopers intended to relieve threats to the right-wing rear, including those to the horses. All of this is consistent with tactical prescription. Portions of the right wing could be expected to be kept in reserve for use in timely charges. That is what happened: a reserve unit deployed as L Company controlled other ground from its skirmish line on the hill.

Hollow Horn Bear, Two Eagles, and Lone Bear[94] said that no cavalrymen charged during the battle, but they were on the east side of Custer Ridge and probably did not see any of this. On the other hand, they might have remembered correctly insofar as a rapid movement en masse did not necessarily constitute to them what others might perceive as a classic cavalry charge. Indian references to charges, if they do not derive from the interviewer, must be evaluated in this light.

In any case, the "great roll of smoke" (typical of black-powder loads) indicates a considerable amount of firing, at least by the Indians. In light of archaeology, much shooting must have come from Greasy Grass Ridge. Almost certainly, some soldiers died, or suffered incapacitating wounds, and these deaths account for the memorial stones in upper reaches of Calhoun Coulee. Moreover, those not killed—and now dismounted, according to Bighead and Wooden Leg— retreated toward Calhoun Hill. Probably the sequence of events in this rout began with the firing from Greasy Grass. This so rattled the troopers that they broke. Then Lame White Man, Contrary Belly, Yellow Nose, Comes in Sight, and the others, including those in the Greasy Grass positions, seized the advantage created by the confusion and pressured the soldiers back.

There can be no doubt—historically and archaeologically—that the cavalry foray into Calhoun Coulee ultimately proved unsuccessful. Nevertheless, the dismount procedure suggests an intent to occupy the area and prevent further infiltration. The horses were "standing near" the soldiers.[95] The absence of archaeological evidence for substantial soldier resistance here precludes discerning the nature of the pedestrian deployment. Absence also indicates that the Indian attack was sudden and unexpected. Though the soldiers were initially successful merely through a show of force—the enemy melted away as the company rumbled into Calhoun Coulee—pressure soon forced the troopers to seek safety.

At this point, Red Bird's recollections, mentioned above, are relevant.[96] Clearly, these cavalrymen vacated the coulee via the Calhoun Ridge sector; Red Bird placed Lame White Man's charge there. Hollow Horn Bear, when queried, left his interviewer with the impression that when the men reached the ridgetop, they were "bunched."[97] In fact, his account indicates that at the start of the fight, the soldiers operated in "good order," but they soon became "demoralized" (in the words of the recorder).

Archaeological data around the ridge crest are equivocal in that they reveal either a rapid movement through the sector or a brief stop. Lone Bear said a "short stand" was made here (Calhoun Ridge), but he also said the men were moving along.[98] Lt. George Wallace equivocated at the Reno inquiry, saying that he saw corpses arranged in "some indication of a skirmish line" atop a ridge that "ran at right angles [to Custer Ridge]."[99] His description fits Calhoun Ridge nicely, though Wallace, perhaps confused by the inexact map used in the inquiry, placed these men on Calhoun Hill. Red Bird suggested to Camp that there was a "line" on the adjacent ridge.[100] This may be a product of Camp's translation. In any case, a line could be formed by moving men. In fact, Two Eagles, in response to Camp's prepared questions, said that Calhoun Ridge witnessed nothing more than a moving fight.[101] Some soldiers moved over the sector on horseback, and others went along afoot; the latter had lost their horses.

In answering Camp's queries, Hollow Horn Bear mentioned that the troopers "went" from Calhoun Ridge to nearby Calhoun Hill, implying that they did not stop.[102] He also stated, metaphorically referring to terror and panic, that they were drunk. Thus, it seems likely that no skirmish line existed here. Certainly, archaeological evidence for significant government firearm use is absent. Ultimately, those soldiers still alive must have traversed the ridge, as Runs the Enemy intimated,[103] en route to Calhoun Hill, seeking safety there with other right-wing units. Judging from marker placements on the ridgetop, not many who got out of the coulee made it to the hill. (I estimate that about half of the original 40 or so made it back to the Calhoun Hill position.)

Walter Camp reported that He Dog, a Sioux warrior, attributed the memorial markers in Calhoun Coulee to soldiers fleeing from Custer Hill,[104] an episode that followed action in the Calhoun sectors. Hollow Horn Bear thought so too but did not know for sure.[105] On another occasion, Camp, rendering Curley's testimony, wrote that the stones memorialized men cut off and killed during a charge.[106] Obviously, the Crow scout referred to the cavalry deployment from around Calhoun Hill; reference to a "charge" is notable. Curley, as a scout, surely had some knowledge of tactical maneuvering. He could leave Camp with a reasonably good impression of this action.[107]

Curley erred in claiming these soldiers charged while dismounted;[108] he almost certainly drew on an imperfect knowledge of Sioux and/or Cheyenne oral history. On the other hand, He Dog apparently witnessed the Custer Hill episode firsthand. It is therefore likely that most, if not all, of the markers in the gulch represent both incidents, some of those in the lower reaches marking He Dog's observations and those above resulting from the movement off Calhoun Hill.[109]

There is circumstantial evidence to support Curley's claim of a deployment into Calhoun Coulee. Moreover, the evidence clearly indicates that C Company was the unit involved in Calhoun Coulee (and the ridge sector). Several days after the fight, Sergeant Kanipe (a messenger sent to Benteen) identified the remains of his C Company comrades on Calhoun Ridge—2d Sgt. August Finckle and 3d Sgt. Jeremiah Finley.[110] It is reasonable to assume that these two men, as high-ranking noncommissioned officers, died with their company. The company first sergeant, Edwin Bobo, died in the Keogh sector. In any case, as Joe Sills has pointed out, the locations of these sergeants in no way support interpretations that place C Company elsewhere on the field, most notably the South Skirmish Line.[111]

It is also probable that the nearly complete remains of a skeleton discovered in the upper gully (at the marker numbered 128, shown in fig. 7-1 at lower right) represent a C Company soldier. Age and stature estimates derived from bones found buried there match the vital statistics of nine Custer battalion troopers.[112] Of these, four are listed in C Company (Nathan Short, Frederick Meier, Jeremiah Shea, and John Thadus, all privates). Bodies of the latter three were never identified, or at least not recorded. The remaining candidates include the trumpeter George Moonie and Pvt. Wm. Huber (both E Company), Pvt. Timothy Donnelly (F Company), and Pvts. Elmer Babcock and Francis Hughes (both L Company).

Bodies of four of the nine men were found elsewhere: Short probably miles away on Rosebud Creek,[113] Huber and Donnelly in Deep Ravine,[114] and Hughes on Custer Hill.[115] Moonie is considered an unlikely choice for the marker 128 skeleton because E Company, as I shall show, engaged the foe elsewhere on the field. The marker 128 remains could be those of Babcock, since L Company fought nearby on the Calhoun knoll. But the Company C troopers—Meier, Shea, and Thadus—appear to be the most likely candidates. Thadus's height, in fact, exactly matches the stature estimate median calculated from marker 128 long bones.

Osteological data, the presence of Sergeants Finley and Finckle together on the ridge, the certainty that Companies C, I, and L constituted the right wing, and the fresh interpretation of Indian accounts describing a cavalry movement into Calhoun Coulee, not elsewhere, strongly suggest that C Company rode to counter threats developing in the gully just west of Calhoun Hill. With Calhoun's unit occupied in skirmishing, Captain Keogh, commanding Company I as well as the wing, would certainly dispatch C, not his own company. In addition, Indian estimates of 30 to 40 soldiers are consistent with a company-size action.

Finley and Finckle seem to have died with their unit, and the fact that they were found close together helps substantiate this assumption. There are no other reports of bodies identified by person on Calhoun Ridge (observers tended to identify the higher-ranking people). Captain Benteen, assisting interment details in the Calhoun sectors, helped to bury dead "from different companies" either at the hill or the ridge (his wording is vague).[116] If the latter, Benteen's recollections, in light of the foregoing, seem inaccurate. Nevertheless, the captain may have laid to rest soldiers from Companies C and L (different companies) if he assisted at Calhoun Hill or at both sectors.

Some unidentified soldiers probably occupied the Calhoun Ridge sector briefly and uneventfully early in the Calhoun episodes—well before the C Company deployment and subsequent rout. He Dog told Camp that the fighting began in this sector.[117] The Cheyenne warrior Tall Bull concurred.[118] This, of course, is not exactly the case; the first confrontations, uneventful as they were, began, as noted in chapter 8, in and above Medicine Tail Coulee. He Dog and Tall Bull might have entered the fray late, or both may have understood Camp to mean the latter stages of fighting. In either case, there is certainly little archaeological evidence for fighting along this ridge. In other words, He Dog and Tall Bull meant that the *battle* began at Calhoun Ridge. This is possible. Curley, sharing in the Cheyenne oral history, suggested that as troops arrived in the Calhoun vicinity, some were left on Calhoun Ridge.[119] But he made no conclusive reference to fighting here or to the subsequent dispositions of these troops.[120]

The event involving C Company evidently signaled a substantial change in the fighting postures of the warriors antagonizing the troops. Foolish Elk told Camp that the soldiers unsuccessfully charged the Indians twice, "and then the battle became furious"—that is, he described the transition from lull to frenzy.[121] Foolish Elk's comment is interesting. First, "then the battle became furious" implies rather low-key preliminary action. Second, Foolish Elk, a man Walter Camp found to be anything but fatuous, mentioned two "charges." Clearly, one of these involved C Company. Foolish Elk was probably east of Calhoun Hill at the time, and beyond view, but with a knowledge of oral history, he need not have witnessed the incident to be aware of it. The reference to another "charge" is enigmatic. It would have had to come before the C Company action (before battle became furious). There is no evidence for such an event during the Medicine Tail Coulee operations, a subject that will be scrutinized in part 5. Perhaps the right wing, while near the Calhoun hillock, had earlier mounted a foray with a purpose similar to that of C Company later. Or maybe Foolish Elk saw a movement which he mistook as a charge.

Archaeological investigations indicate that L Company altered its first skirmish position. There seems little doubt the shift was a response to the failure of C Company. Flushed with a resounding and sudden success, warriors west of Calhoun Hill had seized the advantage. Individual Indian pathways link Greasy Grass Ridge with locations below the L Company hilltop position. These individuals, plus other Sioux and Cheyenne, progressed toward the low prominence. Bighead said the Indians "rushed forward."[122] Runs the Enemy called it an "advance."[123] Lame White Man's excursion carried at least as far as the Calhoun Ridge sector.[124] L Company probably redeployed by facing west to cover retreating C Company soldiers and to thwart the Indian assault. Yet the shift must have exposed the left flank of the new line, allowing warriors to the south—those with Gall—to move into the Henryville area and step up pressure. As a result, the new skirmish line suffered from exposure both in the front and on the left.

This predicament may have caused some or all men on the second skirmish line to again shift positions. Lt. Edward Maguire, on duty as a topographical engineer, inspected the hill several days after the battle. He noted that the "men [bodies] and their empty cartridge shells were formed in a semi-circle around the crest. Calhoun and Crittenden were killed here."[125] Today, memorial markers on Calhoun Hill resemble a slightly curved line. There is, however, no archaeological evidence for firing (e.g., .45/55 cartridge cases) from the marker positions. This is not consistent with Maguire's reference to cartridge cases around the bodies, nor does it accord with Capt. Myles Moylan's observations. Moylan wrote Lieutenant Calhoun's brother a week after the Reno fight, reporting that "as high as 40 cartridge shells were found around some of [Lieutenant Calhoun's] men."[126] Nearly three years later, while testifying at the Reno Court of Inquiry, the captain stated that he saw 28 shells around one man, with scattered shells "between the bodies," and further stated that Calhoun's men died in the regular position of skirmishers.[127]

Perhaps relic collecting around the markers has obliterated evidence for the amount of shooting implied historically. Nevertheless, historical accounts seem to hint that this line existed. Moylan referred to it as "the last line," implying that at least one other existed first.[128] He did not offer anything further. Thus, it is possible that L Company formed three skirmish lines. Alternatively, the two skirmish lines identified archaeologically form (roughly) a backward *L,* which can be construed as a semicircle. This seems more likely, particularly if men fell on both lines, neither of which today coincide with markers. It is also pertinent to note that Stands in Timber, in compiling Cheyenne oral tradition, reported that Calhoun's soldiers "were facing [customary] west at the last."[129]

Either other officers did not notice more than one skirmish line or they did not mention such. Lieutenant Wallace, without pinpointing locations, saw piles of 25 to 30 cartridge cases at "one or two places" on Calhoun Hill.[130] Captain Benteen noticed a "good many" spent casings lying about, but he did not describe patterning, if any.[131] On the face of it, these accounts, and those of Moylan and Maguire, would indicate either of two scenarios: intense firing of short duration, or moderated fire over a protracted period. Extant archaeological residues on the hill do not resolve the options. Indian descriptions do, however, indicating that firing residues accumulated from a mixture of protracted exchanges (the period of subdued encounters) and intense firing (the later furious activity).

It is the intense firing—the furious activity—that led native informants to later report that they suffered the heaviest casualties in the Calhoun sectors, particularly at the hill.[132] Prompted by the developing predicament of C Company, shooting escalated, as we know from the documents. But archaeology reveals firing intensity as well. When sectors are compared, spent cartridge numbers about Calhoun Hill make it clear that L Company troopers fired the most. Indeed, Hollow Horn Bear, obviously referring to the furious developments, said the fighting was hardest here.[133] Sgt. John Ryan, who helped bury Custer's dead, evidently did not notice signs of firing on Calhoun Hill. But he did write of the field in general, revealing no small measure of incredulity in the process. "Strange to say, none of the saddles or horse equipment, not even a strap that I could see, *nor cartridge shells*, could be found on the field [except several shells found beneath Custer's body; emphasis mine]."[134]

If Ryan saw virtually no evidence for soldier firing, Lieutenant Wallace at least saw, in spent cartridges, a distinct disparity between Calhoun Hill and the other sectors. When asked during the Reno inquiry if he had observed many government cartridge cases at locations other than the L Company position, Wallace indicated there were "very few."[135] So as organized skirmishers, the troopers in the L Company lines at Calhoun Hill evidently mustered considerable firepower. But despite their attempt to stem the tide here, it is also clear, on historical as well as archaeological grounds, that tactical disintegration ensued.

With Company C routed and the newly formed Company L line pressured heavily from the west and south (front and left flank), the entire right wing began to fall apart. Hollow Horn Bear left the impression that collapse came very soon after the fighting intensity increased.[136] Escalation began with the Company C provocation. Two Moons helped to break the "line of soldiers" on the Calhoun knoll.[137] This process—erosion in unity—is discernible archaeologically, as bunching, and is evident as well in the historical record, although it has never been recognized as such. Runs the Enemy's account, to my knowledge, is the most complete and graphic source available. It is not contradicted by any other testimony. Much of the Calhoun episode story given by Runs the Enemy, evidently aptly named, is reproduced here, for it encapsulates the transition from tactical stability to disintegration. Note the implied reference to frenzied fighting preceded by calm (although "no firing" is incorrect).

While Custer was all surrounded there had been no firing from
either side. The Sioux then made a charge from the rear side,
shooting into the men, and the shooting frightened the horses
so that they rushed upon the ridge and many horses were shot.
The return fire was so strong that the Sioux had to retreat back
over the hill again. . . . Just then I returned to my men and the
soldiers were still on the hill fighting, with some of their
horses near them. Just as I got back some of the soldiers made
a rush down the ravine toward the river. This retreat [move-
ment] of the soldiers down the ravine was met by the advance
of the Indians from the river, and all who were not killed came
back again to the hill. After the soldiers got back from the hills
they made a stand all in a bunch. Another [Indian] charge was
made and they retreated along the line of the ridge [Custer
Ridge]; it looked like a stampede of buffalo. [138]

"Custer" here refers to the battalion. Runs the Enemy had returned to the
Calhoun areas after confronting the left wing in the northern sectors. Then he
saw C Company dash into the ravine and subsequently return to Calhoun Hill.
Runs the Enemy's statement "after the soldiers got back from the hills" should
read "back to the hill" and is probably an error in translation. This is evident
from the previous sentence, which reads "came back again *to the hill*." The
important aspect, though, is that he described bunching among the soldiers.
Normally an Indian reference to "bunch" as a combat behavioral clue might be
regarded lightly. A company in column formation, for example, may appear to a
warrior, unfamiliar with tactical organizations, as a "bunch" of soldiers, or
translation difficulties might obscure the intended meaning. Archaeological
data, however, and the predictable behaviors of men under extreme combat
duress confirm the observation of bunching behavior. Though it might be more
comforting to cling to the notion of gallantry—perhaps soldiers attempting to
rally—the weight of the evidence is wholly at odds with aggrandizement. Tactical disintegration—the most common behavioral tendency of men under
extreme duress—is entirely compatible, and indeed predictable, given the sud-
denness, force, and proximity of the Indian attack.

There can be no doubt—look at the archaeology and now the history—that
these cavalrymen suddenly suffered from the debilitating effects of extreme
combat conditions. A considerable number of the soldiers must have been on
foot, for Runs the Enemy's account, Cheyenne oral history, and other native
testimony indicate that many horses were shot or captured during the episode.
Additional historical accounts describe more dead horses, or bones of horse, in

the Calhoun area than elsewhere.[139] Two Eagles, in fact, stated that "most" of the troopers who fled through the Keogh sector were dismounted.[140] While the dismounted soldiers gathered, Indians pressed the assault, according to Runs the Enemy, and archaeology shows that various soldiers in the bunch resisted. Individual soldier pathways demonstrate that some, and by inference probably all, tried to flee toward the Keogh sector—"like a stampede of buffalo" according to Runs the Enemy. Indian pathways demonstrate that warriors gave chase. Given the Plains Indian knowledge of bison ethology, Runs the Enemy's phrasing is eloquently explanatory. Two-thirds of the right wing had disintegrated.

10
THE KEOGH
EPISODE

Just like this [intertwined fingers], Indians and white men.
—Horned Horse[1]

We have seen in the archaeological record of the Keogh sector compelling reasons to believe that the action here was devoid of tactical unity. Plumbing the historical documents accordingly, we find, contrary to patronizing accounts of this episode, a stunning picture of mayhem—full disintegration within the right wing. But unlike Calhoun's force and C Company, both of which gave way under pressure, the right wing at this sector moved from stability to chaos primarily from the infectious nature of panic. Fear and disorder emerging from the Calhoun episodes spread to the Keogh portion of the field. About this time, emboldened warriors, finding soldiers in the Keogh sector confused and vulnerable, pressed the attack.

The episode, so named because Captain Keogh died at this time, ended with right-wing soldiers in complete disorder. Several of Reno's officers viewed the Keogh sector in the aftermath of battle. Lieutenant Wallace thought, on the basis of body positions, that the dead men had been running in file and fighting at intervals, but not in skirmish order.[2] Lieutenant Maguire,[3] like Lieutenant Edgerly,[4] thought he saw "some sort of a skirmish line." Despite hedging, these men, guided by emotions and military training, saw tactical stability that did not exist. But their legacy has survived to this day. It is (and traditionally has been) very popular to see in the markers at the Keogh sector evidence of a fierce and organized defense.

Indian testimonies are replete with reference to the skirmishing on Calhoun Hill and the role of L Company. Now, with the help of archaeology, their references to C Company can be understood. But Company I remains virtually invisible in the historical record until the moment when warriors seized the advantage afforded by collapse. Native accounts suggesting that Company I deployed in a battle line of any form are wholly absent. And there is no evidence of such deployment in archaeological traces. These observations are revealing; they strongly indicate that right-wing elements held intact in the rear of Calhoun Hill (north of the Company L skirmish lines). Company C doubtless accompanied

Keogh's troop, serving in a reserve role as well. Only as threats increased did the wing commander commit C Company, sending it from reserve into the Calhoun Coulee action. Before this, the wing had deployed exactly in the formation prescribed by tactics.

This posture—L on a battle line with two companies, C and I, in reserve—should not be unexpected. Clearly, the wing experienced subdued fighting for some time before collapse. In a combat environment such as this, reserve unit tactics could and would be implemented. That is why Keogh's outfit, minus Calhoun's company, remained where it did—in what is essentially a hollow between Custer Ridge and the next ridge east—rather than taking high ground. There was no pressing need to commit the entire force. And the presence of I Company in the reserve force is predictable. Captain Keogh commanded I, and his role as senior wing officer virtually assured his presence with the reserve. The two inactive companies doubtless held in the rear—perhaps, as tactics specified, around 300 yards behind skirmishers active on Calhoun Hill. After the excursion by Company C into Calhoun Coulee, disintegration evidently struck so quickly that Company I, as archaeology shows, could not effectively mobilize its firepower.

Indeed, one of the two left-wing companies, as we shall see, also held in reserve. The left wing was operating not too far away, that is, west of Custer Hill. As it turned out, and this shall be examined, Yates's left wing eventually received the few who survived the right-wing disintegration. Like L Company of the right wing, E Company of the left is highly visible in the historical record; F Company, paralleling the right-wing reserve, is not. The reason? Companies E and L actively engaged in skirmishing, whereas the remaining elements of each wing—the reserves—did not. In their testimonies, warriors naturally emphasized the action rather than those units not engaged. Despite this, there are a few clues, including one of White Bull's accounts, referring to the right-wing reserve units.

After departing the Calhoun area, and before the breakdown in command and control there, White Bull noticed "soldiers [that] were divided into two bunches. "[5] Red Feather reported a similar configuration "on one side of the hill" and noted that Crazy Horse, a Sioux leader, drew some fire when he "rode between the two parties."[6] L Company occupied the Calhoun hilltop, thus the two "parties" on the hillside (east slope of Custer Ridge, or the Keogh sector) possibly were Companies C and I. On the other hand, the two parties, or "bunches," might have been Companies C and I in one group and Company L in the other. The former option seems likely, however, since Two Moons saw three "branches" of the right wing, each "with a little ways between them."[7] These soldiers, Two Moons observed, all dismounted, and some led the horses over the hill. No doubt he saw the L Company horse holders and the right-wing reserve.

Infiltration from the north (the right-wing rear) had started shortly after Indians began moving up Calhoun Coulee (west of the right wing). Gall told D. F. Barry that Crazy Horse and Crow King feared the soldiers would move north and attack the Indian encampment. (They were more or less right, although the attack never materialized, for reasons discussed in part 5.) To prevent this, these two warriors and others left the engagement with Reno, then well under way, and proceeded north down the Little Big Horn Valley. They arrived, wrote Barry, after the right wing had established its positions in and around Calhoun Hill and before its collapse. Crow King, however, left Crazy Horse, most likely at Medicine Tail Coulee, and crept into Calhoun Coulee, which brought him to a position west of Keogh's wing. The Crazy Horse contingent proceeded farther down the valley, crossed the river, and went over Custer Ridge to its east side.[8]

According to Flying Hawk, he and Crazy Horse "followed up the gulch to a place in the rear of the soldiers that were making the stand on [Calhoun] hill."[9] Crazy Horse had infiltrated the right-wing rear. Eventually warriors here, as elsewhere, got very close to Keogh's troopers. Two Eagles, apparently among or near them, said they infiltrated the draws just below the crown of Custer Ridge.[10] White Bull informed Stanley Vestal, in an unabashed attempt to denigrate Crazy Horse's role, that he led the daring rides between right-wing units.[11] Whatever the case, it is clear a few events of this type took place. Such descriptions serve to cement the notion that otherwise not much happened as warriors, mostly exercising caution, crept about. But, sometime after these personal deeds of bravery, the Indians did attack. By this time the foe held positions west (at Greasy Grass Ridge, Calhoun Coulee), south (Gall and others), and northeast (Crazy Horse, White Bull, and others) of the right wing.

Flying Hawk indicated that after a while, Crazy Horse (and others) fired on Calhoun Hill, whereupon soldiers "broke and ran as fast as their horses could go to some soldiers that were further along the ridge toward Custer [Hill]."[12] His account leaves the impression that rapid entropy during the Calhoun Hill episode resulted wholly from Crazy Horse's assault. This cannot be possible, since command degradation, as I have shown, began west of Calhoun Hill (Greasy Grass Ridge, Calhoun Coulee). More likely, Crazy Horse's thrust took advantage of Lame White Man's successes on the other side of Custer Ridge. In fact, Runs the Enemy mentioned an attack against bunched-up soldiers on Calhoun Hill after the Lame White Man push.[13] Archaeology shows that cavalrymen, clustered together, broke and ran from Calhoun Hill.

Lame White Man's foray spurred other attackers in addition to Crazy Horse. In the confusion wrought by C Company as it tried to escape from harm, Gall and those who rode with him, some of whom breached Calhoun Hill via the Henryville position, almost certainly pounced. Gall's role is obscured hereafter.

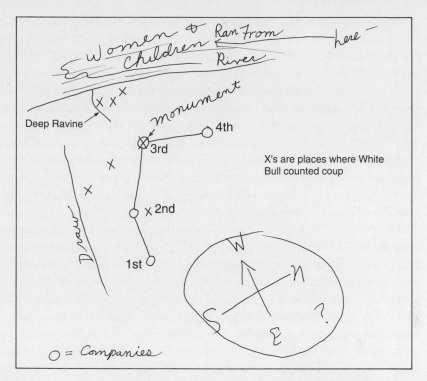

Fig. 10-1. Stanley Vestal's sketch drawn during an interview with White Bull, ca. 1932. White Bull's first, second, third, and fourth cavalry units, or companies, are indicated. "Deep Ravine" is added. "Monument" is Custer Hill. "Draw" is probably Deep Coulee. Women and children ran from the village north to the point labeled "here." "River" is Little Big Horn. Aspects of the sketch are briefly discussed in note 77, chapter 11. Adapted from a copy in Vestal (n.d.e:59) of the original in the University of Oklahoma Libraries.

But White Bull's is not. In testimony transcribed and sketched (fig. 10-1) by Stanley Vestal, White Bull briefly described the effects of what must have been a fearful experience. His party "charged [the] first company," whereupon "the [first] bunch run [*sic*] to the second bunch and the second run to the third."[14] Right-wing survivors had spilled from Calhoun Hill (first bunch), through the Keogh sector (second bunch) toward Custer Hill (third). Once again seized with immodesty, White Bull claimed the attack materialized only after he started out. But the credit, as best as can be determined, should go to Lame White Man, the spearhead of an assault that ultimately included contingents with Gall, Crazy Horse, Yellow Nose, Contrary Belly, White Bull, Comes in Sight, Two Moon, Runs the Enemy, Crow King, and probably other notables unknown to us.

Like Flying Hawk and White Bull, Runs the Enemy also described panicky flight by the soldiers into the Keogh sector.[15] The exodus doubtless proceeded toward I Company. From his position farther east, Wooden Leg saw a "band" of soldiers on the east side of Custer Ridge (Keogh sector).[16] During the period of subdued fighting, he had fired into this group from a distance, intimating that other Indians—their numbers are unrecorded—near his position did the same. Two Moons evidently was one of these. Later in the Keogh episode, he helped kill a "troop" of soldiers.[17] Evidently Two Moons and Wooden Leg assaulted I Company, although its location in the Keogh sector at the time is not certain. There are no details in the documents, and archaeology did not reveal concrete evidence for cavalry positions there. Clearly, all of this came suddenly and at a time when Keogh's I Company functioned as a reserve rather than a fighting unit.

Apparently the Crazy Horse group, spurred by the confusion of I Company under attack and soldiers fleeing from Calhoun Hill, pounced at this time. He Dog told Camp the charge "split up soldiers into two bunches."[18] Red Horse said the troopers became separated.[19] Several Oglalas concurred, noting that the rush on the soldiers "cut the line in two."[20] The "line," of course, reflected little more than a stream of men in flight rather than any type of effective tactical deployment. The charge apparently carried some Indians over the crest to the west side of Custer Ridge, where other Sioux had congregated.[21] These warriors, recently involved in Lame White Man's attack and now following the panicky soldiers (as indicated archaeologically by Indian pathways), had moved along Custer Ridge on its west side.[22] Virtually all of these remain nameless except Lame White Man. Friends found his body west of the ridge—opposite the Keogh sector—just below the crest. Indeed, Red Bird made it clear that Lame White Man chased soldiers involved in the Calhoun episodes into the Keogh sector (see note 85, chapter 9), further stating, with reference to Camp's map (fig. 9-2), "From D and G [Keogh sector] there was no [skirmish] line, the soldiers moving right along."[23]

Company I, a reserve unit ill-prepared for a sudden deterioration, quickly disintegrated as the Calhoun panic spread and as emboldened Indians pressed the attack. One result was the loss of horses. The Cheyennes described this loss in general terms.[24] Several Oglala Sioux suggested that here and there a horse would break loose,[25] but that recollection seems to be an understatement. Many steeds scurried away, with some stampeding toward the river.[26] More critically, not every beleaguered soldier lost his mount, however; some retained their horses, and the Indians described the disparity between mounted and dismounted troopers.

Turtle Rib[27] recalled a running fight with soldiers on foot, who, compared with the mounted men, fought cooly. The latter, he thought, seemed to be "stampeded." Two Eagles said it was a moving fight from Calhoun Hill to Custer Hill, with "most of the soldiers dismounted" (i.e., they had lost their horses).[28] Foolish Elk also saw "men on foot . . . shooting as they passed along, but the men on horses rode away . . . as fast as they could go."[29] Not all the dismounted soldiers acted in a composed manner. Some, according to White Bull, "ran like scared rabbits" while others mounted their horses after a bugle sounded.[30] The bugle reference seems to indicate that officers properly responded to the Keogh sector attacks, though with little success.

Apparently most of the mounted soldiers rode north in an attempt to reach Custer Hill,[31] roughly three-quarters of a mile, via the Keogh sector, from Calhoun Hill. Two Moons, and obviously other warriors (as indicated by Indian pathways), advanced as the troopers fled northward.[32] Turtle Rib, though, saw some men riding in the opposite direction.[33] These might have been the four who, according to Indians, tried unsuccessfully to make a southern escape.[34] Soldiers afoot, many also trying to gain Custer Hill, were left to fend for themselves.

Most soldiers in the Keogh sector probably found themselves dismounted.[35] Such confusion developed that Indians could shoot soldiers from behind.[36] Red Horse mentioned hand-to-hand fighting but did not elaborate.[37] Grinnell, interpreting Cheyenne accounts of the close-in fighting, stated that half the soldiers fought with pistols, not carbines.[38] Sioux and Cheyenne warriors led Miller to believe that the dismounted troopers, unlike those with horses, were unable to join in the breakthrough to Custer Hill.[39] Brave Wolf[40] saw it the other way around, but given the number of marble markers at the Keogh and Calhoun sectors, it is apparent that only a few made it to Custer Hill.[41] Many of the markers located on figure 7-12 are shown in figure 10-2, a view of the Keogh sector taken from the Calhoun Hill environs. In this figure, Custer Hill is at the horizon, far left.

As for fighting during the Custer battle, Lone Bear said it was the hardest during the Keogh episode.[42] His reference, however, is the only one of its nature I have found in the primary sources. Even as a relative measure, his statement is likely not accurate concerning firearm use; all evidence points to the most discharges at Calhoun Hill. Flying Hawk suggested that one unit, probably I Company, tried to make a stand and "fired some shots."[43] Two Eagles indicated that it was, as his interpreter put it, a "slight stand."[44] These passages suggest rather disorganized, ineffectual firing, and this is reflected in the archaeological record. After this "stand," according to Flying Hawk, the soldiers "made another stand" before they fled to Custer Hill.[45] This event—the particulars are lost to us—must have occurred after the charge that separated the soldiers into two bunches.[46] Runs the Enemy noted the results of the charge: "On this retreat

Fig. 10-2. Keogh sector looking northward from Calhoun Hill area. Custer Hill is at the horizon, far left. Note the marble markers throughout the sector. Photograph and notations by Ken Roahen, ca. 1940. Courtesy Custer Battlefield National Monument (#C7774).

the soldiers now broke the line and divided, some of them going down the eastern slope of the hill [ridge], and some of them going down to the river. The others came back [fell back] to where the final stand was made [Custer Hill], but they were few in number then."[47]

There are corroborating accounts of soldiers going toward the river. Two Eagles said that 10 or 12 men made a "dash" over to the west side of Custer Ridge, though he did not think they were trying to "run away."[48] In the strict sense, his observation is correct; they were not trying to escape the field. Later discussions show why—these men, like those who fled to Custer Hill, tried to reach safety with the left wing. White Bull also noticed this over-the-ridge movement. After troopers from C and L companies—those still alive—had joined their comrades in the Keogh sector, "some" did not continue to "run straight." Rather than fleeing to Custer Hill, these men ran "toward the river [and they] were all killed."[49]

Runs the Enemy described the other movements of the two bunches of soldiers.[50] The two groups were apparently sufficiently close together for White Cow Bull to fire into both without changing his position.[51] One group made for

Fig. 10-3. Keogh sector looking southward from Custer Hill area. Part of Custer Ridge is to the right. Stones clustered around the Keogh marker are labeled "Keough." Calhoun Hill is the area below this label. "Twin Peaks" is Weir Point. "C" is unknown. Photograph and notations by Frank L. Anders, ca. 1932. Courtesy University of North Dakota (Anders Papers, Elwyn B. Robinson Department of Special Collections, Chester Fritz Library).

Custer Hill; the other went down the eastern ridge slope (i.e., the Keogh sector). Marble markers clustered around the Keogh memorial stone likely represent the latter group. The Keogh cluster is identified in figure 7-12, and though barely visible in figure 10-3, a view of the sector from near Custer Hill, the cluster is labeled "Keough." The marker group also appears in figure 10-2 (below ridge, center right).

Much has been made of this cluster of stones. A number of eyewitnesses saw these corpses and concluded that Captain Keogh attempted to rally his men.[52] Others[53] suspect soldiers in the Keogh group attempted to reach their horses, though probably they lost their mounts early in the episode.[54] Behavior during the breakup of tactical unity, however, presents an alternative explanation.

The distribution of bodies immediately surrounding Captain Keogh has been variously described as a "pile of men,"[55] "all in a bunch,"[56] troopers "piled in a heap,"[57] and "one compact mass."[58] The clustered memorials generally reflect these descriptions, but not exactly. If the bodies were originally in a mass, the 1876 burial parties probably relocated them for inhumation. In any case, shock, sudden confusion, and perhaps a lack or loss of leadership pervaded the Keogh sector as loss of cohesiveness set in. Given a disordered environment, bunching behavior is the most likely explanation for the clustering.

Indeed, marker distributions throughout the Keogh sector do not convey much semblance of tactical order. Instead, they better fit Miller's description of the struggle, taken from Sioux and Cheyenne eyewitness testimony, as "little knots of soldiers" surrounded by Indians.[59] Miller visited the site with his Indian informants, so their testimony may have been indirectly influenced by the marker patterning. But in 1877, before Sweet's expedition, Lt. John Bourke viewed the actual graves, noting they were "scattered in irregular clumps and at intervals about like those in a slaughter of buffaloes."[60] Runs the Enemy remembered that the right-wing flight resembled a buffalo stampede, and Bourke saw the result. There can be little doubt that what we see today in the Keogh sector memorial stones resulted from panic and fear, not from a determined exploitation of tactical alternatives.

The presence of Keogh sector dead from all three right-wing companies complements archaeological and other historical evidence of flight from the Calhoun positions. The mixture is also consistent with confusion arising from disintegration. Stable units normally do not blend together. At least one L Company trooper in the sector (Pvt. Charles Graham) could be identified,[61] and an observer identified 1st Sgt. Edwin Bobo (C Company) near the body of Captain Keogh.[62] Bobo, it appears, had made it through the Calhoun sectors. His presence, as his company's top-ranking noncommissioned officer, is a strong sign that remnants of his unit fled here. On the other hand, Sergeants Finley and Finckle perished much earlier in the rout—on Calhoun Ridge.

Age and stature estimates calculated from skeletal remains at one Keogh sector marker (#200, immediately north of Keogh cluster) fit the profiles of six right-wing soldiers (four from C and two L) and only three from the left wing.[63] Observers identified two of the possible left-wing candidates elsewhere, leaving only one that fits the age-stature estimates.[64] But it is not likely the remains represent this individual. Contemporary observers did not identify any left-wing troopers anywhere in the Keogh sector, or at least did not report such. They recognized only C, I, and L personnel. Those in the Keogh cluster included two I Company sergeants, Frank Varden and James Bustard.[65] Comrades saw Trumpeter John Patton[66] and Corporal John Wild,[67] both from Keogh's company, there too. One I Company private, Edward Lloyd, also died close to his captain.[68]

Like marker patterning, the archaeological record concerning the role of firearms in the Keogh episode is consistent with decampment amid chaos. Physical evidence for firearm use by either adversary is poor. Possibly, artifact collecting among the Keogh sector markers has impaired the archaeological record. But historical evidence, which is consistent with archaeological conclusions, suggests that there was never much for relic hunters to remove. Hardorff made the same observation, though he thought the dearth of firearm residues did not detract from the belief that these troopers fought intensely.[69]

Hardorff's observation probably has a measure of validity. There are no reasons to eliminate hand-to-hand struggles, each intense but certainly individualistic and without unified purpose. And these struggles were reported by some Indian participants. Red Feather recalled the evolution of this episode. According to him, an impression that the soldiers' guns were empty stimulated the warrior influx.[70] Strictly interpreted, this is probably close to correct. Under extreme duress, considerable numbers of troopers must have simply quit using the single-shot carbine. This enticed many Indians to move right in among the soldiers. There they engaged in hand-to-hand fighting, which Red Horse described.[71] Warriors to the east, those who just earlier had fired from a distance, presumably joined in or, for fear of hitting their brethren, ceased shooting. Perhaps this—closeup struggle—is what Lone Bear meant when he characterized the Keogh sector combat as the most difficult.

These developments help explain the paucity of material evidence for the use of Springfield carbines. The single-shot arm, requiring deliberate and repeated loading to achieve optimum operation, had a limited effectiveness in close-in fighting. Therefore, it is likely that many cavalrymen, when closely confronted, abandoned or quit using the weapon. This behavior probably prompted Sitting Bull's[72] and Red Horse's[73] observations that the soldiers could not fire quickly enough and that many, in panic, simply threw down their arms. Indeed, in one incident, a Keogh sector trooper, confronted face-to-face by White Bull, fired and then threw his carbine at the warrior's head.[74] Both attempts missed, but one cannot escape the conclusion that this scene occurred many times.

Gall remembered, "The soldiers threw their guns aside and fought with little guns."[75] Ignorant of the effects of disintegration among tactical units, and of carbine limitations, he erroneously assumed their ammunition supply had dwindled. Grinnell's Indian informants also implied that Keogh sector troopers mainly used the Colt revolver.[76] According to Dewey Beard, an Indian warrior, "some" troopers managed to discharge their pistols at close range.[77] But a poverty of Colt casings at the Keogh sector suggests minimal handgun use. Fighting clearly ended without enough time to reload,[78] or perhaps soldiers had too little time to deliver all six rounds from the sidearm.

In a scene where fleeing soldiers, acting as if drunk,[79] were shot from behind[80] and were jerked bodily from their horses,[81] resistance must have been sporadic and, as might be expected during panicky flight, quite individualistic. In fact, Two Eagles, when asked if the troopers here ran or stood to fight, said, as did Red Bird, that most of the them died while "moving."[82] He might as well have said "while fleeing."

Other accounts suggest that substantial numbers of Indians fought armed with clubs, knives, and hatchets, handy for counting coup on live enemies.[83] Indeed, Indian testimonies are replete with descriptions of coup honors. In the close-in fighting, many of the soldiers were probably killed with these weapons rather than firearms. This helps to explain the relatively few Indian cartridge cases and bullets found in the Keogh sector (compared with the Calhoun Hill vicinity).

Foolish Elk watched the Keogh episode from east of Custer Ridge. He saw that the "men made no stand" as they went toward Custer Hill.[84] Turtle Rib called it a "running fight."[85] Clearly, the weight of archaeological evidence, and those historical accounts that mesh, indicate that events at this time simply represented a continuation, if not acceleration, of the tactical breakdown that had begun in the Calhoun sectors. The entire right wing had crumbled,[86] the disintegration process ending with individualistic, hand-to-hand contests as demoralized cavalrymen ran through the Keogh sector. Indeed, by August 1876, the Indian "grapevine" had carried this story as far as what is now Oklahoma. There, at the Darlington Agency (Cheyenne and Arapaho), John Miles, after hearing Indian reports of the Custer battle, wrote to his superior, "After [Medicine Tail Coulee]—the struggle was a hand to hand fight."[87] This is true enough for the right wing, particularly in the Keogh sector, and as we shall see, it is largely true of the penultimate and final episodes as well.

Rejecting historical data to the contrary, we can no longer believe the myths of group cohesion. Developments during this episode are entirely consistent with expectations derived from behavioral models of soldiers in combat. Men fled through the sector toward Custer Hill, toward cavalry units that remained tactically stable, for the moment. We now turn to these units, the left wing, and to the Cemetery Ridge episode.[88]

11

THE CEMETERY RIDGE EPISODE

The possibility of fighting near the present [national] cemetery location can also be developed from verbal as well as physical evidence.

—Clifford Nelson[1]

The Cemetery Ridge episode is not incorporated in conventional wisdom about the Custer battle, nor in myths and beliefs. In the fatalistic tradition, Custer's battalion is obliterated almost immediately on reaching Custer Ridge. In the purest form, it is said that Custer, under enormous duress, stationed his men at the southern (Calhoun Hill) and northern (Custer Hill) extremities of the ridge—poor locations but the best defensive positions available at the time—and fought it out. One version finds the battalion strung out along Custer Ridge, only to be engulfed from virtually all sides simultaneously. It is then said that the soldiers on Custer Hill—the so-called last stand—fell last. In another twist, Calhoun and Keogh fell first, with the Indians rolling over cavalrymen as they advanced to the north end of the ridge. Then, on the hill, came the last stand, and all was over.

Though erosion in battalion cohesion (and ultimately defeat) occurred roughly in the latter sequence, it did not happen until after the left wing had maneuvered offensively on Cemetery Ridge—and well beyond. After these maneuvers, the left wing returned to the Custer Hill vicinity. Only then did disaster occur. There is a manifest aversion to accepting the idea of an episode on and beyond Cemetery Ridge. To do so implicates Custer himself, for if not driven, the battalion movements are his responsibility. To reject any such notion shifts blame, overtly or otherwise, to his subordinate commanders. Thus, subscribers to the fatalistic theory are often attracted to the argument that at no time did (or could) any element of the doomed column proceed beyond Custer Hill because of overwhelming Indian forces. Yet the evidence for a Cemetery Ridge episode is, in light of archaeological interpretations, substantial and convincing.

On Cemetery Ridge, Companies E and F composed the left wing, with regimental staff members, including General Custer, attached. F Company as a discrete unit is often obscured in the historical record because of what can best be described as an enduring obsession with the "gray horse company." For a variety of reasons, mostly associated with the fatalistic theme, the actions of E Company became shrouded in mystery. Many questions arose, and Indian eye-witnesses had the answers. Only E company, of the five with Custer, rode gray horses. So the best way to inquire about E was with reference to the grays. "What happened to the gray horse soldiers?" early researchers asked Sioux and Cheyenne participants. Where did they go? In the answers, Company F became obscured whenever the two companies maneuvered together as an intact wing. Or, since questions specified the gray horse troop, Company F, which rode bays, lost its visibility when the two left-wing troops operated independently. Despite this, the historical record does contain important clues regarding the operations of both companies on Cemetery Ridge.

Recall that the two wings had departed Medicine Tail Coulee and converged around Calhoun Hill. Lone Bear, from his position near Calhoun Ridge, early on saw the gray horse company mixed with all the others (i.e., the entire battalion) as the battalion moved into the Calhoun sectors.[2] Hollow Horn Bear saw the grays at the first as well. From here, the left and right wings separated. Hollow Horn Bear recalled that the gray horses, either referring to the company or the wing, "kept fairly well together" thereafter. Later he would witness gray horse soldiers "in the last of the fight."[3]

There is little doubt that the left wing, as it detached from the right wing on or near Calhoun Hill, moved north through the Keogh sector en route to Cemetery Ridge. Grinnell's[4] Cheyenne informants observed that after ascending Deep Coulee, the "gray-horse company" (i.e., the left wing) stopped on Custer Hill—but only momentarily, as we shall see. Cheyenne oral tradition indicates that these soldiers passed along Custer Ridge.[5] Foolish Elk told Walter Camp, "The gray horses went up in a body; then came the bay horses [Companies I and L of the right wing also rode bays] and men on foot altogether."[6] The reference to bay horses and men on foot together obviously refers to refugees from the Calhoun and Keogh episodes. The account makes it appear that these men followed immediately after the gray horses. But here either Camp or Foolish Elk has compressed elapsed time. The gray horses, or more properly the left wing, proceeded toward Cemetery Ridge long before the right wing fell apart.

He Dog apparently saw the left-wing movement as well. He informed Camp that "Custer" (the left wing) moved mounted through the Keogh sector without stopping and (presumably) without fighting.[7] The gray horses, here referring to the left wing, remained together at this time. Hollow Horn Bear, east of Custer Ridge at the time, also reported seeing this event.[8] Further corroboration, as I have noted, is derived from one of several accounts of White Bull (Sioux).[9]

White Bull mentioned that the right wing did not proceed along Custer Ridge (a few men did, eventually, but after tactical unity had failed), thus implying that only the left moved farther north beyond Keogh's right-wing positions.

Evidently, the left wing rode to and over Cemetery Ridge and, importantly, without resistance, for there is no archaeological evidence of such. Relevant historical accounts are slightly contradictory, but not one can be presented as evidence for a blocking force or even a modest warrior assemblage. The accounts are, in fact, consistent with the archaeological evidence. Two Eagles simply stated that Indians occupied Custer Ridge before "Custer" (i.e., the battalion) got there.[10] If so, this is hardly a statement of warriors in force. Similarly, He Dog said nothing more than that Indians were all along the ridge.[11] But Cheyenne oral tradition indicates the presence of only a few Indians (40 or 50) during the left-wing trek along Custer Ridge.[12] Evidently these Indians, including Wolf Tooth and Big Foot, had earlier harassed the right wing on Luce and Nye-Cartwright ridges. Lights, a Sioux warrior, remembered that none blocked the battalion front (i.e., along Custer Ridge).[13] And Thunder Hawk's wife, evidently drawing from oral history, reported no warriors to the north of Calhoun Hill.[14] Lone Bear could not say for sure one way or the other.[15]

General statements, such as those by Two Eagles and He Dog, cannot justifiably be used to confirm a massive force—one of sufficient might and, in light of passive infiltration, aggressiveness to stop the left wing in its tracks—surrounding Custer Ridge at this time. Indian accounts that compress time appear to indicate, to the unwitting researcher, the presence of such a force. But this was not the case—most warriors had not even arrived yet. Rather, evidence points toward either an absence altogether or nothing more than a paltry collection of timid warriors. Indians could not have been numerous, and they certainly presented no impediment to the left-wing movement. The calm at this time also allowed Companies C and I to act as reserves while L Company deployed to skirmish from Calhoun Hill.

Cheyenne oral tradition provides a general account of left-wing operations on and beyond Cemetery Ridge.[16] The wing's route, such as can be pieced together in a tentative way from this and other unrelated sources soon discussed, can be followed in figure 11-1. After departing Keogh's three-company force, left-wing soldiers followed the ridge down to where the national cemetery is now located (hence the name Cemetery Ridge). A few Indians (the 40 or 50 with Wolf Tooth) took up positions on or near Custer Hill and began light firing. Undaunted, the troops continued their northwestern movement down Cemetery Ridge toward Little Big Horn River. They went to the vicinity of a ford there; in 1956, John Stands in Timber, then the Cheyenne tribal historian, pointed out this ford to the chief historian at the Custer battlefield, Don Rickey. That ford, based on my

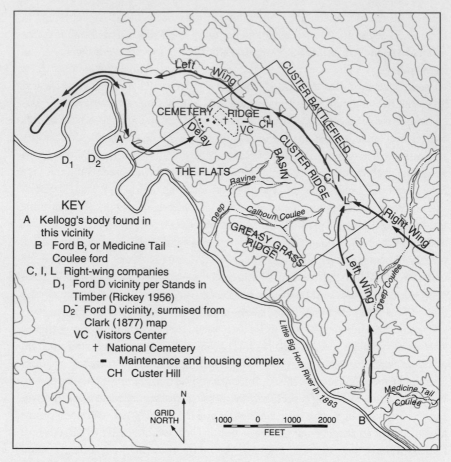

Fig. 11-1. A general representation of wing movements and positions from Medicine Tail Coulee environs to the point of the left-wing delay on Cemetery Ridge.

communications with Rickey, is located on figure 11-1 ("D_1").[17] Warriors in large numbers had not yet moved into this area. The vast majority, at first unaware of Custer's battalion, had responded to Reno's attack on the southern end of the village.

As the left wing neared Little Big Horn River, some Indians crossed and delivered fire of undisclosed proportions. The soldiers turned and moved northward for a time, then returned and occupied selected Cemetery Ridge localities. During this journey, the wing had proceeded some 2.5 miles beyond its counterpart stationed around Calhoun Hill, well beyond visual contact with the right wing, and out of sight of those Indians beginning to congregate in the southern battle sectors. But Two Moons saw the left-wing troopers (or later learned of the maneuver), who rode "beyond where the monument stands [Custer Hill] down into the [Little Big Horn] valley until we could not see them."[18] Here, in the valley, the left-wing cavalrymen found a river ford north of the Indian village.

Later, Lt. Philo Clark, investigating the battle, probably learned of this movement. During the first eight months of 1877, and while commanding a detachment of Indian scouts, he interviewed Custer battle warriors who surrendered at Sioux reservation agencies near Camp Robinson (now extreme northwest Nebraska). Clark submitted an official report (dated September 14, 1877) based on these interviews. A color map accompanied the report (fig. 11-2). The map misrepresents the extent of the Indian village, but correctly identifies the Cheyenne circle as the northernmost encampment (this problem is scrutinized in chapter 18). Most important, however, is the identification of what Clark labeled "ford D," the location of which I have estimated in figure 11-1 (labeled "D_2"). Note that Clark's ford is very close to that identified by Stands in Timber.

Clark's ford D, a Little Big Horn River crossing, is located north of the Cheyenne encampment some distance downriver. Trails on his map are marked in purple as "Trail of troops," or cavalry routes. Custer's route (so marked) leads from Reno Creek to the Medicine Tail ford, then up Custer Ridge to Custer Hill ("Custer found here"). Four routes emanate from Custer Ridge; two of these originate at Custer Hill. Three of the four routes converge below the ridge and lead as one to ford D. The convergent route passes right through Indian strongholds, appropriately drawn in red, which are located between Custer Ridge and Little Big Horn River.

Informants evidently led Lieutenant Clark to believe, or he alone chanced on the erroneous conclusion, that the battalion (Custer's five companies) remained intact throughout (no wing separation). Referencing his map, Clark described Custer's movements:

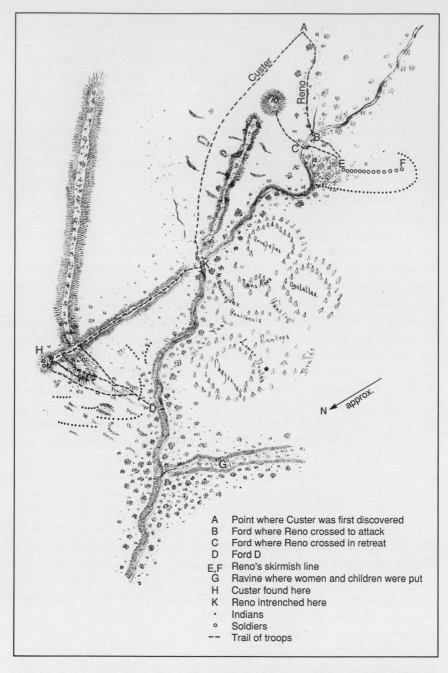

A	Point where Custer was first discovered
B	Ford where Reno crossed to attack
C	Ford where Reno crossed in retreat
D	Ford D
E,F	Reno's skirmish line
G	Ravine where women and children were put
H	Custer found here
K	Reno intrenched here
·	Indians
∘	Soldiers
--	Trail of troops

Fig. 11-2. Map of Custer battle drawn by Lt. William Philo Clark from Indian testimony in 1877. Lower K (center) is Medicine Tail ford (not defined in key); upper K is Reno-Benteen field (in key); H is Custer Hill; D is ford D. Trail of troops proceeds from Medicine Tail ford along Custer Ridge to Custer Hill area, then through Indian positions (which accumulated later) to ford D. The only cavalry position mapped is at Custer Hill. Based on original in National Archives (Letters Received, Department of Platte, 4601 1877, Record Group 393).

> *Custer's column . . . came down [from Reno Creek] and made*
> *an attempt to cross at the mouth of a little stream at K [Medi-*
> *cine Tail Coulee], finding it impossible turned up . . .*
> *[Custer] ridge and then turned again as the trails leading*
> *down [from Custer Ridge] to ford D were reached. The Indians*
> *had massed in the ravines and timber and opened such a ter-*
> *rific fire from all sides that the troops gave way.* [19]

The soldiers headed to Custer Ridge, where Clark mapped a single soldier position in blue—Custer Hill. His report and map seem to have perpetrated a veiled contradiction. He mapped cavalry routes leading to ford D north of the village yet avoided stating that troops actually reached the crossing. Nor did he say how far the column proceeded after turning toward the river. Rather he suggested that the warrior force, mapped in red, thwarted the soldiers while en route.[20] The contradiction suggests a hesitancy on Clark's part to attribute the cavalry routes to Custer's column. But this is easily explained.

Clark copied his map from one drawn by a Sioux informant at Camp Robinson. The Little Big Horn veteran also provided his "description of the Custer massacre," which the lieutenant did not detail in writing.[21] Evidently, the anonymous warrior showed a troop movement to ford D and described how Indians eventually descended on the battalion. Descriptions of the rout no doubt fostered Clark's hesitancy: if warriors had converged on the column, how did it get to the river? Perhaps at this early date the fatalistic tradition had seduced him. More likely, he simply fell into the temporal trap, the "disconcerting jumble of ephemeral, non-chronological impressions" often found in Indian testimony.[22] Clark had evidently failed to differentiate between an early troop movement to the Little Big Horn and later events that resulted in annihilation. Warriors en masse, of course, eventually did converge on Custer Ridge, but only after left-wing troops rode to and from the river virtually unhindered. Despite Clark's confusion, he was clear on one thing. He learned that the column turned off Custer Ridge and went toward a river crossing north of the Indian village—ford D.

Clark's record may be considered among the most trustworthy of all Custer battle accounts. He obtained the map from a participant. Moreover, he acted under orders to gather intelligence regarding the Little Big Horn fight. The lieutenant interviewed scores of Custer battle veterans over eight months. And the testimony he received came within a year of the battle. Most important, Clark compiled his intelligence without prior knowledge of the battle site.[23]

It seems likely, then, that Clark, despite his hesitancy, unwittingly recorded the left-wing journey to Little Big Horn River and back, an event preserved in Cheyenne oral tradition and validated by Two Moons. Sitting Bull too, early on (in November 1877), most likely recorded the journey—or a part of it. Referencing an interviewer's map,[24] the Hunkpapa Sioux leader commented that soldiers (he said Long Hair, or Custer) rode *up* a ridge to Custer Hill.[25] The ridge he pointed to, stretching from the river to Custer Hill, corresponds in configuration and orientation to Cemetery Ridge, though the map Sitting Bull used mistakenly identifies this ridge as the place where C and E companies fell. After relating this incident, he said he was not sure of it. Sitting Bull, who did not participate in the battle, got his story from warriors, so his uncertainty suggests that among the Sioux, this action came to be known principally through hearsay. This is not at all surprising, since there are no accounts putting Sioux in the ford D vicinity. They had all responded to Reno first and then to the right wing (before the left wing returned from the river).

Mark Kellogg, a civilian war correspondent with the expedition, very possibly died during the left-wing trip to the river. Some observers, days after the battle, thought they saw his body, or evidence for such, on or near Custer Ridge.[26] Other eyewitnesses placed Kellogg's remains very near Little Big Horn River ("within a stone's throw"; three-quarters of a mile from Custer Hill and "100 yards from the river"; near the river about "a half mile" from Custer Hill).[27]

Almost certainly, the latter group of observers were correct. Lt. James Bradley identified Kellogg's corpse "some distance from the field of battle," which logically cannot refer to Custer Ridge.[28] Moreover, Colonel Gibbon, en route on June 29, 1876, from his camp to the scene, stated that he found Kellogg alone in a remote gully.[29] The burial details of previous days had overlooked his body.[30] The river course has changed considerably since 1876, but M. B. Moore and M. Donahue, matching Gibbon's narrative with an 1883 topographic survey map, have admirably traced his route.[31] The Gibbon party, intending to survey the battle site, evidently crossed Little Big Horn River at Clark's ford D, or at least very nearby. According to Gibbon, Kellogg lay dead just beyond this ford near the river. The corpse evidently lay in the vicinity marked on figure 11-1.

How did Kellogg end up near the river? It might be argued that he fled the carnage on Custer Ridge, but for nearly a mile into the Indian front? The chances of getting so far under such circumstances seem slim (although evidently Gibbon thought this to be the case). More likely, Kellogg died sometime during the left-wing maneuvers to and from the river. Kellogg, known to be eager to keep up with developments,[32] surely rode with the left wing (more specifically, with Custer's regimental headquarters staff).

In any event, the left wing had gone to a ford north of the Cheyenne circle hoping to find an adequate attack point. But the troops returned from the river, for reasons discussed in part 5, and eventually occupied Cemetery Ridge.

Archaeological remains from The Flats sector make this fairly clear. Indeed, they force us to seek a historical explanation, for from an archaeological perspective, the tactical nature of deployments on the ridge are, due to modern disturbances, hazy at best. Similarly, there is a dearth of military eyewitness accounts pertaining to Cemetery Ridge. Therefore, nothing happened at Cemetery Ridge, or so it is thought. But this is easily explained. After the battle, all attention turned, naturally enough, to the ghastly killing fields about Custer Ridge. Even a cursory glance at the literature makes this clear. Cemetery Ridge received little attention, for few if any dead lay there. But corpses littered Custer Ridge. Thus the silence on Cemetery Ridge.

Also, there are only a few Indian accounts describing Cemetery Ridge action. Early researchers assumed that Indians forced Custer's battalion to immediately take up the best defense possible—an assumption at the heart of various fatalistic theories, which have deep historical roots. That defense, of course, was Custer Ridge, and the battalion got no farther than that. The researchers' biases dictated lines of questioning, and this did not readily provoke informants, if they knew, to discuss what had happened on Cemetery Ridge. In addition, Indian accounts are few because of the scarcity of warriors, particularly Sioux, present during most of this episode, especially during the left-wing trip to the river. Wooden Leg, for example, went back to his camp circle and found it nearly deserted.[33] When Two Moons returned to the Cheyenne lodges, he found mostly women who were busy striking tents.[34] The vast majority of warriors, originally without knowledge of Custer's battalion, had rushed south to meet Reno's anticipated assault on the village.

But some testimony has managed to slip through the barriers, mental and other. Sometimes the few Cemetery Ridge descriptions are not recognized as such, or each is rejected, ignored, or explained away in allegiance to the myth. But now, prompted by archaeological insights, we must address this evidence. Runs the Enemy's recollections offer some initial observations:

> *I left my men there [the Calhoun vicinity] and . . . rushed around the hills and came up to the north end of the field near where the monument now stands [Custer Hill]. . . . From the point that juts out just below where the monument now stands about thirty of us got through the line, firing as we went, and captured a lot of Custer's horses.* [35]

Runs the Enemy's "line" probably stood, at least in part, near the modern visitor center, which is on Cemetery Ridge below and some 750 feet west of the Custer Hill apex.[36] On departing the ridge, Runs the Enemy, after capturing some horses, returned to his original position in the Calhoun vicinity, where he helped to destroy the right wing.[37] Thus it is clear the left wing had deployed on Cemetery Ridge before the onset of disintegration in the Calhoun and Keogh sectors.

The two units composing the left wing—Yates's (F) and Smith's (E) companies—operated independently at this time (before tactical disintegration). White Bull recalled that as the right wing fell apart, men at the Keogh sector struggled to join other soldiers "about where the monument [Custer Hill] now stands."[38] These were the soldiers that Runs the Enemy encountered near the monument (i.e., in the visitor center vicinity). At the same time, White Bull remembered that "another bunch of soldiers were . . . down the hill nearer the river."[39] The body of troops nearer the river was almost certainly F Company, for Two Moons noted gray horses near or atop Custer Hill. Two Moons stated: "I again started [north along Custer Ridge] for the bunch of gray horses on the hilltop. . . . I could not break the line at the bunch of gray horses and I wheeled and went to the left [customary west] down the valley with the line of soldiers facing me as I went, firing at me."[40]

Two Moons's attempt to break the "line" probably occurred at about the same time as the right wing disintegration. After his failure, he rode south, delayed for awhile, and came back again northward along Custer Ridge, noting that nearly all the soldiers (at Calhoun and Keogh) had been killed.[41] During their frontal forays, neither Runs the Enemy nor Two Moons could dent the E Company (gray horse) deployment. The stories of White Bull, Two Moons, and Runs the Enemy, not to mention Cheyenne oral tradition, fairly well confirm left-wing maneuvering over Cemetery Ridge. Before cohesion in the right wing began to erode, E Company held positions on the ridge somewhere below the Custer Hill prominence. And as I shall discuss, F Company held in reserve nearby in a secluded area near the head of Deep Ravine.

But under what circumstances did the left wing come to occupy the Cemetery Ridge positions? Stands in Timber, citing oral tradition, suggested that during the return from the river, the left wing, all together at this time, stopped on the flatter ground of Cemetery Ridge short of what is now the national cemetery site. There the wing paused, perhaps for 20 to 30 minutes.[42]

Chief Gall may have recorded this pause during an 1886 on-site interview with D. F. Barry (the 10th anniversary celebration held at the battlefield). Gall told Barry that "this bunch of soldiers" got about "half way" to the river while headed for the village.[43] The account is usually interpreted as a reference to the battalion operations in Medicine Tail Coulee, and "this bunch of soldiers" is thought to refer to troopers represented by markers at Calhoun Hill. Yet there is support for the argument that Gall instead referred to soldiers on Cemetery

Ridge (who got halfway to the river). The Barry interview took place on Custer Hill. Gall specifically referred to the "bunch of soldiers" represented by the memorial markers there, and not elsewhere. Not until later in the day did Gall accompany Godfrey to Calhoun Hill, which overlooks Medicine Tail Coulee.[44]

Research by Michael Donahue has unearthed a previously neglected map—known as map 1008 (National Archives) and reproduced as figure 11-3—which depicts crucial information consistent with the left-wing pause on Cemetery Ridge. On September 18, 1876, Capt. R. E. Johnston, while at Standing Rock Agency (in present-day North Dakota), recorded Kill Eagle's testimony.[45] Kill Eagle did not fight that day, but he was in the village. His narrative is not particularly informative regarding the battle, but map 1008, which accompanied Johnston's official report, is.[46] It depicts, among other information, the location where "Custer first met the Indians." Though scale is distorted, clearly this location is on Cemetery Ridge, well below Custer Hill. It is, in fact, slightly more than halfway to the river (from Custer Hill). Although Cheyenne oral tradition suggests the initial left-wing/warrior confrontation occurred closer to the river, near ford D, Johnston's map reference at least corresponds to Stands in Timber's mention of the delay below the national cemetery site. It is thus fairly clear that the wing did occupy this Cemetery Ridge position, doubtless firing occasionally at targets below on The Flats.

Eventually the left wing moved on, farther from the river into the Custer Hill environs. The new positions taken up by Companies E and F set the stage for collapse. Figure 11-4 encapsulates the events that occurred after the left wing suspended its delay. Cheyenne tradition relates the course of the left-wing movement, recording its destination as a basin below the west slope of Custer Ridge (between the ridge and river, see fig. 11-4). The wing left Cemetery Ridge, evidently first riding roughly southeast toward a gulch, then turning north by east and finally north, moving up the gully to its head. The tradition cannot refer to anything other than Deep Ravine and the expansive, rather shallow basin that forms its headwater drainage (the misnamed South Skirmish Line lies within the basin): "Custer [left wing] went into the center of a big basin below the monument [Custer Hill], and the soldiers of the gray horse company got off their horses and moved up afoot."[47]

That statement implies that only Company E dismounted and "moved up afoot." Company F is obscured. But another variation of Cheyenne tradition, recorded independently of the first, sheds light on this. Father Peter Powell got this version in the late 1950s while working on the Northern Cheyenne reservation (in Montana). After leaving Cemetery Ridge, "Custer [left wing] retreated [i.e., moved], riding toward a dry gulch and following it up to the center of the basin, below where the monument now stands . . . [and Custer's] . . . men

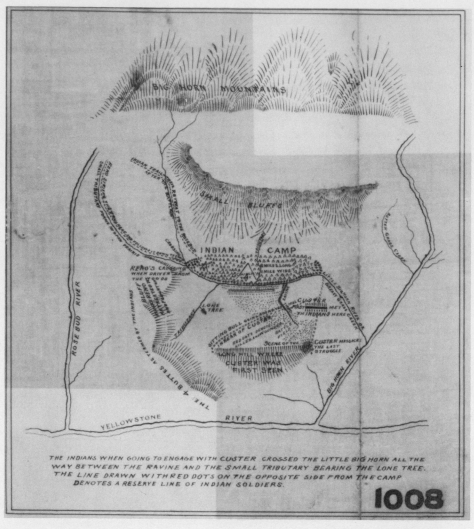

Fig. 11-3. Map of Custer battle compiled by Capt. R. E. Johnston from testimonies taken in 1876; redrawn by officials for clarity. "Tributary" (center) is Medicine Tail Coulee. "Small Ravine" is Deep Ravine. "The Last Struggle" is Custer Hill. The map shows undifferentiated action on Cemetery Ridge ("Custer first met the Indians here"). Reproduced from Map 1008, Tube 530, Record Group 75, National Archives.

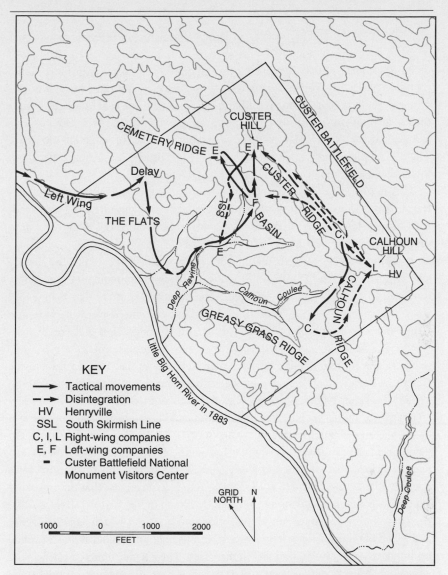

Fig. 11-4. General representation of wing and company movements and positions at Custer battlefield following cessation of the left-wing delay on lower Cemetery Ridge. Solid lines represent tactical movements, dashed lines disintegration.

dismounted. The soldiers of the Gray Horse Company got off their mounts and began to move up on foot."[48]

Powell suggested that Company E moved directly to Custer Hill, there taking up prone positions. The company did, in fact, do exactly that, but not at this moment. Rather, the gray horse soldiers, as is known from Two Moons and Runs the Enemy, took up a position on Cemetery Ridge near Custer Hill. But Powell's account indicates that F Company, now also dismounted, remained in the basin. There is nothing in the archaeological record to suggest its presence here, but this is because Company F did not deploy to do battle.

This is precisely the same configuration first assumed by the right wing. Recall that on reaching the Calhoun sector, and after the left wing departed, L Company deployed in skirmish formation while Companies C and I took to the rear in reserve. Similarly, when the left wing reached the basin, E Company deployed in skirmish formation (the "line" described by Runs the Enemy and Two Moons), and Company F, led by the wing commander, Capt. Yates, remained in reserve. This reserve unit represents the soldiers that White Bull saw "nearer the river." At this time, Companies E and L were the battalion flanks on Custer Ridge while C and I together and F beyond, all sheltered in low-lying areas, followed prescribed tactics by assuming reserve roles.

Cheyenne tradition suggests that "many" warriors had now infiltrated the Cemetery Ridge area, but it also indicates that at this point, the fighting was not "bad."[49] Like the right wing, the left wing could assume the posture allowed by tactics, since Indian activity remained subdued. There are several lines of evidence for this. Runs the Enemy witnessed the right-wing collapse from the beginning, but only after harassing the left wing.[50] Before right-wing decay, as I have described, the warrior force engaged in stealth tactics (infiltration) for a considerable length of time. There are no reasons to suggest that the left wing experienced anything different. Indeed, F Company is historically invisible partly because it remained out of the action until the end, which came suddenly and lasted but a brief time. There are no Indian accounts, other than Cheyenne tradition, that refer to F Company in the basin. This silence tends to validate the company's reserve status. Similarly, only a few warrior accounts allude to the right-wing reserve before unity eroded, yet many describe the right-wing company (L) actively engaged in skirmishing. The same is true for E, the active company in the left wing. But the most compelling argument is archaeological. The absence of physical evidence for organized fighting in the basin (i.e., the South Skirmish Line sector), or anywhere near it, is consistent with a reserve company, and that could only have been F.

The disposition of the gray horses as Company E ascended Cemetery Ridge seems rather straightforward. A few white accounts indicate that the basin contained dead horses, but in some, color is not addressed.[51] Pvt. Theodore Goldin reported dead grays in the basin area, and so did Lt. Charles DeRudio, though General Nelson Miles evidently did not remember any horses in that vicinity.[52] Yet Two Moons recalled gray horses on the hill, or more likely on the ridge, when he tried to break through.[53] In Joseph White Cow Bull's account, which is misplaced chronologically by Miller, he recalled that soldiers were "standing there holding their horses and keeping up a steady fire."[54] And Runs the Enemy recollected capturing some horses in his thrust at the line of soldiers. It appears, then, that E Company men did not leave their mounts in the basin. For the gray horse troop, dismounting and organizing under the cover provided by the basin, and the protection of Company F, served to minimize risks during a momentarily debilitating tactical maneuver. Judging from Two Moons's account, E Company troopers led the grays to Cemetery Ridge. Eventually they lost their steeds; the grays purportedly found in the basin probably wandered there before dying.

The suggestion that the E Company line formed near the modern visitors center site is not certain, although such a position would have placed the wing reserve within a convenient supporting distance. It is likely that Capt. Henry Freeman ran across the E Company position just days after the battle. He witnessed the battle aftermath and made notations, including a sketch map (fig. 11-5), in his journal. Freeman marked on his sketch three places that to him indicated that "they [battalion elements] had dismounted and made a stand."[55] Two of these locations are associated with Custer Ridge. Though Freeman's sketch lacks scale, the other, marked as "1," is indisputably on Cemetery Ridge and beyond Custer Hill—toward the river. Freeman remains silent about what he saw, but no doubt bodies attracted his attention on Custer Hill. As far as is known, few if any cavalrymen died on Cemetery Ridge, so at Freeman's position #1, something else must have caught his eye. He concluded from the evidence he saw that the men fought dismounted. Quite likely, Freeman saw expended government cartridges at intervals suggesting pedestrian skirmishing, or at least a pattern not likely to result from Indian firing.

If this is what Freeman observed, and there appear to be no alternatives, then his observations accord well with pertinent warrior accounts. The fire that Runs the Enemy and Two Moons described almost certainly came from skirmish formations. The line probably faced southwestward for Two Moons recalled that, after his confrontation, he turned to his left and rode down the valley. Some of the government bullets found on The Flats undoubtedly came from E Company skirmishing. But orientations of other bullets on The Flats suggest firing from farther down Cemetery Ridge. Perhaps Freeman saw evidence for skirmishing at the Cemetery Ridge position—the one indicated by Map 1008—

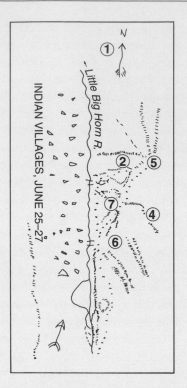

Fig. 11-5. Capt. Henry Freeman's sketch of his observations at Custer battlefield. It shows cavalry action low on Cemetery Ridge (#1, adjacent to top north arrow). Position #6 is Medicine Tail Coulee, #5 is Custer Hill, #4 is Calhoun Hill, #7 is Deep Ravine, "a pocket in which 28 bodies were found." Freeman noted in reference to his map that at #1, #2, and #4, there were indications of dismounted "stand[s]". Adapted from Schneider (1977:225).

occupied earlier by the entire left wing as it delayed. Whatever the case, the widespread distribution of carbine bullets on The Flats could have come only from stable units exercising prescribed tactics. And that, from all the evidence, occurred only on Cemetery Ridge.

Iron Hawk watched at least part of the skirmishing. He had entered the battlefield at the mouth of Deep Ravine. As he proceeded toward Custer Hill, Iron Hawk stopped and watched a daring Cheyenne draw some of the Cemetery Ridge fire. The Cheyenne made several passes, but the troopers failed to hit him. He was bulletproof, Iron Hawk thought. After this, Iron Hawk stood there for "a long time." Then he looked farther up the ridge and saw the gray horses stampeding.[56] Whether the bulletproof Cheyenne dared the left wing in its original Cemetery Ridge position (where the left wing delayed) or dared only E Company after redeployment is not known. Possibly the left wing redeployed during the "long time," though Iron Hawk does not mention it. But E Company had lost its horses now.

Ultimately, gray horses either died or fell into the hands of Indians. Joseph White Cow Bull, like Iron Hawk, saw the daring Cheyenne rush around the soldiers and return unharmed.[57] "A long time" after this brave deed, as just noted, Iron Hawk saw the gray horses break away.[58] Cheyenne oral tradition also includes this stampede.[59] Bobtail Horse, in the words of George Bird Grinnell, recalled that "some of the gray horse company horses got away from the soldiers."[60] White Bull[61] thought that the soldiers let the animals go, which is reasonable, since the Indians had identified horse holders as primary targets.

Lone Bear, in fact, recalled that warriors at times got close enough to separate horses from the unlucky soldiers.[62] White Shield told Grinnell that the gray horse company "held their horses to the last."[63] But here White Shield cannot be taken literally; rather, E Company was among the last to lose its horses. His statement is similar to Two Moons's observation that the "soldiers with the gray horses were the last to fall."[64] This is generally true. Soldiers serving with E, after joining F Company and right-wing survivors at Custer Hill, were *among* the last to die. By this time, most of the horses from at least four companies (F Company excepted) ran loose.

Two Eagles saw the gray horses mixed with others of various colors.[65] What he observed were the "last" moments leading to the Custer Hill episode. Two Eagles was southeast of Calhoun Hill as the right wing disintegrated and could not have seen the original left-wing deployment on Cemetery Ridge. But after chasing fleeing soldiers through the Keogh sector, he came on the "gray horse" company, who by now had lost their mounts. This indicates that pressure on the left wing, or at least on E Company, mounted fairly quickly after the right wing disintegrated.

The timing of the gray horse loss can be worked out, at least approximately. The stampede came at about the time the right wing lost tactical cohesion, or perhaps slightly before. The Cheyennes recorded the stampede in their tradition and remembered that all this happened near the end of the battle. The "suicide boys," a group of young Sioux warriors who allegedly sacrificed their lives that day for the cause, collected on Cemetery Ridge near the national cemetery site. From there, they raced toward E Company, some concentrating on the soldiers while others set about dispersing the grays—"which by then were mostly loose."[66] The young men continued over Custer Ridge into the Keogh sector. Here the suicide warriors are credited with cutting off right-wing soldiers fleeing north toward Custer Hill. Their sudden appearance, as tradition relates, forced some from the right wing to head down the east slope of Custer Ridge (north in the Cheyenne directional scheme).[67] Then the suicide boys moved in for hand-to-hand combat. Two Cheyennes riding with the suicide warriors died in the Keogh sector.[68]

Of course, many other warriors in the Keogh sector engaged in closeup fighting—including those who had initiated the rout of C and L companies. And the traditional account tends to obscure the confusion generated by right-wing remnants in flight. Like the tradition, Runs the Enemy remembered those who fled down the eastern slope (probably those buried at the Keogh cluster of markers), but he also noted that some soldiers crested the ridge while still others made it to Custer Hill.[69] When the suicide boys appeared, the right wing had already fallen apart. The dire predicament perhaps sparked the so-called suicide attack. Or possibly we can consider the timing fortuitous. In any case, the incident served to isolate the two wings and evidently helped prevent many right-wing soldiers from reaching their comrades farther north. Driven by Indians at their rear, the soldiers now suddenly faced warriors in front of them. Very likely, this pincerlike move isolated those who died in the Keogh cluster and may well have caused four troopers to try to escape to the south.

Curiously, Sioux tradition does not mention the suicide element. Yet warrior societies could encourage pledges of stalwart commitment in battle. Perhaps the Cheyenne references to the suicide attack represent an embellishment of such dedication among Sioux that day. Nevertheless, the assault lumped under the "suicide" rubric occurred and included more than just the 20 or so suicide warriors. Two Moons and his outfit participated as well. After helping in the Reno engagement, Two Moons had rushed back to the Cheyenne circle at the northernmost end of the village.[70] From here, he eventually joined Sioux and Cheyenne who rushed beyond the village and then came from the north "up the valley" to block, as he viewed it, any further northward advances. Two Moons's contingent confronted the soldiers with gray horses, which "were all in the open." Like the suicide boys, these warriors spilled over to the east side of Custer Ridge, there joining warriors fighting among right-wing troops.[71] It is here that we earlier picked up Two Moons, who again confronted the gray horse soldiers but could not dent the line. E Company, despite the loss of horses, held firm in the wake of the rupture in right-wing stability.

All of this, from Calhoun Ridge to Cemetery Ridge, shattered the lengthy period of relative calm that had persisted since the wings had separated much earlier. The new developments must have come—as is characteristic of demoralization through shock—suddenly, virtually without warning, and with great surprise, for evidently the left-wing reserve still occupied the basin. Cheyenne tradition relates that when the suicide boys crashed through, soldiers held positions "near the monument site [Custer Hill], with a number of them in the ravine."[72] The references, of course, are to Companies E (near monument) and F (ravine or basin).

So here F Company surfaces, but only momentarily, before sinking again into obscurity. We do know, however, that the company eventually reached Custer Hill. Lieutenant Godfrey counted 39 dead horses there. Some were grays,[73] and a few probably straggled in from the Keogh sector.[74] But most of them likely belonged to the troopers of F, who until now had not been exposed to the Indian tactics. More conclusive are the reports of many corpses of F Company enlisted men on Custer Hill, including the two officers. The F Company remains, those identified by name or unit, represented about half of the 38-man company strength[75] and two-thirds of the 30 or so men (excluding civilians) identified among the swollen, disfigured bodies on and about the prominence. (More than 40 dead lay on Custer Hill, but we do not have identifications for all.) In any case, those identified, which included General Custer and the regimental staff, clearly show that F Company eventually moved as a body to this location.

But how did the two units composing the left wing consolidate on Custer Hill? One of White Bull's accounts bears significantly on this question.[76] Recall how, according to White Bull, the Indians drove the first bunch (C and L companies) and the second (I Company) to the third bunch on Custer Hill (see fig. 10-1). White Bull said that after the fight, he saw General Custer's body in this "third bunch," which he (or his recorder, Stanley Vestal) sometimes refers to as the "third company." The third company in White Bull's scheme is thus F, plus the regimental staff. But White Bull mentioned four "companies." The fourth he identified as the one with gray horses, or E Company. His sketch (fig. 10-1) places E Company below Custer Hill on Cemetery Ridge.[77] White Bull saw (or later learned) that "the fourth comp[any] went to the third co[mpany] in the draw and they don't go any farther [south]."[78] This reflects an assumption that the entire left wing intended to join the right—farther to the south but now in flight. The draw, of course, is the Deep Ravine basin. White Bull makes it clear that E Company by now had lost its grays.

Evidently F Company, functioning primarily in a reserve role, had remained in the basin since arriving. During this time its presence likely discouraged Sioux and Cheyenne from approaching the wing via Deep Ravine. Iron Hawk, in fact, indicated that the Hunkpapa warriors stayed in the lower reaches of the ravine until the gray horse stampede. Only then did they move up.[79] This is entirely consistent with Cheyenne tradition—not until after the suicide attack, which incorporated the gray horse stampede, did warriors move in.[80] Before this, the Indians here, like those harassing the right wing, had generally remained at bay, and probably for good reason. The left wing, after its delay low on Cemetery Ridge, had earlier made a show of force by moving over to Deep Ravine and then up the drainage into the basin.

But now the calm had snapped. E Company (White Bull's fourth company) left Cemetery Ridge under great pressure and went into the basin to join F. The left wing, evidently still intact but severely harried, remained together in the basin for an indeterminate period. The soldiers probably spent an exceedingly short time there, for the situation now doubtless loomed desperate. Pressure on the left wing had increased considerably. The suicide warriors and others had struck. Emboldened by the gray horse stampede, Hunkpapas lower in Deep Ravine moved up. And as we know from Indian cartridge case pathways, other warriors who were released as Keogh's right wing burst now poured into the Deep Ravine area from the Calhoun sectors. Moreover, the right wing was in total disarray, and warriors advanced from the direction of Calhoun Hill. The command was virtually surrounded by a now highly aggressive foe.

We know that the left wing eventually made Custer Hill. The impetus to do so quite likely came from right-wing survivors. Runs the Enemy recounted that some troopers ran into the Keogh sector, others crested Custer Ridge and ran to the west, and still "others came back to where the final stand was made on the [Custer] hill, but they were few in number then. The soldiers *then* gathered in a group, where the monument now stands [Custer Hill]."[81]

A few right-wing survivors reached Custer Hill. Then the left wing joined the survivors, all gathering "in a group." Seemingly, left-wing elements had not occupied Custer Hill, the so-called last stand area, before this. Nor had they been grouped. Runs the Enemy knew this, for he had earlier attacked the left-wing deployment (his "line") on Cemetery Ridge.[82] Runs the Enemy recorded pretty much the same account as White Bull.

Just how the left wing deployed to Custer Hill can be deduced from another of White Bull's observations. After an undetermined length of time in the basin, "[t]he fourth Company [E] start[ed] to run toward the [Custer] hill [and] most of them don't get to the top and they lay down and start shoting [*sic*]."[83]

Here F Company is again obscured by the gray horse troop. My feeling is that F Company troopers, still with their mounts, rode up Custer Hill to intercept right-wing survivors. Slowed by the loss of horses earlier, E Company followed but lagged behind, perhaps covering the F Compay departure. Clearly the left wing had abandoned the basin. Yet they probably did not do so before some right-wing troopers fleeing the Keogh sector, those that Two Eagles, White Bull, and Runs the Enemy described, began spilling over Custer Ridge in hopes of joining their comrades. If any made it, they went along with the left wing up Custer Hill.[84]

So, E Company struggled up Custer Hill on foot, evidently after F had attained the height. But before getting completely to the top ("most of them don't get to the top"), the gray horse troopers took up prone positions on the hill slope and began firing. This area is recognized archaeologically as the west slope of Custer Hill and is now denoted by various marble markers, some of which are shown in figure 6-7. White Bull said "most" lay down. Perhaps the few who did not sprawl on the hillside continued to the top. Presumably they there joined troopers from F bracing for anticipated threats from many directions and perhaps receiving the final few right-wing survivors. Or possibly a few E Company men died in the trek from the basin.

Now the left wing, the regimental staff, and some survivors from the right lay tightly bunched on the hill today bearing General Custer's name. The E Company position on the west slope, though exposed, was about the best that could be expected under the now critical circumstances. This position afforded resistance, certainly poor yet the best possible, against warriors streaming up Deep Ravine and along Cemetery Ridge. We must assume that troopers from F lay above, near the hill crest, there defending against warriors in eastern and northern positions. In effect, each company covered the other's rear—to use military terminology.

Thus ended the Cemetery Ridge episode. Lights, who watched first from north of Cemetery Ridge and then moved into the Deep Ravine area, gave Walter Camp a short account of the final moments. Though at first glance cryptic, the narrative is only superficially so when understood within the context of left-wing operations during the Cemetery Ridge episode, an episode that for more than a century has gone unrecognized. "One company had gray horses, in the retreat around to about K [Keogh sector, see fig. 9-2] they were in the fighting front, at that point they were mixed up with the other horses. At this point the company's [sic] would alternate in covering the retreat of the others."[85]

One company (E) had gray horses. It, so far as Lights knew, was the battalion "fighting" front on Cemetery Ridge. Either he had not seen Company F or he recognized it was not actively engaged. At the time the right wing fled through the Keogh sector, E Company lost its horses, and the grays began to mix with other riderless steeds. After E Company soldiers lost their mounts, the two left-wing units alternated in covering the right-wing flight and their own move to Custer Hill. E Company, because of its nearby position, first covered the right-wing rout as best it could. Increased pressure, and the loss of horses, soon forced E to join F Company, which in turn departed and rode up the hill. Then E Company made it to the prominence. Thus it appeared to Lights, quite correctly, that the two companies "would alternate" in covering "the retreat of the others [i.e., the right wing]."

Moreover, E Company men evidently covered themselves in their move to

Custer Hill. Cheyenne tradition describes prone soldiers covering men as they advanced. At the same time, troopers fired from behind dead horses.[86] Tradition attributes this event to E Company during its earlier movement from the basin to Cemetery Ridge. But here the chronology is confused. Tradition is actually referring to the later move of Company E to join F. Thus Lights's remembrances, and the traditional story, suggest a calculated and orderly response by the left wing to the new, sudden, and now ominous developments.

Thus, in synopsis, the left wing, largely if not entirely intact, eventually retired to Custer Hill, where it received right-wing survivors. Evidently the left wing, after the right-wing collapse, had deployed without serious threat on Cemetery Ridge. Indeed, it had gone to the river and returned, then deployed in accordance with prescribed tactics—one company in reserve and the other on a battle line. Meantime, the right wing had at first maintained the same tactical posture—L on the firing line and Companies C and I in reserve. Relative calm had prevailed. But right-wing disintegration changed everything, plunging the battalion into crisis. Very shortly thereafter, pressure on E Company increased, guaranteeing the loss of horses and precipitating an influx of now emboldened warriors. In an instant, from retrospect, all was lost. Yet it appears that the left wing, as a whole, replied with a tactical acumen sufficient to consolidate the shattered battalion. On the hill, however, all hopes of an offensive thrust had vanished. Cohesion must have suffered in the face of the now critical circumstances. Despite this, officers evidently restored a measure of control, for E Company eventually deployed off the hill. This maneuver, however, ended up woefully unsuccessful, as shall be explained. But first, we turn to the most celebrated of all the battle sectors—Custer Hill.

12

THE CUSTER HILL EPISODE

Q. How long did the fight last on [Custer Hill]?
A. Just a few minutes.
　　—Hollow Horn Bear's response to Walter Camp's query[1]

As battalion unity eroded, slightly less than half the men who had ridden into battle congregated at the knoll bearing General Custer's name. These included the left-wing troopers serving E and F companies, plus the regimental staff, numbering about 82. Judging from markers (corrected for pairing errors and known spurious markers) at the Keogh and all three Calhoun sectors, close to 100 of the estimated 120 right-wing soldiers died at locations other than Custer Hill. The remaining 20 or so reached the hillock, bringing the total there to about 102. Although of necessity an approximation (but one that conveys the gravity of the situation), the size of this gathering is consistent with Two Moons's estimate that about 105 troopers banded together on the prominence.[2] As I shall explain momentarily, however, not all of these soldiers remained on Custer Hill until the end.

Observers after the fight took great pains to identify officers. They found General Custer's body atop the elevation later named for him. Because of a massive memorial obelisk that stands there today (shown in fig. 6-6), Custer Hill is also known as Monument Hill.[3] The general's adjutant, Lt. William Cooke, lay there too,[4] as did another member of headquarters staff, Trumpeter Henry Voss.[5] The regimental sergeant major, William Sharrow, may also have been on the hill.[6] Captain Custer lay near his brother George, as did, probably, Sgt. Robert Hughes of the staff.[7]

Very likely, civilians with the battalion, and its surgeon, accompanied the staff. Of these five, three died on Custer Hill, including Boston Custer—George and Tom's young brother—and the general's nephew, Armstrong Reed.[8] The body of Dr. George Lord, an assistant surgeon, evidently lay on the hillside, probably with his hospital orderly, an enlisted man named John Callahan.[9] In all, 10 of some dozen persons with headquarters evidently died on and around the elevation, except for the scout Mitch Bouyer and the correspondent Mark Kellogg.

Most of those scattered about the general could be recognized, at the least, as personnel who served with F Company. Pvt. Edwin Pickard, a member of F, fought with Reno. He viewed the knoll after the fight, later recalling that a "group" of F Company soldiers lay on the slopes.[10] Dennis Lynch, another Reno battle survivor, also reported, without establishing personal identities, that 14 F Company enlisted men lay around General Custer.[11] Others of F could be recognized by name, including the commanding officer, Capt. George Yates, and his subordinate, Lt. William Reily.[12]

F Company enlisted men identified in the sector included Sgt. John Vickory,[13] Cpl. William Tieman (or Teeman), and Pvt. Gustav Klein.[14] Pvt. Werner Lieman, another member of Yates's company, also lay dead on the hill, as evidently did Pvt. William Lerock, Private Pickard's "bunkie."[15] Lynch told Walter Camp that he had seen or heard of a man named Donovan at this location.[16] Donovan is not listed on the regimental roles for June 1876.[17] Quite possibly Lynch meant Pvt. Anton Dohman, who is listed with F Company. In any case, identification of the two officers, probably a sergeant, a corporal, and perhaps 17 others establishes beyond doubt the presence of F Company as a unit on the hill in this sector. In addition, most staff personnel were there also, and they rode with the left wing.

Of additional enlisted soldiers around the so-called last stand area, a few identities are known. Two men were privates from I Company (John Parker and Edward Driscoll), and two more were from L Company (Francis Hughes and Thomas Tweed).[18] The only E Company body identified on Custer Hill belonged to its commander, Lieutenant Smith.[19] Lieutenant Godfrey might have seen the body of Ignatz Stungewitz, a C Company private, although that is not certain.[20] Otherwise, the only C Company body recognized on the hill was that of Captain Custer, the company commander, but he probably accompanied the headquarters staff on June 25.

Compared with the number of staff members and F Company personnel at Custer Hill, the relatively few bodies from C, I, and L Companies (those identified by name anyway) suggest that not many right-wing cavalrymen survived the earlier assaults and subsequent flight. This observation is in keeping with the calculations offered above. The near absence of E Company men can be linked to the South Skirmish Line episode—the next topic of discussion (chapter 13). In this episode, E Company rushed from the hill, but obviously without Lieutenant Smith, who was evidently then either dead or incapacitated.

Red Cloud recalled that the men who made it to the elevation gathered in a "bunch" after dismounting, "kneeling down and shooting from behind their horses."[21] The horses he spoke of doubtless belonged principally to F Company, for E Company troopers had by now lost most of theirs, as had the right-wing fugitives. Red Cloud's term *bunch* surely refers to the bunching behavior sug-

Fig. 12-1. Western slope of Custer Hill, with stone memorials. The granite obelisk is at the hill apex. Today the obelisk fence is absent, and the markers are enclosed instead. Photograph by Joseph Dixon, 1909. Courtesy Custer Battlefield National Monument (#2468).

gested by markers clustered around the knoll, specifically those now dotting the western slope. They are visible in figure 12-1, a photograph of Custer Hill before the erection of an ornate iron fence around all the memorial stones there (compare with figure 6-6). He Dog hinted at the state of confusion on the field: "gray horses got . . . all mixed up with the others."[22] Turtle Rib, Tall Bull, and Flying By told Camp virtually the same story.[23]

It is appropriate to recall here that aside from the grays of E Company, sorrels were ridden by C Company and bays by F, I, and L.[24] White Bull observed Monument Hill after the battle, noting the carcasses of "sorrels, bay[s] and whites [i.e., grays]."[25] Foolish Elk recalled that after the cavalry mounts of various colors intermingled, including some grays, a great deal of confusion developed among the soldiers.[26] Evidently the disorganization and chaos rampant in the right wing had spread to the left.

When Walter Camp asked where the soldiers had put up the stiffest fight, Hollow Horn Bear diplomatically noted that the soldiers had resisted as hard at the Custer Hill sector as at any other place.[27] Two Eagles, responding to another of Camp's written queries, is recorded as saying that there was a "firm stand" at the hill.[28] But the question put to him—was this the only firm stand?—is blatantly leading. Camp's questions, however, leave little doubt that Two Eagles, when answering, referred to differences between resistance at the hill (from stationary troops) and the "moving" action across the Calhoun and Keogh sectors. When asked the same question that Hollow Horn Bear answered, Two Eagles replied that the soldiers who had died on Custer's Hill fought "the most stubborn."[29] But considering the preceding developments—particularly in the Keogh sector—this is far from saying that they fought stubbornly.

Runs the Enemy described the death scene, recalling that "soldiers were piled one on top of another, dead, and here and there an Indian among the soldiers."[30] Trooper corpses lay thick.[31] Horses lay on top of men, and men on top of horses.[32] Lieutenant Wallace saw four or five bodies "in a heap," with General Custer lying across one of the men.[33] According to Sergeant Kanipe, dead men were "thick" around the general, falling together in a "little heap."[34] Lieutenant Edgerly, noting the absence of tactical stability, stated that "bodies . . . were lying in irregular positions."[35] Postbattle looting (by Indians) and subsequent burial activity at Custer Hill (and elsewhere) probably disarranged somewhat the original body positions. But even though these disturbances perhaps compromised exact individual positions, they should not be considered sufficient to destroy the overall impression of tactical instability, an impression conveyed by the markers clustered there today.[36] Memorial stones and vivid historical accounts of chaotic scenes seem to invalidate Lt. Edward McClernand's eyewitness claim that bodies on the hill lay arranged in a "half circle convex toward the east."[37]

Most historical descriptions referring to this event are consistent with the archaeological evidence (Indian-delivered bullets) that Indians found their targets within a quite small defense perimeter. Also consistent is the restricted distribution of .45/55 cartridge cases. All of this points to an erosion of tactical stability among the troops bunched there. Claims for elaborate breastworks of dead horses, breastworks that portray or imply a coordinated defense,[38] seem grossly exaggerated.

Yet it can hardly be doubted that desperate soldiers sought protection behind their dead horses.[39] Wooden Leg said his brethren seldom actually saw soldiers on the slopes above them but knew where to fire because of the sprawled mounts.[40] Colonel Gibbon saw scattered dead mounts—numerous, he said—on the southwestern slope[41] (more properly the western slope, where the markers are now). Charles Roe, another eyewitness, remembered that this incline was dotted with 25 men and numerous steeds, all mixed up.[42] The same scene met Lieutenant Edgerly, who saw many enlisted men and horses on the hillside.[43]

The hill peak drew the attention of some observers after the battle. DeRudio, during his inspection, found empty cartridge cases and five or six horses at the very top, the horses "laying as if to suggest a barricade."[44] McClernand saw horse remains at the apex in a 30-foot diameter circle, "evidently used . . . as breastworks."[45] Some other white accounts speak of only several to a half dozen or so dead mounts on the top.[46]

Actually, the use of animal carcasses for protection seems to have been more a matter of expediency than deliberate arrangement. Other eyewitnesses, cognizant of the claims for a coordinated defense, saw little or no patterning in horse bodies.[47] Sergeant Kanipe said that he viewed horses "scattered all over the hill."[48] Lieutenant Wallace knew of talk about breastworks, but he did not see convincing evidence of such.[49] Pvt. William Slaper left the impression that each man, where he could, opportunistically secreted himself behind a slain beast.[50] Indeed, postbattle appearances about the hill evidently allowed one to discern just about any imaginable pattern. This is a characteristic typical of nonpatterned, or random, distributions.

Horse and human corpses at the apex and just below do, however, indicate attempts to cover threats from several directions. I noted this possibility—originally an archaeological deduction—in discussing the Cemetery Ridge episode; F Company first took the hill peak and E the slope. But Lieutenant DeRudio thought that the horses—sorrels, he remembered—found on top of the knoll belonged to C Company personnel.[51] This is certainly possible; the hilltop provided a direct route for frightened right-wing soldiers to reach their comrades. Those afoot were less likely to escape the Keogh sector melee than were those who had somehow managed to mount a horse.

During early stages of this episode, surrounding warriors operated with considerable stealth. Finally they did rush in, but only after attrition had taken its toll on the defenders. The bulk of Indian activity constituted more a siege, albeit a brief one, than an assault. Kate Bighead described the furtive warrior tactics, which hardly varied throughout the whole battle. "The warriors . . . were shifting from shelter to shelter, each . . . trying to get close enough to strike a coup blow . . . upon a living enemy." She noted that Indian heads would pop up quickly and then jerk down again.[52]

Wooden Leg, having witnessed the episode, recalled a great many warriors "creeping" around the soldiers.[53] Like Bighead, he noted that the Indians remained hidden except to spring up and shoot. Vegetation had grown thick that year,[54] and in swales and gullies below Custer Ridge, the soon-to-be victors found luxuriant grasses tall enough to hide in.[55] Years later Bighead commented, "The soldiers must have seen many of these heads, but they must have been puzzled as to which ones to shoot at."[56] Most Indian targets "disappeared before a rifle could take aim."[57] These accounts suggest that the fleeting Indian targets drew a desultory fire. Extant archaeological data from the sector, particularly the small number of spent .45/55 casings, do not detract from these and similar accounts, but they do dispute stories of hard fighting amid a barrage of lead from soldiers' pieces.

Testimony provided by Lieutenant DeRudio during the Reno inquiry is revealing in this regard. Referring to the Custer Hill locality, he remembered noticing only a few shells there.[58] The lieutenant, reflecting an official concern of the army during the western Indian wars period, thought maybe the Indians had collected empty cartridges.[59] An 1876 general order required men to save casings expended during target shooting.[60] The army believed that Indians, thought to be adept at reloading, might pirate empties. The directive optimistically required that those casings expended in battle be collected as well. Of course, this did not happen at the Custer battlefield; much more pressing, somber tasks loomed. And there is really little likelihood that the victors collected spent shells, particularly with plenty, even thousands, of live rounds available. If the Indians did collect empties, assuming the worst of variables an archaeologist might encounter, they swept clean some parts of the field and not others, leaving artifact patterns that nicely match their own descriptions of the action. Clearly, DeRudio's observations at the knoll closely conform with the nature of fighting described by Indians and with the archaeological record.

In this siege phase of Custer's last battle, brief as it was, "the Indians all took cover and kept shooting."[61] But the end was near. Young warriors, from time to time, had been dashing up to count coup on the soldiers.[62] After chasing a soldier fleeing from Custer Hill, Turtle Rib returned, at the close of the struggle, to find some troopers firing pistols at close-up Indians.[63] The "waiting soon brought silence."[64] Soldiers stopped firing.[65] The silence seemed to convince the warriors that everyone on the hill was dead,[66] and they rushed in.[67]

But a few cavalrymen still clung to life, and they resisted with pistols, although as Cheyenne oral tradition puts it, there was no time to reload.[68] Runs the Enemy[69] and Waterman[70] helped dispatch the few remaining soldiers. The Indians apparently carried out much of the last killing with clubs and hatchets.[71] Standing Bear recalled, "The soldiers and Indians were all mixed up and there were . . . many guns going off."[72]

At the end, the Indians' frenzy provided a spectacle of fury, more from emotion than from intense combat.[73] The natives, after all, were about to savor their greatest triumph. Emotion was probably what Thunder Hawk's wife saw when she described "quite a fight" at this stage in the events.[74] She had watched from the village. When the Indians finally did surmount the hill, most soldiers were dead or wounded; those still alive were quickly killed. Certainly there is

Custer Monument— ... ... north north

Fig. 12-2. View of Custer Ridge looking north from near Calhoun Hill. Custer Hill is in the distance (at horizon, slightly right of center). The dirt road along the ridge is now a one-lane pavement. Some Keogh sector memorial stones can be seen at far right. Photograph and notations by Frank L. Anders, ca. 1932. Courtesy University of North Dakota (Anders Papers, Elwyn B. Robinson Department of Special Collections, Chester Fritz Library).

neither archaeological nor historical evidence of a swirling, furious finale to the Custer battle—no famous last stand—and as we shall see, the Monument Hill area did not even see the last of the fighting.

Hollow Horn Bear had the impression that the struggle on the hill lasted only "a few minutes."[75] No doubt the final rush was short—there was not much to overrun—but the siege probably lasted a bit longer. Though brief in its entirety—measurable in minutes—danger on the hill, nothing more than a rise at the end of Custer Ridge (see fig. 12-2), loomed quite real throughout. At some point quite early in the episode, about 45 troopers, mostly members of E Company, suddenly dashed downhill toward Little Big Horn River.[76] Their actions constituted what is now called the South Skirmish Line episode. This event accounts for the lack of E Company bodies, with the exception of Lieutenant Smith, identified on the hill.

But others fled at the very end—when it became clear that the warriors would overrun the position. Several doomed troopers evidently bolted to the south, running just beneath the crest of Custer Ridge on its west side.[77] A line of marble markers just below the ridge crest, from 600 to 1,300 feet south of the memorial obelisk, may denote this incident (see fig. 6-8). And like E Company earlier, still others raced down the slope toward the river. White Bull estimated 10;[78] Wooden Leg counted no more than seven.[79] They probably related two separate events. Whatever the number, the last of the men on the hill fled, some after others, hoping to join vestiges of E Company in the Deep Ravine area. Big Beaver had joined the rush on Custer Hill. He remembered that no soldiers remained standing but that "some" lying prone or sitting up did fire. As this episode concluded, Big Beaver recalled, 15 or 20 troopers jumped up and began to run down Deep Ravine.[80] There in the ravine, each of the few men still alive, struggled on his own. These were the only soldiers still alive, and White Bull helped kill them.[81]

Thus, of the 102 or so men originally involved in the episode, about 45 departed early on, this leaving some 57 on Custer Hill, most of them to endure there until the end came. Besides those involved in the South Skirmish Line episode, perhaps 15 other troopers attempted to flee at various times, understandably putting behind them their dead, dying, and doomed comrades—some 40 men in all.[82] Lieutenant Godfrey[83] and Pvt. Thomas Coleman[84] counted 42 bodies on and about Custer Hill several days after the battle, and this figure is generally regarded as accurate. Other estimates place the body count at 40 to 50.[85] The lowest guess I have seen is 30 to 40 corpses.[86]

13

THE SOUTH SKIRMISH LINE EPISODE

*[The soldiers] at Custer Hill were all killed before those were
down along the ravine.*

—Respects Nothing[1]

Data derived from material remains dispute widely accepted ideas about the South Skirmish Line episode. So does history, when viewed through archaeology. All things considered, then, the action here should be called the Deep Ravine episode, but I shall retain the more familiar term. The story starts on Custer Hill.

Two Moons estimated that about 100 men eventually congregated on this hillock. Finally, according to Two Moons, 5 horsemen and about 40 men on foot started toward the river.[2] Many other Indians witnessed the event, Lone Bear and Two Eagles among them. Two Eagles thought that all the soldiers were dismounted.[3] These men, White Bull implied, rushed on foot from the hill; he noted that the fourth company (E Company, see fig. 10-1) "run [*sic*] from the third company [F]."[4] White Bull had seen his fourth company join the third on Custer Hill, and now he saw it vacate the elevation.

Iron Hawk had watched from the lower reaches of Deep Ravine for a long while as the left wing maneuvered on Cemetery Ridge. After the gray horse stampede, as he called it, he went up with friends toward Custer Hill. The soldiers, now confined to the rise, fired. According to White Bull, this was a fierce fire that caused the warriors to take cover.[5] Iron Hawk and his friends scurried back. Then suddenly the yell went up, "Now they have gone." Iron Hawk looked up and saw that "the soldiers all were running toward the Hunkpapas [Sioux] on foot. . . . The Hunkpapas said: 'Hokahey!' and charged at them. The soldiers were running downhill and the Hunkpapas were charging. When they saw us, the soldiers swung down. . . . The Hunkpapas ran right up to the soldiers and encircled them from all sides."[6]

Instead of "all" soldiers on Custer Hill, Iron Hawk had witnessed the E Company rush off the knoll (see fig. 11-4). In a pattern reminiscent of the C Company excursion earlier, the warriors backed off, regrouped, and then attacked. Flight carried the soldiers not to Little Big Horn River but to the ravine at its eroded headwall. Standing Bear said they went "into the side of a hill into a draw," where they tried to hide in tall grass.[7] According to Iron Hawk, the soldiers kept going until they reached "a little creek [i.e., Deep Ravine]."[8] Tall Bull and others manned positions at the head of the gulch; the soldiers on foot ran right through them into the gully, where they were killed.[9] Lights also saw this: "some . . . jumped over the high banks."[10] He Dog and Good Voiced Elk watched the soldiers as well.[11] Many "jumped over the steep bank into this gully."[12] White Bull recalled that the soldiers "were killed down in the draw, the last one . . . close to the river."[13] Little Big Horn River as viewed from Custer Hill is shown in figure 13-1; the route these soldiers took—the South Skirmish Line—is marked by white stones in the middle ground.

General Miles heard the same story from several unidentified warriors while at the site two years after the battle.[14] The troopers rushed over the South Skirmish Line, their momentum carrying them to the ravine head, where most died. A few others died farther west and nearer the river along the south bank of the ravine.[15] But as a body, the men appear not to have stopped en route. The rugged, brush-infested coulee, portions of which are pictured near midcourse in figures 13-2, 13-3, and 13-4, seemed to provide the only hope for safety.

Military men who examined the aftermath identified many, if not most, of the soldiers in the deep gulch as members of E Company. Augustus Devoto, a B Company private who survived the Reno-Benteen siege, remembered there were members of E Company among the dead.[16] And so did Lieutenant DeRudio, an E Company officer attached to Major Reno's command.[17] Capt. Thomas McDougall, on three separate occasions that I know of, stated that he found most of E Company in or near the ravine.[18] The captain, who had formerly commanded the company, could identify by name only a few of the swollen, disfigured bodies.

Presumably, company insignia helped McDougall recognize men from his old unit. Also, dead gray horses (E Company) found in the ravine vicinity may have influenced these men in their identifications. Horses, however, are poor indicators of company whereabouts. The grays had been scattered (or lost) before this episode and could have wandered about. Hardorff has suggested that this probability that the horses wandered led eyewitnesses, confounded by featureless bodies, to erroneously assign dead men in the coulee to E Company.[19] To Hardorff, then, E Company did not participate in the South Skirmish Line episode. But this cannot be true. E Company bodies on Custer Hill are conspicuously underrepresented, and eyewitnesses did not report E Company men anywhere else on the battlefield. These considerations, plus personal identifications by eyewitnesses, suggest that E Company men were, in fact, deeply involved in the South Skirmish Line episode. But primary historical evidence viewed in

Fig. 13-1. View of the South Skirmish Line sector looking southwest from Custer Hill. The stone memorials in the foreground are on the west hillside. The small flags among stones are metal-detector find spots located during the 1984–85 archaeological project. South Skirmish Line stones are seen as small dots running diagonally to Deep Ravine. The ravine mouth is slightly left of photo center at the forested Little Big Horn Valley. Custer battlefield archaeological project (1984–85) photograph. Courtesy Midwest Archeological Center.

Fig. 13-2. A portion of Deep Ravine along its middle reach. The denuded brush is the result of the 1983 range fire. Custer battlefield archeological project (1984–85) photograph. Courtesy Midwest Archeological Center.

Fig. 13-3. Looking up (east) Deep Ravine from near its mouth. Custer ridge is at the horizon; junction of Calhoun Coulee is just below. The 1984 archaeological crew is conducting tests. The absence of brush is due to a 1983 range fire. Custer battlefield archaeological project (1984–85) photograph. Courtesy Midwest Archeological Center.

Fig. 13-4. A stretch of Deep Ravine along its middle reach from above (looking west toward the river). The archaeological crew is conducting tests. The absence of brush is due to a 1983 range fire. Custer battlefield archaeological project (1984–85) photograph. Courtesy Midwest Archeological Center.

light of archaeological results does not support claims of an orderly skirmish line in this sector. Consequently, the episode is misleadingly named.

Indian accounts are clear: a body of soldiers rushed from the hillock, crossed over the so-called South Skirmish Line, and ended up at Deep Ravine. The soldier accounts just discussed leave some latitude as to the unit identity of this body. But other eyewitness recollections offer more detail. Of the twelve bodies identified either personally or by unit at or near the narrow, deeply cut gully, eight (nearly 67 percent) represented E Company troopers. These were Pvts. William Rees, William Huber, and Richard Farrell, Cpl. Albert Meyer, 1st Sgt. Fred Hohmeyer, two E Company men whose names did not get recorded, and probably Sgt. John Ogden, reportedly buried near the river about a half mile from Custer Hill.[20]

No soldiers from C or I Company were identified by person; only two came from F Company,[21] one from L Company,[22] and possibly Sergeant Hughes from the regimental staff.[23] Though not every corpse could be identified, knowledgeable eyewitnesses at the least reported E Company there. These historical circumstances support the presence of E Company as a body in this sector.

The soldiers that Good Voiced Elk saw jump into the deep channel all died there. He estimated that there were from 25 to 30 men.[24] Other estimates range from 20[25] to 50.[26] During the Reno inquiry, eyewitnesses produced various estimates. Lts. Luther Hare and Edward Maguire recalled 28 dead men.[27] Captain Benteen thought there were 22, and Captain Moylan saw "20 odd" men.[28]

McDougall, Lieutenant Godfrey, and McClernand all used the number 28 in later interviews or articles.[29] Walter Camp believed that He Dog's testimony corroborated the existence of 28 dead men in the ravine.[30] So 28 became the acceptable figure among scholarly and military circles, probably with good reason. Lieutenant Hare had helped to bury the bodies.[31] And Lieutenant Maguire, who mapped the battlefield site, had probably accurately counted the bodies because he reported the specific figure within a week of the battle.[32] Captain Freeman recorded a figure of 28 within four days of the event and Lt. Holmes O. Paulding within 13 days.[33] Twenty-eight is less than the 34 bodies allegedly observed by Lt. Richard Thompson.[34] But Sergeant Kanipe, another eyewitness, also claimed that 28 men lay dead in the gully.[35]

Captain McDougall supervised interments around the South Skirmish Line sector. In 1879, he recalled that half the bodies were found in the ravine and half "on a line outside [of the ravine]."[36] Later, in 1909, McDougall remembered that he found most bodies in the gulch and that "only a few men were found on the ground from the extension of the ravine," that is, at its headwall.[37] His later recollection is probably correct. There are today 16 markers on "the ground

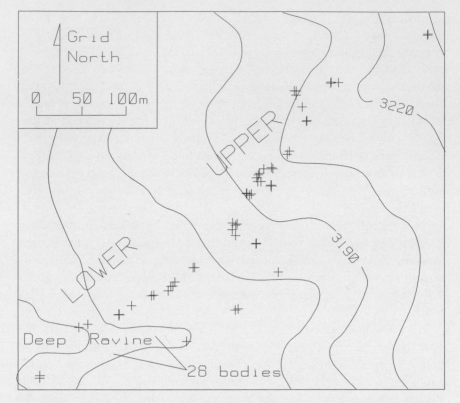

Fig. 13-5. Enlargement of the South Skirmish Line sector depicting marker distributions on the lower and upper segments, and the presumed location of the 28 soldier bodies in Deep Ravine at the ravine headwall.

from the extension of the ravine." They are identified in figure 13-5 as lower-segment markers; the presumed location of the 28 bodies in the deep gully is also depicted.

Lower-segment stones, when corrected for pairing errors, represent the deaths of perhaps 13 soldiers. This line of markers is visible in figure 13-6, where they lead to the edge of Deep Ravine. Archaeological results from two excavated lower-segment markers tend to confirm McDougall's burials on the "line outside" of the ravine. Relatively complete skeletal remains turned up at each location (marker 7 and paired markers 9/10), along with associated buttons, an iron arrowhead, an Indian bullet, and a .45-caliber Colt cartridge case.[38] In figure 13-5, markers 7, 8, and 9/10 are the lower-segment stones closest to Deep Ravine.

In addition to burying men at the lower segment, McDougall interred 28

Fig. 13-6. South Skirmish Line lower segment with stone memorials. View is from a high point along the South Skirmish Line toward the southwest. Deep Ravine is in the background, with the forested river valley at top right. Photograph by Frank L. Anders, ca. 1932. Courtesy University of North Dakota (Anders Papers, Elwyn B. Robinson Department of Special Collections, Chester Fritz Library).

bodies in the deep gully portion of the ravine (fig. 13-5).[39] Lieutenant Hare also helped bury the 28 men "in a coulee [i.e., Deep Ravine]"[40] and "a number more about the coulee [i.e., the lower segment]."[41] Contrary to one claim,[42] none of the bodies in the deep portion of the ravine were carried out.[43] So McDougall and Hare probably buried about 13 men in the shallow swale near the headwall (the extension of the ravine, in McDougall's words, or the lower segment, in mine) and 28 more, including at least five E Company troopers identified by name, within the gully (fig. 13-5).

Miller's Indian informant, Eagle Elk, probably recalled the struggle that led to the deaths of the lower-segment men—the "extension of the ravine" (Mc-Dougall) or "about the coulee" (Hare). Eagle Elk described close-up combat with pedestrian soldiers "low on the western slope of [Custer Ridge] . . . in a shallow ravine." At the same time, according to Eagle Elk, troopers remaining on Custer Hill continued to suffer under the siege.[44]

It appears, then, that McDougall, Hare, and others found about 41 bodies near the ravine headwall, 28 in the deep gully and perhaps 13 in the shallow drainage surrounding the gulch. This total corresponds well with Two Moons's and Miles's estimates of the 40 to 45 men in the Custer Hill group who rushed to the ravine vicinity.[45] Moreover, 41 is consistent with Gibbon's claim that he saw 40 to 50 bodies in Deep Ravine, though he apparently mistakenly recalled that all lay in the deep bottom.[46]

Soldiers buried the 28 men by scraping dirt from gully banks onto the bodies below.[47] There were few shovels in the regiment. Augustus Devoto, who helped in the "very gruesome" task, said the grave diggers "just covered them as they laid using a knife to loosen the dirt, and our hands to cover them."[48] Other eyewitnesses also remarked about the shallow burials, not just at Deep Ravine but virtually everywhere on the field.

Most officers in the Reno contingent had a chance to view the carnage. A few thought that the gully position represented a good place to make a stand, though they offered little convincing evidence in support of this idea.[49] Lieutenant Wallace thought that some bodies lay "in skirmish order" but was reluctant to attribute what he saw to an orderly, tactical deployment.[50] This seems reasonable because other officers noted that the soldiers fell in low positions that allowed assaults from several sides.[51] Benteen, McClernand, and Maguire[52] concluded that the men fled into the ravine to hide, an opinion held by a number of Indian eyewitnesses.[53]

Captain Moylan,[54] Sgt. John Ryan,[55] and Trumpeter William Hardy[56] saw scars on the ravine walls, which indicated to them futile attempts to climb out. McDougall, however, interpreted the scarring as evidence that the soldiers had used the steep walls as breastworks while resisting.[57] This is unlikely, since historical accounts suggest hand-to-hand combat in the gully.[58] If fighting occurred in the gulch bottom, troopers there did not likely use the precipitous walls as breastworks. More likely, soldiers marred the banks when they jumped into the channel[59] or in trying to get out.

Body positions best portray the nature of the deaths of the men in the ravine. Walter Camp often used the word *heap* in rendering eyewitness testimony.[60] In one account based on hearsay evidence, Camp reported "twenty bodies in a heap."[61] Camp's method of interviewing possibly influenced the answers he received. Nonetheless, the fact that witnesses found some bodies bunched together appears indisputable. General Terry, in his initial report on the Custer battle, mentioned bodies "heaped in ravines and upon knolls."[62] One of his ravines is presumably the gully under discussion here. Mrs. Kill Assiniboine heard of or saw the Deep Ravine bodies, "some lying on top of each other."[63] Trumpeter Hardy described an equivalent scene.[64] These accounts imply a breakdown in tactical order that culminated in bunching with little or no unified resistance, an expected behavior under the circumstances.

While at the site in 1878, several warriors told General Miles that the group of soldiers who left Custer Hill "first started in the direction of a small ravine" but, faced with strong Indian fire, "swerved toward the head of a neighboring ravine [Deep Ravine]."[65] Iron Hawk remembered that after warriors met the cavalrymen, the troopers "swung down" to the "little creek."[66] Obviously, E Company diverted toward Deep Ravine. According to Standing Bear, "*after* the soldiers went toward the Little Big Horn they went into . . . a draw [i.e., Deep Ravine]."[67] Apparently, the soldiers departed the hill and first headed toward the river; pressured by emboldened warriors, they "swung down" or "swerved," then went to the deeply cut coulee.

The terms *after, swung down,* and *swerved* are interesting. The terminology, from independent accounts, indicates a planned maneuver, something other than an intent to go to Deep Ravine. Further, E Company, though evidently without its commander, undertook this action as a body. These circumstances strongly suggest that despite the deteriorated situation, officers had reestablished some measure of control on Custer Hill. Indeed, Two Moons recalled that a trumpeter (his account says a bugler) blew commands before E Company departed.[68] Perhaps the rush downhill constituted a charge or a clearing party. Surrounding warriors for the most part exercised great caution then. The poverty of Indian cartridge cases suggests that soldiers on the elevation suffered no immediate heavy pressure, at least by firearms (many warriors had bows and arrows).

Nevertheless, officers, now responsible for a shattered command reduced by half its number, surely perceived the threat raised by a multitude of nearby warriors.[69] In the E Company thrust, they must have tried to alleviate their situation by driving Indians away. But the maneuver clearly provoked the Indians (just as did C Company's earlier penetration into Calhoun Coulee). Miles indicated that Cheyennes met the rush of soldiers with a hot fire;[70] Iron Hawk recalled a Sioux charge that carried Indians right into the soldiers.[71] Here is where the plan, whatever the specific intent, went awry. Faced with serious resistance, the soldiers from E Company could only alter their course. Now diverted, they were driven to the ravine headwall vicinity and were encircled. There warriors killed them with arrows, guns, and war clubs.[72]

Some E Company soldiers discarded their carbines in favor of pistols when they left the knoll,[73] whereas others kept their long arms.[74] They did not, however, use the carbines. During the rush, most apparently fired their pistols indiscriminately.[75] He Dog indicated that some troopers feigned death.[76] On another occasion, He Dog[77] recalled that those on foot "took to the gully [while] the mounted ones tried to get away" by skirting Deep Ravine and riding southward up Calhoun Coulee.[78] Iron Hawk[79] described the soldiers as terrified, and Bear Lying Down[80] said, metaphorically, that they acted as if intoxicated. Camp elicited a similar story from Lights, who had been "near enough to look them in the eyes." Lights stated, "The warriors were taking the guns away from the soldiers, also, the soldiers in running away became so demoralized that they would fire their guns in the air making them easy victims when they were caught . . . [and] . . . some of the men running away had revolvers in their belts that were never used."[81]

After querying his informants about this episode, Miller concluded that most of the soldiers put up no fight at all and let themselves be killed.[82] This is hard to imagine, but when soldiers are seized with panic during combat, such behavior is not at all unusual. The soldiers apparently did rush headlong to the ravine without much, if any, resistance; once there, some found themselves confronted face to face.[83] The paucity of .45/55 casings about the gulch and elsewhere on the South Skirmish Line sector complements the historical record in that soldiers clearly did not make much use of the Springfield carbines. In close-up encounters, such as occurred, the single-shot firearm would have been useless. And in any case, the evidence points to panic. Even with appropriate weapons, resistance would probably have been sporadic. This seems to be borne out in the physical record, including that for the Colt sidearm. The virtual absence of pistol casings indicates only brief fighting; if any soldiers resisted, they had little or no time to reload.

Soldier resistance during this episode, for which evidence is mostly absent archaeologically, became a subject of interest during the Reno inquiry. Most witnesses hedged somewhat. McDougall thought that the troopers had resisted "as best they could."[84] DeRudio said that there "seemed to have been resistance there"; it looked as if they had "made a stand for themselves."[85] Lieutenant Hare found several bodies, all shot in the back, in positions that "indicated a regular skirmish order" or "skirmish intervals."[86] These were probably the men McDougall observed "on a line" (the lower segment), a line that he speculated had been arranged by Indian women after the fight.[87]

This line of men, however, could have resulted from attrition during flight rather than skirmishing. This is more consistent with archaeological and historical data, which reveal a brief, haphazard resistance with little or no tactical cohesion. Thus Captain Moylan's deduction is perhaps more realistic. Moylan viewed the line of dead men just outside the deep gully as casualties suffered in retreat, a retreat that carried men into the ravine. Accordingly, he concluded that the "20 odd" men found in the gulch had been "fighting and retreating."[88]

Some officers saw a skirmish line in the scattered bodies; others did not. But we can definitely state several facts regarding the South Skirmish Line episode. Bullets delivered by Indians clearly define the presence of soldiers. The soldiers' appearance in this sector did not constitute a tactical deployment, least of all a skirmish line, even if only briefly. Historical accounts portray a headlong dash through the area, and this meshes with the lack of archaeological evidence (e.g., government cartridge cases) for any significant army resistance. The flight into Deep Ravine is reflected in the tendency for men to bunch together under dire circumstances. All of this reveals tactical disintegration induced by the Indian assault on the company after it left Custer Hill. That much can be deduced with certitude.

The Fallacy of the South Skirmish Line

Precise locations of the 28 dead men in Deep Ravine remain unknown. Most soldiers probably died near the modern headwall (fig. 13-5) just below the line of dead men (lower-segment markers) referred to by McDougall.[89] Archaeological investigations during 1985 employed geomorphological analyses along the gulch to understand the stratigraphic history and, perhaps if lucky, discover bodies. Though unsuccessful in the latter regard, geomorphology results indicate that the 1876 surface deposits along nearly the entire length of the channel, except within several hundred yards of the headwall, are too shallow to conceal interments.[90] It is therefore likely that those historical accounts locating the ravine dead at various downstream locations are incorrect.[91]

In the headwall vicinity, however, the 1876 surface is more than six feet below the present gulch floor and is sufficiently deep to conceal burials. Ravine geomorphology also indicates the presence of a deep, steep-walled, buried gully just below (downstream) the modern headwall. Over the years, sedimentation has filled the channel. Thus, intermittent stream erosion has not been sufficient to significantly disturb the interments. The opposite is true. Today the bodies are buried deeper than originally—in a gully within a gully. Sediments accumulating from headwall erosion have covered and helped to preserve the ossuary site. For those interested, ravine geomorphology and its enlightening revelations are discussed thoroughly elsewhere.[92]

The gully within the gully is described in several historical accounts. According to Captain Freeman, who inspected the battlefield a few days after fighting ended, the upper end of the ravine—very steep, he said—"formed a pocket in which 28 bodies were found."[93] Theodore Goldin, a private at the time, saw the corpses in positions that "proved to them to be a cul-de-sac."[94] The coulee walls, described by Moylan as almost perpendicular, prevented escape.[95] Sergeant Kanipe saw his fallen comrades in the gulch and on the line outside; he fairly correctly estimated their distance from Custer Hill at about 2,000 feet.[96]

Moylan's placement of the remains at a half mile from Little Big Horn River also roughly matches the location of the ravine headwall.[97] Lieutenant Hare's[98] estimate of 300 yards to 400 yards from Custer Hill is too little, the correct distance being something less than 700 yards. Other sources fail to estimate distance. But Lt. John Bourke, on July 21, 1877, did see seven skulls eroding

Fig. 13-7. Upper segment of South Skirmish Line sector depicting some of the stone memorials there. View is to the north. Custer Hill and stones on its western slope are at the horizon, extreme right. Photograph by Charles Kuhlman, 1937. Courtesy Custer Battlefield National Monument (#5993).

from the ravine, at least four of which lay in a cluster.[99] In 1886, James Carroll, an army hospital steward, collected a broken skull from the gulch (the skull is now curated at the Armed Forces Institute of Pathology). After analyzing the skull, military physicians speculated that fracturing occurred when the victim fell into the ravine.[100]

Although it is virtually certain that the ravine burials are near the modern headwall, there are no commemorative markers in place (nor have there ever been). Stone markers intended for these men were originally, and erroneously, placed on the South Skirmish Line (fig. 13-5, upper segment). There are today 36 markers (36 in 1891, 37 ca. 1910) on the upper segment, where McDougall[101] reported from 6 to (less than) 12 bodies (bodies beyond those he buried in and around Deep Ravine). This indicates that from 24 to 30 of the 36 upper-segment marker locations, some of which are shown relative to Custer Hill in figure 13-7, are phony.

Godfrey[102] recalled, without stating a figure, the presence of only a few bodies in this position, and so did Trumpeter William Hardy.[103] Like these two men, Private Goldin remembered "but very few bodies between [Custer] ridge and the river."[104] Sergeant Kanipe repeatedly told Walter Camp, when they together visited the site in 1908, that he believed too many memorial stones stood on the South Skirmish Line.[105] Richard Thompson[106] also remembered the upper-segment bodies, which he thought numbered 9 or 10, a recollection that narrows the bogus markers to 26 or 27.[107] This calculation is consistent with the 28 unmarked corpses concealed in Deep Ravine.

When Captain Sweet finished marking grave sites in 1890, he had 29 marble markers left over. Sweet eventually placed the remaining memorials, though he did not say where, after "additional and trying work . . . to discover and verify the resting places of the 29 missing bodies."[108] Archaeological testing on the South Skirmish Line upper segment (and elsewhere) suggests that postburial disturbances have scattered the poorly buried remains of the 10 or so men originally interred on the upper segment.[109] Very likely, Sweet placed 29 markers at false locations on the upper segment where he found these scattered bone pieces. Sweet, though he had no way of knowing, should have placed the extra markers in the ravine. Thus, there is and never was a skirmish line—the so-called South Skirmish Line—in this sector.

Recognizing that the numbers can vary a bit either way, we can sum the 1890 marker expedition accordingly. Sweet had with him 246 marble markers (probably around 10 too few)—about 44 meant for Reno's dead soldiers (five of Reno's wounded died elsewhere, during evacuation) and the remaining 202 for Custer's dead. Sweet, instead of marking grave sites at the Reno-Benteen battle site, placed all 246 on Custer's field. The captain probably found about 174 graves, but not those in Deep Ravine. Sweet placed markers at the 174 sites and, in the process, probably overlooked a few. In addition, he erroneously set another 43 or so at the single burial sites presently exhibiting paired markers. By now Sweet had erected 217 of the 246 markers, leaving a remainder of 29. After his "additional and trying work," Sweet placed the remainder (28 or 29 by his count) not in the gulch but on the upper segment of the so-called South Skirmish Line. Here, to the best of our knowledge, only 6 to 10 men died.[110]

White Bull recollected the events following the fatal flight of E Company. According to him, "The third company started running down the [Custer] hill."[111] Here White Bull is referring mainly to F Company. But this cannot be correct, since most of the soldiers remaining on the hill after E Company departed had by now died. White Bull's observation is best interpreted to mean the men still alive at his third company position (i.e., Custer Hill, see fig. 10-1). Thus, as Vestal understood, White Bull saw from his position near the deep gully only remnants of the hilltop defenders rush downhill.[112] It is clear they did so while sporadic fighting continued at the ravine.[113]

Stands in Timber related how an undisclosed number of men fled along the ridge crest. Wooden Leg and White Bull remembered that 7 to 17 doomed troopers raced from Custer Hill toward the ravine. These desperate men, whatever their numbers, and even if dust and gunsmoke obscured their vision, had for some time heard firing in the direction of Deep Ravine. Sensing imminent doom on Custer Hill, they reacted predictably, and understandably, by fleeing in great fear toward their comrades, some of whom died as warriors poured over Custer Hill. Big Beaver remembered this—the 15 or 20 troopers "below where the National Cemetery is now" who jumped up and "started to run towards the river down the [Deep] ravine." They "did not fire back," and mounted Indians killed them.[114]

Thus, the end did not really come at Custer Hill, the last stand of history, the swirling, desperate, gallant defense to the final man. It came more or less ignobly on the slopes beyond and in the tangled ravine underbrush, just as the Sioux warriors Respects Nothing, Flying Hawk, and American Horse said.[115] Austin Red Hawk, another Sioux, said the same and provided a sketch to that effect (fig. 13-8).[116] Here, with Custer Hill overrun, the struggle in Deep Ravine evidently devolved into a hide-and-seek affair. The few remaining cavalrymen, as Big Beaver implied, ceased resistance, at least with their firearms. Mopping up is all that remained to end this famous confrontation.

The eyewitness observations by McDougall, Thompson, Hardy, Godfrey, and others tell us that only a few men, perhaps 10, died on the upper segment, certainly not the 36 or so suggested now (and since 1890) by the spurious markers. Represented among these few, undoubtedly, are some of the 7 to 17 soldiers who participated in the final flights down the hill. Most E Company men evidently died in and next to the deep gulch, though perhaps several dropped on the upper segment while en route. A few might have died even earlier, before the left wing departed the basin for the hill above. Whatever the composition, soldiers found on the upper segment died at various times. No doubt they dropped here and there. In death, the bodies created the illusion that each man had once been part of a skirmish line, a "line" that appeared to extend across the upper segment and downslope to the lower-segment "line" of bodies. This is the so-called, and confounded, South Skirmish Line seen by eyewitnesses.

Kanipe[117] saw this "line" just after the fight, though, as mentioned, he later thought there were too many markers there. McClernand, who went over the battlefield in the immediate aftermath, wrote 51 years later that the "intervals between the dead skirmishers were remarkably regular."[118] But McClernand was a student of the battle. His 1927 account makes it clear that he had access to various materials, no doubt including photos, concerning the Custer battle. It is also possible that McClernand visited the battlefield after the markers were placed in 1890. In any case, a half century is plenty of time to mingle after-the-fact information with dim recollections of personal observations.

Nevertheless, there is ample evidence that the South Skirmish Line theory

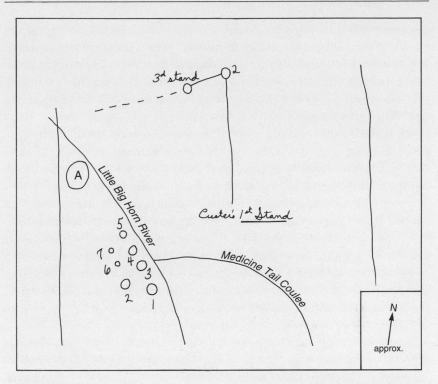

Fig. 13-8. Custer battle sketch prepared in 1906 for Eli Ricker by Red Hawk. Sketch shows that the last fighting occurred in the Deep Ravine area, not on Custer Hill. "Custer's 1st stand" is Calhoun Hill, #2 is Custer Hill, and "3d stand" is Deep Ravine. Sketch notation states: "2nd Stand on Custer Hill, 3rd Stand 3rd stand [*sic*] lower down, about 50 broke thro [*sic*] Indians and ran toward ravine." Sketch also shows prebattle location of Indian village relative to Medicine Tail Coulee (original unlabeled) and Custer battlefield. Cheyenne camp circle is #5; A is "the point to which the camp[']s old men, women & children fled and collected." Adapted from a copy in Ricker (1906a:86) of the original in the Nebraska State Historical Society.

(whatever the twist) arose before marker placements. McClernand likely had access to Maguire's battle reports issued on July 2 and July 10, 1876. He even assisted Maguire in mapping the battlefield.[119] Maguire reported a line of bodies stretching between the hill and the ravine. He thought these represented skirmishers, "as the men fell at skirmish distances from each other."[120] Eight days later, Maguire reported these bodies at "skirmish intervals."[121] What Maguire saw were the upper- and lower-segment bodies. He could see a skirmish line in this distribution, suspecting that men "deployed" on the upper segment might have taken up greater-than-prescribed intervals (which tactics allowed), with some falling in these positions. Alternatively, random casualties at normal intervals would have left, for Maguire's eyes, the same effect in death. These widely scattered bodies (upper segment), plus those buried by Hare and McDougall just outside of the deep gully (lower segment), constituted Maguire's and McClernand's phantom skirmish line.

Lieutenant Godfrey viewed exactly the same scene as Maguire. Godfrey, as much as anyone else, has helped muddle the situation. He reported, "Smith's men [E Company] had disappeared [into Deep Ravine] from the ridge [South Skirmish Line] but not without leaving enough bodies to mark their line."[122] The corpses extending from hill to gulch, of course, did not mark a battle line manned by E Company or anybody. But certainly Godfrey's interpretation is consistent with the military mind. His statement, on the other hand, might provoke the question: how many bodies were enough to leave the illusion of a line—the line that Maguire saw too? The answer is about 23, thinly spread over 600-plus yards, 10 or so on the upper segment and 13 on the lower. This is hardly the picture left by the 52 markers standing, as they have for a century, in what today is called the South Skirmish Line sector.

A year after the battle (before marker placements), Capt. Michael Sheridan reported, without specifics, that he saw a "line of dead" in the South Skirmish Line sector.[123] But Lieutenant Bourke evidently saw no line in 1877, mentioning the graves or bodies at the Calhoun, Keogh, Custer Hill, and Deep Ravine sectors. Except for seeing evidence of 30 to 40 dead beyond the Custer Hill slope (mostly in Deep Ravine), he said nothing about a skirmish line.[124] Similarly, William Allen, a civilian, also went over the field the same year. He too made no mention of the alleged line.[125] Yet he counted the ill-prepared graves elsewhere (again, markers had not yet been erected), reported quite specifically on their numbers, and even deduced (incorrectly) from them the progress of the battle. Surely he saw the few skirmish line graves, for he astutely reported on the others. Why did Allen fail to record these? Evidently he did not see much of import there, at least not enough to influence his deductions. But military men like Godfrey, McClernand, Maguire, and Sheridan, by virtue of their training, were inclined to see in sparsely distributed bodies evidence for a skirmish line.

Revealed through archaeology, the historical evidence reduces the much celebrated South Skirmish Line to nothing more than a minor killing field. Clearly, there are no archaeological data to support a tactical battle line in this sector. Historical accounts, when properly interpreted, find consonance with archaeological reality. Quite clearly also, the thin "line" of bodies stretching to Deep Ravine can be attributed to men fleeing from the Custer Hill sector. Thus, some

28 marble markers on the upper segment of the South Skirmish Line sector are spuriously located; they belong in the ravine.

Parenthetically, body remains found during archaeological excavations at one nonspurious upper-segment marker have been identified (paired markers 33/34, just below the "R" in "UPPER," fig. 13-5). Forensic analyses indicate that the remains are those of Mitch Bouyer, a noted plainsman and scout attached to Custer's staff in 1876. So far as is known, Bouyer, born of Sioux and French parents, was the only mixed-blood with Custer's battalion. The facial bones (maxilla, cheek, nasal cavity, eye orbit) exhibit the peculiar characteristics of a mixed Indian-white parentage. They nicely match Bouyer's facial structure (known from a photograph). What is more, stature and age determinations made from long bones are consistent with Bouyer's age at death and his height. Finally, wear patterns on certain teeth suggest that the victim habitually smoked a pipe, which Bouyer reportedly did. Details of this remarkable example of the analytical power available through archaeology are published elsewhere.[126]

The concern here with markers and bodies is not an exercise in minutiae. The South Skirmish Line sector markers have stood for a century now. They have long been interpreted, particularly on the basis of their fairly linear distribution, as evidence for a tactical deployment, and Maguire's, McClernand's, and sometimes Freeman's accounts are offered as proofs.[127] The most influential of these interpretations has been Kuhlman's[128] hypothesis that C and E companies manned a skirmish line here. With Companies C, I, and L stationed along the length of Custer Ridge, they composed a V-shaped tactical formation—which Kuhlman saw in marble marker patterning—established to receive Benteen when he arrived. Kuhlman's theory is discredited now, but its legacy persists as authors grope to account for the South Skirmish Line markers. Earlier, in introducing the South Skirmish Line hypothesis with its variations, I condemned the tendency to ignore tactics in configuring the battalion wings. The confusion that springs from this tendency is amply illustrated.

McClernand[129] placed C Company on the "line," whereas Moore[130] assigned E Company, both in skirmish roles. In Stewart's version, E Company, rather than originating from Custer Hill, was struck down at the sector as it tried to reach the elevation.[131] Du Bois,[132] in his attempt to account for body distributions, divided E Company into two platoons and sent one from Calhoun Hill to the skirmish line sector, where the enemy overran it. Meanwhile, the battalion moved to Custer Hill. With the fighting force there dwindling, F Company men finally bolted from the knoll, only to join those from E Company in death. Greene[133] believed Indians repulsed Companies C and F deployed on the "line." The men from C perished, but F Company made it back to Custer's position on the prominence. Shortly thereafter, E Company troopers bolted from the hill into Deep Ravine. In most of these versions, the one or two companies stationed on the alleged South Skirmish Line are wiped out by Lame White Man and his cohorts early in the struggle. Again, these scenes are built from battalion configurations predicated on body positions rather than prescribed tactics. As such, they tacitly or, at best, innocently reject the most likely outcome in decisive conflicts—moral defeat.

Utley, seemingly loathe to sully General Custer, is not sure about all of this, but for him the presence of either C or E on the putative skirmish line suffices. He sends the company, whatever its identity, from Calhoun Hill to meet Lame White Man. His is an equivocation that permits him, not without telling limitations, to juggle confusing historical facts and still exonerate the general.[134] Notwithstanding this propensity in Custer battle studies, the various schemes just outlined illustrate the confusion that results from tendencies to ignore tactics in configuring the battalion wings. And all of the various schemes just outlined either unwittingly or purposely qualify as fatalistic interpretations. Indeed, views of action at the so-called South Skirmish Line—conventional wisdom— are a key element in the fatalistic theme.[135]

C Company as a tactical body never even approached the South Skirmish Line sector. It dissolved early in the action, during the Calhoun episode. Moore and Hardorff[136] at least recognize this, but their details, particularly Hardorff's, do not entirely mesh with those presented here. Although E Company operated in the vicinity, it should be clear that its presence in no way approximated a planned, orderly skirmish deployment. The South Skirmish Line hypothesis, illustrated by the variations just mentioned (and there are more), requires an Indian force to overwhelm the deployment. The Lame White Man attack is carelessly plucked from the historical literature, and in the process, its proper temporal and spatial contexts are left behind. In doing so, the importance of Lame White Man's foray and of right-wing disintegration in the battle's outcome is irretrievably lost. Additionally, various renditions of the South Skirmish Line hypothesis, particularly those advanced by Kuhlman and McClernand, assume a degree of tactical stability that simply did not exist in the latter stages of confrontation. The idea of a South Skirmish Line has helped to obscure the reality of this battle, a confrontation that quickly evolved from tactical stability to disintegration.

Iron Hawk encapsulated the whole affair. "Custer's men in the beginning shot straight," he recalled, "but later they shot like drunken men, firing into the ground, into the air, wildly in every way."[137] Following disintegration, cessation of the struggle in Deep Ravine closed the Custer battle. About this time, warriors left Custer's field and moved south to again test Reno's force, now consolidated with Benteen's battalion, both holed up on the Reno-Benteen field. While the two adversaries confronted one another, Indian women stripped the Custer battlefield of useful materials. We know, through archaeology, that leather uppers from high-top cavalry boots were popular items; they could be used to make pouches. From history, we learn that one warrior got a watch, which he threw away when it quit ticking.

And then there is the issue of mutilation. Indian accounts vary as to whether or not the Indians mutilated the dead. So do white stories, but the majority describe disfigurement, ranging from isolated to wholesale. Archaeological results, in instances where sufficient human remains existed, testify to decapitation and dismemberment.[138] Acts of mutilation were, in part, a result of anger and were a practice not restricted to one or another group. But the Indian way also required mutilation for cultural and spiritual reasons. Maimed enemies could not confront you in the hereafter. Also, certain marks on a body showed the ethnic identity of the one who had killed an enemy.

Other stories attendant to the Custer battle abound. In many ways, events and issues precipitated by the Custer fight are as interesting as the battle itself. There is not only the battle scene that Terry's men found but also the burials, burial-improvement details, reburials, marker placements, Indian surrenders, the Reno inquiry, tales related by not just one but scores of "sole" survivors, government policies, personalities, animosities, and the history of theories on the battle, just to mention a few. Some of these have already been touched on. But this book must focus on the battle, and there is more to be said. The story continues with a look at the causes for defeat, including an examination of the soldiers' susceptibility to demoralization.

PART FOUR.
DEFEAT: CAUSES
AND FACTORS

14

PREFATORY AND IMMEDIATE CAUSES

And I earnestly hope that . . . [Custer battle 45th anniversary
ceremonies] may serve to dispel every last, lingering doubt or
criticism that might even tend *to dim the glory of that band of*
troopers and their beloved general, heroes all, who went to
their death with the imperishable valor of the American sol-
dier—fighting a hopeless fight to the last man and the last car-
tridge, at the Little Big Horn. . . .

—Elizabeth B. Custer[1]

In 1905, Fred Huntington, a Billings, Montana, attorney, interviewed an anonymous Sioux who had participated in the Custer battle. The warrior told of an ill-fated soldier charge that within minutes evolved into hand-to-hand conflict. Though Huntington had no idea, his informant had encapsulated the C Company charge and subsequent right-wing rout. Out of this, the informant estimated, only "a dozen or so soldiers" made it to Custer Hill.[2] But before reaching Custer Ridge, and even for sometime while there, no one in Custer's battalion could imagine such an ending. Until C Company undertook its mission, this battalion rode on the offensive, striving to achieve its goal of returning the Indians to reservations.

It is worthwhile now to summarize the Custer battle, in order to examine the causal factors in defeat. After leaving Medicine Tail Coulee, the two Custer battalion wings converged on Calhoun Hill. There the right wing deployed—Calhoun's L Company to skirmish and C and I in reserve. The formation checked warriors, allowing the left wing to continue north along Custer Ridge. The left wing eventually made its way, with little resistance, northwest down Cemetery Ridge to the vicinity of Little Big Horn River. After turning north, the left wing retraced its steps, returning to Cemetery Ridge. Then the battalion waited—some around Calhoun Hill, some on Cemetery Ridge—for 20 or more minutes.

After the left wing departed Calhoun Hill, initial volleys delivered by L Company riflemen sent Indians scurrying for safety. Thereafter, the action settled into the tedium of infiltration punctuated by displays of bravery as daring Indians rode close to right-wing soldiers. Cheyenne oral history describes low-key fighting, which continued for perhaps an hour and a half.[3] Indian estimates of elapsed time should be viewed critically, but clearly the lull in action lasted long enough for the left wing to complete its trip from Cemetery Ridge to the river and back.[4] During this time, infiltration around the Calhoun area escalated as Indians from the west and south crept uncomfortably close. Eventually, safety of the horses was compromised. A number of mounts were killed or lost as horse holders became targets. Ultimately, Indian threats, principally from Calhoun Coulee and Greasy Grass Ridge—not effectively covered by the L Company skirmish line—could no longer be ignored. The right-wing commander sent C Company down the coulee. Its mission was to dislodge warriors from their positions.

The C Company deployment, however, failed. Broken, it was forced to retreat to Calhoun Hill. Response to the C Company provocation proved sudden and fatal. Indians to the west, led by Lame White Man, seized the advantage and pressed an assault. Men on the L Company skirmish line had experienced little activity until this time. But now, about to be exposed on the right flank, they redeployed to cover C Company in its confused retreat. Indians to the south, those accompanying Gall, suddenly found their positions without great threat, and they too pressed in. Compounding matters, Crazy Horse and his contingent, which had infiltrated from the north, sprang from their positions nearby. The action, subdued until now, suddenly became furious. Nearly surrounded, and with Indians upon them, the right wing disintegrated. Some soldiers bunched together and resisted somewhat before the wing fled north toward intact remnants of the command—the left wing.

Pressure, and the rapidly deteriorating situation, forced I Company to move farther north into the Keogh sector. If the intent was to deploy and cover the retreat from Calhoun Hill, the movement failed. I Company came under severe attack from firing to the east, and the unit disintegrated. Panic and terror enveloped the Keogh sector as survivors from three companies fled north. Some had horses, but most did not. The disparity in mobility exacerbated the situation. Some soldiers found themselves cut off as Indians moved in close, many to render their killing blows by hand. Some I Company men, including the right-wing commander, Captain Keogh, bunched together and died. Others lost their lives in flight as right-wing survivors streamed north up the eastern slope and across Custer Ridge. A few made it to Custer Hill, but most failed in their attempt to reach safety. By now, slightly more than half of the battalion had perished.

Somewhat before this massive breakdown, the left wing had moved from low on Cemetery Ridge, up the slope, nearer to Custer Hill. E Company, much like L farther south, manned a tactical line on Cemetery Ridge just below Custer Hill. F Company at the time held as a reserve force in the Deep Ravine basin. Now, on Cemetery Ridge, E Company responded to the right-wing predicament by delivering fire at Indians advancing north along Custer Ridge. But soon E Company itself came under attack, principally from warriors to the west. Some, those in the suicide attack, crashed through the E Company line, spilling into the Keogh sector. Fleeing right-wing men found themselves cut off. A few troops crested Custer Ridge in the direction of F Company.

Company E too returned to the basin to rejoin F Company. The two companies, both still nearly intact, made their way to Custer Hill. Two Moons said they "fell back" to this position as the right wing disintegrated.[5] Here—at Custer Hill—the left wing received 20 or so surviving right-wing soldiers. Left-wing soldiers, and their few remaining comrades, took up positions as best they could, but with little semblance of tactical order. Mostly they formed a makeshift defense, with soldiers tightly knotted about the hill. Some used dead horses as breastworks. Indians surrounded them. A few warriors, those bent on gaining war honors, dashed bravely up to or near the embattled group. But for the most part, the Indians continued to infiltrate. The Custer Hill siege, brief but deadly, had begun.

Officers on Custer Hill restored some measure of tactical control. E Company, perhaps to drive off Indians or to enable horsemen to ride for aid, rushed off Custer Hill toward Little Big Horn River. But the deployment ended in futility. Wooden Leg remembered there were thousands of warriors all around by this time.[6] Badly outnumbered, E Company had no choice but to divert to the head of Deep Ravine. Here, tactical disorganization allowed Indians to throw themselves among the troopers. Not long thereafter, all the E Company men lay dead, including those who had tried to hide in Deep Ravine.

When E Company departed Custer Hill, it left behind some 50 to 60 men. As the gray horse troopers floundered below, this small force dwindled in number. Attrition rapidly took its toll. Finally, the few surviving troopers, facing a hopeless situation, made a desperation dash toward their comrades still struggling in and around Deep Ravine. Just how many fled is uncertain, but best estimates do not exceed 15. Some of these fell along the way, helping to create in death the illusion that troops had deployed along a skirmish line between Custer Hill and Deep Ravine. Others evidently made it to the upper ravine—these were the non–E Company bodies found—only to face death there. With this, the confrontation ended, and all the controversy began.[7]

As time passed, Indian informants, when queried, often testified to the bravery of the soldiers, recalling not just individual actions but a collective courage. Chief Gall, for example, said that all the soldiers fought hard and were brave.[8]

But his testimony came at the site and in the presence of 7th Cavalry officers during the Custer battle 10th anniversary celebration. A reporter there that day even said that only a handsome purse could persuade Gall to speak.[9] Such circumstances hardly inspire a great deal of confidence in Gall's assessment of soldier behavior. An appropriate adage of war states, "The conquered always console themselves with their bravery and conquerors never contradict."[10]

Over the years, a number of other Indians told of bravery as well, often contradicting previous accounts they had given.[11] Some Indian accounts do document brave individual soldiers, but collectively the Custer battle can hardly be offered as an example of gallantry, glory, and resolute resistance in the face of overpowering odds. This image, no better personified than in the chapter epigraph, as much as anything else has colored perceptions of developments during the Custer battle and has impeded proper analyses of the whole affair.

But actions of the 7th Cavalry troopers that day cannot be labeled as cowardly—far from it. Even to enter battle requires immense courage.[12] Cowardice is largely a conscious decision; fear and panic—the terror of battle—is an uncontrollable psychological state of mind. And by the way, so too, in large measure, is bloodlust. Both operated in the Custer fight—one induced by the other—with bloodlust determining the finality of this battle and, in part, the gruesome aftermath.

Military strategists today recognize and grapple with the roles of shock, fatigue, and terror in a combat environment. That a lack of stalwart resistance in battle, even utter collapse, implies cowardice simply does not follow in modern parlance. Psychiatric breakdown is an inevitable result of the nature of war, and always has been.[13] Yet in 1876, the connection between defeat and cowardice was no doubt made, for studied psychological profiles of combat behavior awaited the first of two world wars in the next century. At the time, unsatisfactory conduct on the battlefield, no matter what the circumstances, virtually meant cowardly behavior.[14] Thus in this confrontation, Americans, unaccustomed to the face of battle, selected unwittingly from only two options: courage or cowardice. Collectively, they chose a glorious defeat, which is not surprising and is at least forgivable, and so provided the very foundation for an American myth.

More realistically, however, the Custer battalion as a body exhibited behaviors entirely predictable under the circumstances. The weight and abruptness of the Indian attack induced disintegration. Like those in many a battle where one side loses and the other wins, these soldiers succumbed to a normal process in battle—psychological debilitation. Viewed from this perspective, cavalrymen in the Custer battalion generally suffered from an erosion in their perseverance, not from an exhibition of cowardice—the complete absence of any willingness to fight. If the nineteenth-century citizenry could not comprehend this, the experienced Little Big Horn soldiers could, for they were steeled in the nuances of battle. Many must have sensed the true nature of the Custer battle, although for the most part, their inner thoughts remained private or suppressed.

Paints Himself Brown was at the battle as a young warrior. Years later, Frank Fiske rendered the Indian's brief but succinct description of the rout: "Pretty soon the soldiers started to run and we went after them, but it wasn't long before they were all killed or wounded."[15] There is no mention of a fight to the end here. Captain Benteen and Lieutenant Hare, familiar with the grim nature of tactical breakdown, saw it the same way, though their impressions are largely ignored in favor of more gratifying perceptions. As men buried the dead, Benteen went over the battlefield to determine how the fight had unfolded. He reported, in 1879 at the Reno inquiry, "It was a rout, a panic, until the last man was killed."[16] Of course, in life, Benteen had detested Custer, so in some circles his view is and has been summarily dismissed. Lieutenant Hare's is simply ignored. Shortly after 1900, Hare confided to Walter Camp, "The men were struck with panic and did not fight well."[17] But these perceptions hit the mark. Archaeology has demonstrated this and has allowed a more realistic interpretation of the historical documentation of the Custer battle. Such reality prompts some inquiry into the causal factors that brought about defeat. This chapter and the following one probe these issues.

The search for causes in the Custer defeat has been long and involved, and numerous theories have been proffered. In general, reasons for defeat may be categorized as prefatory and immediate. Those in the prefatory class are factors that precipitated battle; immediate causes are believed to have determined the outcome. The former category contains, among others, issues involving General Custer's decisions to commit his troops to battle, the motives behind those decisions, and the manner of commission. The latter class includes contentions that defeat came through better-armed Indians, the mechanical failure of the soldiers' carbines, exhaustion of the ammunition supply, or overwhelming odds.

Prefatory causes are not susceptible to archaeological analysis. These, and the issues derived therefrom, deal with Custer's decisions and the factors (such as his knowledge of the tactical situation) that influenced his decision processes. Although it is often possible to deduce factors involved in decision making from archaeological data, or at least to advance relevant hypotheses, archaeology in this instance is of little use. There is no archaeological record of what precipitated the battle.

Although archaeology cannot directly address the prefatory domain, we should at least touch on such issues. They deal with the circumstances before the onset of battle—that is, strategies and decisions that placed Custer's battalion in jeopardy. Because strategic matters and related issues are the focus of part 5, prefatory causes assume importance. Custer's knowledge of Indian strength, for example, is relevant to the idea that hordes overwhelmed his battalion, thereby sealing its fate. This notion—hordes of warriors—is a linchpin in fatalistic interpretations. Moreover, conclusions reached in part 5 reflect on the nature of Custer's military mind, on whether or not he properly supported Major Reno, and on the effect of dividing his command. And in the final analysis, the question of why the 7th Cavalry attacked, still hotly debated, illustrates the contentious nature of the historical record.

Obviously, there is an archaeological battle record that, augmented by historical documentation, is relevant in examining immediate causes of defeat. It is possible, as this chapter shows, to test the contention that some of the traditionally invoked immediate causes (carbine failure and ammunition supply) are ill-conceived, whereas the remaining causes (overwhelming odds and superior armament) did play a role in defeat. Discussion of the latter determinants, however, focuses on the roles of overwhelming odds and armament in the loss of tactical unity. This approach contrasts with traditional perceptions of struggling soldiers overcome by hordes of Indians armed with superior weapons. On the contrary, manpower disparity combined with warrior infiltration tactics is better seen as the spark that caused the Custer battalion units to disintegrate. The role of firearms in the Custer battle, moreover, is not a matter of any innate superiority or inferiority between armaments but is rather a consequence of the type of fighting that developed.

Prefatory Causes

In Custer battle studies, emotions run high when appealing to prefatory causes. All too often, these issues are marred by the biases of pro- and anti-Custer adherents, a tendency I have already mentioned. Custer's critics charge, typically with malice, that Custer's decisions were brash, reckless, and baseless. Apologists take the opposite point of view. Neither side seems to have much trouble in finding historical "proofs" to defend its position. This is not surprising. On the matter of Custer's culpability, the historical record is extraordinarily ambiguous. Ambiguity not only has fueled critic/apologist debates but also has made it extremely difficult for most people to objectively assess the nature of the Custer battle.

T. M. Coughlan, who roundly condemned Custer's actions at the Little Big Horn, dissected the Custer battle in a 1934 article. Coughlan incorporated, in one form or another, most of the issues involved in debates over Custer's culpability in defeat, though he ignored the popular "glory hunter" issue, which addresses the role of Custer's personality.[18] The latter is encountered repeatedly in the many analyses of the Custer battle and is discussed here. So also are the issues of Custer's knowledge of the Indian strength, the division of the regiment into separate battalions, Custer's obedience to General Terry's orders, and the issue of whether or not his battalion properly supported Major Reno's attack on the Indian village.

Other matters of culpability include the issues of inadequate reconnaissance and contentions that Custer, as commander, erred in taking a front-line role in the engagement. Rather, it is said, he should have coordinated the battle from the rear. This is a minor issue that is arguable only in retrospect. There is, in fact, no way of knowing if different results might have accrued had Custer commanded from a distance. So there is little need to examine this further.

The reconnaissance issue includes the charge, which is discussed later, that Custer failed to ascertain the Indian strength. It also incorporates a claim that a poor understanding of the terrain on which his regiment was about to engage the enemy contributed to defeat. Failure to scout the country before attacking, however, merits little attention. It is true, as critics charge, that the ground on which Custer's battalion met its fate provided a poor defensive position, particularly in comparison with the Reno-Benteen defense site. It is also true that the dissected terrain east of Little Big Horn River was poorly suited for cavalry operations. Nevertheless, Custer had no intention of engaging the Indians on the broken uplands. He had sent Reno to attack in the river valley, an area quite conducive to cavalry maneuvers, and as I shall demonstrate, Custer himself intended to descend into the valley.

That these plans were foiled is a testament to the tenacity of warriors who seized the opportunity to fight rather than escape. Thus, it was the Indians who unexpectedly selected the battle ground. The Custer battalion found itself engaged on terrain that provided an advantage to its adversary, and even a thorough knowledge of the country could not have prevented this. Indeed, so far as can be deduced from parts 2 and 3 of this book, disintegration came at a time when the battalion expected to complete the offensive so clearly evident in Reno's charge. How else can the setting that led to sudden collapse be explained? All of this, of course, is contrary to fatalistic ideas. But from the perspective of the soldiers' strategy, the actual battle site came about entirely through chance.

The Orders

Custer had received written orders from General Terry, his immediate superior.[19] These orders[20] directed Custer to scout various drainages while ascending Rosebud Creek and then proceed to the Tongue River headwaters. He did neither, instead diverting, as we know, westward to Little Big Horn River. But Terry had given Custer considerable discretion. He wrote that it was impossible to give definite instructions, and in any case, such precision "might hamper [Custer's] action." Terry felt that his specific directions should be obeyed unless there was "sufficient reason" for departing from them.[21]

Was there sufficient reason? Many, such as Lieutenant Edgerly,[22] argue in the affirmative. The march up Rosebud Creek followed a large Indian trail. Thus, there did not appear to be a need for scouting diversions once the Indian trail had been established. On the other hand, had Custer performed his scouts and marched to the Tongue, he probably would not have been in a position to attack before the expected arrival of Terry's and Gibbon's forces. It is argued that in ignoring the scouting instructions, Custer subverted the timetable in a master plan that required coordination among all three forces (although unknown to Terry and Custer, General Crook, after the Rosebud battle, had retired from the field). Coughlan, in fact, charges that this was the primary cause for defeat.[23]

General Terry later maintained that the spirit of the instructions he penned essentially prohibited Custer from following the Indian trail if it led to Little Big Horn River.[24] The trail, of course, did lead to the river, leaving Rosebud Creek near present-day Busby, Montana. Custer followed it. Was Terry's claim valid, or was it mostly an after-the-fact ploy designed to exonerate him? Here is but another example of the ambiguity surrounding Custer's orders.

Yet there is a twist. Were there verbal instructions that augmented or superseded the written orders? The answer to this question, as might be anticipated, vacillates either way. General Nelson Miles, a western frontier campaigner and Custer supporter who was not involved in the 1876 campaign, maintained that there were verbal communications. Miles claimed to have an affidavit sworn by a person who allegedly overheard General Terry say to Custer that Custer should use his own judgment and do what he thought best should he strike the Indian trail. The conversation allegedly took place on June 21—the evening before Custer departed Yellowstone River for, as it happened, the Little Big Horn. Miles for many years refused to name the affiant, but in 1911, over 20 years after Terry's death, he identified Mary Adams, Custer's black servant.

W. A. Graham, however, later uncovered evidence that Adams never left Fort Abraham Lincoln and could not have been on the Yellowstone with Terry's command in Montana Territory.[25] Thus, it is alleged that Custer apologists manufactured the affidavit in an attempt to shift blame for defeat from Custer to Major Reno and Captain Benteen.

Further stirring the matter, Jack Manion assembled evidence that Custer and his wife, Libbie, employed two black servants, one named Mary Adams and the other Maria Adams. General Custer's brother Tom allegedly paid Maria with a check while on the Yellowstone. Thus, as the argument goes, though Mary remained at Fort Abraham Lincoln during the summer of 1876, Maria accompanied the expedition.[26] She, not Mary, overheard Terry's remarks giving Custer greater latitude than some might read into the written instructions.

The Indian Strength

How much the 7th Cavalry staff knew of the Indian strength is muddled. Eventually the Custer battalion met a sizable warrior force assembled in a village with perhaps 8,000 inhabitants. Custer had apparently expected a force of about 1,500 fighting men. The size of the Indian trail and associated camps on the Rosebud had suggested the presence of around 1,000 warriors. Custer, relying on official reports of Indian agents, anticipated that other Indians, including an additional 500 able-bodied men, had left the reservation to join the Indian village.[27] Evidently, agency communiqués badly underrepresented the number of Indians absent from the reservation. The discrepancy arose because of Indian agents' practice of inflating reservation populations in order to maintain a large supply of government-sponsored goods, the surplus of which could be sold illegally at a tidy profit. Sometimes too, government contractors would skim from provisions.

But further information regarding Indian strength did surface during the course of the march. Custer's original estimate of 1,500 warriors had been formulated on June 22. In the early morning hours of June 25, while on the divide between the Rosebud and Little Big Horn River, regimental Indian scouts advised Custer that a huge force of Indians lay camped along the Little Big Horn. The mixed-blood scout, Mitch Bouyer, reporting personally to Custer, noted that it was the largest concentration of Indians he had ever seen in his many years on the plains. This information came with the 7th Cavalry still about 15 miles from the Little Big Horn.

After leaving the divide, and about a mile from it, the command again halted. At this point, Bouyer reiterated his belief about the size of the Indian body, and is said to have warned against attacking. Bloody Knife, an Arikara scout, agreed. Nevertheless, after receiving the new intelligence, Custer divided his regiment into battalions and continued on a westward march toward Little Big Horn River. Shortly thereafter, he issued the attack orders.

Custer reportedly berated Bouyer for his hesitancy, accusing him of timidity. This incident is perceived as "proof" that Custer, now well aware of the number of Indians assembled, conveniently ignored his scouts' information and advice. This is possible. On the other hand, it may be that Custer entertained no such idea and merely berated Bouyer as a matter of principle. The scouting reports, in fact, had been none too convincing. No one had actually seen the Indian village or any portion of it. While on the divide, Custer himself, using field glasses, had searched in vain for the Indians. The scouts had ascertained their location and deduced the size of the gathering by campfire smoke and a large dust cloud raised by the Indian horse herd. But other than general impressions, there was at the time no concrete evidence of the village. Thus it is quite possible that at this point, Custer placed more faith in the official reports and clues read from the trail.

Whatever the case, there is sufficient fodder in the historical record to support either side in the argument over Custer's knowledge of the Indian strength. Apologists can claim that faulty and vague intelligence led to incorrect decisions, whereas Custer's critics can argue that he arrogantly rode to his fate with full knowledge of the circumstances.

The Glory-Hunter Hypothesis

Critics argue that from the very moment Custer left the Yellowstone, he intended to strike in order to gain all the glory for himself. The "glory-hunter" hypothesis is based on interpretations of Custer's psychological makeup, often portrayed as notoriously egotistical and ambitious. As evidence, it is routinely claimed that he aspired to the presidency. That has recently been demonstrated to be false,[28] but the psychological argument, free of anti-Custer passions, merits some consideration. There is little doubt, as his career indicates, that Custer considered victory to be synonymous with attack, but the extent to which this attitude influenced his decisions at the Little Big Horn can only be surmised. Perhaps he attacked in a blithe confidence, based on past experiences, that a small, well-organized body of cavalry could defeat much larger numbers of Indians. Whatever the case, few analyses, reasoned or biased, ignore Custer's character as a factor in various aspects of the battle, and one scholar has conducted a psychobiographical analysis of Custer's role in the famous battle.[29]

From the perspective developed here, however, the most important aspect of the psychological argument is that it highlights the malleable nature of the historical circumstances surrounding Custer's famous battle. It often portrays his decision to attack as reckless and stands in contrast to the contention that his decision derived from entirely calculated options. As might be expected, there is some historical evidence for the latter contention. Apparently the regiment, nearly to a man and including the officers, fully expected the Indians to flee. It is then argued that, regardless of Custer's knowledge of the Indian strength, the fear that village inhabitants might escape in large measure accounts for his decision to strike instead of waiting for Terry and Gibbon. Indeed, early on June 25, scouts and officers spotted several groups of Indians—and they saw the soldiers. Some started off toward the Indians camped on Little Big Horn River. These observations apparently convinced Custer that his quarry might quickly disappear. About this time, with the element of surprise apparently lost, Major Reno rode off in the advance with his assault instructions.

Support or Nonsupport

Custer ordered Major Reno to engage the Indians, adding the assurance that Reno would be supported by the entire outfit. Apparently, nothing more was said. The major attacked at the southern end of the camp on Little Big Horn River. He had expected Custer's support to come from his rear and later testified to that, during the 1879 inquiry. Instead, as we know, the general turned north with his battalion, riding to the Medicine Tail Coulee area and beyond.

Custer's northern move has led to much debate. On the one hand, military strategists argue that Reno had justly expected the promised support at his rear, since military battle principles dictated such action.[30] Thus, it is said, the regimental commander was responsible not only for Reno's rout from the valley but also for the separation of the two battalions beyond distances that allowed mutual support. On the other hand, Custer's actions are defended on the grounds that the Indians were believed to be fleeing,[31] making it necessary to hurry northward to strike the enemy either in the flank or in the rear, where escape was possible.[32] As we shall see, Indians, at least the noncombatants, were scattering downriver, and they attracted the general's five companies.

Division of the Command

We have seen that after leaving the divide between the Rosebud and the Little Big Horn, General Custer split the regiment. As a safety precaution, Captain McDougall, with one company, some scouts and packers, and a mixed lot of troopers from other companies (about 130 men in all), remained in the regimental rear to guard the supply train. Benteen, with three companies, received instructions, apparently without explanation or elaboration, to march in a southern direction. Unknown to Benteen, his course took him generally away from the village. This maneuver is usually interpreted as a measure to prevent Indians from escaping in that direction. Alternatively, when Custer issued Benteen's orders, he clearly had no exact knowledge of the Indian camp arrangements. Perhaps he sent Benteen off because he suspected a series of small villages spread up and down the valley. That is what the general had unexpectedly encountered at the Washita (Indian Territory, present-day Oklahoma) some years earlier, and it had very nearly cost him a defeat.

In any case, Custer later (after he saw a single village) sent for McDougall and Benteen (the combined forces are usually referred to as the Benteen battalion), but they never arrived. The 200-plus men, counting the pack train, instead joined Reno on the hilltop. Reno's battalion consisted of three companies, whereas the Custer battalion comprised five. The regiment entered combat in this configuration.

Was Custer justified in dividing his command? This issue too centers on the line of reasoning that each researcher chooses to adopt. Fred Dustin, for example, found it hard to believe that Custer would have made the division had he realized what he was about to meet.[33] But Dustin, an anti-Custerite, blamed him for his refusal to believe the scouts. Others maintain that Custer ended up a victim of faulty intelligence, or they argue that his conviction that Indians might escape made it necessary and prudent to separate the command.[34]

Captain Benteen, who, to put it mildly, was no admirer of Custer's, flatly stated that the sole reason for defeat was the fact that his commander fragmented the regiment, leaving none of the units within supporting distance of another.[35] The implication, obviously, is that maintaining a consolidated regiment would have saved the day. Typically, however, supporters of this argument seldom offer reasons why this should be. John Gray[36] has pointed out that no one can determine the results had the command remained intact, and he, along with du Bois,[37] argues that claims such as Benteen's rest on nothing more than hindsight. Lieutenant Godfrey also believed that disaster could have been averted had the entire outfit remained together.[38] But Godfrey, one of the early Custer apologists, found no fault with the decision to split the column, implying that had Major Reno pressed his attack—instead of retreating—the battle could have been won.[39]

In the end, the century-long debate over this issue is predicated on faulty ideas about how the battle unfolded—mainly fatalistic themes. If we accept this conclusion for now, probably the most cogent observation is that command division arguments pro and con are premised on hindsight. In retrospect, it is obvious that fragmentation weakened regimental strength, and strength ultimately became a factor. There is also no doubt that Custer's personality is imprinted on this battle. In addition, we can see, looking back, that intelligence information was imperfect. And Reno did retreat, thereby freeing warriors to confront Custer's battalion. And Benteen did not join up with Custer. But all of this took place in an ever changing strategic environment so complex that it has heretofore gone unrecognized, except perhaps in bits and pieces. A unified, explanatory structure must await part 5, a section that may allow the reader to pass judgment on the command division debate and other prefatory issues. First, we need to examine immediate causes, for without them, the nature of the fighting already described, plus the strategies and decisions that precipitated the battle cannot be fully appreciated.

Immediate Causes

Numerous cuts in authorized strength after the Civil War had reduced the U.S. Army's manpower, in Utley's estimation, to an expensive skeleton in proportion to effective strength.[40] One immediate result of the Custer battle was a clamor for increasing armed forces manpower, and this included the cavalry. Less than two weeks after the battle, an *Army and Navy Journal* editorial severely criticized Congress for earlier initiating cuts in the military budget.[41] Five weeks later, in the same journal, a critic complained that the authorized strength of a cavalry company stood at 70 men, yet on the frontier, commanders found it tough enough to scrape up 35 to 45 soldiers.[42] Indeed, partly because of, and within several months, after the Custer disaster, Congress authorized the cavalry to enlist an additional 2,500 men to raise company strengths to 100 troopers each.[43] The congressional act also provided for an increase in Indian scouts.[44]

Although public unrest nudged Congress into action, this increase in strength amounted to little more than a knee-jerk reaction to a poorly understood, complex problem. Indian fighting required reforms in troop training, logistics, tactics, and strategies and fundamental changes in perceptions of the roles of cavalry and infantry. Such reforms and changes came about fitfully, and in the end, the "successful" conclusion to western Indian "problems" resulted more from Indian attrition than from any effective and insightful political or military leadership.

Though in retrospect an inadequate measure, the call for additional manpower came in an atmosphere that did not question the combat behavior of soldiers who rode with the 7th Cavalry, particularly those in Custer's battalion. As I noted, the public and the policymakers generally assumed that their troopers fought well, or as well as possible under the circumstances, and this heroic image ultimately determined the nature of questions asked about immediate causes of defeat. If the soldiers were not to blame, then external factors must be sought. So people turned to causes that were beyond the control of the 7th Cavalry. In doing so, they tacitly exonerated their dead, at the same time understandably confirming their gratifying assumptions of gallantry under impossible circumstances.

The Issue of Carbine Mechanical Failure

Immediately after the Little Big Horn fight, the belief prevailed that the Model 1873 Springfield carbines had malfunctioned, thereby hastening, if not ensuring, the fate of the Custer battalion soldiers.[45] Coughlan identified this as a causal factor in defeat and attributed it to neglect among higher authorities who had, just a few years earlier, selected the carbine as the standard cavalry firearm.[46] The explanation is so appealing that Edgar Stewart, a noted Custer battle scholar, considered it a major factor in defeat.[47] Sgt. Charles Windolph, who had fought in the Reno-Benteen battle as a private, concluded, without documenting his case, that carbine failure may have been the "indirect" cause of the Custer disaster.[48]

The identified defect was the failure of the carbine extractor mechanism to eject, after firing, the spent .45/55 cartridge. The source of this problem was attributed to the cartridge case, to design deficiencies in the carbine breechblock mechanism that, when opened, extracted and ejected the fired cartridge, and to mechanism fouling because of dust and dirt. Dust prevented proper closure of the breechblock.[49] When clean, the breechblock, it was alleged, occasionally closed improperly, leaving a space between the cartridge case head and the end of the block. When the user opened the block, the cartridge head tore away, leaving the cartridge cylinder inside the chamber.[50] Breechblock problems were noted by the 1872 board of officers, which selected the Springfield carbine over other models, but according to Major Reno (a member of the board), only a minority of officers objected to its selection.[51] In any case, the Springfield carbine, after its introduction in 1873 and with various modifications, remained the official cavalry firearm for 20 years.

Cartridge cases manufactured for the .45 Springfield carbine were made of copper (actually gilding metal, which is mostly copper), which expanded when fired. After repeated firings, heat-expanded casings sometimes jammed in the chamber, causing the extractor to tear through the soft copper casing rim or sever it completely.[52] Dirty or corroded cartridge cases also caused jamming.[53] Verdigris allegedly promoted corrosion, which developed from a chemical reaction between leather cartridge-case belts and the copper cartridges, though cavalrymen may have used web canvas belts during this time.[54] Major Reno also thought that a lack of uniformity in cartridge-case rims might also occasionally prevent the extractor from removing spent cartridges.[55]

Primary historical accounts indicate that extraction failures occurred during the Custer and Reno-Benteen engagements, but from documents alone, the impact of such failures is not at all clear. Pvt. Daniel Newell said that during the Reno-Benteen fight, "most" of the carbines in M Company experienced extraction failure when the weapons got hot.[56] He and Capt. Thomas French, the company commander, had to use a knife or cleaning rod to remove the casings. But Lieutenant Godfrey, also on the hill during Reno's fight, placed no particular emphasis on extraction failure, stating merely that dirty cartridge cases stuck in the chamber and adding that when the cases were clean, no particular problem arose.[57] Major Reno reported, in a letter dated July 11, 1876, that extraction failure rendered 6 of 380 carbines used during the hilltop defense unserviceable, but he did not mention the failure frequency. Reno's letter,[58] which was extracted in the *Army and Navy Journal*,[59] seems to have initiated the idea that extraction failure caused, or promoted, the defeat of the Custer battalion. Of course, Reno needed to deflect criticism. But this is a venerable belief, so much so that it has even surfaced in recent fictional literature (where it belongs).

Flashman, the swashbuckling womanizer created by George MacDonald Fraser as one of the many "sole" survivors of the Custer battle, swore that jammed carbines helped seal Custer's doom.[60]

Extraction failure continued as a concern immediately after the Custer battle and during the remainder of the 1876 campaign against the Indians. Capt. C. E. Dutton queried 37 officers about the alleged problem; all had seen at least one instance of failure. Some reported witnessing as many as seven extraction failures.[61] Capt. O. E. Michaelis examined one carbine that was used in the Reno/Benteen fight and that contained a cartridge case stuck fast in the chamber.[62] After the Custer battle, men from Colonel Gibbon's command reported finding an undisclosed number of carbines with defective shell extractors (and some with loaded cartridges in the chamber) on the battlefield.[63] These finds are mentioned elsewhere, with the quantity described as "dozens."[64]

Several Indian accounts also describe instances of extraction failure. After the battle on the Little Big Horn, the Cheyenne warrior Wooden Leg saw a Sioux with a carbine that had a cartridge stuck tightly in the chamber. The Sioux, after unsuccessfully attempting to dislodge the casing, finally threw the gun into the river.[65] Years after the battle, White Bull, a Sioux Indian, told Stanley Vestal that he had gotten a "good gun" from a dead soldier, a gun that did not have a problem with jammed cartridges.[66] Vestal, a student of the Custer battle, surely knew of the extraction failure theory, but it is not clear to what extent, if any, he influenced White Bull's observation.

Through an interpreter, Gall, in a June 26, 1886, newspaper interview, said that "the soldiers [in the Custer battle] got shells stuck in their guns and had to throw them away," fighting then with pistols.[67] Gall, of course, witnessed the battle. His story implies that extraction failure was a significant problem for the soldiers during the fighting. The claim, however, must be viewed with skepticism, for there are contradictions in Gall's testimony. In the June 26 interview, Gall also stated that the soldiers "ran out of ammunition early in the day."[68] Moreover, in another account published three weeks later, Gall said the soldiers exhausted their ammunition (caliber .45/55) and had to fight "with little guns."[69] There is no mention of extraction failure in the second account.[70]

Both of these stories (extraction problems and ammunition exhaustion), which shift the "blame" to external factors beyond the soldiers' control, exhibit Gall's understanding of the white man's desire to view the Custer battle in heroic perspectives. The interviews were conducted during the 10th anniversary of the Custer battle, a time when emotions undoubtedly ran high. Like Gall's stories of collective courage, the claims must be evaluated critically. As for problems with the carbine, it is one thing to observe, as Wooden Leg did, that extraction failure occurred, but it is quite another to make a blanket claim that soldiers had to discard their carbines because of malfunctions. Gall's earlier story raises suspicions that he shared in the white man's Custer battle traditions, at least peripherally. By 1886, the extraction failure theory circulated widely, and Gall, an important man among the Sioux and perceived by whites as a leader in the battle, had been interviewed often. It is quite possible that he picked up the extraction failure story or at least succumbed to leading questions. Gall's contradictions, plus his adroitness in assuaging his white audience, bear directly on his credibility as a witness in the matter of extraction failure during the Custer battle.

The extraction failure story apparently circulated among the Sioux. Rain-in-the-Face, a Lakota Sioux warrior, repeated it while in New York City during 1894, implying that jammed cartridges contributed to the defeat of Custer's battalion.[71] Both Miller and Mari Sandoz[72] got the story during their interviews with Sioux participants in the battle. At Reno's valley fight, Crazy Horse ostensibly admonished Indians around him to save their ammunition and make the soldiers shoot rapidly so that their carbines would malfunction. Miller placed this incident during Reno's panicky flight from the valley to the hilltop; Sandoz claimed it happened while the Reno battalion manned the skirmish line in the valley.

In the Sandoz version, Crazy Horse, before charging the skirmish line, remembered (in Sandoz's words) "all the jammed guns [carbines] they got" from soldiers at the Rosebud fight with Crook eight days earlier. This prompted Crazy Horse to advise his comrades to "make them [the soldiers] shoot three times fast, so their guns will stick." Then Crazy Horse rode about, drawing rapid fire from the soldiers. Soon the cavalrymen began, in Sandoz's prose, "to jerk at their guns, making loud words." Finally the Indians charged, and the scared soldiers, "many" of whom were killed in the rout, broke and ran to the brush and trees near Little Big Horn River.[73]

Sandoz's rendition confuses Reno's move to the timber with the subsequent rout in which the battalion fled from the woods onto the hilltop. More important, there are significant historical problems with her story about extraction failure. Only a few carbines, probably less than a dozen, fell into the hands of the Indians as the result of the recent Rosebud fight.[74] These few certainly could not have furnished Crazy Horse with a priori information about problems with carbines. Also, the idea that three rapid firings would cause carbine malfunction is an element of the white man's extraction failure theory.[75] These problems suggest that a theory that originated with the white man came to be regurgitated through Sioux oral history. It is also important to note that Cheyenne oral history does not contain the extraction failure theory.

In his July 11, 1876, letter to the army chief of ordnance, Major Reno wrote that an Indian scout with the battalion saw, from his hiding place, troops in a sitting posture under fire, these men "working at their guns."[76] Later Reno identified the scout as Curley.[77] The major interpreted this to mean that Custer's soldiers experienced extraction problems. This was confirmed (in Reno's mind) by an unspecified number of broken knife blades (presumably broken while attempting to extract jammed cartridges) lying near the bodies on Custer field.[78]

On the matter of extraction failure, then, there is a conspicuous contrast in primary historical accounts. Seventh Cavalry soldiers describe instances of jammed cartridges, but the extent of the problem is never made clear. Most relevant Indian testimonies seem to suggest that the problem loomed significantly in defeat. But such accounts smack of white beliefs. So was the problem prevalent? Were later theorizers, those who left a plethora of secondary accounts based on hearsay, justified in their claims that extraction failure caused defeat?

The issue of extraction failure can be directly tested in the archaeological record by examining cartridge cases for torn and severed heads as well as for microscopic evidence of pry and scratch marks. The problem can also be approached inferentially by other evidence of forced extraction. Presumably, widespread extraction problems would result in the loss of several, if not many, knives. Archaeological sampling at the Custer battlefield, however, did not recover knives or knife parts (only five specimens were found at the Reno-Benteen battlefield). Perhaps the Indians did a thorough job of collecting knives from the Custer battlefield, but the absence suggests that cartridge jamming was not prevalent.

As for the former category of evidence, only 3 of the 88 (3.4 percent) .45/55-caliber cartridge cases recovered from the Custer field exhibit pry or scratch marks; none displayed a ripped or severed cartridge-case rim. The cases with pry marks represent 3 of the 69 individual carbines (4.3 percent) discerned on the basis of firearm identification analysis. With a figure of 210 carbines in the Custer battalion, 4.3 percent would suggest that about 9 carbines used at the Custer battle could have experienced extraction problems.

Slightly different calculations are derived from analysis of cartridge cases recovered archaeologically from the Reno-Benteen battlefield. Seven .45/55 cases (out of 257, or 2.7 percent) exhibited pry marks or torn cartridge-case heads. These cases represent 4 of the 60 individual Springfield carbines identified at Reno-Benteen (or 6.7 percent). With Reno's report of 380 carbines used in the Reno-Benteen fight, 6.7 percent suggests that extraction problems may have affected up to 25 of the carbines of the hilltop defenders. The combined Custer and Reno-Benteen data indicate 5.8 percent, or 34 of approximately 590 carbines in the regiment, may have experienced jamming due to extraction failure.

Paul Hedren also discussed the issue of extraction failure among the 7th

Cavalry soldiers.[79] Of 1,625 .45/55-caliber cases that he examined, only 6 bore evidence of pry marks or gouged casing heads. This represents slightly over a third of 1 percent of the total number of cases examined. The cases came not only from the Custer and Reno-Benteen battlefields but also from areas surrounding the battlefields and between them. Hedren's results are not directly comparable with the archaeological data discussed here, for two reasons. First, there is no suggestion that he employed microscopic examination techniques. If not, it may be that some evidence for extraction failure went undetected. Second, Hedren did not have the ability to differentiate between individual firearms, thus his data cannot be manipulated to project potential numbers of carbine failure at either battlefield site. Nevertheless, his results are roughly in line with those determined archaeologically in that extraction failure did not appear to occur frequently.

Archaeological analyses of cartridge cases from the two battlefield sites lead to the conclusion that extraction failure was not a significant factor in the defeat of Custer's battalion, at least from the traditional perspective of masses of men rendered helpless by widespread carbine malfunctions. Perhaps not so clear is the effect that lesser degrees of extraction failure might have had on the coolness of 7th Cavalry soldiers under fire.

During the 1873 Modoc war, Maj. Charles Hardin, whose troops used Spencer and Sharps carbines (which also occasionally jammed), commented on this effect.[80] In his July 11, 1876, letter discussing extraction failure, Reno left the impression that such problems might have affected the composure of his men, who "were not as cool perhaps as they would have been fighting a civilized foe."[81] Here Reno obliquely addressed the ever present danger of tactical disintegration among fighting men. In doing so, he hinted at the state of moral preparedness of the 7th Cavalry.

From the perspective of the potential for tactical collapse, however, extraction problems at Reno-Benteen proved to be insignificant. The projection of only nine extraction failures during the Custer battle also seems insignificant in this regard, particularly if such problems occurred randomly in time and space, which is likely. It is also probable that of the nine potential extraction failures, some occurred as Indians used captured carbines.[82]

Thus, as both Hedren and Scott[83] concluded, extraction failure as a causal factor in Custer's defeat is rejected on archaeological grounds. There simply is not sufficient physical evidence to argue otherwise. The archaeological data overcome vagaries found in soldiers' primary accounts. Furthermore, these data not only refute Indian stories on this issue but also serve to validate the supposition that some warriors, notably Sioux Indians such as White Bull, Gall, Rain-in-the-Face, and those queried by Miller and Sandoz, quite agreeably incorporated non-Indian perspectives into their stories.

Exhaustion of the Ammunition Supply

Did the soldiers simply run out of ammunition? The troopers, it is sometimes said, fought hard, exhausted their ammunition supply, and were subsequently overcome. This notion also arose in an atmosphere that tended to view the Custer battle in a heroic light. The best example of this idea is an account written by John Finerty, a *Chicago Times* war correspondent. Originally published in 1890, the story portrayed gallant soldiers holding their positions against all odds but finally succumbing after expending all of their ammunition, first from cartridge belts and then from the saddlebag reserves.[84]

The issue assumed importance during the Reno Court of Inquiry as Lt. Jesse Lee, the court recorder, asked numerous questions regarding evidence (i.e., spent cartridges) for ammunition expenditure among the soldiers.[85] In doing so, he tried to establish how well the soldiers had fought. Walter Camp, in the decade following the turn of the century, turned to the issue on numerous occasions, querying Indian informants about evidence for ammunition exhaustion.[86] And of course, testimonies such as Gall's flatly state that Custer's soldiers ran out of ammunition.[87] The principal military players in the Custer drama who analyzed the battle, soldiers such as Godfrey,[88] seldom offered ammunition exhaustion as an excuse, nor did later students such as Coughlan and Graham.[89] And recent studies of the Custer battle tend to ignore the idea.[90] Nevertheless, the issue remains alive.

There are two archaeological lines of evidence, each derived from the Custer field, that can be brought to bear on the ammunition question. Each is based on data provided by .45/55 cartridge cases. One is quantitative in nature; the other is distributional. The quantitative argument as an absolute measure of ammunition depletion is difficult to formulate, but some observations can be made. Perhaps more convincing is the distributional nature of carbine cartridge cases. Distributions indicate that from the soldiers' perspective, the carbine was mostly useless during much of the battle. Taken together, these two lines of evidence form a solid basis for evaluating the conflicting historical accounts on the issue of ammunition usage.

Viewed from the quantitative perspective, .45/55-caliber cartridge cases recovered archaeologically from Custer's field represent approximately a 20 percent sample of the total, 88 cartridge cases of 440. The total obviously does not reflect ammunition expended by troopers before reaching what is now designated as the Custer battlefield. Moore calculated that from 700 to 800 expended

.45/55 rounds have been reported by relic collectors on the ridges in the Medicine Tail Coulee area.[91] Allowing for ambiguities, and to err on the safe side, I shall use 1,000. Also, over the years, relic collectors have reported as many as 30 cases from Deep Coulee.[92] Very little fighting occurred at the mouth of Medicine Tail Coulee,[93] and I am not aware of significant numbers of government cartridge cases found in this area. Thus, soldiers fired at least 1,030 .45/55-caliber rounds before the Custer battalion reached its final battle site. These, added to the projected total of 440 rounds on the battlefield, gives a total expenditure of 1,470 rounds, or very nearly 1,500 when including the few casings found on the battlefield before archaeological work.

This total of approximately 1,500 expended rounds is biased to an unknown degree by the fact that unauthorized relic collecting has occurred and by the likelihood that some unauthorized finds outside the battlefield have not been reported to authorities (unlike the 1,030 enumerated above). Furthermore, those finds reported beyond the battle site have been collected in an unsystematic manner and are unfortunately not amenable to sampling projections. Nevertheless, the 1,500 total, as a minimum, is useful in quantitatively addressing the issue of ammunition depletion, provided there is a comparative base by which the minimum can be evaluated. Such a base is available in the historical record.

With one exception, historical accounts indicate that before the Little Big Horn battle, each soldier received 100 rounds of carbine ammunition. The exception is Lieutenant Godfrey, who reported a per-man issue of 150 rounds.[94] Lieutenant Wallace[95] and Captain Moylan,[96] however, stated that each trooper carried 50 rounds in his cartridge belt (on his person) and 50 rounds in the saddlebag. Lieutenant Hare remembered that the belts were full with enough in the saddlebags to "make it 100."[97] Moylan, in fact, stated that General Custer himself decreed this configuration. Scout George Herendeen said that each trooper carried 40 rounds in his belt and 60 in the saddlebags.[98] The 50–50 split is generally accepted. Thus the Custer battalion, which consisted of approximately 210 men, had available as it entered battle some 21,000 carbine rounds.

The minimum of 1,500 expended cartridges represents approximately 7 percent of the total number of rounds available. This percentage, however, is misleading. I have discussed the Indian strategy of stampeding and capturing cavalry horses, and it is certain that the Indians captured large amounts of ammunition in this manner.[99] Indeed, Lone Bear recalled that "considerable ammunition was found in the saddle bags."[100] Two Eagles said there was a "great amount of ammunition in nearly all the saddle bags."[101] Although it is probable that some soldiers had access to their saddlebags at certain points in the battle (particularly those on Custer Hill, where 39 cavalry horses lay dead, and also those in the Calhoun environs, which reportedly contained many dead horses), precise numbers cannot be accurately quantified. Thus it is best, for comparative purposes, to eliminate saddlebag ammunition (10,500 rounds) from consideration. This leaves 10,500 rounds carried in the cartridge belts and increases the minimum percentage of expended ammunition to approximately 14 percent (1,500 expended rounds out of 10,500 minimum available).

The 14 percent minimum provides a basis for evaluating the ammunition exhaustion thesis. Relic-collecting variables, which cannot be controlled, increase the probability that Custer's soldiers exhausted more than 14 percent of the minimum available. But how much more? If ammunition expenditure is arbitrarily increased threefold, then troopers fired only 42 percent, or less than half the 10,500 rounds available. A fivefold increase (70 percent expenditure) would place the remaining ammunition supply at a critical point, with a seven-fold increase representing exhaustion ($7 \times 1,500 = 10,500$).

A further quantitative resolution can be made on the basis of the Custer battalion composition. The 800 or so expended rounds reported by Moore[102] were probably fired by members of the right wing while on the ridges south of the Custer battlefield. Later the right wing occupied the Calhoun area, where disintegration began. Did these soldiers run out of ammunition? The right wing consisted of approximately 120 men, each with 50 rounds on his person, for a total of 6,000 rounds. The right wing expended a minimum of 16.7 percent of that as it crossed Nye-Cartwright Ridge. Based on sample projections, these troopers expended an additional 3 percent while in the Calhoun area. Minimum usage for the right wing, then, computes at approximately 20 percent.

A threefold increase in ammunition expenditure places the right-wing per-centage at 60 percent, a fivefold increase at 100 percent, or exhaustion, both somewhat less than the increases based on the entire battalion. But in either case, arguments that relic collecting has depleted the data base require substantial increases in proposed ammunition depletion to bring totals up to critical levels and beyond. Thus, on the basis of the quantitative data available, resolution of the ammunition exhaustion thesis depends on how far one is prepared to go in arguing that relic hunters have depleted the archaeological record. With every proposed increase in ammunition used predicated on relic variables, both within and outside of the Custer battlefield boundaries, the force of the argument that the Custer battalion, or elements thereof, ran out of ammunition, or that their supply was seriously dwindled, is proportionately decreased.

Distributional characteristics of the spent carbine cases on the Custer bat-tlefield provide a clearer perspective on the ammunition exhaustion theory. In the archaeological construction of the Custer battle, I noted that few battle sec-tors contained firearm evidence (i.e., spent government cartridges) for significant resistance by soldiers, especially in comparison with Calhoun Hill, where carbines seemed to be used the most. This disparity in relative distributions, in fact, prompted the conclusion that erosion in cohesion developed early in the battle and spread to other sectors. Thus, on a purely archaeological basis, it appears that firearms, particularly the carbine, played a minor role in much of the battle. Given this, it is doubtful that ammunition exhaustion, or even considerable ammunition usage, occurred during the final stages of the fight.

Here the relic-collecting issue emerges again. Undoubtedly some will argue that illegal collecting on the Custer battlefield has created an illusion and that resistance was much greater than that reflected archaeologically. Nevertheless, the distributional nature of carbine casings is precisely that observed by Lieutenant Wallace. He found piles of cases at Calhoun Hill but "very few elsewhere."[103] In addition, Hollow Horn Bear responded, through an interpreter, to Camp's prepared questions by stating, "At the start of the fight the soldiers were in good order, but soon after they became demoralized."[104] Horn Bear's reference to "demoralized" is synonymous with tactical disintegration, which is marked by a tendency to offer little resistance. So it appears that the archaeological distributions in fact reflect the true nature of the soldiers' involvement in the Custer battle.

Moreover, as already pointed out, few spent government rounds, including carbine casings, were available to relic collectors. This paucity seemed painfully evident to early observers, who concocted various explanations for what must have been a disturbing reality. Lieutenant DeRudio told the Reno court that he had found but "few shells . . . [and on Custer Hill] there were a few shells of our caliber," and he tendered the possibility that Indians had retrieved spent casings.[105] Another explanation also circulated. Charles Roe, a 2d Cavalry officer and student of the Custer battle, wrote, "Much fatigued and worn out, the men may not have been able to fully exert themselves, which some say was evidenced from the fact that very few cartridge shells were found, while others state that the Indians picked them all up."[106]

The Indians had not collected shells. Four or five months after the battle, Wooden Leg and his war party returned to the battlefield. They searched only for live rounds (and found some) but saw more empties than loaded cartridges.[107]

A third line of physical evidence relevant to the ammunition exhaustion claim is also available. Indians used Springfield carbines captured during the Custer battle against defenders at Reno's hilltop position. Of 528 carbine bullets found during the 1985 archaeological investigations there, those found within the cavalry defense perimeter, some 350, came from captured arms.[108] These represent but a fraction of the actual number delivered by Indians. A fivefold increase, or about 1,750 bullets, is consistent with the 20 percent sampling strategy. This projection—a minimum—represents more than 8 percent of the 21,000 carbine rounds that Custer's battalion carried into battle. Of course, some captured ammunition came from the battalion saddlebags. But data from the Reno-Benteen site, coupled with the foregoing discussions, suggest that the Indians enjoyed a windfall, which is congruent with neither the exhaustion theory nor critically low ammunition levels.

Provided with a sound archaeological base, we can reinterpret the Custer battle historical documentation. The historical-archaeological construction in part 3 of this book indicates that for much of the fight, soldiers found their carbines useless. Indians used close-in fighting, in many cases hand-to-hand combat, which rendered the single-shot carbine ineffective. This happened, in particular, at the Keogh and South Skirmish Line sectors, where over half of the Custer battalion died, and during the latter stages of the Calhoun episode. Rain-in-the-Face, in fact, generally implied that the soldiers could shoot only once, that the soldiers' inability to reload allowed the Indians to knock troopers down with war clubs.[109] Little is known of the fighting intensity on Cemetery Ridge, but apparently cavalrymen on Custer Hill resisted sporadically, for only a few Springfield casings turned up there. Lieutenant DeRudio noticed this early on; he saw few spent casings there.[110] His observation does not conflict with Indian accounts describing the nature of the fighting on Custer Hill.

Thus historical data, when approached using a sound archaeological base, provide convincing evidence that fails to support an ammunition exhaustion theory. Indeed, archaeological evidence, complemented by historical accounts, suggests exactly the opposite. During disintegration, many soldiers, mostly those in the right wing and later the E Company troopers, ceased using or abandoned their carbines. This, despite the impact of past relic collecting, largely accounts for the paucity of spent .45/55 casings at various battlefield sectors.

Numerous Indian recollections bear on the ammunition expenditure issue. Unfortunately, the accounts, with one exception, are general statements about the amount of ammunition found on soldiers' bodies after the battle. They are not useful in determining whether or not ammunition expenditure varied among battle sectors, although archaeological evidence and several accounts by military observers suggest that the greatest firing came from L Company on Calhoun Hill. The exception is at Custer Hill, where two specific accounts are contradictory. In responding to Camp's prepared questions, Hollow Horn Bear remembered that soldiers' bodies at G (Custer Hill on Camp's map, see fig. 9-2) "had plenty of ammunition."[111] On the other hand, Lone Bear, also in answer to one of Camp's questions, stated that "ammunition found on the men at 'G' was not plenty."[112] He Dog also recalled that those men at the end of the ridge (presumably Custer Hill) did not run out of ammunition and that cartridges were found on the dead soldiers.[113] Horn Bear's and He Dog's observations are probably correct, since they are consistent with the archaeological evidence. So also are DeRudio's[114] observation and various Indian descriptions of the fighting at Custer Hill.

Some general accounts pertaining to expended ammunition are similarly contradictory. The Sioux warrior White Bull, for example, told Vestal that after the fight there were many cartridge belts and that few of the shells in them had been used.[115] In another interview with Vestal, White Bull stated that there were few cartridges in the belts.[116] Interestingly, it is the latter account that Vestal chose to publish, thereby continuing the heroic tradition.[117] Two Moons, a Cheyenne, also offered contradictory evidence. During one of his interviews, he recalled that there were "not many cartridges on the soldiers."[118] On the other hand, Two Moons told Vestal that there was "lots of unfired ammunition on the soldiers" after the battle.[119] Again, on the basis of quantitative and distributional archaeological evidence, White Bull's and Two Moons's generalizations about little ammunition found on soldiers' bodies can be discarded.

Gall's[120] generalizations that the soldiers ran out of cartridges can also be discarded on the basis of archaeological data. To be sure, Gall was asked leading questions about this matter.[121] But it is also interesting to note that Gall participated in (or witnessed) the hand-to-hand fighting, for he noted in the 1886 interview that the "braves ran up to the soldiers and killed them with hatchets."[122] He must have seen many soldiers abandon their carbines, a rather peculiar behavior in the heat of battle. A natural and immediate explanation for such behavior would be that the soldiers ran out of ammunition. Later Gall probably learned of the extraction failure theory and incorporated it and the ammunition exhaustion notion, both of which conformed nicely with what his white audience wished to hear in his story.

Rain-in-the-Face also participated in the hand-to-hand fighting. In 1894, while in New York City, he parroted the extraction failure theory (though he did not mention ammunition exhaustion), apparently as an explanation for the paucity of firing among the soldiers.[123] Neither Gall nor Rain-in-the-Face seems to have recognized the limitations of the single-shot carbine in close-in fighting and the propensity among terrified men to abandon arms altogether. We have seen that other Indians posited ammunition depletion as well. At face value, these accounts are worthless. They do, however, highlight how utterly foreign terror-filled combat behavior was to the nomadic Plains warrior.

Archaeological conclusions on the nature of fighting and the issue of ammunition usage provide a basis for evaluating valid historical accounts. Red Horse, in describing the Custer battle, noted that the soldiers became foolish, many throwing away their guns, or became "panic-stricken," throwing down their arms.[124] Red Horse also took a soldier's gun and two cartridge belts, one of which had two cartridges missing and the other five. He further stated that Custer's troops "used very few of their cartridges."[125] Flying By told Camp that the soldiers, when killed, had "plenty" of ammunition.[126] Camp solicited a similar response from Foolish Elk, who, in Camp's words, said that the Indians "got much ammunition out of the saddles and out of the belts of the killed and wounded."[127] Left Hand claimed he found a cartridge belt with "many" cartridges in it.[128] But perhaps the most succinct statement was Wooden Leg's: "In all of the belts taken from the dead men there were cartridges. Some belts had only a few left in them. In others the loops still contained many, an occasional one almost full. I did not see nor hear of any belt entirely emptied of its cartridges."[129]

Wooden Leg's remembrance seems to reflect the fact that some soldiers fire their weapons more willingly than others. In addition, the Custer battle sectors varied in fighting intensity, as reflected archaeologically. In either case, archaeological data make it clear not only that soldiers did not exhaust their ammunition supply but also that, in most instances and as documentary sources indicate, they either forsook their carbines in panic or, as close-up fighting developed, did not have much opportunity to use them. The nature of demoralization and collapse seems to favor the former scenario.

The Issue of Armament

After the Custer battle, outraged critics immediately began to question the trustworthiness of the Springfield carbine, charging that because of mechanical failures, in particular the jamming of cartridge cases, the weapon was inferior to those possessed by Indians.[130] Nevertheless, criticism directed at the carbine and its reliability soon abated, at least among army officials, and the weapon performed adequately until replacement in the early 1890s.[131]

More persistent, however, was the charge that the carbine, even in good mechanical order, was simply inferior to weapons used by Indians. This concern had developed long before the Custer battle, and it usually centered on inept government officials and their alleged involvement in illegal arms trading. Shortly after the Custer battle, but before the disastrous news reached the East, an *Army and Navy Journal* editor quipped sarcastically, "To be sure the redskins are somewhat badly off for field artillery; but with another year of Interior Department mismanagement and corruption, we do not despair of seeing them supplied with a battery or two of Gatling guns in time for the campaign of 1877-8."[132]

News of the Custer battle provided fuel for the critics, and the criticism took several forms. Some were vague claims, with little or no supporting evidence, merely stating that the Indians had better armament or that the carbine proved ineffective in comparison.[133] Among more specific critiques, one observer argued that the carbine was useless beyond a 300-yard range.[134] Others campaigned for a firearm capable of increased range without additional weight and barrel length.[135] Another detractor claimed that the Montana dust fouled the carbine mechanism.[136] The most vituperative charges, however, argued that soldiers armed with single-shot carbines were no match for Indians with modern repeating rifles. This contention was so strong that Col. Ranald MacKenzie, an experienced cavalryman and Indian fighter, unsuccessfully applied to have the Springfield carbine replaced with a Winchester repeating rifle.[137] Even Gen. John Gibbon argued for the adoption of a repeating firearm, which he thought would be more easily manageable on horseback and, when the soldier dismounted, more competitive with the Indian's weapon at long range.[138] In 1890, Finerty went so far as to say that if the 7th had carried Winchesters, the Custer battle might have turned out much differently.[139]

In the main, remonstrations against the efficacy and reliability of the Springfield carbine grew out of the desire, however subconscious, to deflect responsibility for defeat from Custer's soldiers to factors they could not control. By 1879, the Indian armament issue rose to such a pitch that the U.S. Army Ordnance Department attempted to obtain specimens of the "superior arms" allegedly in possession of Indians.[140] The concern over the role of the repeating rifle in the Indians' victory over Custer did not lack some validity, although as Utley has pointed out, the anomaly of Indians using Winchester repeaters to gun down soldiers carrying single-shot carbines is considerably exaggerated.[141] Nevertheless, within four months of the Custer battle, Kill Eagle reported that he and the other Indians had been armed not only with Sharps, Spencers, muzzle-loaders, and revolvers but also with .44-caliber Henry and Winchester Model 66 repeaters.[142] Dr. W. A. Allen inspected the Custer battlefield on August 18, 1877, noting evidence (cartridge cases) for Winchester and Henry repeaters as well as "Long Toms," Spencers, and .50-caliber rifles.[143] A survivor of the Reno-Benteen fight, Sergeant Windolph, stated that although many warriors carried bows, arrows, and lances, some had old muzzle-loaders, and perhaps 25 percent to 30 percent carried "modern repeating rifles."[144]

Although historical records confirm suspicions, then and now, that the Indians possessed repeating arms, they offer only vague impressions of the extent of Indian armament. Archaeological data (cartridge case signatures) and procedures (firearm identification analysis) help to resolve these vagaries. The .45/55-caliber cartridge case signatures represent 69 individual Springfield carbines. This indicates that sampling procedures proved successful in identifying nearly a third of the approximately 210 carbines that Custer's battalion carried into battle. (The sample may be slightly biased by carbines captured by Indians during Reno's valley fight.) The one-third percentage may be used in quantifying individual Indian weapons used in the fight.

Firearms identification procedures, including cartridge case signature, caliber, and morphological analyses, discerned 132 individual Indian firearms (excluding captured carbines and Colt pistols). This figure represents the minimum number of Indian firearms. Based on a one-third percentage, the minimum number represents a total of 396 individual Indian firearms. More specifically, cartridge case signature analyses identified 7 Model 1873 Winchester repeating rifles and 62 of the Winchester's predecessor, the .44-caliber Henry repeater. Projected totals are 21 Winchesters and 186 Henrys, totaling 207 repeating rifles. Again, these totals are minimums because the area studied is only a portion of the area occupied by Indians.

These quantitative projections seem to suggest that the Indians possessed considerable numbers of repeating rifles, at least when compared with the size of the soldiers' force. The projected total of 207 repeating firearms represents nearly one for every cavalryman who participated in the Custer fight. From a technical perspective, however, the contention that repeating rifles were innately superior to the Springfield carbine is so exceedingly tenuous as to be without merit. Army ordnance tests conducted in 1879 demonstrated that the carbine, compared with repeating rifles of the time, was clearly superior in range, stopping power, and accuracy.[145] Colonel MacKenzie's request that his regiment be equipped with Winchesters was rejected by army officials on precisely these grounds.[146] Lt. Charles Varnum, who had fought at the Reno-Benteen battle, stated during testimony at the Reno Court of Inquiry that the effective range of the carbine exceeded that available from the Winchester by 400 yards.[147] Though other range estimates, predicated on reasonable accuracy, varied from 600[148] to 1,000 yards,[149] the carbine range clearly exceeded the 300-yard guess made by the uninformed critic.[150]

Range, stopping power, and accuracy combined to make the Springfield carbine technically superior to any repeating rifle of the day. The long-range Springfield effectively kept Indians at distances beyond their normal abilities as riflemen.[151] But this clearly did not occur at the Custer battle. At the Henryville position, Indians, who attained ground within 400 feet of the L Company line on Calhoun Hill, were armed primarily with .44-caliber repeaters (see fig. 14-1). At this point in the battle, few warriors had captured carbines. Similarly, the C Company charge into Calhoun Coulee came within 600 feet of Indians behind Greasy Grass Ridge, where there is abundant cartridge-case evidence for

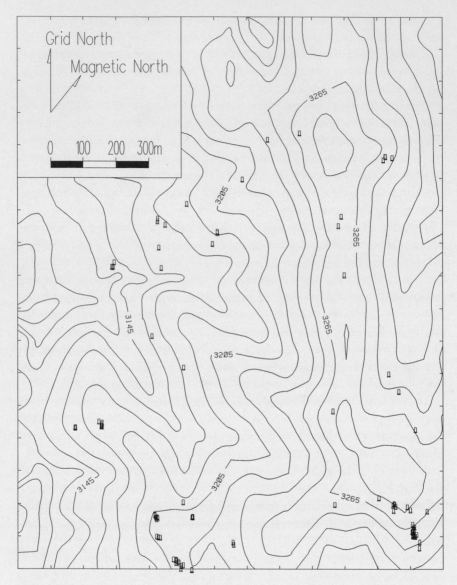

Fig. 14-1. The distribution within the Custer battlefield study area of .44-caliber cartridge cases discarded by Indians using Winchester and Henry repeating rifles.

repeating rifles (fig. 14-1), and probably much closer to those Indians who had infiltrated the coulee.

Thus, the proximity of warriors to soldiers rendered the repeater more effective than the carbine. In effect, the single-shot limitation peculiar to the Springfield became a distinct liability especially during close-in fighting, which developed during the initial stages of destroying Custer's battalion. At this point, the importance of range, accuracy, and stopping power diminished considerably, and rapidity of fire assumed importance. Proximity combined with rapidity of fire appear to have escaped the attention of those who debated, on technical grounds, the relative merits of the carbine and Winchester. Nor has it been considered during the 100-plus years of wrangling over the Custer battle (before the archaeological investigations).

The effect of repeating rifles on the soldiers in the Calhoun sectors in particular, and elsewhere on the field as well, lay not only in the killing but also in the shock that such weapons can deliver at close range. Marshall, for example, noted that the moral fortitude of fighting men endures only so long as the chance remains that their weapons will deal greater death, or fear of death, to the enemy. "When that chance dies, morale dies and defeat occurs."[152] Moreover, area (or saturation) fire, such as that available from repeating weapons, is psychologically effective, particularly against inexperienced troops.[153] We shall soon see that experience levels, particularly given the type of fighting that developed on the Little Big Horn, did figure in the outcome.

Judging from markers corrected for pairing errors, perhaps only 4 or 5 soldiers (of approximately 40) died during the C Company charge into Calhoun Coulee, and not more than 30 men (of approximately 120 in the right wing) were killed during the Calhoun episode. Most of the remaining troopers in the wing, some 70 in all, died farther north, in the Keogh sector. Thus, the repeater as an instrument of shock, coupled with the liability of the single-shot carbine in close-in fighting, probably contributed significantly to demoralization among the right-wing men and, ultimately, the entire battalion. The shock effect was magnified by the likelihood, based on archaeological data, that the Indians had at least 200 repeating rifles.

In an account related by Godfrey, Gall described how Indians "moved to the foot of the knoll held by [Lt.] Calhoun."[154] There the Indians would jump up and shoot, drawing a return fire. These and additional warriors (Godfrey described them as a "mass") then rushed at Calhoun Hill, their momentum carrying them, and presumably surviving soldiers, to the Keogh sector. This is a straightforward historical account, and it nicely fits with the flow of battle deduced archaeologically. But concerning the arms possessed by Indians at the "foot of the knoll," it lacks the detail provided by archaeology. The position described by

Gall was without doubt Henryville, a completely unknown position before the archaeological research. Archaeological determinations have shown that warriors who occupied this position carried mostly repeaters. So it is very likely that L Company, and the remnants of C as it fled, suffered greatly from the shock effects delivered by repeating rifles. This terror must have figured significantly in the onset of demoralization and, ultimately, in the overwhelming disorganization. Loss of tactical cohesion, in fact, allowed Gall and other warriors, including those accompanying Crazy Horse and Lame White Man, to rush on the soldiers.

Repeaters are emphasized here, but during these crucial moments, warriors used other arms as well, simply heightening the shock potential. After the Calhoun episode, the role of warriors' firearms of any kind, including repeaters, diminished somewhat, as Indian cartridge-case distributions illustrate. These distributions, like those of carbine cases, are generally consistent with historical descriptions of hand-to-hand fighting. Beyond the Calhoun Hill sector, there simply are not many spent cartridges representative of either side. This reflects, for the most part, the bloodlust that seizes combatants who suddenly find their terrified adversaries helpless. At least one side—the terrified—tends not to resist much at all. Such circumstances provided a special incentive for the Plains warrior intent on gaining war honors.

Coup counting as an element of Indian tactics has been largely overlooked by Custer battle students. Indeed, even at the Reno-Benteen battle, groups of Indians continually attempted to close in on the embattled defenders, some often getting within a stone's throw. Timely charges drove them away. Their inability to make contact with the soldiers—and thus gain war honors—probably, as much as any other factor, played in their decision to abandon that siege. There came a point when there was simply no social value in persisting. In fact, when asked why they chose to leave Reno while enjoying the upper hand, some Indians responded that they had already counted enough coup during the Custer battle. For them, there was no need to reap more war honors (although Indian leaders also knew that General Terry was approaching). For this reason, there are few spent Indian cartridges among the markers that denote fallen soldiers. Warriors preferred instead to jump among the fugitives and count coup (though documents make it clear that before disintegration, Indians did fire from a distance).

Thus, the issue of armament is a relevant concern, but certainly not from the historical perspective of the controversy over the utility of the Springfield carbine. Compared with repeating rifles, such as the Winchester, the carbine possessed superior technical merits; army officials reaffirmed this by retaining it in the inventory. Certainly, repeaters could be more easily managed on horseback, but by this time, army authorities used cavalry more as mounted infantry, and in pursuit. The traditional shock role of the cavalry had diminished. These officials, and concerned observers, did not understand the nature of the fighting that developed during the Custer battle. The popular perspective of the time, which persists today, envisioned hordes of Indians working methodically, nearly non-stop, at loading levers and mowing down tenacious soldiers until none stood to resist. Although the repeater did play a role, its effectiveness, measured in terms of the shock provided by rapidity of fire, resulted from the close-in positions attained by Indians and not from any innate superiority. These positions vastly exacerbated the limitations of the carbine single-shot capability and helped to induce a massive breakdown in tactical stability. Subsequently, the cavalrymen offered little in the way of effective firearm resistance.

The Issue of Manpower Odds

Size estimates of the Indian warrior force vary widely. A generally accepted minimum estimate is 1,500.[155] In his historical treatise *Centennial Campaign,* Gray used the figure 2,000,[156] and Sergeant Windolph, who was at the battle, estimated that 2,000 to 3,000 men took part in the fight.[157] Mrs. Spotted Horn Bull's husband, after some deliberation, decided on 5,000 warriors,[158] an estimate that falls roughly midway between the 4,500 to 6,000 range offered by the historian Edgar Stewart.[159] A *Chicago Times* correspondent by the name of Charles Diehl learned from Crazy Horse, in 1877, the number of lodges and wickiups in the Indian village. On this basis, he calculated that 7,000 warriors raised their cudgels, and whatever else, against Custer.[160]

Immediately after the Little Big Horn fight, Captain Benteen guessed that he had faced 1,500 to 1,800 warriors.[161] Later, in 1879, Benteen drastically changed his estimate to 8,000 or 9,000 fighting men.[162] Thus, estimates of warrior strength, like nearly everything else related to the Custer battle, are befuddling. They range from 1,500 to 9,000 warriors, and the upper limit may be increased— if pulp novels spawned by the Custer battle are to be believed—to many more than 10,000 "maddened hostiles." Generally speaking, the more sensational and inaccurate the story, the greater the number of Indians, which is in keeping not only with the heroic tradition but with explanations of how "savages" bested a "superior" people.

The difficulty in pinning down warrior strength is not hard to understand. Most estimates derived by white men are based either on hurried estimates formulated under battle conditions or on the number of lodges in the camp multiplied by the estimated number of people per lodge. Regarding the latter, and not surprisingly, there is little agreement on either figure (lodges or persons per lodge).[163] Indeed, and this is a matter for later scrutiny, virtually all calculations made over the years are based on a village roughly double its actual size.

As for the Indians, they had no reason to establish an accurate census for the entire camp, one that consisted of not only various Cheyenne bands but also numerous bands within each division (e.g., Sans Arc, Oglala) of the Sioux. The large gathering remained assembled only a short time, and in any case, various groups departed or arrived daily. Elders probably had reasonably accurate counts of the people in their own bands, for such knowledge is critical in nomadic hunter-gatherer societies. But no one ever solicited specific information of this type. Had early white chroniclers done so, it might have been possible, by summing individual band compositions, to establish a reasonably accurate picture of overall village population and warrior strength. Instead, questions invariably focused on camp numbers as a whole and on the total complement of warriors, information that no inhabitant could possibly have possessed.

Despite the wide-ranging estimates, the Indian force that faced Custer's battalion was clearly superior in number. Using the minimum-size estimate for the warrior contingent and assuming, for convenience, that all 1,500 participated en masse (though they did not), we find that the Custer battalion, made up of some 210 men, faced odds of seven-to-one. This disparity did not escape the public awareness.[164] Many sensational accounts of warrior hordes originated in the media, magazine articles, and books (as well as Hollywood's celluloid tabloids), which often portrayed odds as 20- or 30-to-1.

Such figures are born of stupendous ignorance and are irresponsibly inflated. Most informed students of the battle now accept an Indian force of somewhere around 2,000 men—maximum. Overwhelming odds are invariably listed as a major factor in defeat (or victory, depending on the perspective). Lieutenant Godfrey, without quantifying warrior numbers, considered strength disparity as a primary factor contributing to failure, although he remained confident that had the regiment operated intact, the mission could have been achieved.[165] Graham disagreed, arguing that even a united regiment would have been hopelessly outnumbered.[166] According to Coughlan, the disaster was the "legitimate result [of the] great superior strength and armament of the enemy," among other factors.[167] Many similar perceptions abound, but there is no need to address all of them. Suffice it to say that many Custer battle authors, past and present, assume that great hordes of Indians simply rose up and quickly crushed Custer and his men. The question to be asked is, to what extent is this assumption valid?

One way of answering the question is to briefly examine the Reno-Benteen battle. Thousands of Indians laid siege during that battle. Benteen formulated his lower estimate (1,500 to 1,800 warriors) while ensconced on the hilltop. Little Buck Elk, an opposing warrior, stated that "the Indians were as thick as bees"; there were so many that they could not all take part in the fight at the same time.[168] Yet Reno's soldiers managed to hold their enemies at bay. Occasional charges drove away those who crept too close. But over the course of the siege, the carbine successfully kept the Indians at desirable distances, thus fulfilling its role as an effective long-range weapon.[169]

In contrast, warriors engaged with Custer gained positions close to the troopers on Calhoun Hill (within 400 feet), and C Company rode to within 200 yards or less of Indian positions at Greasy Grass Ridge (and presumably closer in Calhoun Coulee). I have already discussed the impact of proximity, but in this context it requires emphasis. The military strategist Ardant du Picq, a French contemporary of Custer's, noted that when one or two hundred meters separate adversaries, "everything hangs by a thread."[170] He referred to the potential for tactical disintegration. Decades later, S.L.A. Marshall, drawing from his World War II studies, arrived at the same conclusion: in the near presence of the enemy, "troops will always let down at every opportunity."[171] Whether axioms or not, these observations from the nineteenth and twentieth centuries provide an important insight into the Custer battle. Without a doubt, the proximity of the Indians, some armed with repeating firearms, contributed to the demoralization that developed in the Calhoun sector.

It is perhaps a bit unfair to compare the Custer battle with the Reno-Benteen defense. The latter site, compared with Custer's field, was a superior position. But from the perspective of proximity, the issue of manpower odds and its role in the Custer battle diminishes somewhat in importance, at least from the popular perception of thousands of Indians striking en masse. For instance, the C Company deployment into Calhoun Coulee could not possibly have encountered 3,000, 2,000, or even 1,500 warriors. Warriors nominally associated with Gall were positioned farther to the south, where they could not have observed this charge or the counterattack led by Lame White Man. Similarly, Crazy Horse and many more combatants were east of Custer Ridge and well beyond Calhoun Coulee. And other Indians were probably harassing the left-wing troops at the Cemetery Ridge sector. Still others, and this is yet to be discussed, had not yet arrived. Thus it is clear that many, if not most, of the Indians were not positioned to respond to the provocation ignited by the C Company charge, if that is what it was.

Nevertheless, historical accounts[172] suggest there were at least hundreds of warriors in the Calhoun Coulee and Greasy Grass ridge area, certainly many more than the 40 or so soldiers involved in the deployment. These odds, the firepower of the Indians, and as much as anything else, the Indians' proximity to the soldiers almost certainly combined to break cohesion among C Company troopers. The soldiers' flight to Calhoun Hill, and the confusion it engendered among other elements of the right wing, prompted nearby Indians to engage in combat. These warriors included the Gall and Crazy Horse contingents and others already mentioned.[173] Soon many more warriors, originally at a distance, seized the advantage provided by the demoralized right wing and joined the fray. The left wing moved to stem the tide, joining with the few right-wing survivors at Custer Hill. Ultimately, these soldiers did face a thousand and more warriors.

This approach downplays the role of a numerically superior Indian force in the Custer defeat, and it certainly is at odds with images of swirling hordes, whether 1,500, 3,000, or more Indians, attacking as one and crushing a stubborn resistance. The interpretation does not deny the presence of superior warrior numbers, particularly to the east, south, and west of Calhoun Hill. Rather it emphasizes the disruptive effect that proximity can have on tactical cohesion—an effect similar to that demonstrated with regard to armament. Considering the Indian force, the most important aspect is the fact that warriors were able to infiltrate and position themselves near the troopers. They did so mostly on foot; Benteen remembered he saw only two dead Indian ponies on the field.[174]

After deployment, the closeness of C Company to numerous Indians in the Calhoun Coulee area played a crucial role in undermining company unity. Once the soldiers were routed, the nearness of Indians east and south of Calhoun Hill allowed them to respond quickly to the developing confusion, as Indians were likely to do during moments of weakness and indecision.[175] The disintegration process, which typically occurs quickly,[176] enveloped the Custer battalion within minutes. At this point, the numerical strength of the Indians precluded reorganization, negated escape, and ensured the well-known outcome.

Summary of Immediate Causes

Proximity to the enemy often induces shock, and shock is the prime ingredient in loss of tactical stability. Although Custer battle students occasionally recognize that Indians attained positions close to the soldiers, the concept of proximity as a causal mechanism in defeat has escaped attention. The impact of the near presence of the enemy in battle cannot be realized without the holistic approach to combat behavior formulated herein. At the Custer battlefield, this impact is highlighted by the archaeological discovery of the Henryville Indian position. Indian positions at Greasy Grass Ridge were generally known before the archaeological research. But these locations assume a new importance in light of the reevaluation, based largely on archaeological deductions, of Lame White's role, not with E Company but with C. The C Company deployment places the Greasy Grass warriors (and those in Calhoun Coulee) much closer to elements of the right wing than heretofore suspected. Moreover, controlled, systematic recovery of archaeological data, and unique analytical procedures, demonstrate the extent to which Indians at these positions were armed with shock-inducing weapons.

Two Eagles's account leaves no doubt about the nearness of the Indian adversaries and is consistent with the numerous Indian testimonies considered in part 3. During the entire action from Calhoun Ridge to Custer Hill, the soldiers and Indians were "quite close to each other."[177] The proximity of warriors magnified their numerical superiority from sector to sector, a factor that undoubtedly increased the effects of shock. Major Reno reported, in an understatement, that the "uncivilized" foe, fighting in an unconventional manner, affected the composure of his men.[178] Clearly, face-to-face confrontations with unconventional enemies produced similar debilitating effects on the cavalrymen in the Custer battle. Close-up positions provided an increased effectiveness in Indian armament, not only as a medium of death but also, in the case of the rapid fire available from repeaters, as an instrument of shock. Conversely, the distance between soldier and Indian only exacerbated the single-shot limitation of the carbine. Moreover, nearby Indians were in advantageous positions as the right-wing troopers began to display weaknesses. Many warriors found themselves able to respond quickly to the confusion by routing the soldiers in Calhoun Coulee and on Calhoun Hill. Ultimately, they initiated hand-to-hand combat in their own style.

The popular claim that malfunctioning carbines led to the deaths of many troopers cannot be substantiated archaeologically. Consequently, there is little chance that jammed carbines contributed to the disintegration process. Similarly, the soldiers neither ran out of cartridges nor saw the ammunition supply dwindle below a critical point, one that might cause soldiers to panic. This is clear from the paucity of expended government cartridge cases recovered archaeologically. These data are useful in resolving conflicting historical accounts regarding the degree of ammunition depletion among the troopers. Indeed, this aspect of the material record suggests that lengthy fighting remained subdued before demoralization and that thereafter the carbine (and the Colt pistol) played only a minimal role in the battle.

Using archaeological data and deductions as a point of departure, we can discern the nature of fighting in a conflicting and confusing historical record. The weight of the evidence indicates that Custer's battalion disintegrated in the face of nearby warriors, many of whom were armed with repeaters. The shock effect these weapons provided was magnified by proximity. The ability to infiltrate, apparently either undetected or without any great concern on the part of the soldiers, provided the advantage to the Sioux and Cheyenne. How and why this situation developed are addressed in part 5. For now the soldiers, as the next chapter shows, rode into battle highly susceptible to shock and thus predisposed to tactical disintegration.

15

CONTRIBUTING
FACTORS

Battle, therefore . . . is essentially a moral conflict.
—John Keegan[1]

No man or woman, however steeled, escapes the deleterious psychological effects of shock in combat. Because of this, it is axiomatic that armies engaged in combat, without exceptions, are subject to disintegration. Some are more susceptible than others, depending on the degree and type of training, armament capabilities, the mental and physical state of the soldiers, and the nature of fighting they endure. I have explained how men in the Custer battalion suffered from shock, apparently to an enormous degree, and how this mental state culminated in defeat. It is possible to evaluate, at least generally, the extent to which the these troopers were predisposed toward the tendency to disintegrate under pressure.

Training

It is difficult to rate recruit training in the U.S. Army of 1876 as anything more than perfunctory, particularly compared with training today. Indeed, results of the Custer battle, and other botched campaigns of the time, stirred movements toward reform in the training of newly enlisted men. Some people even called for the army to employ frontiersmen, rough characters thought to be well schooled in Indian war tactics, to take over the job of fighting Indians in the West.[2] By 1881, training depots provided recruits with four months of basic training before assignment to a line unit.[3]

Before this, in the late 1860s and through the 1870s, recruits, if exposed at all to training before assignment, received only rudimentary instruction in drill, the manual of arms, and mounting of the guard.[4] Training philosophy hinged on the premise of European-style traditional battle, that is, the clash between standing armies.[5] In reality, the 1876 U.S. Army approach to prosecuting war did not differ much, in procedure and practice, from the Civil War fought a decade earlier, except that close-order formations widened to accommodate technical advancements in firearms. Whatever instruction the recruit assimilated in 1876, he set out ill prepared for the guerilla-like sorties prevalent on the western frontier.

According to Graham[6] 30 percent to 40 percent of the 7th Cavalry enlisted men in 1876 were recruits, but this proportion seems a bit exaggerated. Perhaps 210 men, or a third of the regiment, had been assigned to the 7th Cavalry in the six months before the 1876 campaign. Of these, approximately 150 boasted no prior military experience. Some 60 recruits joined the regiment only a month before departing for the Little Big Horn.[7] Aware of this, Douglas McChristian recently estimated the "raw" recruit level at 15 percent of regimental strength.[8] Still, newcomers unfamiliar with battle composed roughly a quarter of the regiment. They certainly lacked combat readiness, measured by even meager standards, when sent to meet the Sioux and Cheyenne that spring.[9]

Army-wide, new enlistees who moved from the depot directly to their operational company could, theoretically, expect some training while at the post. But exigencies of post life, particularly among the undermanned units that characterized the frontier army, usually precluded organized, intensive, and meaningful instruction. Both Rickey and Utley[10] have noted that such requirements as fatigue duty, guard posting, and daily routines of life left little time for marksmanship practice, horsemanship training, and drill. The 7th Cavalry regiment, which in the months before the 1876 campaign lay scattered between several posts, did not escape this predicament. Stewart[11] charged that all manner of military proficiency languished because Major Reno had neglected training during the 1875–76 winter. (General Custer had spent much of the winter in New York City and Washington, D.C., arriving at Fort Abraham Lincoln only a week before departing for the Little Big Horn.) Reno probably had little choice, given the practical demands of post life during a Dakota winter. In any case, he had no direct supervision over 7th Cavalry companies quartered elsewhere.

The proportion of newly inducted soldiers among the 7th Cavalry regiment is often cited as a contributing factor in the defeat of the Custer battalion. There is some validity to this contention. "Green" troops are more likely to flee the field than "seasoned" soldiers simply because the former have not become accustomed to the extraordinary conditions of battle.[12] But what is it that prepares "green" troopers for this experience? There are two factors: combat skills and the moral element. Proficiency in such technical skills as horsemanship, tactical maneuvering, and marksmanship hone the ability to fight. The moral element, as we have seen, shapes the individual's will to fight. Maintenance of tactical stability or cohesion within an army and the prevention of demoralization among individuals are dependent on the strength of moral commitment. These two concepts are discussed with respect to their influence on the 7th Cavalry's vulnerability to disintegrative processes.

Technical Skills

Though it is difficult to accurately assess skill levels of 7th Cavalry troopers (training records do not exist), it seems certain that many of the soldiers, particularly recruits, lacked staunch preparations for combat. Acquisition of the mechanical skills of warfare fosters confidence at the individual and unit levels, which in turn builds the moral element. This aspect of training, or deficiencies thereof, and its role as a contributing factor in defeat are sometimes emphasized in Custer battle studies. The concern is valid, but the emphasis may be slightly misdirected.

Poor training in drill is occasionally cited. Such training, however, only orchestrates tactical maneuvering; it does not ensure that men will fight. In any case, archaeological evidence suggests that Custer's battalion operated smoothly for some time. A portion of the right wing—L Company—routinely established its skirmish deployment on Calhoun Hill. Until the C Company charge, it appears the remainder of the right wing did not deploy along battle lines at all, certainly a formation in accordance with tactical prescription. Historical data indicate that warriors in and around Calhoun Coulee posed threats. Company C, acting properly and as designed in a reserve role, dashed down the gully and initially drove antagonists into the more remote recesses. Accounts of deployments of the left wing are not common, but it appears that the two companies maintained a strong cohesion long enough to assist the right wing. Before that, Companies E and F assumed postures identical to the right-wing skirmish and reserve roles. Thus, it does not appear that drill deficiencies contributed to defeat.

Horsemanship is often perceived in terms of riding skills. Accomplished riders are of course essential to cavalry but primarily in the classic, offensive shock role. Adept mounted men can maintain the unit cohesion necessary for successful charges and harassing maneuvers. But the battalion, while on Custer Ridge, acted principally (and through design, as shown in part 5) as mounted infantry, dismounting there and thus abrogating, at least temporarily and certainly not intentionally, its offensive capabilities. Even so, riders seem to have experienced little trouble in urging their chargers on during the mounted thrust that C Company initiated. All in all, poor riding skills seem to have had little bearing on defeat.

Considered in broader terms, however, horsemanship probably figured somewhat in the processes that broke cohesion. Historical documents suggest that Indians operated effectively in stampeding or capturing cavalry mounts. Horse holders, particularly among the right wing and those of E Company, found it difficult to control their riderless animals. This predicament arose principally from the Indians' determination to separate the prized beasts from their masters. The likelihood that some stock had been newly acquired and thus was unaccustomed to a combat environment probably exacerbated control problems, for cavalry mounts too underwent training. It is possible also that each horse holder monitored more than the normal complement of four animals in order to release some men, normally assigned holding duties, for more active combat roles.[13] If so, horse-management difficulties probably increased even more.

Whatever the exact events, various sources leave no doubt that led horses were mismanaged, ultimately impairing mobility. Some soldiers in the right wing lost their mounts; others did not. Indian accounts vividly describe the confusion that developed among riderless and mounted soldiers, particularly in the Keogh sector. It is reasonable to suggest that disparity in mobility, particularly as perceived by anxious pedestrian soldiers, helped induce much terror within battalion elements, if not the whole command. As tactical unity began to evaporate, left-wing soldiers to the north retained possession of their animals. Though some of these men soon lost their steeds, a disparity in mobility between wings must have further excited the situation.

A similar argument can be made for the contention that poor training in marksmanship contributed to defeat. Were the soldiers simply bad shots? Coughlan, remarking in the 1930s that the regiment had received little target practice before embarking on the 1876 campaign, rated poor marksmanship high among his causal factors.[14] But it is doubtful that substandard abilities in aiming and firing had much to do with defeat. The initial salvos at and near Calhoun Hill, whether they found targets or not, successfully forced warriors back, at least temporarily. Judging from Indian descriptions, the volleys had the same effect as that achieved through volume fire, the principle that most modern armies espouse. Fire is massed against the enemy or against positions where he is presumed to be.[15] The shock effect of volume firing, as much as the wounding or killing, prevents closer contact. The corollary maintains that an undue emphasis on ammunition conservation poses as great a danger to safety as does an excess expenditure.[16]

According to Indian accounts, however, fighting (firing) slackened considerably after the initial shots from Calhoun Hill—the period of subdued fighting. Evidently, warriors respected the firepower of L Company, taking pains not to unduly expose themselves, though they continued infiltrating. Indians describe how, during the Calhoun episode, each soldier tended to fire only when a careless warrior provided a target. Archaeological results also reflect rather timid exchanges during this period, since evidence for other skirmish deployments or organized battle lines is absent from the field. In addition, other Indian accounts, validated through archaeology, describe plenty of ammunition on soldiers' bodies. Judging from the historical-archaeological perspective, there is little that lends credence to the idea that poor marksmanship contributed much to defeat. If anything, a failure to maintain regular fire appears to have allowed enemies to creep closer. Evidently, the corollary to volume fire prevailed during the period of subdued activity.

While shooting abilities, poor as they might have been, very likely had little to do with the defeat of the Custer battalion, the lack of practice in using the carbine (and revolver) probably did. Along these lines, McChristian recently wrote that neglect of training on the firing line rendered men of the 7th ill prepared to function in the Custer fight, since training involves much more than hitting a target.[17] During the 1870s, economic strictures allowed soldiers only a few cartridges per year for practice.[18] Consequently troopers, particularly new inductees such as those who populated the 7th regiment, found few opportunities to become intimately familiar with their weapons. This deficiency may have affected the composure of the Custer soldiers, for moral fortitude endures only so long as confidence in weapons persists.[19] Practice breeds familiarity and confidence in weapons, not just accuracy.

Conversely, poor firearm training can adversely affect moral strength. Lieutenant Varnum, a participant in the Reno fight, told Coughlan that during the hilltop siege, officers found it necessary to instruct defenders in aiming and firing.[20] If widespread deficiencies of this nature existed in the regiment, then a substantially diminished level of confidence in the carbine surely prevailed. Such a detriment would have adversely affected Custer battalion soldiers, particularly when they found themselves closely confronted with an unconventional enemy armed, in part, with repeating rifles. Thus, a substandard familiarity with and a halting confidence in firearms, as opposed to the narrower perspective of marksmanship, can fairly be considered as a factor contributing to defeat, especially as pressure on the battalion escalated—those moments when everything hangs by a thread.

The Moral Element

S. L. A. Marshall[21] observed that "tactical strength is unlikely to be any greater than . . . moral strength," faintly echoing Napoleon, who is quoted as saying that in war, "the moral is to the material as three is to one."[22] Training deficiencies, viewed from the perspective of their influences on the moral strength of soldiers in combat, probably left the Custer battalion morally weaker than desired. Military success—and failure—moves between two basic forces: the courage and skill of individuals; and the cohesiveness, the steadfastness, of the tactical body.[23] Cohesion, which develops as moral strength increases, is not entirely instilled by honing the combat skills of fighting men, skills such as firearm training. Armies depend on other elements as well. Principal among these are normative forces that act on individuals at three levels: the primary group, the military unit, and the individual's sociopolitical concepts. These three are more important in fostering cohesion than any other force.

Normative forces manipulate the individual within his or her social context. Today the primary group is emphasized, usually the four-man squad, where moral standards are set and enforced within the group. The soldier responds in battle through a mutual sense of solidarity, responsibility, and friendship within the group.[24] The stronger the bonds, the greater the combat potential. In the military unit—an aggregate that contains primary groups—esprit de corps bonds and motivates individuals. This level of moral responsibility can develop through unit pride or a sense of common derivation such as that found in regional volunteer units.[25] Finally, the soldier's personal commitment to abstract societal values, such as patriotism, also helps instill moral fortitude.[26]

Tactics utilized in 1876 orchestrated men in sets of four, yet the primary group concept did not exist in the U.S. Army, even though du Picq, drawing from his experiences in the French army, advocated similar principles as early as 1870.[27] During the Indian wars, if squad composition remained intact for protracted periods, members could foster some degree of familiarity. Usually, though, squads did not remain intact. Overall, primary group unity did not emerge as a factor in shaping tactical cohesion within the 7th Cavalry regiment or any other army unit of the time.

Similarly, it is doubtful that societal values, including patriotism, had much impact on cohesiveness in Custer's command. Many regimental members were recent immigrants, soldiers of fortune, or miscreants seeking anonymity in military life. Often they came to the service illiterate. Moreover, young men commonly sought security in the army, however fragile, during the troubled economic times of the 1870s.[28] The varied backgrounds of enlisted men, and the diverse motives for selecting army life, precluded a common social experience. Cohesion built on abstract social values languished. By default, therefore, the U.S. Army in 1876, including the 7th Cavalry, relied nearly exclusively on the military unit concept for its moral commitments, although coercive forces, such as the prospect of severe punishment for cowardice and disobedience, loomed ever present.

How effectively did the military unit concept shape an individual's moral steadfastness and promote cohesion within the frontier army? Army units were often widely scattered, and the largest group to which a soldier most commonly affixed an identity—the regiment—seldom came together in its entirety. Companies made up regiments. Thus, the job of dictating loyalties and fostering cohesion fell to company pride and esprit de corps.[29] Writing about the frontier U.S. Army in general, Utley noted that pride and spirit were maintained despite a continuing turnover in manpower and an inferior quality of enlisted men.[30]

Possibly this was true for the 7th Cavalry regiment, for it was then (and is now) often perceived as a crack outfit. But a contrary argument can be made. An individual will normally experience the forces that instill pride and esprit de corps only as an active member of the unit. Shared experiences in combat are most important, and so are fraternal relationships that develop in time. Recent arrivals in the 7th Cavalry, of whom 70 percent can be labeled as recruits, had had no opportunity for shared combat experiences and little time to absorb whatever unit values existed.

It is difficult, if not impossible, to measure accurately the effects of the new 7th Cavalry members on previous levels of unit pride and esprit de corps. But in assessing the propensity of the Custer battalion toward disintegration, we should note that military scholars today agree that all three normative forces are essential in achieving the utmost from moral commitment. The 7th Cavalry lacked exposure to two of these, including the primary group concept, which has dominated military thought since World War II and which is usually considered to be the most effective in shaping the moral element.[31] The concept was first articulated by Marshall, who argued that tactical unity depends on cohesion within the four-man squad.[32] Cohesion springs from the same things that induce men to face life—friendship, loyalty, responsibility, and confidence.[33]

Sharing primary group standards is effective in subjugating ethnic, social, economic, and political differences among new soldiers. These standards replace idiosyncrasies with common values that encourage the individual to recognize that his welfare and that of the group are interconnected.[34] Such values are imparted effectively only through intensive, formal training programs. It is true that the U.S. Army in 1876 utilized four-man squads, but again the concept, implemented to improve tactical maneuverability, was a mechanistic innovation. In any event, it has been noted that formal military training in the 1870s, considering the frontier foe, was generally substandard. From the perspective of primary group training, this deficiency affected not only the new recruits assigned to the 7th Cavalry but also the veterans, who constituted the larger proportion (some 75 percent) of the regiment. They too lacked training in the moral element. Given the diversified backgrounds of 7th Cavalry regimental members and their varied motives for choosing army life, it is therefore doubtful that strong, resilient bonds of commonality developed.

Of course, the Custer battalion's defeat cannot be fairly ascribed to any failure, in 1876, to emphasize primary group cohesion. The concept did not gain favor until military scholars demonstrated empirically (in the Korean War) that primary group training dramatically improved the moral commitment of men in battle.[35] But by comparing standards of yesterday with current knowledge in military training, we can illustrate the level of tactical cohesion achieved by the

7th Cavalry. Since the study of moral preparedness for battle, and thus of building and loss of cohesion, is a legitimate historical issue,[36] the comparison is hardly Whiggish history. It is an eminently justifiable approach to this matter. Therefore, using measures employed today, we can fairly say that tactical cohesion in the Custer regiment was substandard. Even when judged by criteria of the time, certain training imperfections in combat skills indirectly lowered moral potential. The introduction of new recruits at inopportune times probably diluted the reservoir of esprit de corps and unit pride within the regiment. Moreover, cohesion and stability suffered because of a lack of unanimity in subscribing to abstract societal values. In launching its campaign, the regiment was therefore ill prepared normatively and technically, and as a body it entered battle acutely susceptible—especially when faced with an unconventional enemy—to agents that provoke dissolution of moral unity.

Fatigue

It is generally accepted that the 7th Cavalry column suffered in some measure from fatigue before entering battle. In his detailed history of the ill-fated expedition, Stewart concluded that exhaustion had engulfed both men and horses.[37] Lieutenant Godfrey intimated as much, noting that lengthy marches spread over only four days had totaled 113 miles.[38] Actually, the marches took place over about 72 hours, from approximately noon on June 22 to shortly after noon on June 25. A private soldier riding with the column, William Slaper, considered the marches "forced," causing horses to play out.[39] Theodore Goldin, then a private, made the march too; he remembered "weary" men the night before hostilities.[40] When considered in Custer battle studies, however, the impact of fatigue has been largely obscured in generalities. And to my knowledge, the issue has never been considered formally with respect to its adverse effects on tactical cohesion.

That weariness in battle is deleterious cannot be denied. Lessons drawn from modern armies show that soldiers sapped of energy—soldiers who are tired, hungry, and thirsty—can quickly break, even under moderate stress.[41] Keegan described the terrible effects of this condition among the French and English armies that clashed at Waterloo in 1815.[42] As happened at Waterloo, fatigue will drain fighting strength as quickly as any other condition, for with it comes fear, reduction in the moral force, and erosion of tactical stability. Moreover, physical exhaustion will strike at tactical efficiency from two directions simultaneously. Fatigue not only destroys physical responses to crisis, subverting courage and deadening mental acuity, but also results in negative emotions, ranging from resentment to rebellion. Troops fight less willingly for their commanders or not at all.[43]

In measuring degrees of exhaustion, we should know the prior health and physical conditioning of the subjects. Forensic analysis of human remains (bone elements representing 33 soldiers) recovered archaeologically detected few pathological abnormalities and only several cases of trauma. If this sample is representative of the regiment, then general health can be rated as good. Physical preparation, however, is an unknown factor for the 7th Cavalry soldiers. It is evident that no formal opportunities exclusively for strengthening the body arose during basic training. At posts, regularly scheduled exercise programs designed to enhance fitness did not exist, and men acquired or maintained conditioning, to the extent possible, principally through daily labor. Most 7th Cavalry enlisted men were young (mean age was approximately 22) and presumably physically fit. But this can only be surmised.[44] Nevertheless, it seems clear that whatever the level of conditioning, the 7th Cavalry regiment entered the battle tired.

Others, not just Godfrey, noticed this. Captain Freeman, with Terry's column when it relieved the beleaguered Reno, had ample time to observe conditions of many soldiers as well as converse with a number of them. He described these men (and horses) as "worn out" and thought that had Custer's men been fresh, they might have made good an escape.[45] Of course, he saw the Reno-Benteen survivors after nearly two days of combat had taken a toll. Nevertheless, his firsthand account of worn-out men is revealing, though he failed to comprehend the relationship between fatigue and cohesion. Major Reno also commented on the exhausted condition of man and horse. Like Freeman, he emphasized weary men as a factor in Custer's defeat.[46] And Lieutenant Roe equated a scarcity of spent cartridges with spent men.[47]

Similar evidence for fatigue exists in Indian testimony. It is doubtful that these comments resulted from leading questions. In a patronizing fashion, White Bull said that the soldiers fought to the end, but he did note that the "soldiers looked tired."[48] Sitting Bull said essentially the same thing.[49] Sitting Bull's comments are interesting because he did not participate in the battle. He must have received this information from other Sioux who had noticed jaded men among Custer's troops, not just some but collectively.

Improper nourishment aggravates the physical condition and hastens the tired state.[50] Reno, in discussing the fatigue factor, commented that the men were not fed before battle.[51] Actually, they had probably snacked, as Stewart surmised,[52] but the available fare—consisting of field rations (hardtack, bacon, and coffee)—can hardly be considered delectable. In fact, field rations constituted much of the men's diet after leaving Fort Abraham Lincoln and apparently all of their diet during the march up Rosebud Creek (June 22–June 25). Although such morsels, sometimes augmented with game, composed the typical menu while on the march, dietetically these portions undoubtedly constituted inadequate nourishment. This, coupled with what, for many, proved to be exhausting marches in the final days, must have helped to heighten weariness.

As I noted, exhaustion is occasionally mentioned in Custer battle studies, but largely in passing and without explicit reference to tactical cohesion. Viewed from a cohesion perspective, however, fatigue in the regiment probably detracted from an already diluted pool of moral commitment provided by unit pride and spirit. Possibly it fostered some resentment among the men. It is difficult to accurately measure the extent of weariness in the regiment, though clearly by June 25 the men were tired. Judging from the emphases that modern military authorities place on conditioning programs and the conservation of human energy while on campaign,[53] physical fitness and dietary requirements are of considerable importance in maintaining tactical cohesion during battle. Affected by fatigue, untold numbers in the regiment entered battle somewhat more depleted of their moral potential.

Summary of Contributing Factors

When Reno's command of some 130 soldiers, guides, and scouts fled the woods, crossed Little Big Horn River, and scrambled in disorder up the steep bluffs to a refuge on the hilltop, tactical stability had vanished entirely. In discussing their departure from the timber during the Reno Court of Inquiry, members of the battalion disagreed on the safety provided by the trees and brush. Some felt that the area provided an adequate position for a prolonged defense; others believed that eventually the location would have become untenable. A dwindling ammunition supply and the uncertain prospect of replenishment helped shape differences in opinion. Nevertheless, the retrospective discussion centered on the security of the timber over the long run. As it turned out, the commander eventually elected to retire. At the moment that cohesion vanished, however, the position remained secure. The panicky escape across the river proved possible because Indians, though pressing Reno's flanks and rear, had not yet formed in his front (the east bank of the river). The river also hindered pursuit.

Blame for the sudden collapse of Reno's column is often placed on leadership, specifically that of the major himself. When Reno decided to leave the timber, he ordered his soldiers to gather. They did so in good order (some did not hear the order and were left behind). Then a small group of warriors emerged from nearby and approached to within 50 or so feet of the gathering. They delivered some volleys. One shot hit the Arikara scout Bloody Knife squarely in the head, splattering blood and brains over Major Reno, who became highly agitated. Reno's emotional state, it is often claimed, led directly to the panicky flight. Certainly, leadership is instrumental in determining whether or not men will stand to fight or remain in order.[54] But overlooked in assessing culpability in this incident is the fact that the near point-blank attack also badly rattled the major's men. Though few died with Bloody Knife, most, like Reno, quickly bolted in panic.

Clearly the majority, not just Reno, suffered the effects of shock engendered by the unexpected Indian assault, and this is to be expected in extreme and sudden circumstances. Leadership qualities are only part of the equation. A prominent and contentious aspect of Custer battle studies, Reno's role in the evaporation of cohesion within his command has become a partisan issue. But such partisanship merely obscures the complexity in situations where several forces conspire to dissipate unity, forces that transcend the actions of a single individual. Reno's agitation alone did not cause demoralization. There are no primary historical data that even begin to demonstrate that poor leadership during these moments played a central role in the terror that infected Reno's men. And flight, once under way, is impossible to contain in an instant. Reno fell victim not just to himself but to soldiers badly prepared for this type of experience. Certainly, there is little to criticize in Custer's ability to lead, yet nothing better than a simplism emerges when biased reasoning reduces the defeat to one of weak (Reno) versus strong (Custer) leadership.

I have argued that the 7th Cavalry regiment rode into the Little Big Horn Valley undesirably exposed to disintegration processes. Reno's episode in the timber seems to substantiate this contention: panic, which developed from a harrowing but hardly hopeless experience, rather quickly overwhelmed all in the command. Custer's battalion as a body surely harbored similar inclinations. The only alternative is to argue that Custer took the seasoned soldiers and left the other leaders with the green recruits, but that does not reflect well on the regimental commander. What is left is the realization that members of both battalions shared common deficiencies in readiness for combat. Esprit de corps and unit pride, the single normative force on which the U.S. Army in 1876 depended for tactical cohesion, could not have been strong. Most, if not all, recruits had experienced inadequate training in basic combat skills, a deficiency that detracted from their potential for moral persistence in battle. Veterans and recruits alike had received little practice in basic skills. These factors further reduced the level of cohesion by eroding confidence levels. Neither the veterans, though experienced, nor the recruits boasted any intensive exposure to the training that best promotes cohesion. Fatigue probably increased the potential for the development of fear and, with it, a breakdown in cohesion. And finally the soldiers, collectively inexperienced in Indian fighting, confronted an unconventional foe.

Reno's and Custer's battalions rode into battle susceptible to the deleterious effects of shock. Limitations in moral fortitude, caused by weariness and normative deficiencies, adversely affected cohesion. Unity in both battalions collapsed under the effects of shock magnified by the proximity of Indians. At the Custer battle, shock intensified because of the reduced effectiveness of carbines in close-in confrontations. Inexperience and lack of practice in using the weapon doubtless exacerbated the situation. An inability to control many of the horses produced disparity in mobility, an extremely dangerous situation among cavalry units. These factors contributed to the loss of cohesion within the Custer group, first as unity in C Company disappeared, then as stability failed in the right wing and finally the battalion.

It is fair to say, in comparing the two fights, that cohesion within Reno's column decayed in the face of a less precarious situation and under more feeble pressure. Despite being outnumbered (estimates of the Indian force in the timber vicinity range from 200 to 900 warriors), the soldiers held a position among the trees that remained tenable, certainly for a while longer. The close-up attack on Reno's force as it assembled for departure probably did not approximate the severity of that suffered by Custer's right wing as the moral element wavered. Moreover, Reno's column found the luxury of escape after breakdown. This lucky advantage largely reduced, if it did not eliminate, the role of poor combat skills in disintegration. The Custer battalion, on the other hand, found itself effectively held in place as cohesion began to dissipate, leaving the men few options other than reliance on their combat skills in a highly stressful environment. Still, the similarity between the two engagements—collapse under shock effects amplified by proximity—is persuasive evidence that the regiment harbored a latent propensity for disintegration. It is thus not surprising, given the unconventional nature of each confrontation, that both battalions fell apart. Once again, current standards measure this disintegration, but they offer no basis for condemnation.

PART FIVE.
FATE, BLAME,
AND STRATEGY

16
FATE VERSUS CHOICE

Most impediments to scientific understanding are conceptual locks, not factual locks.

—Stephen Jay Gould[1]

Having described and ordered Custer battle episodes, identified immediate causes in defeat, and outlined factors contributing to defeat, we need now to consider events leading to the ruinous end. Why and under what circumstances did the precarious situation that ultimately confronted Custer's battalion develop? Such questions address what many consider the most fascinating and perplexing of all issues in Custer battle studies. As might be expected, there are diverse opinions, and for good reason. Circumstances leading to the demise of Custer's battalion cannot be adequately addressed without a circumspect understanding of the battle itself, heretofore lacking in detail and construction. I believe that archaeology, focused through combat modeling, and history have provided such an understanding. The results, which reinterpret and reorder Custer battle events within the parameters of a stability/disintegration model, afford insights unavailable from either archaeological or historical analyses alone.

With this new "how?" background, the "why?" questions begin to bear fruit. So in part 5, I will contest in detail the fatalistic scheme (this and the next chapter) and follow with an alternative answer (chapter 18). All of this is concerned with strategy. The subject of the brief discussions in Chapter 19—Where was Custer?—is an unavoidable consequence, no matter what the battle, of ruminations on strategy. I use history here, for we have not, except at the Reno-Benteen site (not applicable here), dug beyond the Custer field. But I offer this reminder: insights here have their origins in the ground.

The Medicine Tail Coulee Episode

In opening this book, I introduced the "fatalistic" theme, a dominant concept in Custer battle studies and an element integral to the myth. Various twists of the theme purport to answer the how and why questions. Why did Custer suffer defeat, and how did that destiny come about? Major Reno failed, it is said, releasing warrior hordes and thus sealing the fate of Custer's battalion. In this way, "Why?" is answered. But this perception, however argued, is wholly unsatisfactory. Its flaws are exposed in the next chapter. As for the second element—"How?"—it is argued that the ill-fated battalion had no choice but to defend and that the defense took place on Custer Ridge, inadequate indeed though the best-available defensive position. The predicament developed in Medicine Tail Coulee. This part of the fatalistic argument—fate instead of choice—is addressed here.

In fatalistic schemes, "How?" answers can incorporate any or all of four major elements: a doomed cavalry force *driven* by *superior* numbers of Indians who *quickly* mounted a savage, unrelenting *onslaught*. Doom began at or near the mouth of Medicine Tail Coulee. Custer's battalion entered Medicine Tail, then split into wings. The left wing, attempting to reach Little Big Horn River, rode to the coulee mouth while the right remained on ridges above. Stewart's approach explains what happened next.[2] He argued that both wings (battalions, to him) came under heavy attack in Medicine Tail Coulee, an attack that forced the command to take up the strongest defensive position available. That was Custer Ridge, which the troops occupied in sequence from its southern (Calhoun Hill) to northern (Custer Hill) extremities. Many other serious students of the Custer battle have put forth similar arguments.[3] In addition, popular accounts—those based on the heroic tradition but riddled with inaccuracies and sensationalism—subscribe to the fatalistic theme. Sadly, the popular bunk persists, illustrating the power of myth. Of these, one of the more recent attempts—published in 1990—is in *Glorious Defiance*.[4]

There is some documentary evidence that purportedly supports fatalistic arguments, although the accounts create an illusion, as I shall explain. Gall, through a newspaper correspondent, reported that the soldiers were "forced back step by step" to Custer Ridge.[5] Standing Bear's account, rendered through Walter Camp, described soldiers attempting to cross Little Big Horn River at a ford opposite the mouth of Medicine Tail Coulee. According to Standing Bear, resistance checked the advance and forced the troops back to Custer Ridge.[6] This account is not unlike that of Tall Bull, who also told Camp that Indians drove the soldiers away from the coulee mouth, forcing them ultimately to the ridge.[7] Other similar Indian accounts exist.[8]

In a variation on the theme, the command, although not under heavy pressure, sensed the gravity of the situation as the left wing maneuvered near the mouth of Medicine Tail Coulee. The realization necessitated rejoining the wings on Custer Ridge and formulating a defensive strategy. Du Bois[9] found it "obvious" that decisions made immediately after linking up resulted in the deployment of Yates's "battalion" (left wing) to the northern end of Custer Ridge (Custer Hill). At the same time, Keogh's "battalion" (right wing) took up the southern extremity (Calhoun Hill). (Du Bois's composition of the left and right wings, or "battalions," as he calls them, differs from mine.) With the defense in place, the battle began in earnest.

Hardorff's[10] construction is similar to du Bois's but with a twist. He believed that the battalion, on attaining Custer Ridge, still maintained an offensive but shortly thereafter found itself forced into a defensive posture. Under pressure, Yates's "battalion" (left wing), stationed with the right wing as the pressure escalated, eventually pushed from Calhoun Hill to Custer Hill, where it assumed a defensive stance. Utley's version also moves Yates's battalion (i.e., the left wing) from Calhoun Hill, now entrusted to Keogh's right wing, northward to Custer Hill, all the while fighting along the ridge.[11] But unlike Hardorff, Utley invokes the fatalistic theme to get Yates from Medicine Tail ford to Calhoun Hill. (Meanwhile, Keogh saw Yates's predicament and, though not threatened seriously, moved the right wing to effect a junction.)

Utley, like others, uncritically accepts three of the thematic elements: soldiers driven by a superior force which quickly massed at the crossing.[12] As for an onslaught, the warriors, except at the ford, are primarily relegated by Utley to the role of infiltrators,[13] a role that in due course will emerge as one of many chinks in the fatalists' armor.

I should point out that the fatalistic tradition has a long and enduring history, beginning as it did virtually as the gunsmoke wafted from the field. It is the foundation of the myth. Modern analysts tend to exercise restraint in invoking the fatalistic theme, but in the extreme, sensational form, Custer's troopers hold out, sometimes for hours, to the last cartridge and last man—often the general himself. Whatever the trappings, however, in all variations hapless (or soon-to-become hapless) soldiers, after leaving Medicine Tail Coulee, are decisively overwhelmed.

But based on the historical-archaeological construction formulated herein, one or another of the fatalistic twists hardly seems likely. The construction recognizes that after Custer's battalion attained Calhoun Hill, the left wing departed. It moved along Custer Ridge, then down Cemetery Ridge, and finally to the vicinity of Little Big Horn River (Clark's ford D). This movement seems highly improbable had the battalion been relentlessly driven to Custer Ridge by Indians hordes bent on destruction. The same is true for variations on the fatalistic theme that place the battalion on the defensive either immediately on reaching Custer Ridge or soon thereafter.

What is more, after leaving the river vicinity, the left wing paused on Cemetery Ridge, according to Cheyenne tradition, for as long as 20 to 30 minutes. I have argued that it is difficult to accept Indian estimates of elapsed time at face value. What is important here is that a delay occurred and that it came after an indeterminate but surely lengthy amount of time expended in the left-wing river trip. Thereafter, part of the wing deployed on and about Cemetery Ridge, not on Custer Hill. Only then did the fluid situation place the battalion in jeopardy. None of this adds up to a fatalistic argument.

In the mid-1950s, Don Rickey, Jr., formerly the Custer Battlefield historian, compiled Cheyenne battle traditions as given to him by John Stands in Timber.[14] But traditional accounts became available in published form only after the late 1960s.[15] Ready availability in earlier years might have influenced Custer battle studies, but this is doubtful. Research in the past two decades has virtually ignored that part of Cheyenne tradition that refers to the left-wing sojourn from Custer Ridge.[16] In other parts of the Cheyenne accounts, there are clear errors, providing a convenient excuse for rejection *in toto*. Basically, Cheyenne tradition is discarded because it does not fit with presuppositions about the battle, principally the popular fatalistic view.

The reluctance may also be the result of an inclination to discount descriptions given orally by a person removed in time from an event. Somehow, if written down, an account is better. Indeed, in Custer battle studies, it is not unusual for researchers to ignore or reject Indian oral traditions while at the same time appealing to the white testimony, which in large part is nothing more than oral tradition written down. This neglect is unfortunate; the value of oral tradition as history has been demonstrated elsewhere.[17]

One is struck by the thematic undercurrent in Cheyenne tradition, a theme of bewilderment, amazement, and even disbelief. The Cheyennes thought that the battalion could have made good an escape to Reno. So why did they not? Why did they wait? Of course, the Cheyennes did not perceive a battalion on the offensive. Yet these are quite natural ponderings, questions that arose from the grim aftermath, the finality of annihilation. The soldiers all got killed. Why? The Cheyennes were well aware of the lengthy period of subdued fighting. Thus, the delay doomed the troopers. Hesitancy, or so the tradition relates, spelled defeat. This is classic cause/effect reasoning, perhaps the most normal mental process. Though short of explaining a protracted pause, Cheyenne traditional references to the Cemetery Ridge episode cannot logically be overlooked.

Logic may not be altogether convincing, but historical links to Cheyenne tradition have already been revealed. Archaeological remains tend to validate Indian descriptions of troop maneuvers on Cemetery Ridge. And artifact evidence accords well with other accounts, which are usually assiduously ignored but which complement the tradition. White Bull located two cavalry units on and about Cemetery Ridge. Captain Freeman evidently mapped a position of one. So did Captain Johnston, at least generally, when he noted that fighting (left wing) began low on Cemetery Ridge. Runs the Enemy remembered attacking an organized unit. Lights described, albeit cryptically, the left-wing reaction to the right-wing collapse. Two Moons, a Cheyenne, eventually encountered the troopers on Cemetery Ridge; he later remembered that the soldiers had previously ridden into the valley and out of sight. Sitting Bull, though not altogether certain, reported that troops had come from the river *up* Cemetery Ridge. And Gall, it now seems certain, pointed out one position where left-wing troops deployed after their return from Little Big Horn River.

Historical threads that support claims for a cavalry engagement on Cemetery Ridge lend validity to Cheyenne traditional accounts of soldiers who went to the river and returned. Lt. Philo Clark, in compiling fresh Indian testimony, recorded the same. An informant mapped the cavalry route between Custer Hill and the ford *north* of the Indian village. Others too probably told Clark of this movement, recounting how eventually warriors overran the army. Though Clark's official report is hesitant, the gist is clear. Custer's column, as he called it, went toward the river, intending to reach the ford. This outfit, the left wing as we know it, did reach Little Big Horn River, although that fact, for reasons already discussed, evidently escaped Clark's comprehension.

In questioning the fatalistic theme on archaeological grounds, as well as historical, we need to resolve the contradictions raised in various documentary sources. As noted a few paragraphs above, the accounts of Gall, Standing Bear, and others, filtered through interpreters and non-Indian writers, describe driven soldiers and imply the involvement of masses of Indians. Here are two of the four elements of the fatalistic theme.

There is no doubt that the left wing moved from near the mouth of Medicine Tail Coulee up Deep Coulee to Calhoun Hill. Clearly, the right wing traversed the eastern ridges (Luce and Nye-Cartwright) on the way to Calhoun Hill. In both cases, Indians followed and, at the very least, harassed the movements, drawing resistance in the process. It is not surprising, then, that the Indians considered themselves to be "driving" or "forcing" the soldiers back. No doubt the result of the battle had a lot to do with the development, over the years, of this perception as well. But whether or not the soldiers perceived themselves as being driven is an entirely different matter, one to which the Indian cannot speak. In fact, given later developments, which included the left-wing excursion, the soldiers most certainly could not have shared the Indians' viewpoint. Each side considered itself to be on the offensive, which is not at all uncommon as adversaries collide.

Warriors did not drive the left wing, or the battalion, to Custer Ridge. The Sioux warrior Lights, known also as Runs After the Clouds, said as much in response to Walter Camp's prepared questions. Fighting as the soldiers (left wing) moved from the ford to Calhoun Hill "[was] not very vigorous, but shooting was indulged in by both soldiers and warriors."[18] As for the issue of superior numbers of Indians, it is adequately documented, here and elsewhere, that the Custer battalion eventually faced overwhelming odds. But these masses accumulated over a period of time (not quickly) and primarily through infiltration tactics rather than an onslaught (the remaining two elements of the fatalistic theme). Perhaps only 50 Indians initially confronted the right wing in the Medicine Tail Coulee vicinity. Fighting, which consisted of long-distance shooting, was brief.[19] As the wing moved north toward Calhoun Hill, apparently a few other Indians joined distant skirmishing, but without casualties to either side.[20]

The right wing evidently executed its movement from Luce Ridge across Nye-Cartwright to Calhoun Hill with military precision. Cartridge cases found on the ridges during the 1940s suggest this. E. S. Luce,[21] then the battlefield superintendent, believed that casings found at about nine-yard intervals belied mounted skirmishing; those at three-to-four-yard intervals suggested, to him, skirmishing on foot. These he discovered in roughly linear distributions. Technically, skirmish intervals remained the same in either posture, but variations can and ought to be expected, particularly in horseback skirmishing. Though the findings are poorly documented from an archaeologist's perspective, I am inclined to accept Luce's observations of tactical deployments. Indian accounts of this action suggest the same. These two lines of evidence have led to a consensus among informed Custer battle researchers about the nature of action here. Clearly, the right wing deployed, when necessary, in prescriptive fashion against a rather small force that presented no serious threat.[22] Indications of defensive behavior during the right-wing movement are entirely absent.

It seems that many warriors eventually gained Custer Ridge after crossing Little Big Horn River opposite the mouth of Medicine Tail Coulee. But documentary evidence rather clearly suggests that few Indians remained at or even near Medicine Tail ford when the left wing arrived. Utley estimated the number of Indians at about 30—a slight inflation.[23] Most others had responded to Reno's attack on the south end of the village. For the most part, only those warriors without horses remained near the ford.[24] According to Foolish Elk, Indians eventually got across the river, but not before going west to the horse herd to secure mounts.[25] Many others in the vicinity responded to the new threat by escorting women and children out of the village.[26] Still more, according to He Dog, had gone west to "get ready."[27]

Standing Bear echoed He Dog.[28] He described 15 or 20 Sioux near the ford, some on the east side of Little Big Horn River. Several Cheyennes told Grinnell that initially only 10 warriors had resisted the advance.[29] Joseph White Cow Bull, a Sioux, was among those at the ford. He heard one Indian advise the small party not to attack the more numerous soldiers. Later, according to White Cow Bull, "hundreds" of other Indians accumulated near the coulee mouth.[30]

And as it turns out, a number of Indian accounts indicate light and short fighting near the crossing. Two Eagles, for example, said the scrap was a short one.[31] He Dog did not recall an intense fight at the river; the antagonists exchanged only a "few shots." He stated, "Not much shooting there."[32] Because they were few in number, the eight or so Indians with Bobtail Horse and Calf reportedly had to shoot fast.[33] The tiny force intended only to prevent the soldiers from charging across Little Big Horn River into the village, parts of which lay directly across the ford. And in their minds they did just that (after all, the soldiers did not cross and attack)—a perception that will be scrutinized later.

Accounts of few Indians and little shooting are difficult to reconcile with fatalistic views. Nevertheless, Utley, for one, is not prepared to abandon the theme. In defense, he cites evidence for a heavy fire that "greeted" the left-wing arrival. "Our young men rained lead across the river," wrote one journalist who rendered Sitting Bull's story.[34] "The bullets flew so thickly," claims Utley,[35] that, as Horned Horse's reporter put it, "the command reeled back."[36] No more than a handful of secreted warriors accomplished this. If true, the troopers were plenty skittish, but I doubt this is the impression Utley intended to convey. These accounts are laden with bias imparted by interviewers who helped mold the Custer myth. There is nothing at all in the legitimate literature that portrays Indians who "rained lead" and a command that "reeled back." But it is the type of evidence seized by fatalists.

A few accounts suggest that warriors swarmed across the river to turn back the soldiers.[37] These accounts are typically invoked, sometimes in lieu of the dubious argument for heavy Indian fire, to provide the mechanism that turns an intended cavalry charge into ignominious retreat. Grinnell's Cheyenne account, for example, left this impression, but even it is contradictory. Either numerous Indians caused the cavalry to fall back, or shooting at the river took place with "neither party giving back."[38] Camp believed that the left wing intended to charge. But it obviously did not. So he "made" Standing Bear say that Indians crossed and turned the wing away. In fact, all this business about intended charges and soldiers driven back is as much the interviewer's persuasion as the Indian's perception.

Meanwhile, scant attention has been paid to warrior accounts that clearly state that Indians who crossed at Medicine Tail followed on after the left wing began to leave.[39] It seems the more timid Indians dared not risk fording at Medicine Tail in the immediate presence of troopers. And probably for good reason. While at the ford, troopers obligingly returned the Indians' fire.[40] Goes Ahead, a Crow army scout posted on an elevation above the ford, heard volley fire and saw horse holders behind firing lines.[41] None of this suggests a harried command, one "greeted" at the ford by intolerable blasts of raining lead.

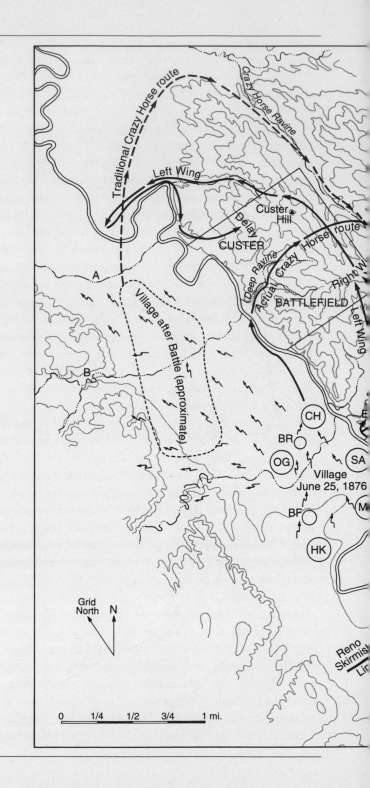

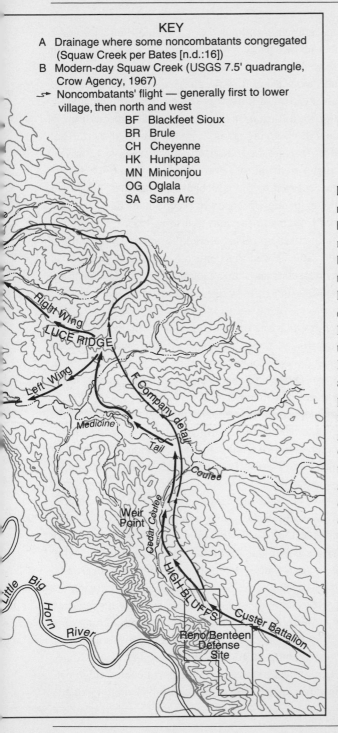

KEY

A Drainage where some noncombatants congregated
   (Squaw Creek per Bates [n.d.:16])
B Modern-day Squaw Creek (USGS 7.5' quadrangle,
   Crow Agency, 1967)
⟿ Noncombatants' flight — generally first to lower
   village, then north and west

    BF Blackfeet Sioux
    BR Brule
    CH Cheyenne
    HK Hunkpapa
    MN Miniconjou
    OG Oglala
    SA Sans Arc

Fig. 16-1. General representation of Custer battalion wing movements from the high bluffs to the Custer battlefield area before the left-wing delay on Cemetery Ridge, including E and F Company positions near the mouth of Medicine Tail Coulee and a proposed F Company advance detail route. Also shown are general representations of Crazy Horse's actual and traditionally accepted battlefield-access routes. The map depicts the prebattle Indian village and the noncombatant exodus through and from it, in relationship to the relocated postbattle village. The Little Big Horn River channel is taken from the 1883 Blake map (on file, Custer Battlefield National Monument).

Rather, it is indicative of a deployment planned and executed with purpose. Brave Wolf's observation that neither party gave back in effect says that Indian firing did not deter that purpose.[42]

The trooper volleys came from a knoll between Medicine Tail and Deep coulees and a position below this toward the river. The positions are located in figure 16-1, along with additional information that maps out other discussions in part 5. As for the Medicine Tail volleying spots, both commanded the ford at distances near enough to direct fire into the Indian village—just across Little Big Horn River.[43] F Company occupied the hillock and E Company the flat below.[44] An E Company detachment deployed to the riverbank. Rather than pursue an attack, this small party quite evidently advanced to reconnoiter. Charles Eastman, a Sioux scholar, learned from his informants that some troopers examined the riverbanks.[45] They, or some of them, also entered the water—apparently to test the riverbed. White Cow Bull viewed their entry as a charge,[46] but this is nonsense made excusable by expectations of an attack into the village. The main body remained behind (including the right wing) while most of the left wing covered the detachment.

Indian bullets might have dropped one or two soldiers into the water.[47] Like White Cow Bull, many have linked these possible casualties with a hurried departure from the river and the subsequent retreat of the wing. Though in retrospect ominous, armies are schooled to expect and accept such losses, minimal as they were, and if true nothing much should be made of this. Rather, if casualties coincided with the departure, it is equally plausible that the detachment had obtained sufficient intelligence by that time. Indeed, eyewitness testimony describes advanced conduct of tasks crucial in determining the suitability of a river ford and nothing more. Hardly pressured, the detachment simply retired—for good reasons, as we shall see.

Of some concern might have been the appearance of an unspecified number of warriors to the right of and behind the wing. Two Moons said that these Indians had crossed before the left wing arrived at the river.[48] Other testimony indicates that the few warriors caught in Medicine Tail Coulee as the wing descended beat a hasty retreat across the river.[49] So warriors who appeared on the east side likely had crossed at places below Medicine Tail ford during the left-wing occupation there. Nevertheless, a show of force as the wing departed for Custer Ridge evidently cowed the would-be antagonists, and nothing happened.[50] The two companies, as a precautionary measure, evidently employed a "to fight on foot" formation, keeping in good order during the Deep Coulee ascent.[51] Apparently, protecting flankers posted on the north coulee ridge paralleled the movement.[52] Edward Curtis's line of march up this ridge evidently represents the flanking route.[53] The deployment seems to have been thoroughly professional.

Increasing numbers of warriors vacated the village side of the river, crossing after the left wing retirement.[54] It is, however, impossible to determine from the vague descriptions just how many Indians crossed, or when, or how rapidly the warrior strength increased relative to the left wing's progress toward Calhoun Hill. Accounts leave the impression, as I indicated, that the soldiers were driven from the Little Big Horn. Many Custer battle students assume that the bulk of these warriors, however numerous, actively engaged in brisk fighting as the wing climbed to Calhoun Hill via Deep Coulee. Elsewhere, though, the Indians employed furtive tactics, and many, if not most, warriors began infiltrating the nearby coulees, but remaining out of the skirmish. Bighead and Wooden Leg, in fact, described this as the tactic used as Yates's wing moved eastward to Calhoun Hill.[55] Subdued fighting and infiltration continued, of course, for a lengthy time after the battalion reached Custer Ridge. A few Indian accounts relate "attacks" on the left wing during the movement, leaving the impression of a gigantic battle.[56] But it was not, and Lights remembered the less-than-vigorous exchanges. The wing merely covered its movement to Calhoun Hill, as one might reasonably expect, and few, if any, soldiers died. There is an unconfirmed, vague report of several open graves, presumably of soldiers, found years ago near Medicine Tail ford.[57] Two Eagles suggested that "a few" soldiers died here.[58]

The Cheyennes agreed, telling Grinnell that some soldiers fell as the "gray-horse company" (i.e., the left wing; here F Company has already lost its identity) made its way up Deep Coulee to Custer Hill.[59] We are not told where or when or how many soldiers died, and in any event, we have no reliable confirmation of any deaths.[60] More important, as Grinnell's informants described it, during this ascent the left wing "opened so heavy a fire that the Indians fell back."[61] This is a generic or blanket description of the nature of fighting during the ascent to Custer Ridge, and it is clearly consistent with infiltration tactics. Flying By's account is similar to that of the Cheyennes. During his approach to the scene, he found "Custer fighting Indians and driving Indians back toward the river."[62]

Evidently the warriors, no matter their number, felt no great compulsion to mix it up in force. The situation in Deep Coulee was no more serious than that under way at right-wing positions. Lone Bear, while retrieving his horse, heard "considerable" shooting as the two wings moved to converge.[63] The cavalrymen in both wings dispersed those Indians who dared get too close, and the soldiers no doubt ably kept the Indians at bay with controlled, periodic firing, just as they had done at the ford. Surely, battalion officers sensed their enemy's reluctance and, maybe aware of growing numbers, likely even relied on it. The soldiers were witnessing classic Indian tactics (including individual daring dashes up close), and they almost certainly knew it. Rather than consternation, urgency, or doom, their emotions must have ranged from exhilaration to determination, as well as the agitation that can attend fire fights. These circumstances, though still consistent with Indian perceptions of an enemy being driven, are not the stuff of a battalion on the defensive.

Other accounts describe many warriors who, after leaving the Reno fight, crossed the river at the mouth of Medicine Tail Coulee. But they make no mention whatsoever of the left-wing encroachment near the river.[64] Although these are invariably used, usually subjectively, as evidence for masses of warriors driving soldiers from the river, these accounts seem to be nothing more than general statements identifying the coulee mouth as an infiltration route to the Custer Ridge vicinity. Though useless in determining the rate of infiltration, such accounts at the least suggest that not all of the warriors who eventually participated in the Custer battle arrived at the same time.

There is confirmation for this suggestion that the warrior force at the Custer battle accumulated over time. Gall, and presumably his followers, did not arrive until after the left wing had departed from its position near the mouth of Medicine Tail Coulee, for he later asserted that no part of the Custer battalion got anywhere near the river.[65] His account and others that make similar assertions[66] contradict those that state that soldiers (the left wing) marched down Medicine Tail Coulee to the river. The seemingly contradictory testimony has for a long time created confusion in Custer battle studies regarding the movements of troopers in Medicine Tail Coulee. Some students argue the soldiers went to the river; others claim they did not. Both groups can cite supporting evidence. Yet the confusion disappears when it is recognized that some Indians were present when the left wing approached the river, whereas many others, Gall included, did not arrive on the scene until after the left wing departed. Moreover, other Indian accounts make no mention of any activities in Medicine Tail Coulee. They do not refer to any Indian or cavalry operations, including the left-wing ascent to Calhoun Hill and the right-wing maneuvers on the ridges east of the river.[67] Some accounts, such as J. K. Dixon's rendition of Two Moons's story, refer vaguely to the cavalry and warrior routes through the Medicine Tail Coulee environs.[68] The references, however, seem to indicate that such knowledge accumulated after the battle, when oral histories circulated. The Bighead and Wooden Leg accounts reflect this.[69]

Thus, it seems clear that many Indians returning from the Reno engagement did not cross the river until after the battalion had reached Custer Ridge. Crazy

Horse was one of these later arrivals. His contingent approached the Calhoun and Keogh sectors from the north and in the absence of the left wing. Hollow Horn Bear recalled, "Quite a little talk was indulged in before an attack was made on [the] Custer [battalion] after [it] first came in sight."[70] Presumably involved in these discussions, he does not pick up the story until sometime during the Calhoun Hill episode. Crazy Horse evidently delayed so long in camp while invoking the spirits that many of the warriors with him became impatient.[71] Also, the majority of warriors who infiltrated Calhoun Coulee via Deep Ravine did so in the absence of the left wing and after the right wing was well established on Calhoun Hill.[72]

It is pertinent to note also that some warriors apparently did not enter the battle until after the fighting on Custer Ridge began in earnest. Standing Bear told Camp[73] that the left wing was forced back, but his account given to Neihardt[74] suggests he approached with later arrivals. Dewey Beard probably also arrived late. After leaving Reno's column, he, like Wooden Leg, had returned to the village to prepare for battle.[75] Other Indians, unprepared when Reno attacked, also went back to invoke their medicine and prepare their bodies before reaching the Custer battle site. Wooden Leg did not join the fighting until the Keogh episode. His account describes the battle from beginning (Calhoun episode) to end (Custer Hill episode) but does not, with few exceptions, utilize a first-person, eyewitness narrative until the Keogh action.[76] His descriptions of earlier action seem to have been compiled from oral histories.

It is therefore reasoned that the many Indians who were eventually involved in the Custer battle accumulated over time. Thus, historical data seemingly inconsistent with a rejection of the fatalistic argument can be resolved. From the troopers' perspective, the right and left wings of the Custer battalion arrived on Custer Ridge under no great pressure. No great masses of warriors drove them there, although infiltration steadily increased. Indians did not force these troopers on the defensive, nor was their demise imminent. Instead, the right wing assumed a position on Calhoun Hill. The left wing departed to the north, obstructed by only a handful of warriors here and there, and eventually approached Little Big Horn River before returning to occupy Cemetery Ridge. Archaeology suggests desultory fighting during this time—a rather tame combat environment. Archaeological observations, independent historical sources, and time-consuming movements of the left wing validate Cheyenne accounts of subdued activity for a lengthy period of time.[77] Moreover, it seems clear, on historical-archaeological grounds, that three-fifths of the battalion remained in reserve while on Custer Ridge, a rather unusual posture for a beleaguered command.

According to Cheyenne oral tradition, the time consumed by left-wing opera-

tions proved fatal because "many more" Indians took the opportunity to infiltrate.[78] These included the warriors, among them Lame White Man, who infiltrated Calhoun Coulee. Eventually the right wing, initially confronted only by
early arrivals, had to contend with these encroaching adversaries—the tinder. C
Company was deployed. Provoked by this deployment, Lame White Man led the
attack that sparked disintegration. Gall and his nearby warriors seized the
advantage provided by the spark. Crazy Horse fueled the fire, moving in from
the north. Quickly, a conflagration erupted. As the right wing collapsed, survivors fled north toward the left wing, stationed on Cemetery Ridge and below
in the basin. The left-wing soldiers also came under fire but moved to assist the
right wing. All remaining soldiers congregated at Custer Hill, where they were
surrounded by overwhelming numbers of warriors and where the final episodes
unfolded.

17

FIXING BLAME

*Bad generalship won his [Custer's] first Indian fight and lost
him his last.*
                                        —*Frederick Van de Water*[1]

*I protest the name of Major Reno [on the Reno-Benteen battle-
field monument].*
                                        —*E. S. Godfrey*[2]

Dispositions, the feelings exemplified by the chapter epigraphs, have
always fueled Custer battle inquiries—and likely always will. The controversy
over Major Reno's culpability in the demise of Custer's battalion is as old as the
event itself. It survives today in vigorous, usually rancorous debate. Custer
apologists, of course, finger Reno himself and often Benteen. The latter, Custer's
defenders claim, failed to comply with orders directing him to rejoin the Custer
battalion.[3] But Reno is by far the most popular target. In fixing blame, Reno
detractors point out that the major did not press his charge as ordered (he abandoned his valley skirmish line), thereby completely and irreversibly thwarting
the plan of action (a plan that is misunderstood or only vaguely sensed). Alternatively, it is said that disintegration among Reno's column (while in the timber)
released hordes of warriors, enabling them to move quickly downstream and
overwhelm the hapless Custer battalion. This should sound familiar. It is, as
pointed out earlier, the "Why?" part of the fatalistic theme. Why? Because Reno
failed. Inalterably confronted with this reality, the only consolation available to
Custer defenders is a futile but gallant, even triumphant, defense flung at the
face of betrayal. Thus was born the Custer myth, and thus does it prosper.

Often Reno supporters do not disagree with the idea that warriors in great
numbers drove Custer's battalion to the ridge, where it was overwhelmed. That is
an indication of how pervasive the fatalistic notions have come to be. To counter,
though, they point out that Custer rejected good intelligence (about warrior force
and village size), unwisely dispersed his command, ordered Reno to an impossible
task, and in any case, failed to support the major's charge. Even though Reno
faltered (characterized not as failure but as a reasonable alternative to certain
death), Custer brought it all on himself. The result is a polarization of views, one
that in my experience, no matter the issue, invariably results in two wrongs.

In contemplating the issue of blame, not everyone has succumbed to the constraints of polarization. Writing in 1886, J. P. Dunn slipped these shackles in a curious way. The Indians, expecting an attack, planned a complicated trap. Cleverly, they divided into two huge warrior bodies. These two, each an overwhelming force, pounced on the two widely separated cavalry columns simultaneously.[4] Neatly, no one is to blame. Dunn neglects to mention why the trap did not include Benteen's battalion and the packtrain. In any case, warriors did not attack en masse simultaneously; there was no trap. Not only did Reno's charge come as a surprise, but so too did Custer's column when its presence later became known. That both columns surprised the Indians is beyond contention. There is much more wrong with Dunn's solution. But it does, in a naïve way, represent the problems in determining event sequences on the Little Big Horn that June day.

Indeed, a great deal of studious labor has gone into determining temporal relationships between movements and actions of the two battalions, particularly concerning the timing of Custer's arrival in Medicine Tail Coulee.[5] Some Custer apologists conclude that Reno's appearance on the hilltop coincided with the arrival of the general's five companies in Medicine Tail Coulee.[6] Others allow a little more time but not enough for the left wing, after separating from the right, to escape a massive confrontation at the mouth of Medicine Tail.[7] In either instance, the timing of Reno's disintegration controlled the destiny of Custer's battalion. Hopelessly confronted at Medicine Tail ford, the battalion ended up driven to Custer Ridge by an aggressive Indian horde bent on destruction.

Lubricating the analytical machinery with fatalistic grease results in nothing more than a simplism. Simplistic solutions must be avoided in examining the complex issue of blame. This is what Wayne Wells had in mind when he examined the timing of Custer's appearance at Medicine Tail ford—an early or late arrival.[8] Wells cogently argues that Custer's battalion, after separating from Reno, proceeded without significant delay to Medicine Tail Coulee and thence to its mouth (the left wing). Further—he shows—the few Indians who confronted left-wing troops at the coulee mouth must have done so very shortly after warriors in substantial numbers raced to meet Reno. And Wells notes that many warriors who eventually returned from the Reno engagement arrived too late to see the left wing at the river. Most compelling are Wells's deductions based on movements of the Crow scouts serving the regiment. Clearly, some of them saw the left wing at the river. Then they rode south *unhindered by enemy warriors* and joined Benteen *before* he linked with Reno. Wells (whose agenda is unbiased) neatly concluded that the left wing most likely arrived at the river early, much too early to have been confronted by warrior throngs and then forced to Custer Ridge.[9]

Wells uses arguments similar to mine, adding others that substantiate an early left-wing arrival at the mouth of Medicine Tail. Summarizing, I have argued that teeming warrior hordes bent on destruction and raining lead neither drove the battalion to Custer Ridge nor enveloped it immediately on arrival. Indeed, it is even possible to argue, citing accounts by One Bull and Young Two Moons, that many Indians stayed out of the Custer battle altogether.[10] Still, a large force ultimately did participate. No one disputes this. White survivors of the Reno fight, in fact, testified that after reaching the hilltop, they were not harassed by Indians for up to an hour. Still, the warriors did not move en masse to confront Custer's battalion at the mouth of Medicine Tail, nor did they collect there in great numbers on short notice. Of those who did not respond to the Reno threat, only a few warriors manned stations near Medicine Tail ford. Others escorted women and children well away from the village. Later, more and more warriors arrived. Some left the Reno engagement early, others later, as word of Custer's presence circulated haphazardly. Some of these warriors were mounted. Others, taken too much by surprise when Reno attacked the village, did not have time to secure a horse. Of these, some moved downstream to intercept on foot. Many returned to the village to select a mount. Some warriors took circuitous routes to the Custer field, whereas others proceeded as directly as possible. Flying Hawk said that able-bodied warriors accompanied the wounded back to their camps.[11] Many delayed there to gather fresh mounts, renew their medicine, or prepare for battle.

It should not be surprising, then, that the large warrior force that eventually overwhelmed the battalion on Custer Ridge took considerable time to accumulate. Few Indians were in positions to meet the left wing at the river. Some showed up to follow (not drive) the soldiers to Custer Ridge. Others gathered while the battalion prepared to continue operations from Calhoun Hill. Still more, altogether ignorant of the left-wing trip to the river, arrived on Custer Ridge after the wing departed. Others, like Wooden Leg, did not appear until after warriors began fighting in earnest. Thus, when the wings separated at Calhoun Hill, the second split since Medicine Tail, a favorable strategic environment prevailed.

This opportunity—to again separate—stemmed not only from substantially less than overwhelming manpower odds (which accrued later) but also from the warrior tactics of cautious infiltration. Thus, battalion operations from Custer Ridge—the left-wing trip to the river while its counterpart remained on Calhoun Hill—clearly started at a time when the command did not perceive a serious threat. Otherwise, it is unlikely that a decision would have been made that resulted in two widely separated wings. Although fatalistic arguments, whatever their twists, deteriorate in light of this explanation, it might still be argued that the influx of warriors after wing separation led to the downfall of Custer's battalion. Here there is some merit. Nevertheless, as with any complex event, there is seldom, if ever, a single causal factor. If the warrior release made possible by Reno's failure is weighed heavily, then other factors must be evaluated, factors that can be gathered from the historical archaeology construction and its insights.

There was, for example, apparently little perception of the threat, now so clear in hindsight, taking shape while the battalion occupied Custer and Cemetery ridges (after the river trip). The virtually unhindered mobility that the left wing enjoyed before occupying Cemetery Ridge probably influenced this perception. But the dissected topography that characterizes portions of the field of battle provided excellent concealment, which in turn promoted infiltration. The command, however, seems to have been poorly informed regarding topography and the Indian strategy, for many warriors, particularly those in Calhoun Coulee and on Greasy Grass Ridge, got very close to the soldiers before being detected— or at least confronted. C Company eventually deployed in an attempt to rid the coulee of these Indians, but historical archaeology shows that before then, neither C nor I had deployed in battle formations. Similarly, F Company constituted the left-wing reserve unit, and only two (E and L) of the five companies stood actively skirmishing.

Procedurally, these are sound deployments indicative of perceptions of a favorable tactical and strategic environment. It is unwise, however, to assume that concealment prevented officers from getting some idea, if only general, of increasing enemy manpower. Much of the field of battle, mostly to the south and east of Custer Ridge, is little broken (much of this area is beyond the national monument boundaries). In many places, particularly viewed from Calhoun Hill, growing warrior numbers probably became obvious. If so, it is impossible to estimate the degree of concern this generated (except to note that eventually C Company did deploy). But if we assume a high degree of concern, the nature of Indian tactics must be considered. The fruits of these tactics may be measured in threats (proximity, danger to the led horses), not in perceptions of impending doom. And these threats developed over time. All the while, only a small portion of the Indian force scampered about on horseback, keeping at a distance, except for an individual's daring thrust from time to time. Skirmishing remained light as Indians chose to infiltrate rather than launch an assault. In the main, warriors showed little fight, hardly a grave situation. This behavior clearly continued even as the left wing, after departing the river environs near ford D, returned to Cemetery Ridge. Thus, notwithstanding manpower odds, this type of prolonged fighting doubtless influenced not only the decision to remain about Custer Ridge but also the decision to stand poised with reserve deployments.

Separation of the wings, though it occurred under favorable conditions, ulti-mately contributed to erosion in the strategic environment. All contact between the two wings vanished as the left wing journeyed to the river. After its return, and during the delay, intervening high terrain prevented visual contact between the two units. Distance seriously impaired timely communication, although it is reasonable to suspect, in the absence of evidence, that wing commanders exchanged information. But neither group could know exactly—from moment to moment—the other's tactical situation, which for the right wing evolved into a serious predicament. For most of this period, the left-wing status remained comfortably stable, creating an overall illusion of security.

This fallacy, this illusion, came to be understood, but only at a critically late moment. That moment may be confidently deduced from the historical archae-ology construction of events on Cemetery Ridge. The left-wing delay low on Cemetery Ridge—related in Cheyenne tradition and supported by independent historical and archaeological evidence—does not appear to be the stuff of a battalion in distress. It is hard to imagine that a command, if officers thought it beleaguered, would remain divided—at a distance of over a mile as the horse goes, and beyond voice and signal communication. The left-wing movement up Deep Ravine, which brought the wings nearer, might at first glance qualify as the moment of realization. Still, F Company, after completing this move, held in reserve. Evidently, concerns had heightened but not to the extent that thoughts of an offensive had been abandoned. If we eliminate these phases, it becomes clear that the moment of realization—the moment when all hopes of an offensive vanished—must have coincided with the onset of disintegration in the right wing.

There is no doubt that dispersal represented a key element of an offensive strategy implemented well before the onset of actual hostilities. This simply cannot be denied, it never has been denied, and it is often pointed to as a factor in defeat (by pro-Reno/anti-Custer forces, of course). While the entire regiment descended into the Little Big Horn Valley, and while undeniably on the offense, orders left McDougall and his packtrain behind, directed Benteen on his scout to the south, and sent Reno into the river valley. Dispersal had begun. The Custer battalion contributed further to dispersion by moving well northward. The bat-talion itself dispersed in wing formation for a while in Medicine Tail Coulee. Such strategic continuity is a compelling barometer. It should not be terribly shocking to find the dispersal strategy repeated even after the battalion vacated Medicine Tail Coulee. But this squares neither with the myth nor with certain biases and so will probably not influence many, even in the face of historical-archaeological evidence and insights.

In sum, Indians released from the Reno engagement thwarted the strategy employed by the Custer battalion. The warriors, when provoked, did stand to fight, and as cohesion crumbled, they rushed the cavalry in considerable numbers. Surely, the no-show of reinforcements (Benteen and the packtrain) obviated any alternative to the outcome, whatever that might have been. But although these factors perpetrated a desperate predicament, as we so well know in hindsight, poor judgment in confronting a fluid strategic environment may also be implicated. Miscalculation of Indian tactics (infiltration), failure to perceive or anticipate the enemy's resolve (after all, the cavalrymen were about to attack the Indians' families), inattentiveness to potential threats posed by odds, and the vulnerability of stationary cavalry in such situations, all coupled with maintenance of a dispersal strategy until too late, reflect singularly poor judgment while operating from Custer Ridge. So in the end, the enterprise of fixing blame is not so simple as one might expect. The subtle but fatal interplay between complex variables resulted in the sudden disintegration and subsequent annihilation of the Custer battalion. To fully appreciate the role of strategy in this defeat, we shall examine that subject in greater detail.

18

STRATEGY

*[At the Washita in 1868] the command . . . was divided into
four nearly equal detachments [and dispersed]. . . . By this
disposition it was hoped to prevent the escape of every inmate
of the village.*

—*George Armstrong Custer (1874)*[1]

Continuity in the offensive strategy of dispersal, established at the
onset of hostilities and maintained nearly until the end, is far too compelling to
ignore. Yet in pondering strategy, and why the events of June 25, 1876, all came
about, there is still more to consider. Discussions until now have made the case
that the battalion collapsed on Custer Ridge while on the offensive. Clearly,
then, old concepts—fatalistic in nature—about events and strategies leading to
the famous finale must be rethought. If the command was not driven, doomed,
and overpowered by hordes of Indians released when Reno faltered, what then
did happen?

Guided with the new framework provided by archaeology, we can wrest
substantial details regarding strategy, and the tactical environment within which
it evolved, from the historical record. These details involve battalion actions on
Custer Ridge and beyond, prior events at Medicine Tail Coulee, and circumstances encountered even earlier—before and after reaching what I call the high
bluffs. These bluffs are defined as the terrain stretching from the Reno-Benteen
field northward to Weir Point (fig. 4-2 or 6-1). Precipitous and elevated—the
highest land—they are a unique part of the Little Big Horn scene. The river here
and there cuts into them from below, in many places over 300 feet below. Here
on the high bluffs, a single Indian village—large indeed—first came into Custer's
view. And here is where he began to shift his focus from the encampment. That
focus is encapsulated in figure 16-1, a visual guide to the strategic environment
that led the general and his battalion ever northward, farther and farther toward
disaster. The map may be used to follow ensuing discussions.

On Custer Ridge and Beyond

The Custer battalion wings, most assuredly on the offensive, left Medicine
Tail, rejoined at Calhoun Hill, and again separated. The right wing remained
while the left undertook its journey to the ford D environs—north of the village.

Most likely, the purpose of the left-wing trek was intelligence gathering, which pivoted on villagers' reactions to Reno's attack. Such critical intelligence could not be obtained with precision before reaching Custer Ridge. The tortuous meanders of Little Big Horn River deceive from a distance, and crossings can be explored for suitability only close-up. Moreover, dense floodplain vegetation had probably precluded a view, except for occasional glimpses, of goings-on in the valley. Surveillance capabilities doubtless improved steadily as the battalion made its way north. But still, village limits, terrain characteristics, disposition of the quarry, and fording places needed to be determined.

The right-wing deployment on Calhoun Hill effectively checked Indian harassment already under way from the south, thereby covering the left-wing excursion. Positions here also prevented further separation from Benteen's battalion, now presumed to be on the way, as earlier ordered (messengers were dispatched before entrance into Medicine Tail Coulee). Once the necessary intelligence had been gathered, and on Benteen's arrival, the force could attack. Quite likely it was hoped that the opportunity could come soon. Custer Ridge provides a panoramic view of Little Big Horn Valley through the west and north. The river here hugs the eastern bluffs. Forest vegetation tends to obscure the stream and its immediate environs. But an expansive floodplain sweeps to the western tablelands in full view of the observer on Custer Ridge. No doubt the commanders, on attaining the ridge, for the first time clearly saw the magnitude of their task, a village in flight—women and children, aged and infirm, thousands of them, escorted by older men who had not responded to Reno's attack, fleeing north downstream and westward to the faraway hills.

Though Reno did not succeed in pressing his attack, his startling descent on the village had resulted in precisely the anticipated reaction. Warriors raced to the confrontation while vast numbers of noncombatants hastened from the camp. Indian accounts describe the exodus, much of which the men in Custer's column surely witnessed from their distant vantage point on Custer Ridge. Flying Hawk mentioned that the ridge placed soldiers "right above the women who had collected down the river."[2] Indeed, some Indian women testified they could and did watch the battle from their river sanctuaries.[3] Custer's five companies were now in the right place. And the timing was right. Reno had struck. The alarm sounded through the village well before Custer's battalion reached the ridge now bearing his name. There is no doubt that the exodus had by now developed fully, although late in the battle, with the outcome assured, many fugitives returned to the village.[4]

Alarmed by Major Reno's assault, some noncombatants raced west to help corral the pony herd.[5] A few doubtless tarried in the village, which, thanks to the major's surprise appearance, now virtually lacked warriors.[6] Before Custer's two wings appeared, some women evidently trailed up the bluffs to watch what was happening in Reno's hilltop fight.[7] Others in small numbers eventually followed Gall to the Custer battle scene.[8] But at first alarm, the large majority of noncombatants scurried away—west and downriver toward the north.[9] Little bunches of women began running into the hills.[10] Some went beyond the village "a considerable distance."[11]

With this scene looming beyond, it became imperative for troopers to leave Custer Ridge and go to the river again, to continue marching toward the north. Corralling the noncombatants would effectively bring the warriors to bay, thereby neutralizing manpower superiority, now clearly known to be in the Indians' favor. The campaign would be a success. Custer had learned this much in 1868 at the Washita. A strategy to capture women and children had figured in a hollow victory over Black Kettle's Cheyenne village. So did the multiprong attack plan (using widely dispersed forces) devised by Custer.[12] But here, on the Little Big Horn, intelligence remained to be gathered. Clearly, to intercept the fugitives, the soldiers needed to cross the river. Leaving the right wing behind, Captain Yates's left wing departed Calhoun Hill and rode off on its northern, or more precisely northwest, course into the valley.

During this trip beyond Custer Ridge, the left wing, viewed from a military perspective, encountered light resistance, for few warriors held positions ahead. For convenience, I previously described the left wing march rather generically as along Custer Ridge and down Cemetery Ridge. But when Yates and his men departed Calhoun Hill, they evidently rode along the east or backside (away from the river and village) of Custer Ridge—following, as He Dog represented it, a "hollow."[13] Two Moons said essentially the same thing: the soldiers came from behind Custer Ridge, then rode out of sight into the valley.[14] Quite likely the wing continued not atop ridges, but using a broad coulee behind or north of Cemetery Ridge as cover. This drainage, which leads directly to Clark's ford D vicinity, is denoted by the left-wing route marked on figures 11-1 and 16-1.

The route choice—drainages—served to shield wing movements from observers in the valley and from warriors who had followed from Medicine Tail Coulee. Most of the latter, proceeding as they did with considerable stealth, probably missed the wing as it slipped into the hollow. But Gall at least saw it depart, recalling—through Lieutenant Godfrey—that "other" troopers moved rapidly "toward Custer Hill."[15] From his position (south of Calhoun Hill), Gall might have seen the two-company column continue on—the quote says "toward," not "to," the hill. But most Indians assumed the wing stopped at Custer Hill, for that is where the "other" soldiers were at the end of the battle. All this—the right-wing deployment and the left-wing departure—occurred early in the period of desultory, long-distance fighting, indeed well before great throngs of warriors had congregated around Custer Ridge (most accounts come from late arrivals who missed this altogether). The left wing, even at a slow gait, would probably consume no more than 30 minutes in its three-mile round trip.

Only a handful of Cheyennes confronted the left wing on its river journey, and it is no coincidence that details of this movement come to us only through the Cheyenne tongue. The record makes it abundantly clear that warriors who followed the two wings as they left Medicine Tail, and for the most part those warriors joining up later, proceeded no farther than the right-wing position. Keogh's wing did its job not only with firepower but also with its presence alone; many warriors, even if they saw the left wing move out, had to remain; they could not leave this force unattended. Quite likely, bullets discouraged others from following on. But in the final analysis, the warrior force present as the left wing departed simply was quite small. Meager numbers, combined with stealth tactics on both sides, considerably reduced chances of detecting the departure, as evidenced by the paucity of accounts concerning the departure. The vast majority of Indians arrived in the Custer Ridge vicinity after the battalion split up, and these warriors encountered only Keogh's complement. They had no knowledge of the river reconnaissance, for the troops that composed Yates's column, as Two Moons recounted, had disappeared.[16]

Ironically, Crazy Horse and his warrior band were among the tardy. Learning of the Custer battalion while engaged with Reno, he returned to the village, delaying there to prepare his medicine and invoke the spirits.[17] Extremely concerned for the women and children, Crazy Horse, with other warriors who had waited impatiently during his lengthy preparations, finally raced to Custer Ridge, there taking positions close to and northeast of Calhoun Hill.[18] Now there were Indians north and south of the right wing, and west too as the Greasy Grass/Calhoun Coulee region began to fill. But when Crazy Horse arrived, the left wing had already disappeared into the valley toward the fugitives, and Crazy Horse knew nothing of it. Once in position, he and those with him sniped at the right-wing rear (to block any further northward movement toward village refugees). Crazy Horse eventually helped break these soldiers, who then fled toward Custer Hill. Of course, by then the left wing had departed the valley to occupy the Cemetery Ridge/Deep Ravine basin environs.

Numerous fatalistic versions place Crazy Horse's initial attack at Custer Hill. Gall and Crazy Horse, it is often said, crushed the battalion simultaneously from opposite ends of Custer Ridge—Calhoun Hill (Gall) and Custer Hill (Crazy Horse).[19] Utley (like some others) does not accept the simultaneous version. Rather, cognizant of the facts, he has Crazy Horse strike first at Custer Hill, then moves him on to the right wing at Calhoun Hill.[20] A Custer Hill first-strike is, however, nothing but a surmise, one made necessary in the face of fact. That

Crazy Horse first attacked the right wing, not at Custer Hill, is indisputable. Flying Hawk's description of Crazy Horse's action cannot be misunderstood; Foolish Elk and White Bull also describe it.[21] And Two Moons related the story as well.[22]

As much as anything else, Crazy Horse's actions—his first-strike at right-wing positions—leave no doubt that the left wing journeyed to the river. In the meantime, Crazy Horse arrived on Custer Ridge to confront Keogh's wing, missing the other soldiers altogether. Just like earlier, when Custer's entire battalion had gone undetected for some time, the strange quirks so common to battle had intervened. Crazy Horse, a victim of timing, topography, and tactics, entirely missed the force that posed an immediate threat to fugitive Indian families scurrying through the valley.

Crazy Horse's route to the battle scene had taken him right past the vacant Cemetery Ridge and Custer Hill localities. His route, however, is commonly misinterpreted. Gall said that Crazy Horse crossed Little Big Horn River at the extreme north end of the Indian village—at the time delimited by the Cheyenne camp.[23] And Flying Hawk recalled that he and Crazy Horse, after crossing, "came to a ravine; then we followed up the gulch to a place in the rear of the soldiers [i.e., the right wing]."[24] From these accounts, researchers typically conclude that Crazy Horse swept well to the north in accessing the battlefield. After he forded, it is thought, he ascended what is today often called (for obvious reasons) Crazy Horse Ravine. Figure 16-1 traces this traditionally accepted route up Crazy Horse Ravine. The drainage heads near Calhoun Hill, flows northwest parallel to Custer Ridge on its east side, and then continues in that direction for a mile to join a larger tributary of Little Big Horn River.

There is no doubt (e.g., Flying Hawk, quoted above) that Crazy Horse and his party, in attacking the right wing, did utilize the upper reaches of the ravine unofficially named after him. But they evidently did not follow it continuously from the river valley, as typically thought.[25] Using such a route, Crazy Horse would probably have collided with the left wing, which most likely rode into the valley behind (north) Cemetery Ridge. That no such encounter materialized strongly indicates that Crazy Horse's party used another route.

The most likely candidate is Deep Ravine.[26] Though later that evening occupants moved their village downstream, its north end on June 25—the Cheyenne camp circle—lay, as the battle unfolded, quite close to the mouth of Medicine Tail Coulee (approximately as shown on fig. 16-1). It is from here—the first encampment—that noncombatants fled. Figure 16-1 also illustrates this exodus, the one that beckoned Custer northward. More than a few Indian accounts attest to this village location, in sketch as well as word,[27] and some of the crude drawings are reproduced here (figs. 13-8, 18-1, 18-2, 18-3, and 18-4). Compare these with figures 9-2, 11-2, and 11-3, three non-Indian portrayals of the village.

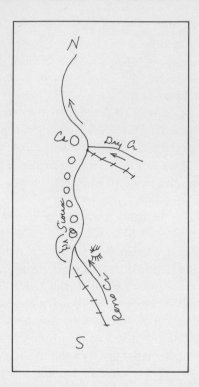

Fig. 18-1. George Bird Grinnell's sketch (based on Solider Wolf's testimony in 1908) of the prebattle Indian village relative to Medicine Tail Coulee (here, "Dry Cr."), Reno Creek, and Little Big Horn River (unlabeled). The Cheyenne camp circle (here, "Cs"), or northern end of the village, is nearly directly across from the mouth of Medicine Tail Coulee. The hatched lines show Custer's advance, above, and Reno's advance, below. From a copy in Grinnell (1898a:201) of the original in the Southwest Museum, Los Angeles.

Interpretations of this nature, and there are many more, invariably distort size and location to the extent that an inflated village has become fact. But the Indians had camped in a much smaller area. So Crazy Horse, before he and the others with him exited the village, went to a Cheyenne camp located very near where Medicine Tail empties into Little Big Horn River.

Going "to his right" (i.e., fording the river) at the Cheyenne circle (north end of camp),[28] Crazy Horse proceeded up a ravine that Eastman described as projecting "east [customary] from [Crazy Horse's] crossing" place.[29] Mrs. Spotted Horn Bull, watching from the village outskirts, allegedly saw Crazy Horse enter the ravine.[30] Gall described it as "a very deep ravine."[31] Deep Ravine is the only defile meeting all these descriptions—very deep, visible from and close to the

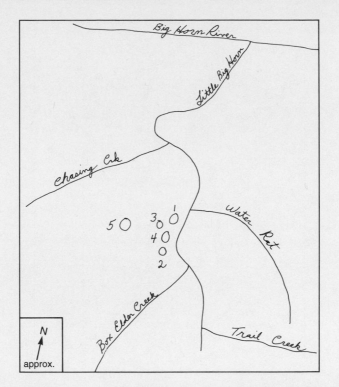

Fig. 18-2. Sketch of Custer battlefield vicinity prepared by Respects Nothing for Eli Ricker in 1906. Sketch shows the prebattle Indian village, with the Cheyenne camp circle (northernmost, here #1) located nearly directly across from the mouth of Medicine Tail Coulee (here, "Water Rat"). Adapted from a copy in Ricker (1906b:1) of the original in the Nebraska State Historical Society.

June 25, or prebattle, village site, and projecting east from the river.[32] So what is wrong with the traditional route, the one shown on figure 16-1? The answer lies in the village, which inhabitants relocated after the battle.[33] Figure 16-1 also approximates the postbattle village site. Notice that if the Crazy Horse party is made to set out for Custer Ridge from the northern end of the later or second village, it did indeed use the traditional route. But that did not happen, for no encampment yet existed there. All of this points exclusively to Deep Ravine.

Precipitous and narrow, Deep Ravine, compared with neighboring drainages, is in fact uniquely deep, hence the name. Short in length, it heads at the west slope of Custer Ridge (the basin), providing quick access from the river. Indeed, three Oglala Sioux with Crazy Horse recalled that they crossed over Custer Ridge from its west (river) side.[34] It appears, then, that the accomplished Sioux leader forded near Deep Ravine, passed up or along it, and then crested

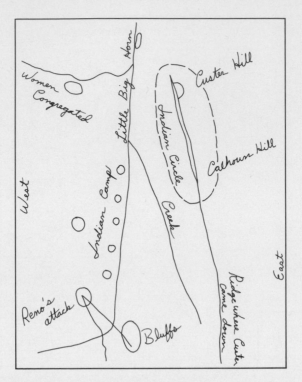

Fig. 18-3. Sketch of the Custer battlefield vicinity prepared by Eli Ricker on the basis of his interview with Standing Bear in 1907. Sketch shows the prebattle Indian village relative to Custer Ridge and the mouth of Medicine Tail Coulee (here, "Creek"). It also locates a point where noncombatants (here, "women") from the village congregated. Adapted from a copy in Ricker (1907:56) of the original in the Nebraska State Historical Society.

Custer Ridge to take up positions behind the right wing. Active, but encountering little resistance, the left wing could not be detected audibly as Crazy Horse made his way to the ridge. When he rode north through the valley, dense vegetation blocked views of the left wing. His contingent, the numbers unknown to us, forded roughly a mile distant from Yates's wing. During his ascent toward the right wing, ridges obstructed, as they do today, views of the forested river environs below.

So, for all Crazy Horse, or most any other warrior, knew at the time, the northern threat was ensconced on Calhoun Hill, harassed by cautious Indians who had originally followed from Medicine Tail Coulee. Later, as other warriors raced piecemeal from Reno, they too could see and hear the right-wing skirmishing. Ignorant of the left, they, like Crazy Horse, wanted to get between this

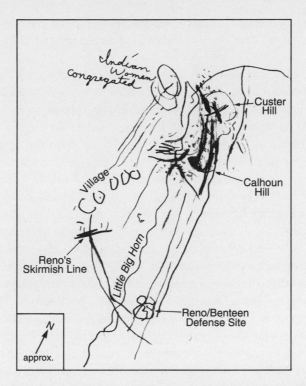

Fig. 18-4. Sketch of the Custer battlefield vicinity drawn by Flying Hawk during an interview with Eli Ricker in 1907 ("marred a good deal by the pencil in explaining"). Sketch depicts the prebattle Indian village relative to Custer Ridge, plus lines of flight from the village to a point where noncombatants (here, "Indian Women") congregated. Adapted from a copy in Ricker (1907:42) of the original in the Nebraska State Historical Society.

force and their refugee families. So others followed Crazy Horse, using Deep Ravine as an infiltration route.[35] Some eventually showed up after the left wing had returned to Cemetery Ridge—the Hunkpapas and Cheyennes described by Iron Hawk.[36] Stymied by the soldiers' presence, they had gathered at the foot of the deep gulch, not daring to go any farther. And for the most part, they did not go farther until induced to do so by the great collapse.

When the left wing returned to Cemetery Ridge, both sides must have been surprised. Warriors, in the absence of the undetected left wing, had been using Deep Ravine to get at the right wing. But then these other soldiers appeared on Cemetery Ridge. This accounts, in part, for the government bullets strewn over The Flats and for the Indian firing remains there. So also does the left-wing show of force at Deep Ravine and its march up the defile into the basin. In all, the record fairly well establishes Deep Ravine and the vicinity as a common point of infiltration. That Crazy Horse crossed here should not, then, seem at all remote.[37]

The left wing had probably reached the river by the time Crazy Horse appeared. If still behind Cemetery Ridge, the left wing might have been revealed by dust, a telltale sign more likely to be inhibited by lush grasses in the valley. In addition, the floodplain forest could obscure whatever the column kicked up, making it all the more "invisible" to warriors focused on troops (right wing) that they could clearly see and hear. And in any case, fugitive families racing through the valley raised their own dust clouds—everywhere down the valley, said one witness. With all this commotion, the missed connection is little wonder.

It is said among the Cheyennes, when relating their traditions, that during this wing's excursion, an undisclosed number of Indians who were secreted in the floodplain forest fired from ambush. Traditional accounts vary as to the effect of this encounter. Indians either unhorsed a left-wing soldier or "killed a couple."[38] The soldier column then returned to the Cemetery Ridge area. Cheyenne tradition continues, stating that the Indian ambush forced a retreat.[39] But again, this is doubtless an impression evolved principally from the grim outcome. Tradition may not tell us how many Cheyennes greeted the left wing, but there are certainly no eyewitness accounts of the action. Virtually everyone had rushed to engage Reno. So my guess on number would be a mere handful—just like at the Medicine Tail ford. Captain Johnston also learned that the initial encounter occurred on Cemetery Ridge (fig. 11-3), not before. So whatever happened near ford D must not have amounted to much, though the fact that traditional stories seem to make more of it is understandable. Oral tradition is more than just word-of-mouth history; it is an ethnic glue.

The wing did not retreat; the feeble "ambush" likely caused little concern. This was an army, and earlier a part of it—Reno's command—had been sent against what anyone, after crossing the divide on June 25, could have guessed to be a larger force. No reasons exist to expect that the left wing would waver the second time it reached the river. Cheyenne tradition remembers that while there, the column reached a ford, the one John Stands in Timber pointed out to Don Rickey.[40] Clark's ford D location, as I have noted, seems to correspond closely to that identified by Stands in Timber.[41] Both locations are shown on figure 11-1, near where Colonel Gibbon found Mark Kellogg's remains. The colonel, in order to inspect the battle aftermath, crossed at this ford, which he described as shallow.[42] Very likely, the left wing saw a natural, well-used crossing that did not require a lengthy, detailed inspection.[43]

Views from this vicinity probably gave left-wing officers an accurate fix on the northern periphery of the village, or at least knowledge that it lay a considerable distance south of the crossing.[44] The wing had entered the valley north of the ford and had marched along the floodplain in a southwest direction to reach it. Once finished there, the column turned northward, returning by roughly paralleling its original route to the river.[45] In all, the left-wing trip had established the existence of a suitable ford, had determined that the ford lay at a comfortable distance (1.5 miles) from the village, and had allowed a nearby assessment of the fleeing families. Striking here would block a village exit, facilitate capture of the noncombatants, and deny the many warriors still busy with Reno upriver access to them. (Warriors were thought to be still busy because a tiny threat at ford D would create that impression. No doubt that impression changed somewhat on return to Cemetery Ridge, but not appreciably, as we have seen.)

With vital intelligence gathered, the left wing turned about and rode back to Cemetery Ridge, there to await Benteen's arrival—not because a Cheyenne ambush forced them back. Reinforcements, including the packtrain and its escort, would effectively double the force (over 400 men). Also, noncombatants clearly had scattered and were still scattering, creating the impression that Reno had been successful. Perhaps his battalion would soon appear as well. The decision to remain on Cemetery Ridge, nearer the right wing, allowed continued assessments of the situation in the valley directly below and stymied enemy access via the Deep Ravine environs. But it also unwittingly placed the battalion in fatal jeopardy. It appears that for some time, options other than tarrying on the elevations existed. The wing could have resumed its northern march; the ease of the earlier left-wing movements virtually assured this, at least initially. But evidently the exodus had not reached much farther north. The left might have returned to the right wing. Both could have marched off toward Reno (south), an option that Stands in Timber thought possible,[46] mostly because of passivity, for by now warrior numbers had increased. But because an offensive posture prevailed, no one considered these options. When the situation deteriorated, the options were no longer available.

Custer desired the assistance of Benteen's force as much for sheer numbers as for additional firepower. Borrowing one Indian's description of how warriors eventually fell on Custer, we can suppose that the villagers must have swarmed like ants from their hills when Reno attacked. No interviewer asked a question that might have elicited such an answer. But the scene can be fairly reconstructed from existing testimony. Answers Camp received to his question about the villagers' reaction to Reno's assault describe utter confusion and intense excitement. Many other accounts describe the same reaction. Women and children started for the benchlands; they "scattered down the stream, and up in the hills."[47]

One sanctuary is known to be a tributary or gully of the Little Big Horn—commonly known as Squaw Creek—located north of the village and west of the river.[48] Some Indian-derived sketches reproduced here seem to indicate this haven (see figs. 10-1, 11-2, 13-8, 18-3, 18-4). Squaw Creek as mapped in earlier times might have differed from that identified on modern maps, so two locations are depicted in figure 16-1 (likely both harbored refugees). Notwithstanding the exact identification, there seems a tendency to believe, when the crucial issue of noncombatant reactions is considered (which, due to the fatalistic bias, is exceedingly rare), that all women and children sought safety in a single creek bottom.[49] But this does not seem possible. Descriptions of the confusion, excitement, and scattering of little bunches militate against a lone haven. No one in the village exercised authority or implemented a standing evacuation plan, although when Reno attacked, some inhabitants evidently hurriedly received instructions to break camp and move out.[50] Fugitives, caught by surprise, clearly scattered in any direction so long as flight carried them away from Reno's assault. Some accounts say fugitives ran to the west, others propose downriver, some describe benchlands, and hills and coulees too—like swarming ants. Indeed, Flying Hawk recalled, "Women [and] children . . . ran in every direction."[51]

It is not hard to imagine the tactical problem that widespread scattering presented—a village of thousands on the run. Here was a cavalry regiment determined to corral the whole lot and forcibly return all to reservation life. But villagers in staggering numbers—as many as 6,000 (see note 11)—began scurrying in many directions at once. Custer's battalion of 200-plus just might, barely, succeed at its task—or maybe, even probably, not. But double the size of the battalion, and chances for success increased immeasurably. A partial victory, capturing just a portion, like at the Washita, could not be accepted in light of the singular campaign objective—to bring all the "recalcitrant" Indians to bay. But rounding up a widely scattered population required dispersal of forces. Either Custer's small battalion would be spread too thinly, thus increasing vulnerability, or there simply would not be enough men to accomplish a thorough task. More were needed; Benteen and McDougall were (presumably) on their way, as ordered. So far as anyone in the Custer battalion could anticipate, these two groups would provide the extra manpower necessary to effect apprehension. In addition, their appearance would compromise the warrior positions steadily accumulating around the right wing, which could not now be easily disengaged to assist the left in rounding up their quarry. So, in effect, at this crucial time, only the left wing—not the entire battalion—remained free for the task at hand. But even though the strategic environment had evolved since Benteen's recall, help could be expected. The battalion waited.

Before entering Medicine Tail Coulee, Custer sent two couriers from his battalion with dispatches to McDougall and Benteen. The first dispatch—verbal instructions transmitted by Sergeant Kanipe—ordered McDougall, and Benteen if encountered, to bring the packs overland straightaway. The second, specifically recalling Benteen with the pack animals, conveyed essentially the same sense of immediacy. The regimental adjutant, Lieutenant Cooke, penned this command, and Trumpeter John Martini relayed it. Often, Custer's written order is perceived, in hindsight, as a portent of great danger: "Benteen. Come on [straightaway]. Big village [overwhelming force]. Be quick [we are in immediate danger]. Bring packs [ammunition needs are critical]."

This common interpretation [in brackets], which of course is the fatalistic approach, was not at all the case. Instead, the message reflects not only village size but a single encampment ("Big village"), plus a legitimate concern that many of the Indians therein might escape ("Be quick"). Further, it shows a desire to remove the packtrain from isolation ("Bring packs"). The supply column had earlier that day remained well behind when the three battalions had moved out toward Little Big Horn River. Alone, the train remained terribly vulnerable to infuriated warriors who might choose, once noncombatants had been secured, to maraud rather than submit. Custer had learned that lesson after capturing some women and children at the Washita eight years earlier. Unable to recall his supply wagons, he anxiously hoped warriors would not discover the wagons (luckily they did not).[52]

At least this much could be anticipated when officers in Custer's battalion first glimpsed the village on the Little Big Horn. Peering from the high bluffs even before reaching Medicine Tail Coulee, they doubtless learned of the growing confusion in the encampment.[53] The soldiers had little or no concern for the village proper; it could be destroyed later. But many, many fugitives, and warriors too, could be expected, and to handle the situation simply required a larger force. Consequently, General Custer issued his celebrated orders recalling McDougall and Benteen, then continued well to the north and, of necessity, chose to wait for their arrival—and perhaps Reno's too—on Custer and Cemetery ridges.

That the two wings waited, expecting Benteen and doubtless the packtrain, is not speculation. At the time, Custer knew (1) that Benteen was on his way, (2) that Benteen ought to arrive earlier than originally expected, (3) that the trail was open, and (4) that Martini had surely delivered the message directing Benteen to Custer. He could be confident of all this, for Boston Custer had left the packtrain and joined his older brother while the battalion maneuvered in Medicine Tail Coulee. The younger Custer, twenty-seven years old then, served the expedition as a civilian packer, and he brought with him valuable information.

Along the way, Boston first encountered Benteen's column and next Martini, who was ferrying the recall orders to Captain Benteen.[54] But as it happened, the captain, no longer probing to the south, had already returned to Custer's trail—on his own volition.[55] Boston knew this, and the elder Custer surely learned of it. Having covered the same ground, the general's youngest brother could also say about where he had met Benteen, allowing an estimate of the latter's time en route. And Martini, Custer knew, doubtless used the trail that Boston previously had negotiated safely—and alone. The trumpeter would make it, easily (he did). Further, the packtrain had been only about a mile behind when Boston had ridden by Benteen's column.[56] With Benteen already on the trail and close to the packs, Custer could expect him to be quick once Martini delivered the orders. On the strength of such knowledge, the general could afford to wait, particularly considering the daunting task ahead. There, on Cemetery Ridge and around Calhoun Hill, he and his men did just that.

To and on the High Bluffs: Scatteration and Strategy

It is appropriate to view in greater detail the nature of Custer's strategy. Crazy Horse, who granted an interview less than a year after the battle, stated that the women and children made a stampede in a northern direction.[57] In fact, many Indians figured it this way.[58] One of these—Crow King—matter-of-factly summarized the Indian intent. Unaware of Custer's battalion, warriors rode to hold Reno in check so that villagers could scatter in the hills.[59] Speaking of Custer's thoughts as he first glimpsed this village from the high bluffs south of Medicine Tail Coulee, Lieutenant Godfrey theorized:

> *He must, then, have expected to find the squaws and children fleeing to the bluffs on the north, for in no other way do I account for his wide detour to the right [i.e., to Custer Ridge]. He must have counted on Reno's success, and fully expected the "scatteration" of the noncombatants with the pony herds. The probable attack on the families and the capture of the pony herd were in that event counted upon to strike consternation into the hearts of the warriors, and were elements for success upon which Custer counted in the event of a daylight attack.*[60]

That the general at some point expected "scatteration" can hardly be denied. Very early on June 25, near the Rosebud/Little Big Horn divide and some distance from the village on the Little Big Horn, Custer had learned of various Indian sightings. He concluded from these that his regiment had been detected.[61] To him, it was just a matter of time before these outlying Indians notified their people in Little Big Horn Valley. So Benteen, under orders, took his battalion to the left, en route either to block a southern escape up the Little Big Horn or, perhaps, to intercept encampments scattered throughout the valley. Custer and his subordinate, Major Reno, continued east toward the Little Big Horn, following down Reno Creek. Shortly thereafter, about when the major received his attack orders, intelligence reports of fleeing Indians began reaching Custer. Lieutenants Hare and Varnum had led advance scouting parties to the river valley. Varnum reported his observations several times, the last report delivered in person "probably two miles from the river."[62]

Lieutenant Hare reportedly sent notes, the contents of which are not known. But George Herendeen, a scout riding with Hare, supposed that the lieutenant reported Indians in flight, for that is what everyone in the scouting party seemingly observed.[63] Fred Girard, another scout, reportedly told Custer—minutes before Reno received his attack orders—that Indians were "running like devils."[64] Girard had evidently seen a few scores of Indians hastening beyond an outlying campsite. Located on Reno Creek several miles east of the main village, this camp is now most commonly called the Lone Tipi site (also Burning Tipi) because only a single lodge stood where many more had been. Occupants had abandoned this small encampment, by all indications, just hours earlier.

Shortly after Girard's declaration, the Crow scout Half Yellow Face reported (to Custer) fleeing Indians as well—perhaps those seen by Girard.[65] Counting on surprise, the general thought that his fears had been realized. But as it turned out, and though there are isolated accounts to the contrary, Reno caught the villagers completely off guard.[66]

It is important to emphasize here something I have previously only touched on. We know that the Indians inhabited a single, rather large village. Peering from the Rosebud/Little Big Horn divide, the scouts possibly thought as much. But this intelligence seemed to lack conviction, at least among officers. So it is possible that no one in the regiment, while marching from the divide down Reno Creek, counted on only one village. Thus, as Mike Moore has commented to me, some decisions—perhaps the one that resulted in Benteen's scout to the left—could have been predicated on the possibility of a number of small villages spread widely along the valley. That, of course, proved to be the configuration that Custer encountered at the Washita eight years before the Little Big Horn. Under such expectations, the problem of "scatteration" would have posed an even greater concern.

In any case, heading down Reno Creek, the two battalions (now without Benteen's command) roughly paralleled each other on opposite sides of the stream. The general soon (near the Lone Tipi site) waved the major over, telling him, through Adjutant Cooke, to move his outfit ahead "at as rapid a gait as prudent, and to charge afterwards, [and you will be supported by the whole outfit]."[67] As Reno complied, Cooke coincidentally advised that Indians in the valley 2.5 miles distant were "running away."[68] This communication belies, with official force, Custer's assessments at the time. Indeed Reno, like Godfrey, understood that his commander fully believed the Indians were scattering.[69] Very likely, Custer had learned that Indians even then were fleeing north.[70]

As Lieutenant Varnum delivered his last report, Custer told him of Reno's impending attack. Custer either had already issued his subaltern's orders on the strength of earlier intelligence or decided to do so even as the lieutenant reported. In any case, Varnum noted that he told Custer the valley was "full of Indians."[71] Varnum's last communication, as it is recorded, does not specifically reflect an escaping quarry.

Indications are that subsequent intelligence further modified initial perceptions. Girard had ridden with Reno on the attack. After crossing Little Big Horn River, he could see warriors spilling out to meet the major's three companies. The Indians came from the village, which, until now, had not been spotted in any form by anyone with the 7th Cavalry. The enemy had decided to confront the soldiers. Understanding that Custer presumed otherwise, Girard recrossed the Little Big Horn and reported this to Lieutenant Cooke, at that moment riding ahead of Custer's battalion.[72] Although it is not recorded, there can be no doubt that Cooke turned about, rode back, and told his regimental commander of these developments.

Custer's attack instructions indicated that he would support Major Reno—the entire outfit in support. Adjutant Cooke had ridden briefly with the major after delivering the orders. Then, according to Reno, the adjutant stated, "We [Custer's battalion] are all going in with the advance [Reno]."[73] Reno had expected this support, in accordance with military convention, from his rear.[74] Instead, as we know, Custer went north. Shortly before reaching the river, the general and his column veered sharply right (north)—off Reno's trail and onto the high bluffs.

Had Custer intended to support Reno's rear, he obviously changed his mind. Some 100 Indians on the more northern high bluffs and ahead of the column must have sparked his turn to the right. Sergeant Kanipe, then with Custer but shortly to act as messenger, said the battalion turned north immediately after spotting them and quickened the pace.[75] The command ascended the high bluffs, which overlooked Little Big Horn Valley and the southern village limits. On reaching this height, the soldiers found that the 100 or so Indians (I use the highest of varying estimates), evidently those first seen near the Lone Tipi site, had disappeared.

Major Reno, along with Benteen, would soon establish his hilltop defensive position atop these same bluffs. But at the moment, he and his battalion had entered the valley floor below. From the high bluffs Custer, or his officers, could see only a part of the village (their first view of the south end).[76] Otherwise, accounts of sightings are generally contradictory. There are reports that the village was peaceful, unaware, and that Reno could not be seen or heard.[77] Others saw various stages of Reno's valley attack.[78] No doubt both versions are correct—observations by different people at various vantage points and/or at different times. Some soldiers with Reno, in fact, at various times caught glimpses of the battalion above.[79] Fairly clearly, the major's outfit appeared in Custer's view soon, but sometime after the general's battalion attained the heights. Now provoked, warriors in the valley sallied forth, and evidently a handful of them also spotted Custer's battalion above but, not sure of its intent, reacted instead to Reno's immediate threat.[80] Sometimes fatalists illogically translate these few sightings into widespread knowledge; according to this view, warrior throngs immediately turned about and quickly intercepted Custer's battalion at Medicine Tail Coulee.

Nonetheless, we know that Reno's charge immediately sent village inhabitants into confusion and flight.[81] Custer probably could not have avoided seeing clear evidence of, or receiving information about, these initial results. "Everything was a scramble" with "dust rising everywhere down [north] the valley," two of his Crow scouts said later.[82] If not, he doubtless by now expected classic Indian tactics—rear-guard skirmishing designed to provide the main body time to escape—and in effect, that is what emerged from Reno's attack.[83]

Whether or not Custer, or the command's eyes and ears, actually saw Reno's halt—a deviation, it is said, from orders to charge the village—has been a focus of controversy.[84] But even that event could have been anticipated. The general knew early on, thanks to Girard, that the warriors, instead of fleeing, had responded to Reno. He also knew, through two couriers sent by Reno, that the opposition was (or would be) "strong."[85] Girard's information surely reached Custer by the time he was on the high bluffs, probably before, and perhaps before his turn to the north, for it appears that Cooke accepted the message while he was still in Reno Creek, well ahead of his regimental commander.[86] Moreover, Reno's couriers (at least the first) located Custer minutes after Cooke reported Girard's observations. This seems evident because Girard, backtracking to rejoin Reno and before again crossing the Little Big Horn, evidently met the first messenger hurrying east up Reno Creek.[87]

Though deviating from earlier intelligence reports of an entire village in flight, warriors and families all, these developments—rear-guard tactics—nonetheless played into Custer's hands. They provided an opportunity to intercept fugitives, now rendered largely defenseless as warriors, still ignorant of the Custer battalion, began engaging Reno. The situation had changed somewhat, as might be expected in a fluid strategic environment. But the fact that Custer recalled McDougall (packtrain) and then Benteen while on the bluffs is consistent with all this. No need now to jeopardize the packtrain, given finalization of the strategy and expectations of success. Further, developments now largely precluded a southern escape route, which Benteen at the moment ostensibly blocked. And besides, Benteen's forces from here on would be useful, particularly now that the nature of the villagers' reactions could be anticipated. Custer, through Lieutenant Cooke, sent Trumpeter Martini with the now famous "Come on—Big Village" message recalling Benteen. Martini, through Camp, later reported that just before he left the battalion, "Custer . . . made a speech to his men saying, 'We will go down . . . and capture the village.' . . . the consensus of opinion seemed to be among the officers that if this could be done the Indians [warriors] would have to surrender when they would return [from the Reno fight], in order not to fire upon their women and children."[88]

Notice here the clear reference to the warrior forces *now* being brought to bear against Reno. To continue, if capturing the village represented the intent at this time (as the column reached the high bluffs), then that changed too, as we have seen. As the passage intimates, however, noncombatants represented the primary target. So probably the village proper never did figure prominently in Custer's intent. A low-ranking private, Martini may not have anticipated flight from the village (which clearly occurred). But certainly Custer and his officers expected abandonment, and they by now knew of it. Clearly the general's strategy, whatever it might have been earlier, hinged on these fugitives, and nothing he saw along the way—whether in Medicine Tail Coulee, later at its mouth, then along Custer Ridge, or finally near ford D—changed the situation as he perceived it. On the contrary, he observed a largely deserted village at the coulee mouth, a fully developed exodus at Custer Ridge, and "scatteration" at the ford D vicinity. And nothing foiled the plan—no massive attack in Medicine Tail, no retreat to the ridge, no swift denouement—until disintegration unexpectedly dissolved the offensive.

At Medicine Tail Coulee

Battalion operations while in Medicine Tail Coulee are striking in that they mirror, in structure if not in detail, those undertaken thereafter—on Custer Ridge and beyond. It is thus reasonable to suppose that these sequent operations reflect uniformity in a strategy developed as Indians reacted to Reno's attack. This reaction—flight under cover of rear-guard fighting—fueled strategic operations in Medicine Tail Coulee. Surely anticipated, and witnessed during initial stages, these events led Custer's battalion northward, seeking access to fugitives. The appearance of the battalion in Medicine Tail Coulee, whether intended or not, blocked a potential escape route.

Vacating the high bluffs, Custer's battalion, the wings not yet separated, trailed into Medicine Tail via Cedar Coulee, arriving some distance from the river (nearly two miles). Seeing the battalion, several Indians there scurried down to the village. Initially marching down the creek, the entire command eventually occupied an adjacent high ridge overlooking Little Big Horn River (on Luce Ridge about a mile distant, see fig. 16-1). Subsequently, the left wing undertook its trek down Medicine Tail to the river ford. During this time, the right wing remained stationary, occupying the ridge crest. A familiar posture, this is seen again during battalion operations on and beyond Custer ridge.

Several Indian accounts suggest that while at the river, the soldiers attempted to ford and attack the village.[89] The claim—though forgivable, given the finality of subsequent events—is so unlikely as to be without merit. These are Indian impressions in the genre of "soldiers driven back." They do not necessarily reflect the troopers' intent. Indeed, as already noted, only a small soldier party approached the river. Meanwhile (again see fig. 16-1), the two left-wing companies remained behind, one on a rise (F Company) some 500 yards from the Little Big Horn and the other (E Company) below on flatter ground midway to the river.[90] So far as is known, some few troopers at the stream, thought to be from E Company, actually entered the water. Doubtless this action created the impression of an attack, for it is reasonable to assume that an attack is what the few nearby warriors expected. After all, their village lay directly across the river. Nevertheless, the nature of the wing deployment at the time seems ample proof that the left-wing deployment, for the moment at least, was only an exploratory probe.

Of course Yates's wing did not implement an attack while at the ford; it is clear that F Company began its movement to Calhoun Hill from its original position on the rise. The whereabouts of E Company as it withdrew with F is less certain, but it is unlikely that it would have been sent to an attack alone. Indeed, the entire wing, we know, numbered only about 80-plus men. Nevertheless, the "planned but thwarted attack" belief prevails in Custer battle studies. We have already viewed much of the evidence cited in support. In sum, the evidence includes enormous Indian resistance, ominous soldier deaths, the timely arrival of additional warriors, and the fact that some Indians forded to harass the rear and right flank of F Company. A few Indian accounts even suggest that many, many warriors, instead of simply offering a stiff defense, attacked first.[91] But again such accounts, if not outright fabrications, are hazy explanations for the grim outcome. As such, they do not bear on strategic intent. Except for Indian impressions, there is no known evidence at all—material or historical—that supports a foiled attack at Medicine Tail ford.

Thus it remains equally probable, indeed most likely, that the left-wing mission functioned, precisely as did the later trip to ford D, to gather intelligence. An attack across Medicine Tail ford cannot be construed as anything other than an option—viable only if intelligence proved that such an action was strategically feasible. Considering the subsequent operations, a thrust by the left wing alone, indeed the entire battalion, seems exceedingly doubtful. Certain of the conditions necessary for an optimal strategic environment had not been fulfilled. Even with a vulnerable village, which is certainly the case at this stage in events, Benteen had not yet arrived. Clearly, Custer had early on anticipated that Benteen's assistance would be necessary. If desiring to attack from the Medicine Tail ford, the left wing, as it did in the Custer Ridge environs, would have withdrawn to within supporting distance of the right, with both wings remaining there to await Benteen.

But that did not occur, and the actual events give rise to two important implications. First, the left wing did not return east to the right-wing position on Luce Ridge—no less suitable for defense than Custer Ridge. Rather, it went farther north. Indeed, the right wing moved that way too. Yet at the time on Luce Ridge, the warrior threat, by all accounts, hardly constituted anything serious. Actual events seem curiously odd if warriors repulsed a river attack, shifting the battalion from offense to defense. Under such circumstances, one might expect the right wing to stay put and the left to beat a hasty retreat to Keogh's wing. This did not happen. What is more, the battalion, after separating from Reno, had just marched over ground wholly uncontested by the adversary. If we assume the battalion was suddenly and overwhelmingly placed in jeopardy—as in the fatalistic tradition—Custer could have guessed that Reno too had been checked. The major could not reasonably be expected to appear downstream. Thus, for a defensive command, backtracking loomed as the best option. This action would have closed the gap between widely separated commands, including Benteen, who Custer had reasons to believe was on the trail. Presumably not yet engaged, Benteen could render relief to a beleaguered Custer. But none of this occurred because the general's battalion had no reason to abandon the offensive.

More liberal fatalistic versions posit a repulse at the Medicine Tail ford but allow the battalion to maintain an offensive up to Custer Ridge (operative here is the reasonable conclusion that an army does not necessarily lose the initiative simply because it is checked). There all is lost, nearly immediately, and backtracking is not possible. But this scenario does not work either—because of the second implication. Actual events, viewed in an optimal strategic environment, indicate that Benteen was not the only missing ingredient. Had he been, there can be little doubt that, rather than further distancing himself from reinforcements (going to Custer Ridge), Custer would have waited in Medicine Tail Coulee. In spite of a village inadequately defended at Medicine Tail ford, the general could see that something else was missing—people. Fugitives remained the principal objective: one could not return an empty village to reservations. Control of the village proper meant nothing without first apprehending its inmates. In any case, seizing a vacant camp would not neutralize the warrior strength, certainly by now presumed considerable even though at the moment meagerly constituted in Custer's front.

The case for an exodus from the village has already been made here, in general terms. Evidence points to a sequential development. When Reno attacked, according to several Indian accounts, most noncombatants in the upriver camps, ignorant of Custer's battalion, fled north to and toward the Cheyenne circle at the lower village.[92] Others, as noted earlier, scrambled west to the horse herd. Eventually, according to Kill Eagle—he remained in camp during the entire fight—the upper camps lay deserted.[93] These were the "signs" that Custer's men read from atop the high bluffs—signs of flight, from their vantage point.[94] Then, somewhat later, Indian women foraging east (north in the Indian scheme) of the river spotted Custer on the bluffs. They quickly brought word of his impending approach to the lower village,[95] as did, perhaps, five Sioux warriors driven by the left wing as it descended Medicine Tail Coulee.[96] Excitement intensified.[97] As word spread through the lower lodges, "most" of the women and children congregated there "stampeded."[98] By many accounts, they fled, with Medicine Tail blocked, west and farther north. It seems also that some raced southward—back through the village.[99] Some of these refugees notified the warrior body, then busy with Reno, of Custer's surprise appearance. The word spread haphazardly (not immediately throughout a dispersed group). As this new information circulated, warriors, when they could, returned to assay the new threat.

Thus as it turned out, the left wing at Medicine Tail ford could see not only a sparsely populated lower village but clearer signs of full flight. Custer now found himself immersed in a trend that extended his strategy not so much in design as in space. His appearance contributed to the trend, which now virtually dictated a northerly extension. Conversely, an attack from Medicine Tail had become much less attractive. Even viewed from the ford, the village apparently sprawled still farther downstream. Curtis, early in the 1900s, heard from Indian informants that some soldiers had looked around, as might be expected, from a "fairly" high point near the ford.[100] If the floodplain forest did not intervene, village extent might have been estimated. An attack here should have netted some captives; by some accounts, the village was not wholly deserted. (Later, shortly after the left wing departed Medicine Tail ford, Wooden Leg found the Cheyenne camp virtually deserted.)[101] But such action would largely preclude rounding up fugitives already farther north, beyond the village limits (possibly visible at times but certainly predictable). Given these circumstances, potential dangers in entering the village probably figured little in the decision not to attack here. And arguments that an impassable ford precluded an assault are also rendered moot.

Like Curtis, Walter Camp learned from three Crow scouts that officers (presumably), to enhance surveillance, climbed a low bluff near the crossing.[102] Surely this happened. Would not a military man take advantage of high ground? What anyone could see of Reno from Medicine Tail ford is speculative—but probably nothing because of forest, lodges, and dust. Heavy firing upstream is sometimes offered as a portent of danger left unheeded. But in battle, such can be expected, and I do not see any omen here. Custer could have charged into the village from Medicine Tail to support Reno, thereby sandwiching the warriors. But they would easily have slipped the trap, joined their families, and escaped, all the while harassing pursuers, if any cared to bother, with rear guards. In that case, both forces would have lost; the Indians their village and the regiment its captives. I noted earlier that Custer possibly knew, and might have suspected, that Major Reno had stalled (not quit). But at Medicine Tail ford, Custer encountered nothing more than light warrior resistance (in numbers, then tactics), proving that the major had successfully occupied adversaries. Meanwhile, the quarry was escaping, and Custer remained free to pursue them.

The two wings operated independently while at Medicine Tail Coulee, so it is not unreasonable to suspect that strategic options were formulated before separation at Luce Ridge. One of these, the attack option predicated on Benteen's arrival, did not materialize, for reasons just enumerated. In this event, the strategic plan called for the left wing to undertake a maneuver to high ground farther north. The right wing, under this option, was to join the left. There is strong support for this scenario. The right wing *did not* begin its northern movement to Calhoun Hill via Nye-Cartwright Ridge until *after* the left wing began its withdrawal.[103] Clearly, alternatives required the passive right wing to respond to actions of its counterpart.

Moreover, independent evidence suggests that strategic options, in lieu of an attack at Medicine Tail ford, called for a rendezvous and that the location had been established before the two wings separated. Two Eagles, while referencing Walter Camp's map, said that a small detachment ("a few") proceeded from an elevation east of Custer Ridge ("E" on figure 9-2) to Calhoun Hill. Evidently, they did so before the left wing departed the right for Medicine Tail ford ("B" on Camp's map).[104] Camp got a similar story from "an intelligent Sioux woman" who reported a small party "in advance of the 5 companies and further to the east."[105]

One of Pvt. Peter Thompson's recollections fits nicely with Two Eagles's and the unidentified Sioux woman's statements. Originally with the right wing (in C Company), Thompson—thanks to an exhausted mount—lost contact with the battalion somewhere in Medicine Tail Coulee.[106] Eventually he had to return south (as it happened, to Reno's position on the hilltop). But as he backtracked, and from a position in or above the coulee, Thompson saw "5 men of Co[mpany] F going, away out on the side of the slope beyond Dry Creek [Medicine Tail Coulee] . . . riding at a fast gallop."[107] The five had not yet reached Calhoun Hill when Thompson spotted them. Still, it is evident from his phrasing—going "away out" beyond—that they headed in that direction, away from the battalion and Thompson. The private did not remember names of these scouts.[108] But like Two Eagles's account, his story indicates that this event occurred before separation into wings.[109] My interpretation of the scouts' trail appears on figure 16-1.

Thompson's account, particularly concerning the Reno-Benteen siege, which he survived, is often lightly regarded by Custer battle historians. However, there are independent corroborations (Two Eagles and the Sioux woman) of the advance detail. Indeed, under the circumstances, an advance scouting party is entirely plausible, even prudent, no matter what anyone might have thought would occur at Medicine Tail ford—or anywhere else for that matter. Earlier, when Benteen had received instructions for his scout to the left, Custer had also ordered him to throw out an advance party (well-mounted officers with about six men).[110] Moreover, Thompson's reference to F Company is especially relevant. In another interview, Thompson told Camp, "Company F was next to Headquarters [Custer's regimental staff] on [June] the 25."[111] As Brian Pohanka has noted, it makes sense that an advance party would be drawn from this company.[112]

In addition, the advance party appears as a discrete unit as early as at the Lone Tipi.[113] Leaving that site, the five- or six-man detail reported to headquarters staff after Custer's battalion had reached the high bluffs.[114] From here, they went ahead to reconnoiter, according to Thompson, who thereafter began lagging behind.[115] There can be little doubt that the advance detail rode to Medicine Tail Coulee, there establishing a contact point for the battalion—probably on or about Luce Ridge. Then, after the battalion arrived, the advance again rode ahead—eventually to Calhoun Hill, an elevation providing excellent downstream surveillance.

Riding from Medicine Tail Coulee, the advance went ahead of Custer's battalion well before hostilities began and before any event that can be even remotely construed as producing doubt, hesitation, or an acute awareness of danger. Whatever their route, these forward scouts clearly did not set out searching for a good defensive position. Further, observations by Thompson, Two Eagles, and the anonymous Sioux woman show that a Medicine Tail attack was an option, not a singular intent. These accounts support a strategy that pivoted on the apprehension of fugitives, and they reveal a battalion on the offense.

Seeking optimum conditions, the battalion implemented the nonattack option. The wings departed the Medicine Tail environs. Soon thereafter, the two units rendezvoused on Calhoun Hill. While there, those in the know doubtless communicated intelligence obtained at Medicine Tail ford to all concerned. Advance party scouts reported what everyone now could see for himself—the exodus. Peering into the valley from this vantage point, the troopers could confirm all suspicions, anticipations, and expectations, if any remained. In response, the commander determined that the strategy employed in Medicine Tail would be repeated, whereupon the left wing again undertook its journey even farther toward the north.[116]

What functions the advance detail—if not now absorbed by the left wing—performed at this time are unrecorded (at least I have not found any further mention). But in Medicine Tail Coulee, Yates's left wing, not the advance, went to the river. I have shown that his wing conducted this task again, this time from Custer Ridge all the way to ford D. Meanwhile, the right wing—harassed initially by only scores of furtive Indians, then more and more—remained on Calhoun Hill to function precisely as it had while positioned above Medicine Tail Coulee only moments before (Luce Ridge). On Calhoun Hill, the right wing facilitated contact with Benteen, checked Indians, and provided the left wing with the luxury of unhindered mobility.

The left wing certainly took advantage of the opportunity. Officers fixed the northern extremity of the village, determined the tactical requirements posed by a mass of fugitives, found a ford providing access to the fugitives, and discovered little resistance—thanks to Reno's diversion. An attack here, when the time came, would serve to lessen exposure to the battalion, would prevent Indians from escaping north, and assuming a successful capture, would render warriors helpless. Pending attack, the regimental commander elected to leave the river environs a second time and station his wings on Custer and Cemetery ridges. Results of this decision, complicated by other events, have already been described. Finally, experienced observers may see reflected in all this some measure of General Custer's military temperament.[117]

19

THE WHEREABOUTS OF CUSTER

[Custer's] body had not been touched, save for a single bullet hole in the left temple near the ear, and a hole in his left breast.
—Charles Windolph[1]

What about this second trek to the river? Fugitives were all over the valley. The soldiers weren't in a position to round up everyone, but surely the left wing would have seized some hostages before going back to the ridge, right? Obviously it didn't. Look what happened: all the soldiers died. Captives would probably have prevented that. So this business about another trip doesn't make much sense.

Aside from practical objections, the course charted above is by now a familiar tack—it derives from what happened. But I prefer to flip the reasoning. Custer's battalion did collapse, or fall, or whatever one wants to call it. So Yates's wing had not apprehended anyone (at Medicine Tail too). What does this mean? It reveals an air of considerable confidence, an atmosphere generated by a host of factors already discussed—Reno's results, favorable prospects, Benteen's imminent appearance, little resistance, and ease of mobility. When the left wing departed the ford D environs, nothing desperate loomed. Instead, things looked rather good, so no need for hostages—even as a hedge.[2]

Viewed this way, implications of strategic operations regarding the whereabouts of General Custer and the point at which he fell seem clear. First, throughout the affair, he and his staff—regimental headquarters—had doubtless attached to the left wing. Repetitiveness and continuity of events in a favorable strategic environment indicate this. And Private Thompson implied as much in noting that F Company (part of the left wing) rode next to headquarters.[3]

In addition, Lieutenant Cooke made a revealing statement to Major Reno before the latter began his attack. While on Reno Creek, Custer had given the major his attack orders, adding that Reno would be supported by the whole outfit. Reno separated. Cooke, Custer's adjutant and thus attached to headquarters, rode for a while with Reno after separation. During that ride, the adjutant offhandedly told Reno, "We are all going with the advance [i.e., Reno], and Myles Keogh is coming too."[4] Evidently, Cooke understood that Custer intended (at that time) to go in with Reno. But the statement reveals more. First, it is clear that wing assignments in the Custer battalion had already been made, with Keogh commanding one (the right wing, as we know). Second, it is implicitly clear that the two wings of the Custer battalion could operate independently as tactics allowed (otherwise, there would be no need to mention Keogh). Finally, and important here, Cooke cryptically revealed the wing affiliation of headquarters. By specifically mentioning Keogh, he identified a left-wing association. Had it been otherwise, the adjutant would have ended his comment not with reference to Keogh but with "and George Yates is coming too"—or something similar.

So Custer (headquarters) can be assigned to the left wing (and he did not alter that affiliation). One argument to the contrary is predicated on cartridge cases. Proponents sometimes point to brass .50/70-caliber cartridge cases found on Nye-Cartwright Ridge (which, possibly excepting the advance party, only the right wing traversed). Assuming that only Custer used brass cartridges (in his .50-caliber Remington sporting rifle), they conclude that Custer rode with the right wing. But Indians used them too; archaeology demonstrates that they not only are found all over the battlefield but also came from many guns.[5]

Thus, it seems, brass casings are poor indicators of Custer's whereabouts, unless he went everywhere.[6] And in the final analysis, decisions on where and when to strike, which constituted the Custer battalion strategy previously outlined, properly belong to the commander. They are best formulated from first-hand assessments of the tactical situation, particularly, as on the Little Big Horn that day, in a situation that is fluid and rapidly changing. In the Custer battalion, the task of gathering intelligence clearly belonged to the left wing. It is doubtful that the general would have relied on another's judgment in making the critical decisions required in an ever changing strategic environment. The strategic role of the right wing was passive, ill suited to Custer's well-known temperament; not so the left wing. Thus his presence with the right wing can probably be dismissed.

By now it is evident that preoccupation with General Custer's whereabouts is more than just minutiae. The subject is integral to the myth. With which wing did Custer ride? If the left, it is convenient to fell him at Medicine Tail ford, thereby absolving him of blame for the ensuing slaughter. Loyal soldiers then toted him, dead or mortally wounded, to his final resting place on Custer Hill. By placing the general with the right wing while in Medicine Tail Coulee, proponents shift blame for disaster to Yates. As left-wing commander, he failed to press the alleged attack at Medicine Tail ford. The right-wing option has the added advantage of allowing the charismatic commander to organize a gallant fight, of no making of his own, which is necessary if the myth is to prosper. Of course, Custer detractors do not accept either option, preferring instead to resign the battalion to its fate by virtue of decisions made much earlier (e.g., separating the command, attacking without sufficient intelligence, and so on).

And so go these alibis. Although I believe that the strategy arguments advanced herein constitute an insightful claim for a left-wing affiliation, let me offer some other circumstantial evidence in support. If Custer died early, or suffered incapacitating wounds, Captain Keogh undoubtedly took over, as prescribed by rank and seniority within rank. Keogh eventually died, but not with the regimental staff. Rather, the captain died with his company (and most of his wing) in the sector now bearing his name. Like the general's corpse, headquarters staff bodies were found on Custer Hill. It seems quite likely, then, that the general made it there in able condition, tending to scuttle the "died early and carried to the hill" claim, which in any case is sorely speculative. (Claims by certain Indians—usually distorted or embellished by their chroniclers—that "I killed Custer" on the hill are also unverifiable.) As we learned in chapter 12, as many as five bodies lay knotted with Custer's. Here is a classic behavior in precarious combat situations—bunching around a leader, in this case one about to die on Custer Hill (there hardly seems any survival value in clinging to a dead man).

The fatalistic theme, as we know, gets the entire battalion to Calhoun Hill under considerable or at least increasing duress. Ultimately, developing threats from the north forced the left wing through the Keogh sector to its defensive position on Custer Hill. That, of course, is where Custer lay in death. Indian and other evidence for the left wing's river sojourn, and its subsequent deployment on Cemetery Ridge, are for obvious reasons rejected, ignored, and defiled. They do not square with myth or bias. So surely the general detached from the right wing, after preparing a defense at Calhoun Hill, and moved with the left to Custer Hill. Later, warriors overran the right wing, and the few survivors joined the left on Custer Hill. Notice the advantage here—Custer is elsewhere when the right wing falls, furthering jeopardy.

But is this acceptable? The fatalistic theme demands rather brisk fighting in the Calhoun sectors and a healthy measure of opposition faced by the left wing during the nearly three-quarter mile push to Custer Hill. Did not a few in the left wing die along the perilous way? Evidently not. Except for one (Trumpeter Henry Dose, found in Medicine Tail Coulee), the entire staff, presumably at the vanguard of the alleged push, lay scattered about Custer Hill. Among them were two of the four civilians riding with headquarters (the two others were found west of Custer Ridge). Not one staff or civilian body was found in the Calhoun and Keogh sectors. What is more, not a single E or F Company (left-wing) body lay in these two sectors (so far as could be identified). With the fatalistic vision of dire circumstances, what are the odds for this? Possible, but mighty slim in my opinion.

Issues of whereabouts and blame are legitimate, but only in the context of revealing truths, so far as can be known. In seeking truths, we cannot admit biases designed to exalt one by vilifying another. Each must draw his or her own conclusions while trying to keep a fair and open mind. So in deciding, consider this. Archaeology renders useless the brass cartridge-case theory, formerly thought to be nearly ironclad, and prompts inquisitive reflection. The disperse-and-reconnoiter strategy, established even before the village came in sight, is indisputably that of George Custer. Uniformity in strategies, even deployments, until forced on the defensive strongly suggests continuity in decision making. We might deduce that he made these decisions all along. Other evidence does not erode this observation. Indeed, body positions, the chain-of-command argument, Lieutenant Cooke's comment, and Custer's intrepid character are entirely compatible. Much circumstantial evidence indicates that the regimental commander rode exclusively with the left wing, making the decisions throughout, and that he died on Custer Hill during the denouement but only in the wake of a bold offensive thrust that sputtered while on Cemetery Ridge. To contend otherwise seems to require elaborate arguments that ultimately exceed the bounds of parsimony.

Historical-archaeological analyses of the Custer battle portray an offensive-minded battalion suddenly caught up in the most often deadly process of disintegration. This understanding demanded a reexamination of what happened before the battalion reached Custer Ridge. Results refute the heroic myth and its backbone ingredient—the fatalistic tradition. As for the subject of whereabouts, the implications should be clear. Benteen, following Custer's northern trail, ran into Reno's distressed command. Heeding Reno's pleading order (allegedly, "For God's sake, Benteen, halt your command and wait until I can organize my men"),[7] he did not reunite with his commander's battalion but stopped to provide help.

While the general's column awaited Benteen's arrival, Indians infiltrated the cavalry positions. Enemy numbers grew steadily, ultimately jeopardizing the soldiers' safety. Though Reno's presence had encumbered nearly all these warriors at first, his departure from the valley contributed to the general's predicament. Conversely, poor judgment in assaying a deteriorating strategic environment exposed Custer's soldiers—as a body vulnerable to the deleterious effects of inadequate military policies largely beyond their control—to the perils of disintegration. This happened not only with each wing offensively deployed but also with the two rather widely separated—another patently offensive posture. It is extraordinarily hard to escape the conclusion that at the Custer battle, right to the end, decisions made and actions undertaken by each of the leaders—some from beyond the battlefield—figured prominently in the celebrated outcome. Nothing productive comes from haranguing the players now, but much good flows from our dispassionate attempts to find out what happened. I hope you see this as such an attempt.

PART SIX.
CLOSING

20
CONCLUSIONS

It becomes apparent that the work of all historical disciplines really leads to construction and synthesis, not reconstruction and resynthesis.

—W. O. Taylor[1]

The Custer battle as I perceive it provides the forum for discussing the value of archaeology in historical studies. I conclude this book by discussing views on the relationships between archaeology and history. I also assess the utility of the archaeological approach outlined here to battlefield studies in general. This leads to some ideas on future applications of archaeology in historic battlefield studies.

The past few years have afforded people time to reflect on the infusion of archaeology into Custer battle studies. Some rather strong reactionary views have surfaced. I will speak of them generally as trends in thinking—kind of a distillation of everyday thoughts and professional philosophies. They are good barometers of the place archaeology holds in history, vernacular and academic. No more subtle examples exist than in the emotional realm. The site itself—the place—inflames passions as much as the event. More than a few people feel that archaeologists have somehow violated hallowed earth. In other words, "feel free to use the library but let the bones lie." You can see the reasoning here. Archaeology is a nonhistorical discipline. Usually there is no conscious agenda, merely a powerful mental undercurrent, though one that saps reason all the same. But if archaeology can serve history, then the quest for knowledge is derailed by the impassioned mind.

I have run into several people who harbor the quaint notion that archaeologists must serve a long apprenticeship before their ideas about Custer's last battle can be taken seriously. If only a perplexing documentary record were available, then I would agree. The notes and manuscripts, the testimonies and documents covering this affair, have taught me that much. But I have found in the physical remains a mediator, and hopefully that is apparent. Other historians are only lukewarm, viewing archaeology as a "handmaiden" to history. Now and then, they say, an artifact or two might lend support to a particular historical theme. Or some finds might militate against one or another option. I have talked about this a bit already. Lost in this practice is context, the most important of archaeological data. But context is not lost to archaeologists. It is their bread and butter, and that is why archaeology is a different way of knowing, not simply a historical tool.

A few people adopt a "why bother?" attitude—what can archaeology add to what we already know? You cannot combat this over lunch, or even in an article. There is always some counterclaim, something overlooked, something wrong. The answer requires a book, and that is what I offer. Here is a unified account, a coherent explanation, of the Custer battle, first how it happened and then why it happened. I hope it serves to expose the narrowness of various views of archaeology and the utility of archaeology in explicating the past. In fairness, it is indeed refreshing to find some historians, professional and avocational, who hold the archaeological approach to battlefield studies in higher esteem. Nevertheless, the opinions distilled here reflect current perspectives on the relationships between history and archaeology. Whatever philosophical bent one might hold, these are legitimate concerns.

History and Archaeology

There is a widespread belief that archaeologists somehow write something other than history. An anecdotal display of this attitude comes from a recent conference of Custer aficionados. The opinion was stated there that archaeologists should just make available their findings and leave interpretations to knowledgeable historians of the battle. This attitude is hardly different from that of the 1960s, when the role of archaeology in history began to be debated among professionals—historians and archaeologists alike.[2] Discussions coincided with the rise of historical archaeology as a distinct discipline. For the most part, a belief akin to J. C. Harrington's prevailed: archaeology had until then contributed significantly to historical data but "relatively little" to history.[3] Harrington wisely hesitated to conclude that such a situation resulted from limitations inherent in archaeological data and reasoning. Since that time, archaeologists have confirmed his wisdom, not only in researching historical settings largely or wholly insulated from historians because of meager documentation or none at all, but also in melding comprehensive documentary data with a rich archaeological record. Nonetheless, when archaeology is at all considered, it is still viewed as an adjunct to historical studies by many nonarchaeologists. Material data are, it is thought, useful in historical analyses, but archaeologists are not historians.

In probing connections between the two disciplines, I maintain that although archaeology might, from time to time, usefully serve history in an auxiliary role, the practice is by no means thus limited. But sorting out these connections requires an examination of the aims of archaeology and history. In doing so, I am indebted to James Deetz, who has treated the two disciplines as partners with common goals.[4]

Obviously, archaeology deals with the past. Archaeologists provide constructions of former events, not reconstructions. The latter imply recreating the past in its totality, an impossible goal. Dealing as they do with a fragmentary material record, and working in fragile depositional environments, archaeologists seem to know this intuitively. Historical constructions, guided by various theoretical concerns, are influenced by the cultural values of their writers. Paraphrasing Deetz, then, we can define the practice of archaeology as the value-laden construction of past actuality based on fragmentary remains.[5] Written records are altogether more seductive than material residues, and once it was common to portray history as reconstruction. But historians now will agree that histories represent constructions of the past and are the product of contemporary values imposed on excerpts of past actuality. History and archaeology thus do not seem to differ in definition. But what are the broad-based goals of each?

In history, constructions of past actuality are undertaken at two analytical levels. First, they serve to explicate culture history by illuminating the complex processes that produced certain segments of bygone times. Second, history involves the search for regularities in cultural processes that might prove instructive in contemporary life. The latter is revealed in the oft-used phrase, "It is wise to know our past to avoid repeating its mistakes." When historians construct culture histories, they engage in historiography; when they seek processual regularities, they engage in anthropology.

Archaeologists also have strong interests in culture history, which, like historiography, developed from a descriptive, classificatory, and chronological base. Moreover, archaeology has long aspired to an anthropological role. It is not uncommon now for archaeologists to approach their data with the express purpose of determining regularities in cultural processes. It therefore seems that there is a general consonance between the broad goals of historians and archaeologists.

Thus, in one analytical domain, historians and archaeologists engage in writing *culture history*; in another, they practice *anthropology*. Deetz described the way in which archaeologists go about compiling their constructions of past actuality as "archaeography," which contributes to both culture history and anthropology.[6] By implication, so also does historiography, which constitutes the methods of history. Archaeography is a useful concept because it clearly distinguishes archaeology as another way of explicating the past. It is more than a semantic switch. Archaeography is an epistemology independent of historiography—a different way of knowing. Archaeography and historiography are relevant to both goals because the regularities sought in anthropological pursuits are found in the study of culture historical processes.

If historiography and archaeography subscribe to common goals, then how is it the latter is perceived, at worst, as beyond the historical realm, or, at best, as only marginally affiliated with history? The question may be answered in two ways. First, I suspect that archaeology is believed to be relevant to the prehistoric past, but when its procedures are applied to historical ages, the fruits are either useless or somehow restricted in utility. But this defies logic. Historians have no quarrel about the validity of prehistoric constructions; they even use them. So if archaeography constitutes adequate and useful methods in one time period, why not another? To an archaeologist, the distinctions between prehistory, history, and even the present are blurred so long as physical remains are available for study. The temporal range that attracts archaeologists spans millions of years.

Archaeographers focus on material records, historiographers on documentary sources. Wherever archaeology is denied admission to the historical clan, the material base is commonly viewed as inferior on the grounds that it is somehow more difficult to interpret. This distortion results in large part from the seductive nature of documents. They are, it is somehow thought, in closer touch with reality. But Cuyler Young, a historian, has noted that this is not the case. Both mediums pose difficulties in interpretation (for history, look at the Custer battle documents); neither is more valid than the other in our efforts to revive the past.[7]

Considering the aspirations of history and archaeology, we can accept both the physical and documentary records, where they overlap, as complementary rather than separate and unrelated. This pertains to the respective analytical methods. Any site with a recorded past qualifies. But what is the recorded past? In their unique way, physical remains record bygone activities every bit as much as written descriptions of decisions, events, transactions, and the like. Who can disagree that bones, stones, and metals preserve in physical form the events described in documents? The essence, the totality, of the past, so far as we can get at it, must then be found in records *and* residues. As historical disciplines, the two fields ought to assume an equal partnership in constructing the past.

Not all past events leave physical traces. But where they do, the history we write cannot be sealed until the material record is incorporated. That is the thematic thrust of this book. My forum for developing this theme is a history of the Custer battle using archaeography. It is appropriate, then, to synthesize the contributions made here to the history of this event, one that produced not just records but residues too.

At one level of analysis, archaeography confirmed documentary sources and their acceptable interpretations thereof. On another level, it provided information formerly either unavailable or only vaguely accessible. The Henryville position, heretofore unknown, emerged from the ground. Results of excavations at paired markers helped to sort out problems created by extra memorials on the battlefield. Years ago, documents established a force of relatively well-armed Indians equipped with a variety of weapons, including then-modern firearms. Uniquely archaeological methods add to this variety and provide, for the first time, a basis for quantifications.

Historians knew of a skirmish formation on Calhoun Hill, but archaeography defines the presence of at least two and pinpoints their locations. Archaeography highlighted the Indian occupation of The Flats, a sector that has previously received no attention. Forensic analysis of human skeletal remains, discussed only briefly here but explicated elsewhere, agrees with the demographic profile documented for the 7th Cavalry in 1876.[8] Archaeographic analyses flatly contradict contentions that malfunctioning carbines and ammunition exhaustion resulted in the defeat. Any surmise that cavalry units fought on Greasy Grass Ridge is dashed by the coincidental distributions of government and Indian cartridge cases there, as well as by the virtual absence of Indian bullets.

As isolated observations, however, these examples trend more toward demonstrating the value of archaeography in an adjunct role. How, then, has this new way of knowing about Custer's last fight transcended the auxiliary status? In opening this study, I contended that archaeology (now archaeography) served the broader aims of history in a complementary role, and I affirmed that belief in this chapter. The Custer battle construction formulated here is predicated on this approach. Traditional and innovative archaeographic methods, focused by a comprehensive model of combat behavior and applied to the material record, did not support historiographical constructions portraying tactical stability, disciplined soldiers, and resolute resistance in the face of an onslaught. Instead, a different picture emerged, one in which tactical stability eroded. Clearly this is at odds with the myth engendered by the "heroic" tradition and widely believed by the public. More important, this picture forms the basis for a Custer battle construction heretofore unrecognized even though similar information existed, deeply embedded in conflicting and confusing accounts in the documentary sources.

The archaeographic approach to history seems to leave little doubt about the general nature of the Custer battle. Stable units lost cohesion, and the battalion disintegrated. But important details of the fight also emerged, particularly concerning the development of disorder and its impact on the battle chronology. In effect, the fatalistic tradition in all its variation fell by the wayside. Preferably it will stay there, but then sometimes fact is no match for fancy.

Material remains highlighted the significance of Greasy Grass Ridge, a substantial Indian stronghold, and the trooper positions at Calhoun Coulee and Calhoun Ridge. Analyses strongly suggested a disintegration process sparked by action in and near these sectors. Pathways added timing and direction to the sequence, indicating that Indians followed as troopers moved to Calhoun Hill. This interpretation, derived purely from physical residues, prompted a reevaluation of the popular E Company/South Skirmish Line hypothesis. Clearly, historical sources used to support this hypothesis had been badly misinterpreted. In fact, these referred to C Company and its role in the breakup of tactical cohesion within the right wing. Additional documentary analyses revealed how warriors, including Lame White Man, forced C Company back to Calhoun Hill, just as pathways indicate. No such evidence exists at the South Skirmish Line, and Lame White Man did nothing there.

Firearm identification analyses revealed two skirmish lines at Calhoun Hill and showed that the same cavalry unit formed each. Archaeological reasoning prompted the conclusion that the second line formed in response to problems occurring in Calhoun Coulee and Calhoun Ridge. Firearm analyses identified bunching behavior at Calhoun Hill and resulted in the observation that cohesion, represented in the skirmish lines, eventually evaporated. Pathways suggested that soldiers fled to the Keogh sector. It has always been possible to see the disintegration phenomenon in historical sources. But archaeography made it possible to cut through the venerable preconceptions and biases that prevented recognition of disintegration.

Scant material evidence for soldier resistance prompted the observation that flight through the Keogh sector resulted in many deaths, represented by memorial stones. Historical sources painted a graphic picture of the close-up and deadly struggle. Archaeographic analysis resulted in similar conclusions regarding the South Skirmish Line. Written sources revealed in detail the results of panicky flight to Deep Ravine. The nature of material remains at the South Skirmish Line made it clear that markers there could not represent a skirmish line. The clear contradiction between archaeography and standard interpretations resulted in documentary research that indicated that up to 29 markers in this sector are misplaced.

It is a well-known historical fact that the battle culminated at Custer Hill. It is now well known that this fact is wrong, in the popular sense particularly—no defiant last stand on this prominence. The last fighting, such as it was, petered out in and around Deep Ravine. Archaeography did not establish this, but analysis put the battle together in such a way as to make it visible in the documents. Using physical traces from Custer Hill, we could recognize a rather haphazard, even weak, defense there, deriving from failure in tactical organization. Some documentary sources suggest otherwise, describing quite a fight. It is now possible to recognize the validity of contrary accounts, those describing siege tactics and attrition.

So far, I have extracted some examples of complementarity between independent ways of knowing. I have also argued that reasoning from the material record can lead to insights that are not always available from documents. My version of the Custer battle illustrates this. For instance, archaeography led to insights into the effect of proximity and firepower as instruments of shock in the Custer battle. How could this be known otherwise? Indian testimonies do not tell of it, nor do they furnish clues from which it might be reasoned. I showed too, first on archaeographic grounds, that the battalion held an offensive posture at the time chaos developed. How else could a physical record with only a single battle station (Calhoun Hill) be explained?

As judged from the proliferation of fatalistic stories, the insight on offensive posture has not been available through historiography. Neither has the understanding that Custer Ridge became famous as a result of chance, not defensive design. Moreover, the fatal predicament resulted there as much from inaccurate assessments of developing threats as from any other actions, or nonactions, by others. Standing alone, the primary record is simply too incoherent to speak to these ideas. More distressing is the clear realization that incoherence allows tailored explanations. A great deal has already been said about this proclivity, particularly the fatalistic approach. Using the historical record, fatalists first determine the Custer battalion strategy and then proceed to construct results of the battle on this basis. Though details of construction vary widely in this line of reasoning, there is generally only one conclusion. The strategy is determined to be one of beleaguered retreat (or variations thereof) to Custer Ridge. Given the stark reality of how this battle ended, the prestructured conclusion, with all of its unwarranted implications regarding culpability in defeat, cannot be anything other than envelopment followed by annihilation.

This is a poor analytical approach, if only because it stifles alternative scenarios. A more reasonable avenue, one that avoids the tendency to channel conclusions, is first to construct the event. Understanding the nature of a battle facilitates determinations of the strategy or strategies involved. Of course, everyone already knows what, where, and when. But in seeking explanation, we should first determine how. With this in hand, the informed student can then ruminate on why. This is the approach used here, and it began with interpretations of the material record.

Archaeographic observations led to strong suspicions of a rather relaxed tactical posture while on Custer Ridge. These observations promoted the distinct possibility that subdued engagements preceded the onset of catastrophe. Skirmish line data from Calhoun Hill suggested the deployment of only one cohesive unit, very likely of company size. Documentary sources revealed it as Calhoun's L Company. Investigations indicated that other battalion elements never deployed on battle lines. Historical sources identified those in the southern sectors as Companies C and I, two of the right-wing units. The idea of a battalion driven to its fate, however, began to lose luster even without clothing for the skeleton. If there was great pressure, why was there no evidence for it? Ultimately, this lack of evidence allowed confidence in sources describing the role of Indian infiltration tactics, a furtive mode that is widely ignored in favor of the idea of a pitched battle.

Other purely archaeographic observations disputed the picture of a command forced to a hopeless defense. Patterns of carbine bullets on The Flats, with the aid of previous relic finds, posited the presence of cavalry on Cemetery Ridge. Why were bullets found there if soldiers on the defense got only as far as Custer Hill? Or if soldiers were on the defense, why were they so far from troopers at the southern sectors? We now know why, thanks to history, but not before archaeography validated eyewitness testimony, Indian traditions, and other accounts of a Cemetery Ridge episode. Traditional stories mention a delay before the fighting became furious, a pause consistent with other Indian sources describing slow, long-distance fighting over a lengthy period. Given the somewhat relaxed tactical postures in the right wing during this time, no reasons arose to suspect that the left wing on Cemetery Ridge reacted much differently to the docile exchanges. In fact, only E Company deployed to skirmish, leaving F Company to languish, largely because of its reserve status, in historical obscurity—until the so-called last stand, of course.

I speak here of left and right wings, and their makeup, as if all this is common knowledge. History, of course, leaves open the matter of battalion organization. Only through an appeal to tactics, and the standardization imparted by prescription, do identity and composition become available through the documents. I introduced my battalion organization at the onset and maintained it—with the emphasis on *maintained* because my configuration fits every situation, including the chaotic scene left by disintegration. And it fit those "aberrant" accounts that show troopers going to the river a second time.

Indian traditions, as well as Two Moons's story, indicated that the left wing did not stay on Cemetery Ridge after the battalion arrived. Rather, the wing went into the valley before returning to wait. Archaeographical results do not speak to this, principally because of limitations in areal coverage. Yet they do address—positively—the occupation(s) described, in one way or another, by Gall, Sitting Bull, White Bull, Johnston, Clark, Freeman, and Stands in Timber. Why were battalion elements found here, far down the ridge and well away from the right wing? Mission objectives provide the answer. Simply put, it is inconceivable that a force intent on capture would not go toward its quarry. The left wing did; and low-key fighting allowed the trip. The chain of reasoning started by archaeographical observations leads to validation of the ford D journey.

Such are the final stages of Custer's last engagement as displayed in the historical-archaeological context. Nothing of this version squares with a doomed cavalry driven to Custer Ridge by an overwhelming Indian force that quickly mounted a savage onslaught. It simply could not have happened that way. This recognition further prompts insights into the prelude to battle. Much can now be said about earlier strategic operations *beyond* the archaeological study area without ever having to turn a shovelful of dirt in these locales—Reno Creek, the high bluffs, Medicine Tail Coulee, the coulee ford, the Indian village. Logical, coherent, unified, and defensible patterns can now be clearly seen in the thoroughly bewildering array of testimony. It is as if the patterns spring out, leaving all the chaff to blow away.

Reno rode out on the attack. Some Indians appeared on the high bluffs. Custer veered to the north off Reno's trail. The bluffs provided a view of an immense village with many people. All the Indians destined for reservations were in one place—what good fortune for Custer. The warriors, ignorant of Custer's presence, drew to Reno. Thousands of noncombatants began scurrying about. These thousands became the quarry. There was no need now for outlying columns. Verbal and written orders recalled them. The advance detail from F Company went ahead, north to Medicine Tail Coulee. Custer followed, halting the command. The exodus gathered momentum. Plans were formulated. With returning units anticipated, Keogh's wing stayed behind, well positioned above Medicine Tail. Expectations sent the advance guard even farther north. Yates's left wing rode to the ford, causing more and more families to spill from the lower village. The exodus had developed—to the north, the west, the hills, draws, and bluffs. Still, hardly any warriors were seen (Reno had done his job), but a few helpless ones remained in the village. A thrust now would not trap fugitives between two forces. The battalion went farther north.

The left wing departed the river. No sense in capturing an empty village. The right responded, the two reuniting on Calhoun Hill. The advance reported. Nobody to the east—no quarry or danger anyway. But fugitives filled the valley downriver. Everyone could see that now. The wings repeated their offensive strategy. The left rode again to the river. Keogh's wing stayed to welcome Benteen and block Indians. More of the enemy infiltrated. Otherwise, not much happened. Calhoun's troop handled the cautious warriors. Meanwhile, the left wing assayed the situation. More men were needed to effect capture. The wing returned to a position low on Cemetery Ridge. There was still no sign of the recalled units. The battalion waited. Prudence, shaped in part by impatience, soon dictated closing the distance between the wings. The left moved nearer to Custer Ridge and there deployed. Now two companies at opposite ends of the ridge—L and E—manned skirmish lines, a sensible posture. Indians, though increasing, as a body still did not show much fight. Three companies could hold in reserve, and they did.

Then everything crumbled. Historical archaeology has revealed that part— the how—which in turn has revealed some sense of the why. Of course, archaeography alone has not been sufficient for effecting construction, either of the battle proper or of events leading to it, but neither has historiography. One need only point to the current plethora of conflicting Custer battle interpretations, each of which is derived from the same documentary base. Although documents played a crucial role in the present construction, physical data, derived from traditional and new archaeographic methods, provided the analytical point of departure. Facts and insights offered here, ones supported on behavioral, archaeological, and historical grounds, could hardly have been revealed without this departure point. The chain began with the history beneath our feet.

Why has historiography encountered such difficulty in the Custer battle documentary sources? In reviewing problems raised by this question, I intend to shift the discussion to include battlefield historical studies in general, while retaining the Custer theme as a case study.

One way of answering the question is to compare the fundamental difference between documents and artifacts. Both are remnants of past behavior, but documentary sources record human perceptions of affairs. In introducing this book, I noted that battles are extremely confusing events. They are, in fact, the most complex of human endeavors. Eyewitnesses never see everything that happens. Observers are severely hampered in their ability to comprehend what they do see. Seldom do they remember all that they witnessed. The frailties of human perception result in battle descriptions that suffer from incompleteness, confusion, and contradictions.

These problems are by no means peculiar to the Custer battle. Young encountered similar obstacles—including obscurities, interpretive difficulties, lacunae, and irrelevancies—in scrutinizing primary sources pertaining to the Battle of Waterloo.[9] Perhaps Young, like students of the Custer battle, faced vagaries resulting from language barriers, translation difficulties, immense cultural differences, interviewer biases, faded memories, ignorance of military prescriptions, and a tendency for individuals to exaggerate personal exploits.

Material remains, on the other hand, represent residues of behavior. Residues, though a product of human activity, are not produced by human perceptions of events. To be sure, the context in which material remains are perceived and analyzed is subject to cultural values and research interests, but so also is the documentary base. The difference is that the archaeographer begins with a data base untainted by human perception. Although the richness of the historical record is not available, this perception-free record is an important advantage. W. L. Rathje and W. W. Hughes, for example, analyzed food refuse of Tucson, Arizona, residents and then queried them about their consumption habits. In many instances, archaeographic analyses differed substantially from the subjects' perceptions of their habits (the most famous difference was that beer consumption was regularly underreported). They concluded that descriptions of behavior are rarely completely accurate reflections of what actually happened.[10] Therein lies the fundamental difference between records and residues. It is what makes archaeography an independent way of knowing about historical events and not just a collection of loosely knit data that can now and then be plugged into history.

Recollections of battles are by nature unusually susceptible to discordance between the perceived and the actual. Contradictions are inevitable. The many variables that contribute to this incongruity have been discussed. Archaeographic constructions of battles provide accounts of actual behavior within a temporal and spatial framework. They form a structure by which documents produced by fallible human perceptions may be evaluated. The Custer battle construction is full of examples. Archaeography provided the basis for dismissing accounts that describe or imply a determined resistance by the cavalrymen and for accepting those accounts that portray psychological and physical collapse. Seemingly straightforward Indian testimonies, such as those describing "driven" soldiers, could be exposed for what they are—perceptions rather than accurate descriptions. The simple recognition that Indian directional perceptions often differ from customary usage all but destroyed the South Skirmish Line idea, a linchpin of the fatalistic theme. This observation originated in the ground and found fruition in diligent documentary research, despite the perplexity of conflicting perceptions.

There are classic examples of contradictions in the Custer battle record too. Answers to questions about battle duration did not correspond. Some Indians talked of hours, others minutes—clear contradictions. Or are they? No, both are correct, but only when seen in the dichotomy of this battle: laid-back combat, if you will, followed by the furious finale resulting in disintegration. Minutes for the latter, an hour or two altogether. What about observations from the high bluffs? Some soldiers saw nothing, whereas others saw Reno in various stages of his attack. The conflicting observations resulted from different vantage points. No one has ever explained why soldiers from the Keogh sector crested Custer Ridge and went toward the river. Why did they go that way when the rest of the command fought on Custer Hill? Because at that moment the rest did not occupy the hill. Instead, left-wing elements were in the basin. There was also the suicide attack, which cut off troopers fleeing the Keogh sector. This event is not a contradiction, but because of fatalistic ideas, it did not fit in with anything. Now it does.

The soldiers in Medicine Tail Coulee never got to the river. But someone can show, just as convincingly, that they did make the ford. Both are correct, a realization that leads to the most seductive conundrum of all. Custer went to the Medicine Tail ford—*right across from the village*—but he did not attack. So, clearly, warriors fell on him and drove his column back. Some warriors even say so. But the Indians also tell us that the presumed attack would have netted a virtually vacant village. It turns out Custer kept north tracking fugitives, not their camp. So the most abstract of all contradictions finds resolve. Retreat from Medicine Tail Coulee is not in keeping with the general's military temperament. But those qualities that rocketed him to renown are indelibly impressed on a strung-out offensive.

It comes as no surprise that an incoherent data base full of conflicting perceptions can be used to support all manner of biases. Approaching the documentary base equipped with a knowledge of actual behavior gleaned from material remains forces the fair investigator to recognize and shed preconceived notions. In such cases, the archaeographic approach to history represents not only an independent historiographical method but a check against the influence of biases as well.

Thus, the archaeography of battles not only facilitates processes in discovering relevant historical data, identifying irrelevancies, correcting misinterpretations, filling gaps, and rejecting spurious accounts but also renders interpretation much more certain. The result is a much more complete and satisfying construction of past reality, a construction that may lead to additional insights unavailable or only remotely accessible in documentary or material sources alone. The work undertaken here illustrates the utility of applying archaeography in battlefield studies and the value of complementing historiography with the analysis of material remains in the common goal of studying the past. Utley wrote that one day the Indian testimony, if sifted through the right mental equipment, might unlock the enigma of Custer's final battle.[11] He might have included non-Indian recollections as well. But the key is not so much the mental equipment—the organic hardware, so to speak—as it is the fresh analytical approach—the software—the different way of knowing provided by archaeography.

Combat Modeling and Analytical Methods

One goal of this work has been to devise a comprehensive model of combat behavior. The stability/disintegration model emerged from research in military theory. Arguing that behavior in battle can be recognized archaeologically, I formulated analytical methods by which the combat model could be applied to the residues of war. Methods included traditional archaeographic analyses of material remains, as well as a spatial application of firearm identification procedures.

There seems to be little room for argument over the utility of applying the stability/disintegration model of combat to the Custer battle. It provides a comprehensive and detailed understanding of the processes at work in a combat environment—in contrast to Kuhlman's model, which sees only unflagging cohesion.[12] As a consequence of this rigidity, Kuhlman envisioned stability and discipline at nearly every turn of the cavalry column. The construction presented here demonstrates the error of this perception for much of the Custer battle—the decisive phases. Although cohesion can be retained in battle, familiarity with combat processes indicates that disintegration is the most common cause of failure. The analytical parameters of the stability/disintegration model require considerations of this sort.

The idea of stable units devolving into chaotic conditions is not exclusive to archaeology. Other researchers have anticipated the potential for the transition from tactical stability to disintegration in the Custer battle, though only implicitly and generally. They disagree among themselves, however, over when and how the disintegration process began and what impact it had in defeat. Usually they place disintegration at the end, when all is already lost. The interpretive confusion, which may in part result from a peripheral acquaintance with the disintegration process, can largely be attributed to the malleable nature of the historical record. Using the material record as a point of departure, I was able to circumvent confusion in the written sources and illuminate, in some detail, the processes that lead to collapse. Although one may speculate about what might have happened under different circumstances, disintegration proved decisive in this battle.

Refinement included determining the point at which Custer's tactical battalion lost stability, thus revealing the impact of demoralization in the outcome. The spatial application of firearm analysis made this possible. The ability to trace individuals represents an important advancement in battlefield studies. Seldom is such resolution in time and space achieved. Analyses indicated that chaos, and subsequent flight, developed in the Calhoun sectors. Behavioral predictions, confirmed by pathways, made it possible to trace the direction of flight and pursuit through the Keogh sector. Furthermore, quantitative and distributional patterns of government cartridge cases demonstrated little resistance by panic-stricken soldiers, another predictable result of tactical failure. This interpretive foundation made it possible to discern, from documents, the very personal and detailed nature of breakdown in cohesion and the subsequent actions. Out of this emerged a more realistic picture of actual events during the Custer battle.

The success in unraveling the historical record confirms the power of the model and methods devised here. Such confirmation should not be construed as a simple testing of archaeographic procedures by comparing results with documentary data. This ought to be clear from the diverse patterns available in the Custer battle historical record. Rather, the process of establishing complementarity in disparate data bases demonstrates the utility of archaeographic methods applied to material culture within the analytical confines of combat modeling. This process includes feedback, which allows the researcher to make judgments about the efficacy of his or her analysis. The results obtained here suggest that for the Custer battle, feedback is largely positive.

Data preconditions necessary for implementing the approach to battlefield studies advocated here are surprisingly minimal. At the least, analyses require adversaries armed primarily with breechloader or magazine firearms that used self-contained, metallic cartridges. Similar studies might be possible with earlier percussion weapons, such as cap-and-ball firearms, which generally predate firearms using metallic cartridges, but research into this possibility has not yet been undertaken. Differences in armament between opposing forces are desirable, since these differences aid recognition of patterns and distributions through firearm identification analyses. Where combatants were similarly or identically armed, however, supporting contextual data, such as various classes of military equipment, may prove useful in distinguishing positions and movements. At the Custer battle, disparities in armament made it unnecessary to consider ancillary data of this nature.

Other data preconditions are limited. Preservation must be such that firearm identification analyses of ammunition components can identify signatures of individual weapons and types. At the Custer battlefield, bullets tended to oxidize over time, limiting their utility in forensic analyses. Cartridge cases, particularly those of modern alloys, can be expected to be more resistant to corrosion. In any case, casings are considerably more useful than bullets in tracing positions and movements. Of course, it is necessary that combatants on at least one side actually discharge their weapons. Given this, absence or paucity of firearm data representing one side or the other is, as the Custer battle example illustrates, quite revealing in behavioral terms. Data preconditions as they are given here can be expected at battlefield sites dating to the era of modern warfare, including twentieth-century battles.

Results of the archaeographic approach developed to analyze the Custer battle are encouraging. Similar analyses may be conducted at other battlefield sites, especially those of considerable renown. The public has always been fascinated with historic battles, many of which—like Waterloo, Gettysburg, Normandy, Batoche, Isandlwana, and the Custer battle—have risen to prominence in the national or ethnic consciousness. Numerous federal, state, and provincial battlefields have been set aside for the public to visit, enjoy, and understand. The historical archaeology approach to battlefield studies provides an opportunity for site officials to broaden and refine their interpretive programs. Their role in transmitting history on the spot will be enhanced, and visitors will leave with a clearer perspective of a past struggle.

Some Further Considerations

I mentioned earlier in this chapter that in one domain, students of the past write history, whereas in another, they conduct anthropological studies. As a student of the past, I have elected to practice historical archaeology. Is historical archaeology history or anthropology? In pondering this question, Deetz decided that historical archaeologists may legitimately operate in either domain.[13] The analysis presented here is written history, albeit of a brief and particular segment of the past. But the study is basically concerned with processes, specifically those that operate in a combat environment, and not with specific events. The ideas and procedures developed here should therefore be applicable to more expansive research, not only in historical studies but anthropological endeavors as well.

A significant segment of American history has been devoted to the military past, much of which deals with the Indian wars period (ca. 1846–90). This history has generally focused on the Euro-American involvement in the Indian wars. The historical-archaeological approach to battlefield studies requires broadening the scope to include Native American aspects of warfare, including, for example, tactics, the scope of participation in firearm trade networks, and the functions of warfare in social life. This study of the Custer battle prompts such suggestions, but a comparative base is necessary for thorough research into these and other historical interests. Nevertheless, the approach outlined here points out the gaps that need to be filled in.

Concerning the military in the Indian wars, histories such as Utley's[14] and Rickey's[15] deal with complex interrelationships between the decisions of policymakers and army operations in the field. Historical archaeology at battlefields can expose the reality of the processes. I have already discussed some of these aspects, such as training and susceptibility to forces that erode the will to fight. Analyses at the Custer battlefield, for example, suggest that military leaders of the day poorly understood the nature of the fighting and thus were ill prepared to draw from experience. Such research avenues are not restricted to one or another period of warfare. Similar potential exists in historical studies of the Civil War and other battles. Whatever the period, the relationships between practice and policy can be fruitfully investigated in the products of these processes, the battles. Historical archaeology at battlefield sites can contribute to history in the broader sense.

In opening this book, I noted that battles are the laboratories of war. Military analysts such as Keegan and du Picq extracted lessons from history, lessons that might prove useful in modern situations. In doing so, they practiced anthropology by searching—using the comparative approach—for regularities in the complex mechanisms of warfare. But are documentary sources alone sufficient for this endeavor? Keegan, though a military historian, recognized the anthropological potential in the material remains of battle. In evaluating the relevance of Waterloo to warfare today, he argued that the "military facts" and "human experiences" of the battle cannot be adequately resolved without assimilating the "military archaeology of 1815" with the documentary evidence.[16] Keegan expressed wonderment that such attempts had not been made.

The Custer battle analysis represents an initial step in this direction. It also illuminates a number of processes in warfare. The effects of proximity in battle, for example, seem evident. Disparity in mobility may promote disintegration, even among the mechanized cavalries of today. Results of the Custer battle, viewed in light of the military training of the 1870s, offer insights into the moral preparedness for war. On the doctrine of fire discipline,[17] is controlled fire superior to volume fire, or are there circumstances in which either might suffice? What are the lessons to be learned from a confrontation between conventional strategems and guerrilla tactics (infiltration at the Custer battle)? Again, the comparative data required for anthropological inquiries of this nature do not yet exist. Nevertheless, this book's approach to battlefield studies offers a structural and analytical basis, however preliminary, for pursuing studies of military history, the ethnohistory of Indians, and the anthropology of warfare.

NOTES

Chapter 1. Introduction
1. Fish 1978:8, emphasis in original.
2. Marshall 1978.
3. Keegan 1978.
4. Ferguson 1977:57–70.
5. South 1977:79, 158–160.
6. South 1977:158–160.
7. R. Gould 1980:230–232.
8. R. Gould 1980:232.
9. R. Gould 1983:140.
10. R. Gould 1983:139.
11. R. Gould 1983:139–140.
12. Noël Hume 1969:188.
13. Scott et al. 1989:5.
14. Dyer 1985.
15. Keegan and Holmes 1985.

Chapter 2. Archaeology and Objectives
1. Vansina 1985:4.
2. R. Gould 1983:140.
3. Utley 1984.
4. R. Gould 1980:140.
5. E.g., Greene 1986.
6. Deetz 1988a:363.
7. Wesbrook 1980:246.
8. Deetz 1988a:363.
9. Vansina 1985:4.
10. Vansina 1985:4.

Chapter 3. About This Book
1. Quoted in Anders 1939. Taylor fought with Custer's second-in-command, Maj. Marcus Reno, in a separate engagement that day.
2. Stewart 1955:455.
3. Stewart 1955:451.
4. Stewart 1955:452–453.
5. Kuhlman 1951:175.
6. Graham 1926:87–88.
7. Graham 1953.
8. Greene 1986:42.
9. Nelson 1969.
10. Utley 1969:33.
11. Utley 1988b.
12. Utley 1988a:190–191.

13. Moore 1987.

14. Moore 1987:44.

15. Moore 1987:50.

16. Moore 1987:70.

17. Graham 1926. The idea that native testimonies are indecipherable is not an antiquated notion. The latest (1991) explanation of what happened to the Custer battalion, an explanation endorsed by one professional historian as all but unassailable, dismisses Sioux and Cheyenne accounts *in toto* precisely on these grounds (Gray 1991). Another (published in 1990) does not even discuss the Custer battle proper, arguing that to do so is futile speculation, for "no living soldier" survived (Darling 1990:215).

18. Miller 1957.

19. Du Bois 1986:106.

20. In 1876, regiments consisted of companies, which could be divided into battalions. Battalions could operate in two wings, as Custer's battalion did (later addressed in detail). Hardorff (1985:24) correctly configured the companies into two wings but later reassigned remnants of one company to another wing (to account for body positions). Du Bois (1986:103) is most intent on accounting for corpses. He took the liberty of splitting one company into halves (platoons) and then assigned each to a different wing. Greene (1986:33) misconstrued wing organization, thereby incorrectly grouping the various companies from the start. As a result, he placed at least one company at positions on the battlefield where tactics tell us it could not have been. Stewart (1955:448–450) and Kuhlman (1951:174, 179) made basically the same error, but each configured their wings differently. Other authors might be cited, but there is no need. The confusion seems evident.

21. Utley 1988a.

22. Wells 1989:17. See also, for example, Red Horse, Crazy Horse, Low Dog, Crow King, Hump, and Iron Thunder in Graham (1953:57, 63, 75, 76, 78, 79, 88). Elsewhere, MacNeil (1987) has ably documented that Indians were sleeping, eating, fishing, swimming, tending horses, gathering foodstuffs, and doing anything but lurking in a planned state of readiness, ready to spring an ambush, when the cavalry attack came. That the assault caught the natives by surprise will become thoroughly evident throughout this book.

There are very few accounts to the contrary. One is from Flat Iron (allegedly one of the four head chiefs that day and identified as a "Cheyenne Sioux"). If not the newspaper reporter's story, his is an elaborate claim. The Indians knew Custer would be there. The night before, they held a council and mapped out a plan. Custer, they reasoned, could approach the Indian village from only one direction. So when the time came, they took up the appropriate positions. No one would fire until the soldiers reached the snare—then three shots in quick succession would spring the trap. Men in an outer circle had the job of dispatching troopers who escaped an inner ring—the main force, evidently. Anyway, the soldiers pranced in. Three shots rang out, and the fight was on. But the Indians got only part of the troops, for earlier Custer had rather unobligingly dispersed his command (Flat Iron n.d.). This is a great story indeed, as fantasies usually are, and there will be occasion to chuckle over it more as you read on.

23. Stewart (1955:434ff) is an influential proponent of the trap, or ambush, theory. He felt that all troop movements in the minutes before the attack were well known by the Indians, and thus he assumed that the movement to the north was quickly devised to sandwich the Custer battalion. Certainly the Indians had for some days known of a cavalry column in the field, but on the day of battle, contrary to Stewart, the cavalry's approach was hardly common knowledge among villagers, who clearly went about their daily business as usual (see note 22 above).

24. Marshall 1972:148.

Chapter 4. Glances Forward and Back

1. Neihardt 1961:280.
2. In fact, size reduction began in September 1876, not more than three months after the Custer battle. Portions of the Black Hills are also sacred to the Northern Cheyenne.
3. The western Sioux were sometimes interlopers, often encroaching on the Crow reservation (it too dwindled in size). In fact, the Little Big Horn battle took place on the Crow reserve, which had been set aside some years earlier. In addition, some Sioux and Cheyenne occasionally violated other aspects of treaty agreements. By 1876, it seems, some sort of conflict was inevitable. Who started it all? Searching for the instigator is much like trying to solve the chicken-and-egg riddle, except that westward expansion— manifest destiny—clearly precipitated the clash between cultures. But, then, so too did European colonization of the New World.
4. See Greene (1982) for an excellent look at the Slim Buttes engagement.
5. For good overviews of the 1876 campaign, see Gray (1976) and Stewart (1955); for wide-ranging topics surrounding the Custer battle, see Hedren (1991); for a broad view of the Indian wars, see Utley (1984); for in-depth biographies of George Custer, see Monaghan (1959) and Utley (1988a).
6. See Stewart 1955; du Bois 1986; Hardorff 1985.
7. E.g., Kuhlman 1951; McClernand 1927; Greene 1973; du Bois 1986; Stewart 1955.
8. McMurray 1991.

Chapter 5. Models, Methods, and Patterns

1. Wesbrook 1980:246.
2. Marshall 1978.
3. E. Upton 1874.
4. Delbruck 1985:450.
5. Du Picq 1946:144.
6. E. Upton 1874.
7. Utley 1973:10–18.
8. Keegan 1978:298.
9. Marshall 1978:160–161.
10. Wesbrook 1980:251.
11. Keegan 1978:63.
12. Marshall 1978:180.
13. Dyer 1985:135.
14. Du Picq 1946:154; Marshall 1978:195.
15. Du Picq 1946:165.
16. Marshall 1978:195.
17. Beaumont and Snyder 1980:44.
18. Du Picq 1946:131.
19. Marshall 1978:74.
20. Marshall 1978:9.
21. Du Picq 1946:149.
22. Du Picq 1946:161.
23. Marshall 1978:144–145.
24. Keegan 1978:183–184, 194.
25. Weller 1966:132.
26. Du Picq 1946:162.
27. See McDermott 1978:79–98.
28. Godfrey 1896:257–258.
29. Carrington 1983:267.
30. Wesbrook 1980:256.

31. Keegan 1978:271; see also Lewy 1980:97–98.
32. Gabriel 1987:84.
33. Keegan 1978:271.
34. Gabriel 1987:84.
35. Wesbrook 1980:244.
36. Keegan 1978:194.
37. Keegan 1978:194.
38. Keegan 1978:106, 108.
39. Delbruck 1980:264.
40. Marshall 1978:146.
41. Keegan 1978:309; Marshall 1978:150.
42. Allen in Rickey 1963:289.
43. Keegan 1978:298; Wesbrook 1980:246; Gabriel 1987:47.
44. Delbruck 1980:264.
45. Keegan 1978:194.
46. Rickey 1963:230–233.
47. Keegan 1978:71.
48. Keegan and Holmes 1985:24.
49. Gabriel 1987:54.
50. Quoted in Rickey 1963:280.
51. Rickey 1963:280.
52. McDermott 1978:88.
53. Keegan 1978:194.
54. Fox 1984.
55. Scott and Fox 1987.
56. E.g., Hatcher, Jury, and Weller 1977.
57. Scott and Fox 1987; Scott et al. 1989.
58. Scott and Fox 1987; Scott et al. 1989.
59. Scott and Fox 1987.

Chapter 6. Fieldwork, Burials, and Distributions

1. Wertenbaker 1954:454.
2. Scott and Fox 1987:19–30.
3. Scott and Fox 1987; Scott et al. 1989.
4. See Scott et al. 1989:34.
5. Scott et al. 1989:35.
6. The consensus is that Sweet had no choice. At the time, the War Department did not own the Reno-Benteen battlefield. He could not erect stones on the other property.
7. Sweet 1890.
8. Scott et al. 1989:50.
9. Scott and Fox 1987.
10. Scott and Fox 1987 and Scott et al. 1989 respectively.
11. Grinnell 1956:352; Brown 1971:44, 217.
12. Anonymous 1876d:805.
13. Scott and Fox 1987; Scott et al. 1989.

Chapter 7. Custer Battlefield Archaeology

1. Scott et al. 1989:75–76.
2. Hardorff 1985:41–42.
3. Camp 1910a.
4. See Scott et al. 1989:49–56.
5. Greene 1973:55–57.

6. Scott et al. 1989:70.
7. Wagner 1973:238.
8. See Greene 1973:end map.
9. Greene 1973:end map.
10. Greene 1973:end map.
11. Greene 1973:end map.
12. Moore 1989.
13. Hardorff 1985:4.
14. Scott et al. 1989:59–64.
15. Greene 1973:end map.
16. These are recorded on a wall-size USGS master map kept in the Custer Battlefield National Monument archives.
17. Moore 1987:29.
18. Haynes 1985.
19. Du Bois 1986:182.
20. Du Bois 1988:183.
21. Kuhlman 1951:237; Carroll 1974:134; Allen 1903:70–71; R. Upton 1973:110.
22. S. Gould 1991:386.

Chapter 8. Prelude

1. Quoted in DeMallie 1984:192.
2. E.g., Tillett 1976:50–56; Marquis 1967:35–43.
3. I.e., Marquis 1931.
4. E.g., Marquis 1928:250; Godfrey 1927.
5. E.g., Hammer 1976:155–173.
6. E.g., Marquis 1967:35–43; Marquis 1931; Marquis 1976; see also Spencer 1983.
7. Ruehl 1987:34.
8. E.g., Marquis 1976:162, 165.
9. E.g., Keegan 1978:192–193.
10. Stands in Timber and Liberty 1967:205.
11. See Keller (1988:49) for discussions on Custer battle myths and for a dismissal of mass suicide.
12. E.g., Vansina 1985.
13. Vansina 1985:29.
14. See Greene 1973:32.
15. Utley 1972; Nichols 1983.
16. Stewart 1952.
17. E.g., Lone Bear 1909.
18. See Greene 1973:end map.
19. Two Eagles 1908.
20. Miller 1971:33.
21. White Shield in Grinnell 1908b. White Bull (Sioux), though in this citation not speaking of events at the mouth of Medicine Tail, also referred to the grays, the common term today, as "white" (Vestal n.d.d:140). Frank Bethune—who lived with the Crows, knew the Crow scouts who served with Custer in 1876, and shared stories that circulated within their nation—reported the same: the gray horse troop reached the mouth of Medicine Tail Coulee (DeLand 1931:447).
22. Stewart 1955:448; Greene 1973:18.
23. Graham 1953:95.
24. Nichols 1983:715.
25. E.g., Edgerly in Nichols 1983:504.
26. Du Bois 1986:103.

27. E. Upton 1874:73.
28. Hammer n.d.:106; Nichols 1983:235.
29. Stewart 1955:452.
30. Greene 1973:33.
31. From Hammer 1972.
32. Cf. Taunton 1986:2; see Thompson in Brown and Willard 1924:149.
33. E. Upton 1874:271.
34. Godfrey 1879.
35. Hammer n.d.:32, 35. Kanipe last saw the five companies in line formation ordered left to right as follows: E, F, L, I, C; he also said that Keogh's unit included his company (C). Here companies within wings are not positioned exactly by tactics (see chapter 5). Whether or not Kanipe erred in remembering the details, the result is the same—two wings with company affiliations as per tactics.
36. Edgerly n.d.
37. Grinnell 1956:352.
38. Quoted in Hardorff 1985:42.
39. Stands in Timber in Moore 1987:25.

Chapter 9. The Calhoun Episode
1. Quoted in Dixon 1973:176.
2. Tillett 1976:103; Camp n.d.d.
3. Quoted in Graham 1953:103.
4. Graham 1953:89, 126.
5. Graham 1953:103.
6. Hardorff 1985:42.
7. Scott 1920.
8. E.g., E. Upton 1874:507.
9. Graham 1953:103; see also Bighead in Marquis 1967:38.
10. Hammer 1976:163.
11. Hardorff 1985:42.
12. Miller 1957:139.
13. Moore 1987:27.
14. Tillett 1976:98.
15. Tillett 1976:98.
16. E.g., Herendeen in Nichols 1983:286.
17. E.g., Godfrey in Graham 1953:142.
18. DeMallie 1984:185.
19. Tillett 1976:81.
20. Graham 1953:103.
21. Quoted in Graham 1953:103.
22. Graham 1953:220.
23. E.g., Moylan in Nichols 1983:272–273; Maguire in Taunton 1986:11; see also the Nowlan map in Nichols 1983:737.
24. Hollow Horn Bear 1909.
25. E.g., Stewart 1955; Graham 1926:87–88.
26. Hammer 1976:163.
27. Tillett 1976:81; also Eagle Elk in Hardorff 1991:104.
28. DeMallie 1984:186.
29. Tillett 1976:98.
30. Hammer 1976:159.
31. Hammer 1976:167.
32. Quoted in Marquis 1931:228.

33. Graham 1953:103.
34. DeMallie 1984:186.
35. Varnum in Carroll 1980:34.
36. Miller 1971:34.
37. Grinnell 1956:351.
38. Stands in Timber and Liberty 1967:202.
39. Scott 1920.
40. Graham 1953:95.
41. Quoted in Tillett 1976:81.
42. Graham 1953:86–87.
43. Scott 1920.
44. Burdick 1949:25–27.
45. Marquis 1931:230–232.
46. Marquis 1967:37–39; Tillett 1976:50–59.
47. Wooden Leg in Marquis 1931:229.
48. Wooden Leg in Marquis 1931:230–231.
49. Quoted in Marquis 1967:38.
50. Bighead in Tillett 1976:53.
51. Tillett 1976:81.
52. Miller 1957:141–142; Mrs. Spotted Horn Bull in Graham 1953:87.
53. Wells 1989:11.
54. Two Moons in Thralls 1925:573; Red Feather in Scott 1920; Waterman in Graham 1953:110.
55. Mrs. Spotted Horn Bull in Graham 1953:87; Gall in Graham 1953:92.
56. Marquis 1931:230; see also Grinnell 1956:351; White Cow Bull in Miller 1971:34.
57. Wells 1989:11.
58. Runs the Enemy in Dixon 1973:175.
59. Lone Bear 1909; Two Eagles 1908; Hollow Horn Bear 1909.
60. Wells 1988:29.
61. Quoted in Dixon 1973:17.
62. Marquis 1931:230; Marquis 1967:38; Tillett 1976:52–53; see also Red Feather in Scott 1920. White Bull (a Cheyenne also known as Ice) said that warriors obtained "many guns and many cartridges" from Major Reno's demoralized command and turned them on the Custer battalion (Grinnell 1895b). The carbine cartridge cases at Greasy Grass Ridge no doubt represent White Bull's observation.
63. Quoted in Tillett 1976:53.
64. Bighead in Marquis 1967:38.
65. Marquis 1931:231.
66. Marquis 1976:158–159.
67. Dixon 1973:176.
68. Marquis 1931:231; Marquis 1967:38.
69. Vestal 1957:7.
70. Marquis 1976:159; Marquis said 500 yards below the monument, but it is clear he is interpreting, not presenting Indian testimony.
71. Wooden Leg in Marquis 1931:231; see also Graham 1953:105.
72. Marquis 1967:38.
73. E.g., Stewart 1955; Greene 1973; Hardorff 1985; Kuhlman 1951; du Bois 1986; McClernand 1927.
74. Dixon 1973:175–176.
75. Hardorff 1985:59.
76. Hardorff 1985:59.
77. Marquis 1976:159.

78. Quoted in Marquis 1967:38.
79. Graham 1953:105.
80. Grinnell 1956:351.
81. E.g., Foolish Elk in Hammer 1976:198–199; Wooden Leg in Marquis 1931:228.
82. Graham 1953:62.
83. Graham 1953:110.
84. Camp, on the basis of many eyewitness interviews, compiled his map sometime during the first two decades of the 1900s. The portion shown in figure 9-2 is of the Custer battlefield. The entire map extends south to include the Reno-Benteen field and environs.
85. Camp 1918. The relevant portion of the 1918 account states (use fig. 9-2): "Lame White Man charged at C to D [i.e., Çalhoun Ridge] and chased them to Keogh [sector] where he [Lame White Man] was killed." See also Hammer (n.d.:632) for a similar version.
86. Wooden Leg in Marquis 1931:268.
87. Vestal n.d.b:8–11; see also Wells 1989:10.
88. Wells 1989:10, 19. In Waterman's account (Graham 1953:110), Lame White Man is "White Man Cripple." I have also seen "Walking White Man." Variations seem to result from how interpreters and interviewers chose to anglicize the Indian name.
89. Vestal's sketch is reproduced in Wells 1989:10.
90. Wooden Leg in Marquis 1931:232 and Graham 1953:105.
91. Grinnell 1956:351; White Cow Bull in Miller 1971:34.
92. Marquis 1967:39; Marquis 1931:232; Tillett 1976:53; Graham 1953:105.
93. Quoted in Tillett 1976:81.
94. Hollow Horn Bear 1909; Two Eagles 1908; Lone Bear 1909.
95. Bighead in Marquis 1967:39.
96. Camp 1918; see also note 85; also Hammer n.d.:632.
97. Hollow Horn Bear 1909.
98. Lone Bear 1909.
99. Quoted in Nichols 1983:74.
100. Hammer n.d.:63.
101. Two Eagles 1908.
102. Hollow Horn Bear 1909.
103. Tillett 1976:81.
104. Hammer 1976:207.
105. Hollow Horn Bear 1909.
106. Hammer 1976:163.
107. Possibly some of the "cut-off" soldiers fled down Calhoun Coulee into Deep Ravine, where "elements" of C Company were allegedly found; see Maguire map in Taunton (1986:7).
108. Hammer 1976:158.
109. Two Eagles (1908) mentioned that 10 to 12 soldiers went toward Calhoun Coulee from the Keogh sector (more on this western movement of troopers, over Custer Ridge, in other part 3 chapters). Another account suggests the victors dragged dead men into Calhoun Coulee (Hollow Horn Bear 1909).
110. Hammer 1976:95; see also Taunton 1986:20–21.
111. Sills 1988:18.
112. Scott et al. 1989:83.
113. Hammer 1976:120, 126, 137, 146, 248; see also Doran 1987:19–33.
114. Berwald n.d.; Hammer 1976:139.
115. Taunton 1986:20–21; Edgerly in Camp n.d.c.
116. Nichols 1983:569.
117. Hammer 1976:207.

118. Hammer 1976:213.
119. Hammer 1976:158.
120. See Hammer 1976:163.
121. Quoted in Hammer 1976:199.
122. Marquis 1967:39.
123. Tillett 1976:81.
124. Red Bird in Hammer n.d.:632.
125. Quoted in Taunton 1986:11.
126. Quoted in Frost 1976:246.
127. Nichols 1983:263.
128. Quoted in Frost 1976:246.
129. Quoted in Rickey 1956:2.
130. Nichols 1983:76.
131. Nichols 1983:569.
132. E.g., Pope in Graham 1953:115; Red Horse in Graham 1953:60; Wooden Leg in Marquis 1931:379.
133. Hollow Horn Bear 1909.
134. Ryan 1923.
135. Nichols 1983:76. I noted in chapter 7 that I would show how legitimate historical accounts accord well with archaeological interpretations of tactical stability followed by disintegration. Those accounts given by Hollow Horn Bear, Sergeant Ryan, and Lieutenant Wallace are examples. Another is from Crow King, who had infiltrated Calhoun Coulee. When he joined in, "there were so many of them [right wing] wounded or confused that the [battle] did not last very long" (Barry 1916:66). Similar descriptions will follow, particularly various descriptions of soldier behavior during the Keogh and South Skirmish Line episodes.
136. Hollow Horn Bear 1909.
137. Tillett 1976:103.
138. Runs the Enemy in Dixon 1973:175–176.
139. E.g., Koury 1970:41; Hammer n.d.:547; Blummer n.d.; McClernand 1927:51.
140. Two Eagles 1908.

Chapter 10. The Keogh Episode

1. Quoted in Graham 1953:63. It is impossible to assign Horned Horse's portrayal of hand-to-hand fighting specifically to the Keogh episode. Nonetheless, much of the struggle, even to the end, evolved into this type of combat.
2. Nichols 1983:36, 74.
3. Nichols 1983:18.
4. Nichols 1983:520.
5. Quoted in Miller 1971:35.
6. Quoted in Hardorff 1985:49.
7. Quoted in Graham 1953:103.
8. Gall in Burdick 1949:25.
9. Quoted in McCreight 1947:113; more on Crazy Horse's involvement in chapter 18.
10. Two Eagles 1908.
11. Vestal 1957:7.
12. Quoted in McCreight 1947:113.
13. Dixon 1973:176.
14. Quoted in Vestal n.d.d:140–147, n.d.e:59.
15. Dixon 1973:176.
16. Marquis 1931:232–233.
17. Tillett 1976:103; Dixon 1973:182.

18. Quoted in Hammer 1976:207.
19. Graham 1953:62.
20. Hardorff 1985:48.
21. Hardorff 1985:48.
22. E.g., Bighead in Marquis 1967:39.
23. Camp 1918; see also Hammer n.d.:632.
24. Grinnell 1956:351; Marquis 1967:39.
25. Hardorff 1985:48.
26. He Dog in Hammer 1976:207.
27. Hammer 1976:201.
28. Two Eagles 1908.
29. Quoted in Hammer 1976:199.
30. Miller 1971:35.
31. Foolish Elk, Turtle Rib in Hammer 1976:199, 201; Flying Hawk in McCreight 1947:113.
32. Tillett 1976:103; Dixon 1973:182.
33. Hammer 1976:201.
34. E.g., Wooden Leg in Marquis 1931:232.
35. Cf. White Cow Bull in Miller 1971:34.
36. Red Feather in Hardorff 1985:49.
37. Graham 1953:62.
38. Grinnell 1956:351.
39. Miller 1957:142–143.
40. Grinnell 1956:353.
41. E.g., Runs the Enemy in Dixon 1973:176.
42. Lone Bear 1909.
43. Quoted in McCreight 1947:113.
44. Two Eagles 1908.
45. Quoted in McCreight 1947:113.
46. He Dog in Hammer 1976:207; Hardorff 1985:48.
47. Quoted in Dixon 1973:176.
48. Two Eagles 1908.
49. Vestal n.d.d:139.
50. Hammer 1976:207; Hardorff 1985:48.
51. Miller 1971:34.
52. E.g., Graham 1953:89.
53. E.g., Moore 1987:48.
54. Cf. Bighead in Marquis 1967:39.
55. Kanipe in Hammer 1976:95.
56. Graham 1953:91.
57. Graham 1953:88.
58. Bourke in Hardorff 1985:50.
59. Miller 1957:140.
60. Quoted in Hardorff 1985:50.
61. Hammer n.d.:667.
62. Kanipe in Hammer 1976:95; for Keogh, see the Nowlan map in Nichols 1983:737.
63. Scott et al. 1989:83.
64. Hammer 1976:120, 126, 137, 139, 146, 248; Hammer n.d.:107; Berwald n.d.; Taunton 1986:20–21.
65. Nichols 1983:520; Hammer 1976:58; Hammer n.d.:672. But see Hardorff (1989:109) for Bustard in the Indian village—according to Sergeant Kanipe, who was uncertain about this.

66. Hammer 1976:58, 130.
67. Hurt and Lass 1956:fig. 90; but see Taunton 1986:35.
68. Anders 1952:1.
69. Hardorff 1985:65.
70. In Hardorff 1985:49.
71. Graham 1953:62.
72. Tillett 1976:70.
73. Graham 1953:60.
74. Miller 1971:36.
75. Quoted in Graham 1953:91.
76. Grinnell 1956:351.
77. Tillett 1976:94.
78. E.g., Stands in Timber and Liberty 1967:201.
79. Hollow Horn Bear 1909.
80. Red Feather in Hardorff 1985:49.
81. Miller 1957:142, 1971:36.
82. Two Eagles 1908.
83. E.g., Gall in Tillett 1976:75; Dewey Beard in Miller 1971:38; Stands in Timber and Liberty 1967:201; Moving Robe in Vestal n.d.c.
84. Quoted in Hammer 1976:199.
85. Quoted in Hammer 1976:201.
86. Two Moons, Little Knife, and Waukutemonie also spoke about soldier behavior, though, due to vagaries in spatial clues in their statements, only generally. But the accounts fit the Keogh episode. "They acted and shot their guns like something was wrong with them [like they] had too much of that whiskey" (Two Moons in Anonymous n.d.). Little Knife reportedly said that the soldiers (and horses) were unmanageable, firing their carbines and pistols wildly (Grill 1928). Waukutemonie, answering one of Vestal's questions, reported: "Most of the soldiers acted as though they were drunk. Many of them threw their guns down " (Vestal n.d.c). All three Indians were at the battle. Obviously, their accounts metaphorically indicate panic and fear.
87. J. D. Miles 1876.
88. Readers may wish to consult Langellier, Cox, and Pohanka (1991) for a more personal and lasting impression of Myles Keogh. The volume contains an earlier version of this chapter.

Chapter 11. The Cemetery Ridge Episode
1. Nelson 1969:42.
2. Lone Bear 1909.
3. Hollow Horn Bear 1909.
4. Grinnell 1956:351.
5. Stands in Timber and Liberty 1967:199.
6. Quoted in Hammer 1976:199.
7. Hammer 1967:207.
8. Hollow Horn Bear 1909.
9. Miller 1971:35.
10. Two Eagles 1908.
11. He Dog in Hammer 1976:207. White Bull (Cheyenne) said that the soldiers "fell back" to Custer Ridge, where they "met Indians coming from above and from all sides" (Grinnell 1895b). Like the statement by Foolish Elk (see text corresponding to note 6), this is an example of compressing elapsed time (either by Grinnell or White Bull). Eventually warriors did come from all sides, but not until after the Cemetery Ridge episode, which took place before the right wing collapsed.

12. Stands in Timber and Liberty 1967:199.

13. Lights 1909.

14. Camp 1909. This woman's Christian name was Julia Face.

15. Lone Bear 1909.

16. Stands in Timber and Liberty 1967:199–200.

17. Rickey 1990.

18. Quoted in Dixon 1973:181 and Tillett 1976:103.

19. Clark 1877.

20. Thomas Buecker found (at the National Archives) and kindly shared the long-lost maps with me before he published them. Lieutenant Clark's report and his map, modified for clarity, are reproduced in Buecker's (1991) article. The lieutenant submitted his report and map to the military Department of the Platte. Officials there drew a nearly identical map based on Clark's original. Aside from altering the map key, officials made only one other change. Evidently they picked up on the contradiction between Clark's trail of troops to the river as mapped and his confusing narrative. As I said, the convergent cavalry route to ford D led right through Indian positions. The Department of the Platte map brought the route up to the warrior strongholds but short of the Little Big Horn. This, of course, reconciled the map with Clark's description of the attack. Clark's original is the one reproduced here (fig. 11-2). Usher Burdick (1936:8ff.), sketching from Sioux testimony, produced a similar map, which implied that Crow King (and his followers) turned the column back to Custer Hill.

21. Clark 1877.

22. Utley 1962:88.

23. Godfrey stated that Clark, accompanied by Lieutenant Pope, visited the Custer battlefield during the summer of 1877 (Godfrey 1923:199; Graham 1953:115). Utley reiterated the claim (Utley 1962:95). Based on this, it might be argued that Clark saw other cavalry trails, perhaps made by burial parties, for example, and incorporated them in his map. But Camp Robinson post returns (Post Returns 1877) account for Clark, except for a 13-day July absence (at Forts Laramie and Sanders in what is now extreme southeastern Wyoming), throughout the spring and summer of 1877 (see also Buecker 1990). So Godfrey's report is apparently inaccurate.

Clark did travel, between August 6 and August 17, 1876, from Fort Ellis (near Bozeman, Montana) down Yellowstone River to the mouth of Powder River. But he did not visit the battlefield then. Clark kept a journal on this trip. His daily entries account for every day, each entry devoted to the long, arduous journey down Yellowstone River (Clark 1876). I am grateful to John Gray for providing a typescript copy of Clark's entries.

The lieutenant probably first visited the battlefield in 1878 while on detached service at Fort Keogh (present-day Miles City, Montana). Fort Keogh post returns put Clark at a camp near the Custer battlefield in late June of that year (Buecker 1990). Any suggestion that Clark visited the site earlier than this (i.e., before or during his 1877 duty at Camp Robinson), and thus was influenced by personal observations, must account for the fact that he did not map soldier positions other than those at Custer Hill. This glaring omission is tantamount to proof that Clark drew only from Indian eyewitness testimony in preparing his September 1877 report and map.

24. In Graham 1953:64.

25. Graham 1953:73.

26. Godfrey, Burkhardt in Hardorff 1989:121; Slaper in Brininstool 1952:63.

27. Mathey in Hammer 1976:79; Camp in Hardorff 1989:122; Glenn and Thompson in Hammer 1976:136, 248.

28. Bradley 1876.

29. Gibbon 1877:668–669.

30. Hammer 1976:79.

31. Moore and Donahue 1991.
32. Girard in Hammer 1976:231.
33. Graham 1953:105.
34. Graham 1953:102.
35. Dixon 1973:175 and Tillett 1976:81.
36. I deduce this location on the basis of archaeological evidence—or lack of it. There is no material evidence for a skirmish line on the relatively undisturbed slope between Custer Hill and the visitor center (except for a one-lane road, a walkway, and the former site of Fort Phil Kearny reburials). Beginning at the visitor center, and extending down Cemetery Ridge through the national cemetery, maintenance complex, and housing area below, the ground is hopelessly disturbed (see figs. 6-4, 6-6, and 6-7). Michael Moore very recently found indirect evidence (in the Custer Battlefield National Monument archives) for six marble markers that were once located at the visitor center site but that allegedly were removed before construction of that facility (1950s). This information came too late for verification here.
37. Dixon 1973:176; Tillett 1976:81.
38. Quoted in Vestal 1957:7.
39. Vestal 1957:8.
40. Dixon 1973:182 and Tillett 1976:103–104.
41. Dixon 1973:183 and Tillett 1976:104.
42. Stands in Timber and Liberty 1967:199; Rickey 1956; Powell 1969:116.
43. Quoted in Burdick 1949:27.
44. Graham 1953:93. As this book neared completion, a print of a Barry photo surfaced; this photo supports the interpretation that Gall, in this instance, referred to soldiers on Cemetery Ridge. The print is of Capt. Frank Baldwin's infantry unit performing a fire demonstration in 1886 during the 10th anniversary (see Burdick [1929:11] for the same image slightly cropped). A pencil notation (on the photo mount reverse) in Barry's hand explains that Baldwin's unit is "at the point where Custer dismounted and backed up to where the monument now stands." An on-the-ground examination showed that Baldwin's company was located on Cemetery Ridge a few feet north of where the visitor center is now situated. The note (to an anonymous recipient) ends, "You can judge [from the photo] the distance he [Custer] was from the river." This information is courtesy of Douglas D. Scott.

Here it is pertinent to caution that there are two Gall accounts, which can be confused. Both were taken at the 10th anniversary. One does refer to Medicine Tail Coulee. It says (incorrectly) that Custer's battalion never reached the river but met warriors about "half a mile" up Reno Creek (Graham 1953:88). Reno Creek refers to Medicine Tail Coulee (see note 107, chapter 18). The account scrutinized here is similar in that the reference is to soldiers who got "half way" to the river (Burdick 1949:27). But the annotated photo rather conclusively shows that in this instance, Gall referred not to Medicine Tail but to what is now called Cemetery Ridge.
45. Graham 1953:48–56.
46. The version of map 1008 shown here (fig. 11-3) is a duplicate of the original submitted by Johnston, except that his handwriting has been replaced for clarity. Someone at department headquarters evidently made the duplicate after receiving the original. Michael Donahue brought this information to my attention. Brian Pohanka secured negatives of both maps for me from the National Archives, where they are cataloged as Map 1008, Tube 530, Record Group 75.
47. Stands in Timber and Liberty 1967:200.
48. Powell 1969:116.
49. Stands in Timber and Liberty 1967:200.
50. Dixon 1973:175, 176.

51. Rooney n.d.; Hammer n.d.:27.
52. Carroll 1975:116; Hammer 1976:87; N. A. Miles 1969:210.
53. Tillett 1976:103; Dixon 1973:182.
54. Quoted in Miller 1971:34.
55. Quoted in Schneider 1977:65.
56. DeMallie 1984:190–191.
57. Miller 1971:34.
58. DeMallie 1984:191.
59. Stands in Timber and Liberty 1967:201.
60. Grinnell 1956:352.
61. Vestal 1957:8.
62. Lone Bear 1909.
63. Grinnell 1956:352.
64. Camp n.d.d.
65. Two Eagles 1908.
66. Powell 1969:117; Stands in Timber and Liberty 1967:201.
67. Powell 1969:117.
68. Stands in Timber and Liberty 1967:204; Marquis 1931:268–269.
69. Dixon 1973:176.
70. Graham 1953:102.
71. Dixon 1973:181–182.
72. Quoted in Powell 1969:116.
73. DeMallie 1984:194.
74. See DeRudio in Hammer 1976:87.
75. Cf. Taunton 1986:2.
76. Vestal n.d.d:139–143.
77. Vestal's sketch map (see fig. 10-1) locates the fourth company (Company E). The original map, reproduced in an article by Wells (1989:18), is inexact and poorly oriented. The E Company location is best interpreted with reference to the Little Big Horn (labeled as "River"). In this context, the company is clearly on Cemetery Ridge at an indeterminate distance from Custer Hill (which is the third company position, labeled as "monument"). White Bull's first and second company positions are very badly oriented with respect to the third and fourth. The latter two are generally correct in reference to the river. Vestal himself was uncertain of his sketch. He placed a question mark (?) next to the direction arrows. Judged from the relationship between the river and the positions of the third and fourth companies, Vestal's north is about 60 degrees west of true. White Bull reported four companies, not five, because he collapsed two into one bunch (evidently C and L). Stanley Vestal, by the way, is a pen name used by Walter Stanley Campbell.
78. Quoted in Vestal n.d.d:140.
79. DeMallie 1984:191.
80. Powell 1969:117.
81. Quoted in Dixon 1973:176, emphasis mine.
82. Dixon 1973:175.
83. Quoted in Vestal n.d.d:143.
84. Two Eagles 1908; Vestal n.d.d:140; Dixon 1973:176.
85. Lights 1909.
86. Powell 1969:116.

Chapter 12. The Custer Hill Episode

1. Hollow Horn Bear 1909.
2. Graham 1953:103.

3. See Hardorff (1989:97ff.) for a sampling of the many references to Custer's location and condition in death.

4. Glenn, Kanipe, DeRudio in Hammer 1976:87, 95, 136; Wooden Leg in Marquis 1931:240; see also Maguire map in Taunton 1986:7; Nowlan map in Nichols 1983:737.

5. Lynch in Hammer 1976:139.

6. Taunton 1986:11; Hardorff 1985:52, 1989:115–116. But see Camp (n.d.b), where Roe says Sharrow's body never was identified.

7. Godfrey in Hammer 1976:76; Maguire map in Taunton 1986:7; Godfrey in Graham 1953:346.

8. E.g., Edgerly in Graham 1953:220.

9. Hammer 1976:248; Godfrey in Hammer n.d.:609.

10. Stewart 1954:22.

11. Hammer 1976:139.

12. DeRudio in Hammer 1976:87; Sheridan in Nichols 1983:632; Taunton 1986:11; see Camp map (fig. 9-2).

13. O'Neill in Hammer n.d.:53; Lynch in Hammer 1976:139. But see Hammer (n.d.:667), where Creighton says Vickory lay in a ravine between Calhoun and Keogh. As the regimental color-bearer, Vickory might have served on the staff, but the colors had been left with the packtrain (Pohanka n.d.).

14. Rooney 1909; Hammer n.d.:60; Camp map in Taunton 1986:20–21.

15. Lynch in Camp n.d.a; Pickard in Stewart 1954:22.

16. Hammer 1976:139.

17. Hammer 1972:xxiii.

18. Hardy in Hammer n.d.:78; Edgerly in Camp n.d.c; Glenn in Hammer 1976:136; Foley in Hammer 1976:147.

19. Kanipe in Hammer 1976:95; Maguire map in Taunton 1986:7.

20. Godfrey 1876.

21. Dixon 1973:169 and Tillett 1976:91.

22. Quoted in Hammer 1976:207.

23. Hammer 1976:201, 210, 213.

24. Taunton 1986:6.

25. Quoted in Vestal n.d.d:141.

26. Hammer 1976:199.

27. Hollow Horn Bear 1909.

28. Two Eagles 1908.

29. Two Eagles 1908.

30. Dixon 1973:177 and Tillett 1976:82.

31. Wallace in Nichols 1983:36; Kanipe in Hammer 1976:95.

32. Standing Bear in DeMallie 1984:187.

33. Wallace in Nichols 1983:75. Sergeant Kanipe said Custer lay across "a couple of men" (Graham 1953:250).

34. Graham 1953:250.

35. Quoted in Nichols 1983:520.

36. Military eyewitnesses described corpses atop Custer Hill and on the southwest slope. A number of these accounts will be presented shortly. If some markers were originally set on top of the hill, modern construction disturbances there (see figs. 6-4 and 6-6) doubtless required workers to relocate them, probably to the southwest slope, although records of such moves evidently do not exist (but see the Fouch photograph in Brust 1991).

37. Quoted in Hammer n.d.:547.

38. E.g., McClernand 1927:52; Clifford in Taunton 1986:14; Stewart 1955:455.

39. E.g., Bighead in Marquis 1967:39; Wooden Leg in Marquis 1931:235; Red Cloud in Tillett 1976:91; Dixon 1973:169; Slaper in Brininstool 1952:61.

40. Marquis 1931:235.

41. Gibbon 1877:670.

42. Hardorff 1989:103.

43. Graham 1953:220.

44. Quoted in Hammer 1976:87.

45. Quoted in Hardorff 1989:103. See also Adams, R. Thompson in Hammer (1976:121, 247) for similar impressions.

46. Edgerly in Graham 1953:220; Goldin in Carroll 1975:116; Sheridan in Nichols 1983:632; Gibbon 1877:670.

47. Hare in Hammer 1976:68; Kanipe 1908; Sheridan in Nichols 1983:632; Gibbon 1877:670; N. A. Miles 1969:288.

48. Quoted in Hammer 1976:95.

49. Hammer 1976:68.

50. Brininstool 1952:61.

51. Hammer 1976:87.

52. Bighead in Marquis 1967:39–40.

53. Marquis 1931:235–237.

54. Marquis 1975:82.

55. Standing Bear in DeMallie 1984:186. Big Beaver described a Sioux who must have taken advantage of the thick prairie vegetation. Repeatedly he shot at soldiers on Custer Hill, jumping up to fire, then falling down to "crawl ahead again." The last time he jumped up, a bullet struck him in the forehead. Big Beaver, right behind the unfortunate warrior at the time, thought better of all this and "crawled back" (Blummer n.d.; Blummer 1930).

56. Quoted in Marquis 1967:39.

57. Bighead in Tillett 1976:54.

58. Nichols 1983:359–360.

59. Nichols 1983:359.

60. AGO 1877.

61. White Bull in Vestal 1957:8.

62. Eagle Elk in Miller 1957:149; Bighead in Marquis 1967:40, Tillett 1976:54.

63. Hammer 1976:202.

64. Bighead in Tillett 1976:54.

65. Wooden Leg in Marquis 1931:237.

66. Wooden Leg in Marquis 1931:237; Bighead in Tillett 1976:54.

67. E.g., Two Moons, Runs the Enemy in Tillett 1976:81, 104; Dixon 1973:176–177, 183; Wooden Leg in Marquis 1931:237; Bighead in Tillett 1976:54; Marquis 1967:40; Gall in Hardorff 1985:53.

68. Stands in Timber and Liberty 1967:201.

69. Tillett 1976:81; Dixon 1973:177.

70. Graham 1953:110.

71. Stands in Timber and Liberty 1967:201.

72. Quoted in DeMallie 1984:186.

73. E.g., Waterman, Left Hand in Graham 1953:110, 111; Standing Bear in DeMallie 1984:186.

74. Camp 1909.

75. Hollow Horn Bear 1909.

76. Two Moons in Graham 1953:103.

77. Stands in Timber and Liberty 1967:201.

78. Vestal 1984:200.

79. Marquis 1931:237.
80. Blummer n.d.:53; Blummer 1930.
81. Vestal n.d.d:148.
82. Stands in Timber and Liberty 1967:201; Thompson in Hammer 1976:248; McDougall in Hammer 1976:72; Wooden Leg in Marquis 1931:237; Two Moons in Thralls 1925:574.
83. Graham 1953:377.
84. Liddic 1979:124.
85. Gibbon 1877:670; Sheridan in Nichols 1983:632.
86. McClernand in Hardorff 1989:103.

Chapter 13. The South Skirmish Line Episode

1. Quoted in Ricker 1906b:20.
2. Graham 1953:103. N.A. Miles (1969:289) estimated 40 men; One Elk said there were nine horsemen (Hammer n.d.:60); Iron Hawk said "nearly" all were on foot (Neihardt 1961:126).
3. Lone Bear 1909; Two Eagles 1908.
4. Quoted in Vestal n.d.d:142.
5. Vestal 1957:8.
6. Quoted in DeMallie 1984:191. Although Iron Hawk is usually placed by analysts just south of Calhoun Hill or nearby, he was, in his own testimony, "on the field between [Custer] ridge and the river" (Carroll 1979:54–55).
7. DeMallie 1984:186; see also Standing Bear in Hammer 1976:215.
8. DeMallie 1984:192.
9. Hammer 1976:213; see also Grinnell 1898b.
10. Lights 1909.
11. Hammer 1976:207; Hardorff 1985:59.
12. Good Voiced Elk in Hardorff 1985:59.
13. Quoted in Vestal n.d.d:142.
14. N. A. Miles 1969:289.
15. E.g., Waterman in Graham 1953:110.
16. Devoto 1917.
17. Nichols 1983:360.
18. Hammer 1976:72; Nichols 1983:616; McDougall's quote in Hardorff 1989:105.
19. Hardorff 1985:58.
20. O'Toole in Hammer n.d.:28; Berwald n.d.; McDougall in Hammer 1976:72; Graham 1953:377; Hare in Nichols 1983:335; Devoto 1917; for Sergeant Ogden, see Quinn 1876.
21. Lynch in Hammer 1976:139; Edgerly in Camp n.d.c.
22. Rafter in Hammer n.d.:107.
23. McDougall in Hammer 1976:72.
24. Hardorff 1985:59.
25. Ryan in Graham 1953:364; Hardorff 1985:56.
26. Gibbon 1877:670.
27. Nichols 1983:9, 341; Utley 1972:262, 264.
28. Utley 1972:224, 327; Nichols 1983:264, 474.
29. Hammer 1976:72; Godfrey 1923:199; McClernand 1927:52.
30. Hammer 1976:207.
31. Utley 1972:262.
32. Maguire 1876a:155, 1876b:166.
33. Freeman in Schneider 1977:65. Writing to his mother on July 8, 1876, Lieutenant

Paulding, a surgeon who tended Reno's wounded, mentioned that others "had found 28 white men [soldiers] lying dead in a ravine" (Buecker 1982:43–44).

34. Hammer 1976:248.

35. Hammer 1976:95.

36. Quoted in Nichols 1983:616.

37. Quoted in Graham 1953:377. For the same quote, taken from a personal letter McDougall wrote to Godfrey, see Hardorff (1989:105).

38. Scott et al. 1989:73–74.

39. Hammer 1976:72.

40. Quoted in Nichols 1983:341.

41. Quoted in Utley 1972:262; see also Roy in Hammer 1976:116.

42. Lynch in Hammer 1976:139–140.

43. McDougall, Logan in Hammer 1976:72, 140.

44. Quoted in Miller 1957:145–146.

45. Graham 1953:103; N. A. Miles 1969:289.

46. Gibbon 1877:670.

47. Goldin in Carroll 1974:19; McDougall in Graham 1953:377.

48. Devoto 1917.

49. E.g., DeRudio in Nichols 1983:366; McDougall in Graham 1953:377.

50. Nichols 1983:74.

51. Hare, McDougall in Utley 1972:264, 379.

52. Nichols 1983:474; McClernand 1927:52; Maguire 1876a:155.

53. E.g., Standing Bear in DeMallie 1984:187; Good Voiced Elk in Hardorff 1985:59.

54. Utley 1972:224.

55. Graham 1953:364.

56. Hammer n.d.:78.

57. Graham 1953:377.

58. E.g., Standing Bear in DeMallie 1984:186–187; Hardorff 1985:61; Mrs. Kill Assiniboine in Hammer n.d.:347.

59. Cf. Good Voiced Elk in Hardorff 1985:59.

60. E.g., DeRudio, Martin in Hammer 1976:87, 102.

61. Quoted in Hardorff 1985:56; see also March 31, 1909, letter, Walter Camp to E. S. Godfrey, Custer Battlefield research files A312 C11380.

62. Quoted in Stewart 1955:445.

63. Quoted in Hammer n.d.:347.

64. Hammer n.d.:78.

65. Quoted in N. A. Miles 1969:289.

66. Quoted in DeMallie 1984:191–192.

67. DeMallie 1984:186, emphasis mine.

68. Graham 1953:103.

69. Cf. Iron Hawk in Neihardt 1961:126.

70. N. A. Miles 1969:289.

71. DeMallie 1984:191.

72. Standing Bear in Ricker 1907:60; Benteen, McDougall in Nichols 1983:84, 616.

73. One Bull, White Bull in Hammer n.d.:350.

74. Lights 1909.

75. Bear Lying Down in Hammer n.d.:269; Iron Hawk in Neihardt 1961:127.

76. Hammer n.d.:126–127.

77. Hammer 1976:207.

78. He Dog's reference is suggestive. Perhaps the E Company maneuver was in part intended to divert attention from the horsemen, allowing them to escape to the south and secure aid, if available, from the rest of the regiment. It is, after all, difficult to imagine

that some sort of scheme, given such desperate circumstances, would not be tried. In any case, He Dog said the mounted men "tried" to escape. However far one or another rider got (probably to the area of the stone markers set today in lower Calhoun Coulee), none succeeded.

79. DeMallie 1984:191.
80. Hammer n.d.:269.
81. Lights 1909.
82. Miller 1957:137.
83. E.g., Eagle Elk in Miller 1957:147.
84. Quoted in Nichols 1983:616.
85. Nichols 1983:360, 366.
86. Quoted in Utley 1972:264 and Nichols 1983:341.
87. Nichols 1983:616.
88. Nichols 1983:264.
89. Nichols 1983:616.
90. Scott et al. 1989:45.
91. E.g., Benteen, DeRudio in Nichols 1983:360, 474; Maguire maps in Carroll n.d.
92. See Scott et al. 1989:39–48, 224–242.
93. Quoted in Schneider 1977:65.
94. Quoted in Carroll 1974:27.
95. Utley 1972:224; see also Hardy in Graham 1953:364.
96. Hammer 1976:95.
97. Nichols 1983:264.
98. Utley 1972:262.
99. Bourke 1877.
100. Anonymous 1889.
101. Hammer 1976:72.
102. Hammer 1976:77.
103. Hammer n.d.:78.
104. Quoted in Carroll 1975:116.
105. Camp 1908b.
106. Hammer 1976:248.
107. Walter Camp wrote W. O. Taylor (letter dated November 6, 1909), stating that McDougall related finding upper-segment bodies that did not "exceed nine or ten" (in Camp Collection, Custer Battlefield National Monument Archives, A312 C11789). Rather than consulting his notes, Camp might have depended on memory, so possibly he confused McDougall with Thompson, who did mention those numbers. If not, McDougall had refined his estimate of less than 12 and maybe not more than half a dozen.
108. Sweet 1890.
109. See Scott et al. 1989:87.
110. Since making these deductions, I have located a letter Sweet wrote to Walter Camp. The 1912 correspondence confirms that Sweet erected not only single but paired markers as well and that, when done, he had placed 217 markers, leaving 29. Sweet wrote: "On the Custer Field you may have noticed more than one marker at a grave. In that case two or more bodies were buried there. I found the resting places of 217 officers and men had been located only, hence 29 remains were not accounted for, exclusive of Boston Custer [General Custer's brother] and Arthur P. Reid [the general's nephew] and Lieut. Porter, hence my most persistent and scrutenizing [sic] search until the missing remains were found under varying conditions" (Sweet 1912).
111. Quoted in Vestal n.d.d:146.
112. Vestal 1984:200.

113. Vestal n.d.d:145–149.

114. Blummer 1930. Blummer, evidently assuming a South Skirmish Line position, assigned these 15 or 20 men to the "White Horse Troop," or E Company, which is very likely correct but, as his narrative suggests, for the wrong reasons. Big Beaver told Blummer "these men were afraid." One of the two speculated that the men had used up their ammunition (which is not clear, compare Blummer n.d. with Blummer 1930). If this was Big Beaver, he, like other Indians, remained perplexed in 1928 (the year of this interview) as to why soldiers did not shoot back as terror set in. As for Blummer, he had no inkling of disintegration.

115. Respects Nothing in Ricker 1906b:20; Flying Hawk in Ricker 1907:42–43; American Horse in Grinnell 1895a. See the chapter epigraph for Respects Nothing's statement. Flying Hawk recalled, "All the living men on Custer's Hill ran toward the river and were killed by the Indians." American Horse stated, "After we killed those on the [Custer] hill, we discovered that there were some other white men who had got off [the hill]. . . . [The warriors] charged these and killed them all."

116. Ricker 1906a:86. Young Two Moons did not participate in the fighting, yet he related the same story, evidently citing oral history. "One of the companies retreated down a little gulch [Deep Ravine]. . . . Here the last of the soldiers were killed" (Grinnell 1908c). Some of these "last" soldiers were the 15 or so that Big Beaver had seen flee from Custer Hill (Blummer n.d.). On Red Hawk's sketch (fig. 13-8), note the dashed line protruding from the "3rd stand" (Deep Ravine). Perhaps this represents men who tried to flee even closer to the river after the demise of most in E Company. Two Moons, the younger's uncle, described the last fighting in a different way: "The grey bunch [E Company] were the last killed" (Hardorff 1991:138). Julia Face put the final deaths in Deep Ravine (Hardorff 1991:190).

117. Hammer 1976:95.

118. McClernand 1927:52. Private Coleman's June 28, 1876, diary entry indicates that he helped inter E Company soldiers "30 [from the company] in line not 10 feet apart." But he also reported "42 Men of E Company" surrounding "the Bravest General of Modder [modern] times"—in other words, on Custer Hill (Liddic 1979:124). Obviously, Coleman's account of his observations is confused. His reference to an E Company line cannot be taken at face value, though it seems clear he did help bury bodies found in the South Skirmish Line sector.

119. McClernand 1969:64.

120. Maguire 1876a:155.

121. Maguire 1876b:166.

122. Godfrey 1923:199.

123. Quoted in Graham 1953:374.

124. Bourke 1877.

125. Allen 1903:67–68.

126. Scott et al. 1989:73–74, 79–82.

127. Maguire 1876a, 1876b; McClernand 1927; Schneider 1977.

128. Kuhlman 1951:181–183.

129. McClernand 1927.

130. Moore 1987.

131. Stewart 1955:449–450.

132. Du Bois 1986:116–118.

133. Greene 1986:37.

134. Utley 1988a:190.

135. I have used markers not as an analytical foundation but at certain sectors, and then only in supporting roles. Many, if not most, analyses are directly or heavily guided by combat actions seen in the total pattern—the overall distribution of stone memorials or,

early on, the actual bodies (or graves). I have mentioned Kuhlman's idea; his alleged V-formation is evident in figure 6-8 (short and long sides of the V converge at Custer Hill). Notice too, in this figure, the rough oval shape imparted by all the markers. This pattern (corpses as well) has also guided fatalistic interpretations, such as the two noted below. In these, the South Skirmish Line figures into the scheme either near the beginning or at the end.

The very earliest fatalistic theory came from body distributions (from eyewitnesses). All five companies left Medicine Tail (an attack at the ford there was foiled by heavy fire), marched north down Calhoun Coulee (sometimes along the river) toward the Deep Ravine mouth (to attack near there), met a stifling resistance, retreated up Deep Ravine to Custer Hill, and then tried to backtrack to the south along Custer Ridge (to reunite with the rest of the regiment). They did not make it. Soldiers fell all along this route, one or two in Medicine Tail, later a few others (Calhoun Coulee), after that a number more (Deep Ravine headwall), then more (South Skirmish Line), and many more (Custer Hill and Keogh sectors), until the last men died around the Calhoun elevations (e.g., Roe 1927:10). Generally, this theory injects tactical stability into every phase of a clockwise movement (reckoned while facing north in Medicine Tail Coulee).

About all that changes in the latest (1991) theory to use stone memorials is the direction in which a clock's hands move—John Gray's counterclockwise movement. Except at the last, everything unfolds more or less with purpose. But there is a hidden difference. The early clockwise theorists had few or no Indian accounts to draw on. Gray knows there are plenty today but rules out Sioux and Cheyenne testimonies entirely because "they reveal little more than [warrior] attitudes and fighting tactics." So in the end, markers guide everything, hence his literary hedges: for example, "prompts the *speculation* that. . . ."

Gray proceeds. A battalion on the offense left Medicine Tail and reached the Calhoun vicinity. It first faced only light fire, but resistance steadily intensified. Now pressured, the battalion needed to get to "higher ground" (offense is lost; higher ground to the north precludes a more western clockwise movement). Lieutenant Calhoun's men held the south end of Custer Ridge while all the others moved north to Custer Hill. (Not clear is why under "adverse conditions" and "heavy action," only one company stayed behind. Custer Hill, by the way, is hardly higher ground, nor is there any for several miles northward; in addition, Calhoun Hill not only is a more expansive landform but, because of a depressed, saucer-like surface, is a better defensive locale than Custer Hill, certainly more suitable for multiple companies to take up siege positions.)

As the lieutenant's rear guard wavered (and finally crumbled), some northbound troopers tried to get back and help out. This retrograde movement resulted in many deaths and accounts for men from various companies found mixed together (Keogh stones and some in the Calhoun sectors).

Then Custer Hill received the brunt of the attack. Various of these troopers (a mixed lot larger than a company but mostly from E Company) soon proceeded to the South Skirmish Line (according to Gray, a movement due to the combination of a hill too small for everybody plus a scheme to hold the enemy back). Deep Ravine was a "death trap," so no one went into it; accounts of such are not "literally correct" (note here an assumption that does not admit panic into the analysis).

Finally, Custer Hill and the southern line fell nearly simultaneously (archaeology purportedly shows that the South Skirmish line markers are mostly valid), but not before 14 soldiers fled the line in "desperation" (here panic is introduced), across Deep Ravine, then south up Calhoun Coulee, and nearly back to Calhoun Hill, where the last man died (markers along the coulee show this). This completed the counterclockwise movement, which was not always orderly (Gray 1991:387–395).

Gray tabbed his counterclockwise motion a "trial hypothesis." A hypothesis consists of predictions (plural in this case)—derived from a body of theory—which are in need of testing by way of experiment and/or observation. If, through testing, predictions are confirmed, theory may be considered adequate; if hypotheses are rejected, theory might be called into question. (Modifications can also accrue.) Obviously, fatalistic theory, including persistence in tactical stability, guided Gray.

Testing is another matter. Gray elected not to use Custer battlefield archaeological data (except as noted above), which he saw as preliminary—and for this he cannot be faulted. But he eliminated the bulk of the only other testing avenue—Sioux and Cheyenne eyewitness testimony, difficult as it may seem. So in effect, Gray rendered his hypothesis untestable.

I have used both data sets. Though I did not set out to test Gray's clock analogy (published in my eleventh hour), that obviously is a result. In any case, the counterclockwise idea, at least in terms of overall movement, has been around for a while. There is something to it, but only in the most elementary way—that is, limited to a rough direction of motion. Further discussions, particularly in part 5, ought to help in showing that the ticks and tocks of this fatalistic clock, whichever direction the hands may turn, fall well short of explanation.

136. Moore 1987:33–34; Hardorff 1985:46.

137. Quoted in Ricker 1906/1907. Two Moons said: "They acted and shot their guns like something was wrong with them. They surely had too much of that whiskey. That bunch of men [Custer's battalion] should have fought for a long time, but it did not take long to kill them all" (Hardorff 1991:138). Shoots Walking recalled the same, adding that the soldiers did not fight within a system (Hardorff 1991:86n).

138. See Scott et al. 1989.

Chapter 14. Prefatory and Immediate Causes

1. E. B. Custer 1923:143, emphasis original. Elizabeth (Libbie) Bacon Custer married the general on February 9, 1864. She never remarried, defending her husband's honor to the last—dying on April 6, 1933, two days short of her 91st birthday. So that her feelings might be spared—it is often said—the "real story" never came out.

2. Huntington 1959:49.

3. Wooden Leg in Marquis 1931:230; Bighead in Marquis 1967:38.

4. "How long did the battle last?" became one of the most persistent questions asked Indian participants over the years. They possessed none of the segmented temporal concepts familiar to Euro-Americans, particularly with respect to clock time. But their responses, as interpreted by white interviewers, tend to fall into two categories: measured in hours or in minutes. Among Custer battle researchers, this is typically perceived as a contradiction. Actually, both categories are correct, depending on perspective. The period of subdued exchanges (beginning in Medicine Tail Coulee) lasted an hour or so and perhaps a half more; the last of the struggle, the furious scramble developing from collapse, was about 20 or 30 minutes more. Such rapidity, of course, is typical when tactical cohesion is lost, and that is the impression many warriors gave. It was over, some said, before the sun in its travel across the sky could move but a very short distance or before a hungry man could eat his dinner.

One of the most precise elapsed-time figures I have seen for the furious action developing from disintegration is 27 minutes—from the C Company charge to the end. This comes from A. B. Welch, an early Bismarck, North Dakota, resident. Welch provides no clue as to how he arrived at this time, but if not exact, it is at least reasonable. Overall, his description is similar to Huntington's. Welch, who claimed his story came directly from Indian participants, stated, "And so they fought there in . . . a furious hand to hand combat, and within twenty seven minutes after that brave and foolish charge was launched [by C Company, as we now know], not a soldier of Generals [*sic*] charging column was left alive" (Welch 1915).

Another time estimate comes from D. F. Barry, who queried warriors from time to time. He said: "When Crow King [in the Calhoun Coulee vicinity] charged through Custer's men [the right wing, as a result of the C Company provocation] . . . the fight did not last very long. The Indians . . . tell us the fight lasted thirty-five minutes [i.e., the furious activity]" (Barry 1916:66). Barry learned this from Gall. Crow King himself estimated a half hour (Walker 1966:102). And the Sioux who Doane Robinson (1929) interviewed in 1907 emphatically agreed—30 minutes.

It is always fun to juxtapose sober testimonies with mythical fantasies. Elbert Hubbard's 1905 story came down to endurance. Surrounded, Custer saw the handwriting on the wall. So he sent a scout to General Terry, pleading for help. "Noon came and buzzards began to gather in the azure." The afternoon dragged on. The sun sank. "Custer warned his men that sleep was death." Dawn came. Daylight found Terry still struggling against all odds to make it in time. But he was three hours behind. Finally, Custer and his men ran out of ammunition (evidently no one had slept). Then the Indians closed in, and it was over. Sadly, Terry had fallen five miles short of saving the day (Hubbard 1974: 119–120).

5. Quoted in Anonymous 1908:30.

6. Marquis 1931:235.

7. Warriors ultimately rushed Custer Hill and found several wounded soldiers, some of whom attempted to resist. The last fighting, however, bereft of tactical organization, occurred at Deep Ravine.

8. Graham 1953:87–92. Rain-in-the-Face offered another poorly disguised attempt to assuage: "I had always thought that white men were cowards, but I had great respect for them after [the Custer battle]" (Eastman 1916:100).

9. R. Upton 1973:110.

10. Du Picq 1946:63. I have found that this adage applies fairly well to the more prominent warriors, those who had the most to gain or lose in relating Custer battle stories. This may sound familiar, no matter one's nationality or ethnicity. Lesser lights tended to be more forthright but not because of any innate superiority in truthfulness. Mostly, the common Indian had nothing much to sacrifice in relating events as best he (or she) could (victims metaphorically). Conversely, he stood to reap little by appeasement (stalwarts plainly). Consequently, the latter tactic rarely even occurred to him. The temporal factor is also involved. Cheyenne and Sioux who talked about this fight (many flatly refused) harbored more uncertainties early on than they did much later—when it became clearer to them that candor would not meet with retribution among their people or personally. Then memory fallibility became the trade-off.

11. E.g., White Cow Bull in Miller 1971:34; Brave Wolf in Grinnell 1956:353; Low Dog in Tillett 1976:86, Graham 1953:75; Crow King in Graham 1953:77; White Bull in Vestal 1957:9; Sitting Bull in Tillett 1976:69–70; Hollow Horn Bear 1909. Sitting Bull, it seems, once stated a contradiction in the same breath. He stayed out of combat that day but learned from warriors—in his newspaper interviewer's words—that a "great many brave [soldiers were] in that fight, and that from time to time, while it was going on, they were shot down like pigs. They could not help themselves" (Graham 1953:73). On the other hand, maybe Sitting Bull obliquely encapsulated unity ("brave") followed by chaos ("shot down like pigs").

12. Marshall 1978.

13. Gabriel 1987:73.

14. Rickey 1963:301.

15. Quoted in Fiske 1917:118.

16. Quoted in Nichols 1983:473, 475. Benteen did not "manufacture" this scene for the Reno inquiry. Confiding to his wife in a July 25, 1876, letter (exactly a month after the battle), he wrote, "[Custer's battalion] was probably thrown into a panic at the first check

received—and gotten in just the condition that indian [*sic*] would get a herd of buffalo" (Graham 1953:188).

17. Quoted in Hammer n.d.:108.
18. Coughlan 1934:20–21.
19. See Utley 1962:64–72.
20. King 1981:161–162; Coughlan 1934:15; du Bois 1986:42–43 and elsewhere.
21. King 1981:161–162.
22. In Stewart 1955:264.
23. Coughlan 1934:20.
24. Godfrey in Graham 1953:147–148. Readers may wish to consult Taunton (1977) for a balanced treatment of this issue.
25. Graham 1953:282.
26. Manion 1984.
27. Godfrey in Graham 1953:134.
28. Repass 1985.
29. Hofling 1981.
30. See Coughlan 1934:17.
31. Cf. du Bois 1986:102.
32. E.g., Coughlan 1934:18.
33. Dustin 1987:110.
34. Gray 1976:182; du Bois 1986:135.
35. Graham 1953:194. See also Captain Moylan in Graham (1953:141) for a similar contention.
36. Gray 1976:183.
37. Du Bois 1986:135.
38. Graham 1953:147.
39. Graham 1953:147. See also Lieutenant Edgerly in du Bois (1986:132), who in essence agreed with Godfrey.
40. Utley 1973:17.
41. Anonymous 1876c:772.
42. Anonymous 1876e:6.
43. Utley 1973:16; Anonymous 1877.
44. Anonymous 1877.
45. Anonymous 1876a:26; Finerty 1966:211; King in Graham 1926:xxvii.
46. Coughlan 1934:21.
47. Stewart 1955:421, 458–459.
48. Hunt and Hunt 1947:92.
49. Reno in Hammer 1971:5.
50. Reno in Hammer 1971:5.
51. Hammer 1971:5.
52. Hammer 1971:8; Stewart 1955:458.
53. Godfrey in Graham 1953:147.
54. Stewart 1955:459; Chappell 1972:27; but see Hedren 1973:68.
55. Hammer 1971:5.
56. Quoted in Hammer 1971:6; see also Stewart 1955:421.
57. Graham 1953:147.
58. Hammer 1971:5.
59. Anonymous 1876a.
60. Fraser 1982:332.
61. Dutton 1877.
62. Michaelis 1876.
63. Murphy cited in Stewart 1955:459.

64. Thomas 1904:285.
65. Marquis 1931:266.
66. Vestal n.d.e:60.
67. Graham 1953:88.
68. Graham 1953:89.
69. Graham 1953:91; Tillett 1976:74.
70. See also Benham (1914:462–463) for a liberally interpreted version of the accounts.
71. Thomas 1904:285.
72. Miller 1957:107–108; Sandoz 1942:326.
73. Sandoz 1942:326.
74. E.g., Wooden Leg in Marquis 1931:213; MacMillan 1876.
75. E.g., Stewart 1955:458.
76. Hammer 1971:5.
77. Hunt and Hunt 1947:171.
78. Hammer 1971:5.
79. Hedren 1973, 1988.
80. Quoted in Rickey 1963:292.
81. Hammer 1971:5.
82. See Hedren (1973:67–68) for tentative evidence that Indians experienced problems with captured carbines, and see Scott's discussion (Scott et al. 1989:113–115) of extraction failure rates among other Indian firearms.
83. Hedren 1973:68; Scott et al. 1989:115.
84. Finerty 1966:200–202.
85. Nichols 1983.
86. Hammer 1976; Hammer n.d.
87. Graham 1953:88, 89.
88. Graham 1953:147.
89. Coughlan 1934; Graham 1926.
90. E.g., du Bois 1986; Hardorff 1985; Moore 1987.
91. Moore 1989.
92. Greene 1986.
93. He Dog in Hammer 1976:207.
94. Godfrey 1896:257.
95. Nichols 1983:48–49, 83.
96. Nichols 1983:198.
97. Quoted in Nichols 1983:315.
98. Nichols 1983:301.
99. E.g., Foolish Elk, Flying By in Hammer 1976:199, 210; Wooden Leg in Marquis 1931:264; Gall in Graham 1953:89, 91.
100. Lone Bear 1909.
101. Two Eagles 1908.
102. Moore 1987.
103. Quoted in Nichols 1983:76.
104. Hollow Horn Bear 1909.
105. Quoted in Nichols 1983:359–360.
106. Roe 1927:11.
107. Marquis 1931:284–285.
108. Scott et al. 1989:140.
109. Thomas 1904:285.
110. Nichols 1983:359–360.
111. Hollow Horn Bear 1909.

112. Lone Bear 1909.
113. Hammer 1976:207.
114. DeRudio in Nichols 1983:359-360.
115. Vestal n.d.e:60. The Cheyenne White Bull (Ice) told Grinnell essentially the same thing: "[Custer's men] had not used many of their cartridges, some had ten cartridges used from their belts and some twenty, but all their saddle pockets were full" (Grinnell 1895b).
116. Vestal n.d.d:149.
117. Vestal 1957:9. Interestingly, Grinnell, faithful to the myth, did not see that panic overtook Custer's troopers, despite the fact that more than one Indian told him just that. Immediately following his notes on the White Bull statement quoted in note 115, Grinnell theorized: "As it was both commands [Reno's and Custer's] were frightened and retreated. . . . If this account is true both commands were wholly demoralized" (Grinnell 1895b).

In reference to the first sentence, Grinnell wrote in the margin, "no only one." He lined out the second sentence, adding to his marginalia, "untrue" (Grinnell 1895b). Clearly, Grinnell could allow disintegration in Reno's battalion but not in Custer's.

118. Quoted in Thralls 1925:575. Another Cheyenne, American Horse, made a similar claim, rendered by Grinnell: "Many of the belts . . . had no cartridges in them" (Grinnell 1895a).
119. Quoted in Vestal n.d.b:15.
120. Graham 1953:88, 89, 91. So also can American Horse's story given to Grinnell be discarded (note 118).
121. Graham 1953:91.
122. Quoted in Graham 1953:89, 91.
123. Thomas 1904:285.
124. Graham 1953:60, 62.
125. Quoted in Graham 1953:60.
126. Hammer 1976:208.
127. Quoted in Hammer 1976:199.
128. Graham 1953:111.
129. Quoted in Marquis 1931:264.
130. E.g., Finerty 1966:211.
131. Utley 1973:70.
132. Anonymous 1876k:757.
133. E.g., Anonymous 1876h:802; Anonymous 1876b:264.
134. Anonymous 1875:201.
135. Anonymous 1876g:8; Anonymous 1876i:41.
136. Anonymous 1876j:73.
137. Anonymous 1876i:41; Utley 1973:72.
138. Gibbon 1879:238, 243.
139. Finerty 1966:21; see also Coughlan 1934:21; Graham 1926:93-94.
140. Gibbon 1879:241.
141. Utley 1973:72.
142. Kill Eagle 1876:149.
143. Allen 1903:68, 71.
144. Hunt and Hunt 1947:92.
145. Scott and Fox 1987:112. Carbine and Winchester specifications are also contained in Hammer (1971).
146. The idea that repeating weapons encouraged ammunition waste developed during the Civil War (Pohanka 1988). The doctrine of fire discipline (see Marshall 1978:83-84)

also influenced the board's decision, but unlike the facts and figures available from testing, this doctrine and its impact are hard to measure.

147. Nichols 1983:198.
148. Windolph in Hunt and Hunt 1947:92.
149. Varnum in Nichols 1983:198; Brininstool 1952:122.
150. Anonymous 1875:201.
151. Rickey 1963:237.
152. Marshall 1978:67.
153. Weller 1966:113.
154. Quoted in Graham 1953:95.
155. Colonel R. P. Hughes in Gray 1976:355.
156. Gray 1976:182.
157. Hunt and Hunt 1947:92.
158. Graham 1953:84.
159. Stewart 1955:139.
160. Utley 1962:91.
161. Gray 1976:355.
162. Nichols 1983:466.
163. See Gray (1976:346-359) for an admirable attempt to estimate the warrior force based on lodge numbers.
164. Cf. Anonymous 1876f.
165. Graham 1953:146-147.
166. Graham 1926:98.
167. Coughlan 1934:20.
168. Little Buck Elk 1876:165.
169. Cf. Rickey 1963:237.
170. Du Picq 1946:161.
171. Marshall 1978:144.
172. E.g., Bighead in Marquis 1967:39.
173. Cf. Grinnell 1956:351; Miller 1957:131; Rain-in-the-Face in Brady 1971:288.
174. Nichols 1983:475.
175. Cf. du Bois 1986:114-115.
176. Wesbrook 1980:256.
177. Two Eagles 1908.
178. Hammer 1971:5.

Chapter 15. Contributing Factors
1. Keegan 1978:296.
2. E.g., Anonymous 1876f:8-9.
3. Utley 1973:24-25.
4. Rickey 1963:86. Ezra Fuller, a career cavalry officer, recalled that early on (evidently before ca. 1880), the common soldier never received drill in advance, rearguard, or field exercises. Noncommissioned officers "in some commands" could get drilled in tactics once a week. "Once in a long while" officers might receive tactical schooling. Up to 1876 (his tenth year), he did not witness any target practice at all, and thereafter only to a "very limited extent" (Fuller 1916:424-425).
5. Pohanka 1988.
6. Graham 1926:117-119.
7. Stewart 1955:176.
8. McChristian 1981:33.
9. McChristian 1981:33.

10. Rickey 1963:86; Utley 1973:24.
11. Stewart 1955:177.
12. Marshall 1978:124.
13. E.g., Moore 1988.
14. Coughlan 1934:21.
15. Marshall 1978:77; Weller 1966:112, 130.
16. Marshall 1978:81.
17. McChristian 1981:34.
18. Utley 1973:24.
19. Marshall 1978:67.
20. Coughlan 1934:21.
21. Marshall 1978:125.
22. Hauser 1980:187.
23. Delbruck 1985:407.
24. Wesbrook 1980:252.
25. Baynes 1967.
26. Dollard 1943.
27. Du Picq 1946.
28. Rickey 1963:17–32.
29. Utley 1973:25.
30. Utley 1973:25.
31. Wesbrook 1980:256.
32. Marshall 1978.
33. Marshall 1978:160–161.
34. Wesbrook 1980:251.
35. See Marshall 1978:5–10.
36. E.g., Keegan 1978.
37. Stewart 1955:265.
38. Graham 1953:148.
39. Brininstool 1952:63.
40. Carroll 1975:106.
41. Gabriel 1987:52.
42. Keegan 1978:134–137.
43. Marshall 1978:173–174.
44. See Rickey (1963:130–133) for a general discussion on health.
45. Schneider 1977:62.
46. Hunt and Hunt 1947:174. Captain Benteen said the same (in 1877), stating, "Horses and men were jaded . . . too fagged to handle themselves" (Hackett 1916:49).
47. Roe 1927:11.
48. Quoted in Vestal 1957:9.
49. Tillett 1976:69; Graham 1953:71–72. See also Two Bulls in Milligan (1972): "It was like fighting boys, the men were so tired, and their rifles so poor."
50. Keegan 1978:134–135.
51. Hunt and Hunt 1947:174.
52. Stewart 1955:266.
53. Cf. Marshall 1978:173–174.
54. Wesbrook 1980:263.

Chapter 16. Fate versus Choice
1. S. Gould 1991:256.
2. Stewart 1955:449.
3. E.g., Greene 1986:33–37; Dustin 1987:157; Graham 1926:87.

4. Karl 1990:158–182.

5. Quoted in Graham 1953:90.

6. Hammer 1976:214.

7. Hammer 1976:212–213.

8. E.g., Curley in Hammer 1976:158; White Shield in Grinnell 1956:350; Two Eagles 1908; Good Voiced Elk in Hardorff 1985:26.

9. Du Bois 1986:116.

10. Hardorff 1985:39ff.

11. Utley 1988a:190.

12. Utley 1988a:188.

13. Utley 1988a:190.

14. Rickey 1956.

15. I.e., Stands in Timber and Liberty 1967; Powell 1969, 1981.

16. Excluding Sills 1988, Moore 1987, Nelson 1969.

17. E.g., Vansina 1985.

18. Lights 1909.

19. Stands in Timber and Liberty 1967:197–198.

20. Cf. Stands in Timber and Liberty 1967:198; Joseph White Bull in Miller 1957:139; Wooden Leg in Marquis 1931:229; Bighead in Marquis 1967:37.

21. Luce 1943:2.

22. E.g., Utley 1988a:189.

23. Utley 1988a:188.

24. Tall Bull in Hammer 1976:213.

25. Hammer 1976:198.

26. Mrs. One Bull in Vestal n.d.a:27–28; Young Eagle in Vestal n.d.f:56, 58.

27. Hammer 1976:207.

28. Hammer 1976:214–215.

29. Grinnell 1956:350. One of these, Bobtail Horse, said, "The 10 [Indians] were firing as hard as they could" (Grinnell 1908a).

30. Miller 1971:33. Another of the few warriors there at the time was a Cheyenne named Mad Wolf, who cautioned, "No one should charge yet the soldiers are too many" (Grinnell 1908b). Dull Knife (Cheyenne) exclaimed, "Its no use we cannot stop them" (Grinnell 1908a).

31. Two Eagles 1908.

32. Quoted in Hammer 1976:207.

33. Grinnell 1956:350; see note 29.

34. Graham 1953:72.

35. Utley 1988a:188.

36. Finerty 1966:209.

37. E.g., Good Voiced Elk in Hardorff 1985:26.

38. Grinnell 1956:350.

39. White Cow Bull in Miller 1971:34, 1957:129; Foolish Elk in Hammer 1976:198; Curley in Hammer 1976:172; Two Moons in Camp n.d.d.

40. Hollow Horn Bear 1909; Good Voiced Elk in Hardorff 1985:26; White Cow Bull in Miller 1971:33.

41. Libby 1973:160.

42. Grinnell 1956:350.

43. Foolish Elk in Hammer 1976:198; Tall Bull in Hammer 1976:212; Moore 1987:17–18; Graham 1953:96.

44. Moore 1987:17–18.

45. Graham 1953:96.

46. Miller 1971:33.

47. White Cow Bull in Miller 1971:33; Two Moons in Camp n.d.d; Grinnell 1956:350; Bobtail Horse in Grinnell 1908a.

48. Camp n.d.d.

49. Miller 1971:33; Grinnell 1956:350. Bobtail Horse said that five Indians fled down Medicine Tail Coulee in front of the soldiers (i.e., left wing), and these eventually joined him, bringing their number to 10 (Grinnell 1908a).

50. Two Moons in Camp n.d.d.

51. Grinnell 1956:352; Finerty 1966:210; Lights 1909.

52. Curley in Hammer 1976:176.

53. Curtis 1908:44 facing; Curtis was the famous frontier photographer. He got his story from Crow scouts with Custer.

54. E.g., Joseph White Cow Bull in Miller 1971:34; White Shield in Grinnell 1956:350.

55. Marquis 1967:37–38; Marquis 1931:229.

56. E.g., Curley in Hammer 1976:162; Horned Horse in Finerty 1966:210.

57. Hammer n.d.:70–71; Blummer n.d.:44–46.

58. Two Eagles 1908.

59. Grinnell 1956:351.

60. It is likely that at least three soldiers who attempted to escape from the battle on Custer Ridge were killed around Medicine Tail Coulee (Sgt. James Butler, Cpl. John Foley, and Trumpeter Henry Dose). Those Indians who suggested that troopers were killed while ascending Deep Coulee may have seen these corpses and assumed the men died after the left-wing departure from Medicine Tail ford.

61. Quoted in Grinnell 1956:351.

62. Quoted in Hammer 1976:210.

63. Lone Bear 1909.

64. E.g., Bighead in Marquis 1967:37; Good Voiced Elk in Hardorff 1985:26.

65. Graham 1953:90.

66. E.g., Lone Bear 1909; Hollow Horn Bear 1909.

67. Cf. Two Moons in Graham 1953:103; Runs the Enemy in Dixon 1973:175.

68. Dixon 1973:181.

69. E.g., Marquis 1931, 1967.

70. Hollow Horn Bear 1909.

71. Standing Bear in Hammer 1976:215. Crazy Horse, it is said, went to a prairie dog town, gathered some earth, and returned to the village, there sprinkling the soil upon himself and others. In addition, before entering the Custer fray, he prayed and made sacrifices over a fire fueled by buffalo chips (Masters 1951:41).

72. E.g., Crow King in Burdick 1949:25,27.

73. Hammer 1976:214.

74. DeMallie 1984:185–186.

75. Miller 1971:38.

76. Marquis 1931.

77. Cf. Wooden Leg in Marquis 1931:231; Bighead in Marquis 1967:38.

78. Stands in Timber and Liberty 1967:199–200.

Chapter 17. Fixing Blame

1. Van de Water 1934:369.

2. Quoted in Graham 1953:335.

3. Detractors claim Benteen failed to return as ordered. A more moderate view argues that Captain Benteen lost his initiative and obligation to obey Custer's "Come quickly . . ." order when he ran into a desperate Major Reno on the hilltop. Reno in effect ordered Benteen to remain there to help the stricken battalion and share his ammunition. The argument is predicated on an understanding that a subordinate is bound to obey the

latest order received, in this case from Reno (Rickey 1989:5). Detractors counter by suggesting that Benteen did not move out toward Custer as quickly as he might have after aiding Reno.

4. Dunn 1958:529–531.
5. E.g., du Bois 1986:100–118; Nichols 1984.
6. E.g., du Bois 1986:107–108.
7. E.g., Utley 1988a:188.
8. Wells 1987.
9. Wells 1987:84.
10. Wells 1989:11.
11. Ricker 1907:45.

Chapter 18. Strategy

1. G. A. Custer 1962:321–322.
2. Quoted in Ricker 1907:51.
3. E.g., Mrs. Spotted Horn Bull in Graham 1953:85.
4. Standing Bear in DeMallie 1984:185.
5. Mrs. Spotted Horn Bull in Graham 1953:86; Bighead in Marquis 1967:37.
6. For example, Mrs. Thunder Hawk seems to have tarried (Camp 1909). American Horse said "most" of the men went to meet Reno (Grinnell 1895a). Tall Bull said "all" (Grinnell 1898b). White Shield and Bobtail Horse were among the 10 who initially confronted the left wing at Medicine Tail ford. They went to their camp (Cheyenne) before rushing out to meet the wing. On arriving at camp, White Shield noticed that "all the men were gone" (Grinnell 1908b). Bobtail Horse said, "The men had rushed to meet Reno" (Grinnell 1908a).
7. Mrs. Spotted Horn Bull in Graham 1953:87.
8. Mrs. Spotted Horn Bull in Graham 1953:87.
9. Bighead, Wooden Leg in Marquis 1967:37, 1931:217; Mrs. Spotted Horn Bull, Gall in Graham 1953:85, 88, 92; Lights 1909; White Bull map in Vestal n.d.e:59.
10. Black Elk in DeMallie 1984:182.
11. Mrs. Thunder Hawk in Camp 1909. Mike Moore has recently calculated the noncombatant population at around 6,000 (Moore 1991).
12. Hoig 1976; see chapter epigraph.
13. He Dog in Hammer 1976:207.
14. Dixon 1973:181.
15. Quoted in Graham 1953:93.
16. Dixon 1973:181.
17. Standing Bear in Hammer 1976:215; Masters 1951:41. Masters learned details of Crazy Horse's delay—prayer, burnt offerings, and the anointment of earth from a prairie dog hill (see note 71, chapter 16).
18. Standing Bear in Hammer 1976:215; Burdick 1949:25.
19. E.g., Godfrey in Graham 1953:95–96; Ambrose 1975:440–442; Sandoz 1942:329.
20. Utley 1988a:190–191.
21. McCreight 1936:28–29; Hammer 1976:197, 199; Vestal n.d.d:140–142, n.d.e: 57–59.
22. Anonymous 1908:32.
23. Burdick 1949:25, 27.
24. Quoted in McCreight 1936:28.
25. E.g., Eastman in Graham 1953:97.
26. Cf. Hardorff 1985:43; Graham 1953:ix.
27. Wooden Leg account and map in Marquis 1931:252–253, 387; Two Moons in Anonymous 1908:30; Rain-in-the-Face map in Brady 1971:287; Red Hawk map in Ricker

1906a:86; Mrs. Spotted Horn Bull in Graham 1953:83; Respects Nothing account and map in Ricker 1906b:2–4; Soldier Wolf sketch in Grinnell 1897; Flying Hawk narrative and map in Ricker 1907:40–42; White Bird map in Tillett 1976:116–117; Standing Bear map in Ricker 1907:56.

The June 25 village consisted generally of spatially discrete camp circles, with the Cheyenne circle (consisting of various bands) at the northernmost end. Various Sioux bands occupied the other circles. Occupants relocated their village just downstream during the evening of June 25—after the Custer battle (Wooden Leg in Marquis 1931:252–253; Bighead in Marquis 1967:40). Wooden Leg explained that the move occurred, in accordance with custom, to avoid death lodges containing war casualties (Marquis 1931:252–253). Captain Freeman implied that the move provided access to new horse pasturage (Schneider 1977:64). Stanley Vestal also learned—from Sioux informants—of the relocation, allegedly made to avoid the stench of dead soldiers (Vestal 1932:173).

Wooden Leg's map locates the first (prebattle) and second villages. In the prebattle village, the Cheyenne circle is shown no farther than several hundred yards north (downstream) of the Medicine Tail Coulee mouth. Thomas Marquis, who lived with the Cheyenne and knew many of the Custer battle warriors (including Wooden Leg), specifically located the Cheyenne camp opposite the mouth of Medicine Tail Coulee (Marquis 1933; see also Kuhlman 1940:41).

Red Hawk's map (fig. 13-8) locates the Cheyenne circle (prebattle) in about the same position as Wooden Leg's. Grinnell, sketching from Soldier Wolf's testimony (fig. 18-1), put the Cheyenne camp (prebattle) directly across from the Medicine Tail ford (labeled "Dry Cr", see note 107). White Bird did not identify the Cheyenne camp, but like Red Hawk, he spotted the northern village limit (prebattle) just downstream from the mouth of Medicine Tail. Mrs. Spotted Horn Bull's crude sketch puts the northern village limit (prebattle) at the coulee mouth, although she incorrectly labels the Cheyenne encampment as "Minneconjoux." On her sketch, Custer Hill is badly misplaced (too near Medicine Tail Coulee; see also sketch in Buel 1883:594). Two Moons, standing on Custer Hill during an interview (ca. 1908), pointed to the south while indicating the prebattle Cheyenne camp. From this elevation, the mouth of Medicine Tail is only slightly east of south.

Traditional notions of village size have the encampment sprawled for miles down the valley. Surgeon Paulding provided an extreme example—a whopping eight miles long and two or three miles wide (Buecker 1982:42). On the other hand, Respects Nothing, through Eli Ricker, specifically stated, "The Indians were not camped on the Little Big Horn for a distance of five miles . . . [but] were camped on a mile square of land." His map (fig. 18-2) clearly shows this, putting the prebattle Cheyenne camp just upstream (south) from the Medicine Tail mouth (labeled "Water Rat" on the sketch, see note 107). Similarly, Flying Hawk recounted that "[t]he extreme length of the camps [village] was about one and a half miles." Like Respects Nothing's map, Standing Bear's sketch (fig. 18-3) depicts the northernmost portion of the prebattle village slightly upstream from the coulee mouth.

The Rain-in-the-Face sketch, although it does not show Medicine Tail Coulee, locates the entire village (prebattle) some distance south (upstream) of Calhoun Hill. So does Flying Hawk's crude sketch (without showing Medicine Tail Coulee, see fig. 18-4). Although accounts and sketches noted here do not precisely agree on the relationship between the northern village limit (prebattle) and Medicine Tail (where shown), they do (1) put the Cheyenne camp at or very near the Medicine Tail ford, and (2) demonstrate a much smaller village extent than traditionally thought. Thus, the entire battle on Custer Ridge occurred below (downstream from) the northern village limit (i.e., the Cheyenne camp).

28. Gall in Burdick 1949:27.
29. Quoted in Graham 1953:97.

30. Graham 1953:87.

31. Quoted in Burdick 1949:27.

32. Pvt. George Glenn (alias George W. Glease), a Reno fight survivor, mentioned a "Crazy Horse gully" on the Custer field. Today's Crazy Horse Ravine (no marble markers, indicating no deaths there) does not meet Glenn's description of "Crazy Horse gully"—in his words a "washout" that contained "bodies lying thick" (Hammer 1976:136). Glenn surely described Deep Ravine, which, of course, contained 28 dead ("bodies lying thick") near a heavily eroded headwall ("washout"). How Glenn arrived at this name is not recorded, but it is one more evidence associating Deep Ravine with Crazy Horse's route to Custer Ridge.

33. Misconceptions of Crazy Horse's route to Custer Ridge stem from overestimates of village size and extent. This error is not surprising, since the first whites on the scene saw the abandoned prebattle and postbattle villages as one, Captain Freeman excepted. Examining the village right after the fight, he noted, as Wooden Leg explained (see note 27), that the camp had been relocated (Schneider 1977:64; see also Gray 1976:353–354 on this issue). Look carefully at his sketch (fig. 11-5), and though not labeled, the two villages can be seen. The northern limit of the first is represented by five symbols forming a slight arc, these abreast of Medicine Tail Coulee (#6 on his sketch).

The northern limit of the second, or postbattle, village extended well downstream to near Clark's ford D, which is abreast of Custer Hill. This is the camp that inhabitants vacated on June 27. Freeman's astute observation aside, badly skewed estimates of village size and extent come from white chroniclers, not Indians, as note 27 illustrates. See figures 9-2, 11-2, and 11-3, three non-Indian sketches of the village. Indeed, the portion of figure 9-2 not shown here contains even more village. It appears this error arose innocently enough. At first, military eyewitnesses failed to differentiate between the two encampments. Later, some Indians just identified the general ground they had occupied those several days in June. Neither the interviewer nor the respondent thought to differentiate— hence, an inflated village. In the long run, however, gross overestimates of size provided one more neat excuse for defeat—that is, the larger the village, the more warriors.

So, conveniently, misconceptions about the village have been uncritically accepted for over a century. Given this thinking (or lack of it), Crazy Horse is made, on the basis of historical accounts describing his access from the Cheyenne camp, to cross at the north end of the inflated village limits. As I noted in the text, the gully informally known today as Crazy Horse Ravine meets a drainage that flows into Little Big Horn River in this vicinity. Thus, traditionally, Crazy Horse accessed Custer Ridge via the ravine named after him, sweeping well north of the battlefield (i.e., Cemetery Ridge) before entering it (see fig. 16-1).

There are too many "traditional route" adherents to list them all. But it appears that the idea started with General Godfrey (then a lieutenant), an influential early Custer battle theorist and, evidently, the original fatalist (Godfrey 1923:197–198). Mari Sandoz (one of Crazy Horse's biographers), for one, has been instrumental in perpetuating the error (Sandoz 1942).

Warriors did, by the way, circle to the north of Custer Ridge, but not early on, as the "sandwich" notion champions. Artifact finds north of the battlefield boundaries (see chapter 7) show that some Indians got there in time to harass the left wing after its return to Cemetery Ridge. Big Beaver was among the very late arrivals, getting to Custer Hill just in time to help overrun it. He left the village, evidently with some others, and went downriver to cross (where is not mentioned) before circling around to creep up the hill on its north side (Blummer n.d.).

Summing up, I have already made the argument for a gradual accumulation of Indians at the Custer field. That can be refined as follows. Warrior ingress from the Little Big Horn may be seen as sequential, proceeding as it did from south to north. Early arrivals, those following on the battalion's heels, so to speak, crossed at Medicine Tail (generally). Later arrivals, in order to get behind the right wing (between the wing and their families), filtered in from farther downstream, including Deep Ravine. Those arriving even later—in the presence of both wings—forded still farther downriver, then circled north of Custer Ridge (between the battalion and their families).

Of course, infiltrators did not progressively quit using upstream crossings. Nor did they all come from the river side. Still, this general sequence does show how warriors, arriving at different times, responded to an evolving strategic environment. Without this evolution—not seen because of collapsing time—the "northern horde" (Crazy Horse et al.) can be made to appear simultaneously (or nearly so) with the "southern horde" (Gall et al.). And then the construction becomes ever so simple. A beleaguered battalion is crushed from both directions after reaching Custer Ridge.

34. The three Oglalas reported to Gen. H. Scott. Scott's (1920) account suggests that Crazy Horse and his contingent crested Custer Ridge during right-wing disintegration (in the Keogh sector). But all other primary accounts indicate that Crazy Horse joined in this fighting from his position east of Custer Ridge (Flying Hawk in McCreight 1936:28; Eastman in Graham 1953:97; Gall in Burdick 1949:27; White Bull in Vestal n.d.d:139, 142, n.d.e:57; Foolish Elk in Hammer 1976:197, 199; Two Moons in Anonymous 1908:32). So evidently either the Oglalas or Scott collapsed time—probably Scott. He, like so many others, simply assumed that once the Indians drove the hapless battalion to Custer Ridge, they went right to work—in the fatalistic tradition. When we correct for this, the important point that emerges is that Crazy Horse and his band evidently approached their positions from west of Custer Ridge—the Deep Ravine area.

35. E.g., Eastman in Graham 1953:96. At this time, warriors were also leaving the river, creeping up gullies—including Medicine Tail Coulee—south of Deep Ravine. In effect, infiltration at this time did "sandwich" the right wing, but not the entire battalion (see note 33).

36. DeMallie 1984:190–191.

37. Today, access via the Deep Ravine mouth is difficult. Little Big Horn River hugs the bluffs here. Its channel has created a considerable precipice at the ravine mouth. Below, because of the bluffs, the river is not easily fordable. In 1883, the river channel coursed through the valley a bit west of the bluffs and the present ravine mouth (subsequently migrating east to its present position). Then (1883), and presumably in 1876, the topographic configuration of Deep Ravine at its mouth (an alluvial fan rather than a precipice) allowed convenient access. And, coursing through the valley, the river would have been more easily fordable then. See the John Blake map (dated 1883)—brought to my attention by Michael Donahue—on file in the Custer Battlefield National Monument archives; see also Weibert (1985:57), who argues for a suitable ford.

38. Stands in Timber and Liberty 1967:199; Rickey 1956; see also Hammer (1976: 250), where Lieutenant Roe reports a body found near the river which he misidentified as Mitch Bouyer (see Scott et al. 1989:79–83, and chapter 13 herein on Bouyer's repose in death).

39. E.g., Stands in Timber and Liberty 1967:199.

40. Rickey 1990.

41. Clark 1877.

42. Gibbon 1877:672.

43. Clark's 1877 map depicts what is evidently a well-used Indian trail at ford D (fig. 11-2, labeled simply as "Trail"). Quite likely, Indians regularly crossed at the ford when in this country.

44. My estimates place the northern edge of the prebattle June 25 village (the Cheyenne camp) about 1.5 miles above (south) of ford D.

45. Powell 1969:116.

46. Stands in Timber and Liberty 1967:199. Here Stands in Timber is clearly reasoning from hindsight.

47. E.g., Lights 1909; Two Eagles 1908; Lone Bear 1909; Wooden Leg in Graham 1953:104; Standing Bear in DeMallie 1984:185; Powell 1981:1011.

48. Flying Hawk (Ricker 1907:51) said that at Custer Hill, the soldiers were "right above the women who had collected down the river." Red Horse (1916:43) said that women and children ran downriver into a ravine.

49. Cf. Hardorff 1985:25, 43, but see p. 32. Even though the bulk of written Indian testimonies clearly describes helter-skelter flight, sketches (such as figs. 10-1, 11-2, 13-8, 18-3 and 18-4) depicting or suggesting a single sanctuary graphically show, at the least, that fugitives became the magnet that drew Custer's battalion ever northward (downriver). I am inclined to believe that the "lone haven" designations convey symbolic meaning and are not to be taken literally (although I do not doubt that some, even many, fugitives congregated in Squaw Creek).

50. Gall in Graham 1953:88.

51. Quoted in McCreight 1936:37. There are scores of accounts describing surprise, panic, and flight, just a few of which have been treated here. One speaker at the 1991 Little Big Horn Associates conference theorized that Indian leaders, knowing about Custer's column in the field, had met the previous evening (June 24) and designed a plan to ensnare the unsuspecting troopers. Then, perhaps three hours before the cavalry attack, the Indian noncombatants moved to places of safety, leaving an empty village (with the warriors hiding in timber). When Custer's cavalry showed up, the Indians sprang their ambush, which resulted in carnage on Custer Ridge.

There is simply nothing to this, or any of the various trap theories (see also note 23, chapter 3). Such notions betray a shallow grasp of the literature. Nonetheless, trap or ambush explanations, some of which are nearly as old as the battle, have served to naïvely account for defeat at the hands of "savages." How else could a "superior" force lose except by entrapment? Such proponents, usually Custer apologists, fail to think through the implications—a trained army led by an intrepid commander stumbling into a snare set by "primitives"? But then, maybe the Indian leaders were not so backward. An inane idea offered shortly after the Little Big Horn fight was that Sitting Bull had received training in the French military arts.

52. Hoig 1976:135, 142–143.

53. E.g., McLaughlin 1989:148.

54. Edgerly in Willert 1982:295; Graham 1953:290; Hammer 1976:101, 104.

55. Benteen in Nichols 1983:458–459.

56. Benteen in Nichols 1983:458.

57. Crazy Horse in Graham 1953:63.

58. E.g. Iron Thunder, Two Moons in Graham 1953:79, 102.

59. Crow King in W. W. Robinson n.d.:12; Walker 1966:102; see also Low Dog in Walker 1966:99–101.

60. Quoted in Graham 1953:94. In 1892, Gall and others told Doane Robinson (1929) of the chase after noncombatants but thought that Custer had mistaken them for "warriors in retreat."

61. E.g., Wallace in Koury 1968:17.

62. Varnum in Carroll 1982:64.

63. Graham 1953:263.

64. Nichols 1983:93.

65. Graham 1953:13.

66. E.g., Eastman in Graham 1953:96.

67. Reno in Overfield 1971:44; also Graham 1953:226. Reno recorded the order quoted here in his July 5, 1876, official report of happenings (the Overfield reference). He

reiterated the same order essentially verbatim during his court of inquiry, on both occasions adding that he remembered this as Custer's exact words (Nichols 1983:665; Utley 1972:417). Notice there is no mention of charging a village. This exclusion may bear on early knowledge about the disposition of Indians in the valley (hence Benteen's movements).

On the other hand, Reno talked about his orders more than once during his 1879 inquiry. Another time he included reference to the village: "charge *the village* afterwards" (Nichols 1983:645, emphasis mine; Utley 1972:401). Did the major here mix three years of hindsight with Custer's actual instructions? Is this a slip of the court recorder's pen? Whatever, it is definitely one more headache for the Custer battle detective. I incline toward an original order minus the village reference, though not without a migraine.

68. Reno in Overfield 1971:44; Wallace in Nichols 1983:23.

69. Overfield 1971:50.

70. Girard in Hammer 1976:321.

71. Carroll 1982:89.

72. Hammer 1976:231–232; Graham 1953:251.

73. Quoted in Graham 1953:228. One of the scouts, George Herendeen, stated that Custer himself told Reno, "Take the scouts, lead out, and I will be with you" (Graham 1953:263). Then later, it appears, Adjutant Cooke augmented that order with instructions on gait and to charge (see note 67 and corresponding text).

74. Graham 1953:228.

75. Hammer 1976:92; Graham 1953:249.

76. Martini in Hammer 1976:103, Graham 1953:289–290.

77. E.g., Martini in Graham 1953:290, Hammer 1976:100, Utley 1972:312.

78. E.g., Kanipe in Hammer 1976:92; various Crow scouts in Hammer 1976:177, 178; Dixon 1973:167; Libby 1973:159; Graham 1953:13, 23, 24.

79. E.g., Hammer 1976:106, 112, 133; Nichols 1983:171–172.

80. E.g., Gall in Burdick 1949:23.

81. E.g., various Indians in Graham 1953:77, 79, 84, 88; Marquis 1931:217, 1967:37; Grinnell 1956:336.

82. Hairy Moccasin, Curley in Graham 1953:19, 25.

83. Cf. Willert 1982:276; Crow King in Graham 1953:77.

84. The argument here, in basic form, is that if Custer knew of Reno's halt and skirmish line, he should not have continued north. This is another of many arguments proffered from retrospect. Odds are Custer did know of this development, for while joining Reno's line, Lieutenant Varnum could see Custer's soldiers on the bluffs (Nichols 1983:171–172). In any case, it is logical to assume that he knew. Custer got to the bluffs before Reno emerged. He or his officers could not have been ignorant of the size disparity and probably learned as much before Reno. The battalion, or elements of it, remained on the bluffs long enough to witness Reno's charge and halt. Surely, given the size disparity, Custer would have had someone tarry to view results—as it happened, warriors acting as rear guards to protect escapees. In this event, a charge brought up short of the village need not have caused undue alarm (except when viewed in retrospect).

85. Overfield 1971:44.

86. Hammer 1976:321; Graham 1953:251.

87. Girard in Hammer 1976:232.

88. Quoted in Hammer 1976:100.

89. E.g., Horned Horse in Finerty 1966:209; Joseph White Cow Bull in Miller 1971:33. The ford here is (or has been) variously known as the lower ford, ford B, Minneconjou ford, Medicine Tail ford, and middle ford. Lower ford and ford B designations are in reference to Reno's entrance to the Little Big Horn Valley at the mouth of Reno Creek (known as upper ford or ford A). As near as I can determine, the "middle

ford" term disappeared from Custer battle studies some 50 or 60 years ago. J. A. Blummer, for example, called the Medicine Tail crossing "middle ford" in a letter written ca. 1930 (Blummer 1930). The term is referenced to Reno's upper ford and a lower ford below (downstream from) the mouth of Medicine Tail (middle ford). Though rarely seen, this lower ford meant either one near the mouth of Deep Ravine or in Clark's ford D vicinity (about where Gibbon crossed). Its disappearance seems largely due to the power of fatalistic theories, which do not recognize any events (except for Indians fording Little Big Horn River) along the river below Medicine Tail ford.

90. Hardorff 1985:25; Moore 1987:18.

91. E.g., Two Eagles 1908.

92. E.g., the Sioux warriors Kill Eagle, Sitting Bull, and Gall in Graham 1953:55, 70, 88, 92. As for the Cheyenne, "When the Indians [warriors] rushed up to meet Reno, all the women and children gathered down at the lower village . . . [where they] . . . discovered more troops coming—this was Custer's party" (Soldier Wolf in Grinnell 1898a). Evidently, some Cheyenne noncombatants fled the village earlier, when Reno attacked (White Shield, Bobtail Horse in Grinnell 1908b ["people running to hills"], 1908a ["women were running out of camp"]). See also Mrs. Spotted Horn Bull in Buel 1883:595.

93. Kill Eagle in Graham 1953:55.

94. E.g., Crazy Horse in Graham 1953:63.

95. E.g., He Dog in Scott 1920.

96. Grinnell 1956:337–338.

97. Kill Eagle in Graham 1953:47.

98. He Dog in Scott 1920.

99. E.g., Sitting Bull in Graham 1953:70.

100. Curtis 1908:48. According to Curtis, soldiers looked from the eastside point of land adjacent to and north of the ford.

101. Marquis 1931:226–227; Graham 1953:105.

102. Camp 1910b.

103. Flying Hawk in Moore 1987:28, Hardorff 1985:30.

104. Two Eagles 1908; see also Camp 1908a:2.

105. Camp 1923.

106. Thompson n.d.b.,1909.

107. Thompson n.d.a. I have so far found the following alternate names referring to Medicine Tail Coulee—Muskrat Creek, Water Rat Creek, Green Grass Creek, Dry Creek, Medicine Tail Creek, and Reno Creek.

108. Thompson 1914:3. "i [sic] do not recall the names of any of the five Men that investigated the lone tepee all i can say that when they had reported there [sic] find instead of taking there place in the company they was sent to reconiter [sic] to the extream [sic] right of the marching colum [sic]."

109. E.g., Magnussen 1974:120.

110. Benteen in Overfield 1971:39. Lt. Francis Gibson led this detail.

111. Thompson n.d.b:3.

112. Pohanka 1990; see also Magnussen 1974:123. Some of Thompson's story is also in a 1923 letter from Camp to Godfrey. According to Camp, Thompson reported that the advance detail consisted of a sergeant and five men. The detail rode ahead as Custer's battalion ("the 5 companies") approached the river. The detail "cut a wide detour, over toward the east, along the high ridge that lies a half mile to one mile east [of Custer Ridge]" (Camp 1923; see also note 108).

Clearly, this is Camp's recollection of Thompson's story. The entire battalion did not approach the river, as Camp at the time believed. The size discrepancy (five or six men) is of little import; an advance party existed. A circuitous route to Calhoun Hill is not unreasonable. Nothing in Two Eagles's or Thompson's other account (quoted in text) discounts such a route. The highest point around, some 120 feet above Custer Ridge, is on a ridge one mile directly east of Calhoun Hill. A few Indians (the 50 or so, including Wolf Tooth, who first engaged the right wing) entered battle from this general area (Stands in Timber and Liberty 1967:198). Prudence would dictate a check here. Also, attaining the highest point seems logical if only to reconnoiter the exodus then under way in the valley. Seeing this, plus no threats to the distant east (nothing in the literature suggests otherwise, though later Indians did emerge here), the advance reasonably moved on to Calhoun Hill (nearer the valley and where Two Eagles saw it).

On the other hand, Camp or Thompson might have confused directions. Possibly the advance rode as directly as possible to Calhoun Hill—along Luce and Nye-Cartwright ridges. Luce Ridge, for example, is a mile from Custer Ridge, but southeast, not due east. Nye-Cartwright Ridge is also southeast, about a half mile beyond Custer Ridge. My representation in figure 16-1 reflects the circuitous route rather than the direct.

Finally, some primary accounts hint at a messenger who left Luce Ridge (my right wing), ostensibly riding north (e.g., Curley in Graham 1953:19). Some battle students think he carried news of a tense predicament to Terry, or at least definite word of the Indian location. No message of any type ever arrived. One researcher theorizes that the runner died on Rosebud Creek (Doran 1987). Assuming a messenger was sent (from either wing), we might consider that a courier carried information to (and maybe from) the F Company scouts (another possibility has always existed—dispatches between wings).

113. Thompson in Magnussen 1974:119; Thompson 1914:3.

114. Thompson in Magnussen 1974:119.

115. Magnussen 1974:120. For Thompson's account, see also Brown and Willard 1924:132–214.

116. I talked earlier (note 135, chapter 13) about Gray's "counterclockwise" hypothesis. The idea, of course, is a fatalistic solution. But in light of all I have proposed, and since he and I agree on some basics, it is instructive to see how his hypothesis is derived. Also, Gray's is the latest example of an offense maintained up to Custer Ridge but, because of circumstances engendered by an untimely deterioration in Reno's unit, not beyond. He uses a time-motion analysis figured to the half minute.

Gray suggests that while on the high bluffs, the command learned of Reno's retirement to the trees (or could anticipate it forthwith). But contrary to my claim that this did not unduly heighten concern (see note 84), Gray states that such knowledge in fact did cause alarm. Principals in Custer's force knew that the major could hold out, but not for long. So no time could be wasted. The battalion went into upper Medicine Tail Coulee, perfect for the attack because it led to the village center. But while there, Custer received word of Reno's rout from the timber. The index of criticality rose sharply (an astonishing 21 minutes now pass before Custer's first engagement in Medicine Tail).

Urged by this ominous development, Yates's outfit (like mine, Companies E and F) set out for the mouth of Medicine Tail in a "feint" to draw warriors from Reno. This might give the major time to regroup and join with Benteen (earlier recalled in expectations of a "hard fight" requiring "all the ammunition available"—the dire circumstances reading). Together, Reno and Benteen could provide "backup for a stronger attack." (Actually, neither Reno nor Benteen had any idea of the other's whereabouts or orders until the two met quite by accident; we remember they got together but forget it was fortuitous.)

The demonstration at Medicine Tail ford, according to Gray, was exactly that (not a charge turned back) for several reasons: (1) two companies would not be sent alone to the attack; (2) Yates first met meek resistance there; and (3) there is no trail of carnage from ford to battlefield (three more basic points of agreement). Meanwhile, the rest of the command (C, I, and L) deployed on Luce Ridge (agreed), there to await the ammunition and reinforcements (Reno, Benteen, packtrain) should some or all show up that soon.

Expecting all this, the battalion bought time to "enable [the] full regiment to deliver a decisive attack" from somewhere downriver (north of Medicine Tail Coulee) where "less opposition" could be expected.

After Yates's mock threat (successful in the sense that warriors later appear quickly enough to force a calculated but futile counterclockwise motion), all five of Custer's companies vacated Medicine Tail by choice (another agreement). The reunion would have to take place farther downriver (which, of course, never came, as Gray knows, hence his clock analogy). Then the whole regiment—not just five companies—could cross the Little Big Horn below (north of) the village (Gray uses an inflated village—his counterclockwise denouement comes just short of its northern limit), charge back up (south and upstream) the flat floodplain into the village, and capture the women and children there plus destroy all their belongings (Gray 1991:346ff.).

And so we have come to the error in all this, the same one repeatedly made no matter what the twist—an obsession with the Indian encampment. Aside from the observation that Gray's proposed full-regiment charge from the north leaves his village-bound inhabitants a southern getaway, that fixation (noncombatants frozen in an inflated village) effectively blinds people to the many, many accounts of villagers' reactions to Reno's surprise assault and Custer's equally unanticipated appearance in Medicine Tail. For most fatalists, an enemy horde foiled a village attack across Medicine Tail ford. For Gray, fatalistic ingredients for a thwarted thrust there are lacking. An assault did not take place from Medicine Tail because less opposition could be expected downriver. (Although I do not see it explicitly stated, Gray's "less opposition" presumably derives from a feint designed to attract warriors who could at least be expected soon.) Hence the "buy time" move farther north, a move that could also result in consolidation and a much needed stronger command.

However, there was no feint from Medicine Tail Coulee, merely an implementation of the nonattack option. Noncombatant flight from a "deflated" village brought Custer's column out of this all-too-seductive drainage and beyond to the north. (The "feint to consolidate" theory is not at all new. Charles Kuhlman used it 40 years ago [Kuhlman 1951:161–164, 171].)

117. Readers may wish to consult Urwin's (1990) work on Custer's Civil War career; the general's prowess is here painted in scenes of military dash, intrepidity, and daring—plus victory after victory.

Chapter 19. The Whereabouts of Custer

1. Quoted in Hunt and Hunt 1947:110.

2. By "practical objections," I mean that hostage capture would have required fording the river and giving chase. That would have further distanced the two wings, already widely separated. Furthermore, fugitives in general surely knew of the left wing even if warriors now arriving did not. Also, flight by now must have carried refugees away from the wing (just like in Medicine Tail). So it is not as if potential captives were in the wing's back pocket. There is also no reason to expect a village egress entirely devoid of protection, and the left wing was a paltry force of only 80 or so. Ultimately prudence, especially in light of favorable expectations, becomes the watchword.

3. Thompson n.d.b.

4. Quoted in Graham 1953:228.

5. Scott et al. 1989:116–117.

6. During the Reno inquiry, Lieutenant Maguire reported finding, on Custer Hill, a peculiar brass shell, which he and others thought came from Custer's sidearm (Nichols 1983:9). Archaeology work turned up none of these brass shells—reportedly used in his Royal Irish Constabulary pistols (Scott et al. 1989:116). J. S. du Mont quotes a manuscript at Yale University (notes for "With Custer on the Little Big Horn," by W. O. Taylor, no

date given), in which Sgt. John M. Ryan states he found four or five brass cases under the general's body. Custer had used these, thought Ryan, in his Remington (du Mont 1974:67). In 1923, Ryan wrote that he had discovered "five or six shells" beneath the corpse, but he made no reference to metallic composition or the Remington firearm (Ryan 1923).

7. Reno quoted by Martini in Hammer 1976:101. Elsewhere, Martini said that an "excited" Reno "requested [Benteen] to halt his command," in the process exclaiming, "Well I have lost about half of my men, and I could do no better than I have done" (Hammer 1976:105).

Chapter 20. Conclusions
1. Taylor 1948:33.
2. See Schuyler (1978) for an overview of the formative years.
3. Harrington 1978:4.
4. Deetz 1988b.
5. Deetz 1988b:16.
6. Deetz 1988b:18, 20.
7. Young 1988:11.
8. Cf. Scott et al. 1989.
9. Young 1988:11.
10. Rathje and Hughes 1975:163.
11. Utley 1962:114.
12. Kuhlman 1951.
13. Deetz 1988b:19.
14. Utley 1973, 1984.
15. Rickey 1963.
16. Keegan 1978:119.
17. E.g., that espoused by Marshall 1978:82.

REFERENCES CITED

AGO
  1877   AGO General Order 13, February 16, 1876. In *Index of General Orders, Adjutant General's Office, 1876*. Washington, D.C.: Government Printing Office.

Allen, W. A.
  1903   *Adventures with Indians and Game; or, Twenty Years in the Rocky Mountains*. Chicago: A. W. Bowen and Co.

Ambrose, S. E.
  1975   *Crazy Horse and Custer: The Parallel Lives of Two American Warriors*. New York: Doubleday and Company.

Anders, F. L.
  1939   Critical Notes on the Line of March of Troops Serving in the Department of Dakota in the Campaign against Hostile Sioux, 1876. Unpublished MS, Collection of Manuscripts, Frank Anders Papers, A73 Box 1, State Historical Society of North Dakota, Bismarck.
  1952   Letter, Frank Anders to E. A. Brininstool, November 7, 1952. Frank L. Anders Papers, OGL #43-5-1, Elwyn B. Robinson Special Collections, Chester Fritz Library, University of North Dakota, Grand Forks.

Anonymous
  n.d.   Two Moon Rode a White Horse That Day. News article (no source) on an account given to R. Throssel in clipping scrapbook titled "Custer" (p. 222), Montana Room, Parmly Library, Billings, Mont.
  1875   Untitled article. *Army and Navy Journal* 13(13):200–201 (October 31).
  1876a   The Carbine in Reno's Fight. *Army and Navy Journal* 14(2):26 (August 19).
  1876b   Cavalry Reorganization. *Army and Navy Journal* 14(17):264–265 (December 2).
  1876c   Disaster to General Custer's Command. *Army and Navy Journal* 13(48):772 (July 8).
  1876d   Editorial commentary. *Army and Navy Journal* 13(50):805 (July 22).
  1876e   How to Fight Indians. *Army and Navy Journal* 14(1):6 (August 12).
  1876f   Massacred. *Bismarck Tribune*, July 6 Extra.
  1876g   Regulars and Frontiersmen. *Army and Navy Journal* 14(1):8–9 (August 12).
  1876h   Sioux Indian Campaign: General Crook's Battle of the Rosebud. *Army and Navy Journal* 13(50):801–802 (July 22).
  1876i   Untitled article. *Army and Navy Journal* 14(3):41 (August 26).
  1876j   Untitled article. *Army and Navy Journal* 14(5):73 (September 8).
  1876k   Untitled editorial. *Army and Navy Journal* 13(42):757 (July 1).
  1877   *Index of General Orders, Adjutant General's Office, 1876*. Washington, D.C.: Government Printing Office.

1889   Pathological Section Report #12938, Catalog #1001064, Armed Forces Institute of Pathology, Walter Reed Hospital, Washington, D.C.

1908   How the Black, the Gray, and the Red Horse Men Died. *Harness Gazette* 27(6):30–32.

Barry, D. F.
1916   The Custer Battle. *The Teepee Book* 2(6):65–67.

Bates, C. F.
n.d.   *Custer's Indian Battles*. Fort Collins, Colo.: Old Army Press.

Baynes, J.
1967   *Morale: A Study of Men and Courage*. New York: Praeger Publishing.

Beaumont, R. A., and W. P. Snyder
1980   Combat Effectiveness: Paradigms and Paradoxes. In *Combat Effectiveness: Cohesion, Stress, and the Volunteer Military,* ed. S. C. Sarkesian, 20–56. Beverly Hills, Calif.: Sage Publications.

Benham, D. J.
1914   The Sioux Warrior's Revenge: A Reminiscence of the Custer Massacre. *The Canadian Magazine* 43:455–463.

Berwald, F.
n.d.   Statement of Frank Berwald. Walter Camp Collection, Box 6, Folder 12, Brigham Young University, Provo, Utah.

Blummer, J. A.
n.d.   Untitled manuscript. Custer Battlefield National Monument Research Files (A123 C5188x), Crow Agency, Mont.

1930   Undated letter (ca. 1930) by J. A. Blummer probably to R. G. Cartwright. R. G. Cartwright Collection, Hearst Library, Lead, S.D.

Bourke, J. G.
1877   J. G. Bourke's Diary, Volume 21, July 21, 1877, Entry. West Point Military Academy Library, West Point, N.Y.

Bradley, J. H.
1876   Custer's Death. *Helena Daily Herald,* July 25.

Brady, C. T.
1971   *Indian Fights and Fighters*. Lincoln: University of Nebraska Press.

Brininstool, E. A.
1952   *Troopers with Custer: Historic Incidents of the Battle of the Little Big Horn*. Lincoln: Bison Books, University of Nebraska Press.

Brown, D.
1971   *The Fetterman Massacre*. Lincoln: University of Nebraska Press.

Brown, J. B., and A. M. Willard
1924   *The Black Hills Trails: History of the Struggles of the Pioneers in the Winning of the Black Hills*. Rapid City, S.D.: Rapid City Journal.

Brust, J.
1991   Fouch Photo May Be the First. *Greasy Grass* 7:2–10.

Buecker, T. R.
1982   A Surgeon at the Little Big Horn. *Montana: The Magazine of Western History* 32(4):34–49.
1990   Personal communication, February 21.
1991   Lt. Clark's Sioux War Report and Map of the Little Bighorn Battle. *Greasy Grass* 7:11–21.

Buel, J. W.
1883   *Heroes of the Plains*. St. Louis: Historical Publishing Company.

Burdick, U. L.
1929   *The Last Battle of the Sioux Nation*. Stevens Point, Wis.: Worzalla Publishing Company.
1936   *Tragedy in the Great Sioux Camp*. Baltimore: Proof Press.
1949   *David F. Barry's Indian Notes on the Custer Battle*. Baltimore: Wirth
(ed.)   Brothers.

Camp, W. M.
n.d.a   Notes. Walter Camp Collection, Box 4, Folder 2, Brigham Young University, Provo, Utah.
n.d.b   Notes. Walter Camp Collection, Box 6, Folder 8, BYU-217, Brigham Young University, Provo, Utah.
n.d.c   Notes. Walter Camp Collection, Box 7, Folder 5, Brigham Young University, Provo, Utah.
n.d.d   Two Moon's Story of the Custer Fight Given to Throssel in 1907. Walter Camp Collection, Box 6, Folder 9, Field Notes Folder 105, Brigham Young University, Provo, Utah.
1908a   Letter, Walter Camp to C. A. Woodruff, December 10, 1908. Walter Camp Collection, A312 C11776, Custer Battlefield National Monument Research Files, Crow Agency, Mont.
1908b   Letter, Walter Camp to Daniel Kanipe, November 17, 1908. Walter Camp Collection, A312 C1320, Custer Battlefield National Monument Research Files, Crow Agency, Mont.
1909   Statement of Thunder Hawk's Squaw, June 1909. Walter Camp Collection, A312 C11402, Custer Battlefield National Monument Research Files, Crow Agency, Mont.
1910a   Letter, Walter Camp to C. A. Woodruff, April 28, 1910. Walter Camp Collection, A312 C11796, Custer Battlefield National Monument Research Files, Crow Agency, Mont.
1910b   Letter, Walter Camp to C. A. Woodruff, March 3, 1910. Walter Camp Collection, A312 C11792, Custer Battlefield National Monument Research Files, Crow Agency, Mont.
1918   Interview with Little Wolf (Red Bird), August 26, 1918. Hammer Collection, Box 3, Folder 1, Lilly Library, Indiana University, Bloomington.
1923   Letter, Walter Camp to E. S. Godfrey, May 28, 1923. Edward Settle Godfrey Papers, Letterbook IV, Library of Congress, Washington, D.C.

Carrington, M. I.
1983   *Absaraka: Home of the Crows*. Lincoln: University of Nebraska Press.

Carroll, J. M.
n.d.   The Lieutenant Maguire Maps. Unpublished MS in possession of the author.
1974   *The Benteen-Goldin Letters on Custer and His Last Battle*. Mattituck, N.Y.:
(ed.)   J. M. Carroll and Company.
1975   *Custer in Periodicals: A Bibliographic Checklist*. Fort Collins, Colo.: Old
         Army Press.
1979   Who Was This Man Ricker and What Are His Tablets That Everyone Is Talking
         About? Bryan, Tex.: Privately Published.
1980   Varnum—The Last of Custer's Lieutenants by Colonel T. M. Coughlan.
         Unpublished MS in possession of author.
1982   *Custer's Chief of Scouts: The Reminiscences of Charles A. Varnum*. Lincoln:
         University of Nebraska Press.

Cartwright, R. G.
1949   Letter, R. G. Cartwright to F. L. Anders, March 20, 1949. Frank L. Anders
         Papers, OGL #43-5-8, Elwyn B. Robinson Special Collections, Chester Fritz
         Library, University of North Dakota, Grand Forks.

Chappell, G.
1972   The Search for the Well-Dressed Soldier. *Arizona Historical Society Museum
         Monograph* 5.

Clark, W. P.
1876   Memo of a Voyage from Benson's Landing on the Yellowstone, 27 Miles from
         Fort Ellis, to the Mouth of the Powder River. W. P. Clark Diary, Small
         Collections #538, Montana Historical Society Archives, Helena.
1877   Official Report dated September 14, 1877: Clark to AGO, Department of the
         Platte. Record Group 393, Document #4601 1877, Department of Platte,
         Letters Received. National Archives, Washington, D.C.

Coughlan, T. M.
1934   The Battle of the Little Big Horn: A Tactical Study. *The Cavalry Journal*
         42:13–21 (January-February).

Curtis, E. S.
1908   *The North American Indian* (vol. 3). New York: Johnson Reprint Corporation.

Custer, E. B.
1923   Preface to Custer's Last Battle. *Historical Society of Montana Contributions*
         9:142–143.

Custer, G. A.
1962   *My Life on the Plains*. Secaucles, N.J.: Citadel Press.

Darling, R.
1990   *A Sad and Terrible Blunder—Generals Terry and Custer at the Little Big Horn:
         New Discoveries*. Vienna, Va.: Potomac-Western Press.

Deetz, J.
1988a   American Historical Archaeology: Methods and Results. *Science* 239:
         362–367.
1988b   Historical and Archaeological Theory: Walter Taylor Revisited. *American
         Antiquity* 53:13–22.

Deland, C.
   1931′ The Sioux Wars. *South Dakota Historical Collections* 15.

Delbruck, H.
   1980 *Within the Framework of Political History, the Germans: History of the Art of War* (vol. 1). Westport, Conn.: Greenwood Press.
   1985 *The Dawn of Modern Warfare: History of the Art of War* (vol. 4). Translated by W. J. Renfroe, Jr. Lincoln: University of Nebraska Press.

DeMallie, R. J. (ed.)
   1984 *The Sixth Grandfather: Black Elk's Teachings Given to John G. Neihardt.* Lincoln: University of Nebraska Press.

DeVoto, A. L.
   1917 Letter to W. C. Camp, July 24, 1917. Walter Camp Collection, A312 C11336, Custer Battlefield National Monument Research Files, Crow Agency, Mont.

Dixon, J. K.
   1973 *The Vanishing Race: The Last Great Indian Council.* Glorieta, N.M.: Rio Grande Press.

Dollard, J.
   1943 *Fear in Battle.* New Haven, Conn.: Institute of Human Relations.

Doran, R. E.
   1987 The Man Who Got to the Rosebud. Papers of the *Custer Battlefield Historical and Museum Association Symposium*, June 26, pp. 19–33, Custer Battlefield Historical and Museum Association, Crow Agency, Mont.

du Bois, C. G.
   1986 *The Custer Mystery.* El Segundo, Calif.: Upton and Sons.

du Mont, J. S.
   1974 *Custer Battle Guns.* Ft. Collins, Colo.: Old Army Press.

Dunn, J. P., Jr.
   1958 *Massacre of the Mountains: A History of the Indian Wars of the Far West, 1815–1875.* New York: Archer House.

du Picq, A.
   1946 *Battle Studies.* Harrisburg, Penn.: Military Service Publishing Company.

Dustin, F.
   1987 *The Custer Tragedy.* El Segundo, Calif.: Upton and Sons.

Dutton, C. E.
   1877 Report to the Chief of Ordnance, January 14, Record Group 156, National Archives, Washington, D.C.

Dyer, G.
   1985 *War.* New York: Crown Publishers.

Eastman, C. A.
1916   Rain-in-the-Face: The Story of a Sioux Warrior. *The Teepee Book* 2(6):31–32, 99–101.

Edgerly, W. S.
n.d.   Edgerly interview with Walter Camp. Walter Camp Collection, Box 5, Folder 1, Brigham Young University, Provo, Utah.

Ferguson, L. G.
1977   An Archaeological-Historical Analysis of Fort Watson: December 1780–April 1781. In *Research Strategies in Historical Archaeology,* ed. Stanley South, 41–71. New York: Academic Press.

Finerty, J. F.
1966   *War-Path and Bivouac: The Big Horn and Yellowstone Expedition.* Lincoln: Bison Books, University of Nebraska Press.

Fish, C. R.
1978   Relation of Archaeology and History. In *Historical Archaeology: A Guide to Substantive and Theoretical Contributions,* ed. Robert L. Schuyler, 8–10. Farmingdale, N.Y.: Baywood Publishing Company.

Fiske, F. B.
1917   *The Taming of the Sioux.* Bismarck, N.D.: Bismarck Tribune.

Flat Iron
n.d.   Last Chief in Bloody Battle. Unattributed newspaper clipping, Battle of the Little Big Horn, Vertical File #3, Montana Historical Society Library, Helena.

Fox, R. A., Jr.
1984   Suggestions for Archaeological Investigations at Custer Battlefield National Monument. Unpublished MS on file, Custer Battlefield National Monument, Crow Agency, Mont.

Fraser, G. M.
1982   *Flashman and the Redskins.* London: Pan Books.

Frost, L. A.
1976   *General Custer's Libbie.* Seattle: Superior Publishing Company.

Fuller, E. B.
1916   Recollections of an Old Cavalryman. *U.S. Cavalry Journal,* 413–433 (January).

Gabriel, R. A.
1987   *No More Heroes: Madness and Psychiatry in War.* New York: Hill and Wang.

Gibbon, J.
1877   Hunting Sitting Bull. *American Catholic Quarterly* 2:665–694.
1879   Arms to Fight Indians. *United Service Review* 1(2):237–244.

Godfrey, E. S.
1876   Edward S. Godfrey Diary, Part 1. William J. Ghent Papers, Box 24, Folder 9, Library of Congress, Washington, D.C.

1879   E. S. Godfrey Lecture at West Point, February 4 and 11, 1882: Taken from 1879 Drafts Concerning the Little Big Horn Campaign. Edward S. Godfrey Papers, Box 5 (Lectures and Writing File), Library of Congress, Washington, D.C.

1896   Cavalry Fire Discipline. *Journal of the Military Service Institution* 19(83): 252–259.

1923   Custer's Last Battle. *Historical Society of Montana Contributions* 9:144–225.

1927   Copy of Letter, E. S. Godfrey to R. A. Burnside, January 10. Frank L. Anders Papers, OGL #43-5-2, Elwyn B. Robinson Special Collections, Chester Fritz Library, University of North Dakota, Grand Forks.

Gould, R. A.
1980   *Living Archaeology*. Cambridge: Cambridge University Press.

1983   The Archaeology of War: Wrecks of the Spanish Armada and the Battle of Britain, 1940. In *Shipwreck Anthropology,* ed. Richard A. Gould, 105–142. Albuquerque: University of New Mexico Press.

Gould, S. J.
1991   *Bully for Brontosaurus*. New York: W. W. Norton and Company.

Graham, W. A.
1926   *The Story of the Little Big Horn: Custer's Last Fight*. New York: Bonanza Books.

1953   *The Custer Myth: A Source Book of Custeriana*. New York: Bonanza Books.

Gray, J. S.
1976   *Centennial Campaign: The Sioux War of 1876*. Fort Collins, Colo.: Old Army Press.

1991   *Custer's Last Campaign: Mitch Boyer and the Little Big Horn Reconstructed*. Lincoln: University of Nebraska Press.

Greene, J. A.
1973   *Evidence and the Custer Enigma*. Golden, Colo.: Outbooks.

1982   *Slim Buttes, 1876: An Episode of the Great Sioux War*. Norman: University of Oklahoma Press.

1986   *Evidence and the Custer Enigma* (updated version). Golden, Colo.: Outbooks.

Grill, "M.T.L."
1928   Little Knife, Uncapapa Sioux Who Fought Custer, Had His Own Version of Little Big Horn Battle. News article (no source, penciled in date of October 12) in clipping scrapbook titled "Custer" (p. 121), Montana Room, Parmly Library, Billings, Mont.

Grinnell, G. B.
1895a   Grinnell's Cheyenne Notes (1895); American Horse as to the Custer Fight. George Bird Grinnell Collection, Ms. #5, Folder 497, Braun Research Library, Southwest Museum, Los Angeles, Calif.

1895b   White Bull as to the Custer Fight, August 16. George Bird Grinnell Field Notebook #325, Braun Research Library, Southwest Museum, Los Angeles, Calif.

1897   Soldier Wolf as to Custer Fight, October 7. George Bird Grinnell Field Notebook #326, Braun Research Library, Southwest Museum, Los Angeles, Calif.

1898a   Grinnell's Cheyenne Notes (1898); Soldier Wolf, as to the Custer Fight. George Bird Grinnell Collection, Ms. #5, Folder 497, Braun Research Library, Southwest Museum, Los Angeles, Calif.

1898b   Grinnell's Cheyenne Notes (1898); Tall Bull, as to the Custer Fight. George Bird Grinnell Collection, Ms. #5, Folder 497, Braun Research Library, Southwest Museum, Los Angeles, Calif.

1908a   Bobtail Horse and Calf, September 27. George Bird Grinnell Collection, 1908–1909 Field Notebook, Braun Research Library, Southwest Museum, Los Angeles, Calif.

1908b   White Shield Custer, September 23. George Bird Grinnell Collection, 1908–1909 Field Notebook, Braun Research Library, Southwest Museum, Los Angeles, Calif.

1908c   Young Two Moon Custer Fight, September 16. George Bird Grinnell Collection, 1908 Field Notebook, Braun Research Library, Southwest Museum, Los Angeles, Calif.

1956   *The Fighting Cheyennes*. Norman: University of Oklahoma Press.

Hackett, C. F.
1916   Along the Upper Missouri in the '70s. *South Dakota Historical Collections* 8:27–55.

Hammer, K.
n.d.   Camp Manuscript, Transcripts of Articles and Field Notes of Walter M. Camp. MS on file, Lilly Library, Indiana University, Bloomington.

1971   *The Springfield Carbine on the Western Frontier*. Fort Collins, Colo.: Old Army Press.

1972   *Men with Custer: Biographies of the 7th Cavalry, 25 June 1876*. Fort Collins, Colo.: Old Army Press.

1976   *Custer in '76: Walter Camp's Notes on the Custer Fight*. Provo, Utah:
(ed.)   Brigham Young University Press.

Hardorff, R. G.
1985   *Markers, Artifacts, and Indian Testimony: Preliminary Findings on the Custer Battle*. Short Hills, N.J.: Don Horn Publications.

1989   *The Custer Battle Casualties*. El Segundo, Calif.: Upton and Sons.

1991   *Lakota Recollections of the Custer Fight: New Sources of Indian-Military History*. Spokane: Arthur H. Clark Company.

Harrington, J. C.
1978   Archaeology as an Auxiliary Science to American History. In *Historical Archaeology: A Guide to Substantive and Theoretical Contributions*, ed. Robert L. Schuyler, 3–7. Farmingdale, N.Y.: Baywood Publishing Company.

Hatcher, J., F. J. Jury, and J. Weller
1977   *Firearms Investigation, Identification, and Evidence*. Harrisburg, Penn.: Stackpole Books.

Hauser, W. L.
1980   The Will to Fight. In *Combat Effectiveness: Cohesion, Stress, and the Volunteer Military*, ed. S. C. Sarkesian, 186–211. Beverly Hills, Calif.: Sage Publications.

Haynes, C. V.
1985   Personal communication, May.

Hedren, P. L.
1973   Carbine Extractor Failure at the Little Big Horn. *Military Collector and Historian* 25(22):66–68.
1988   Cartridge Extraction Problems at the Little Big Horn: Bloody Fact or Flimsy Excuse? *Greasy Grass* 4:14–16.
1991   *The Great Sioux War, 1876–77*. Helena: Montana Historical Society Press.
(ed.)

Hofling, C. K.
1981   *Custer and the Little Big Horn: A Psychobiographical Inquiry*. Detroit: Wayne State University Press.

Hoig, S.
1976   *The Battle of the Washita*. Lincoln: University of Nebraska Press.

Hollow Horn Bear
1909   Statement of Hollow Horn Bear, June. Walter Camp Collection, A312 C11732, Custer Battlefield National Monument Research Files, Crow Agency, Mont.

Hubbard, E.
1974   The Custer Battle. *The Teepee Book* 1:106–122. In two volumes compiled and edited by J. M. Carroll. New York: Sol Lewis. (Reprinted from the original June 1915 *Teepee Book* 1[6], Herbert Coffeen, editor.)

Hunt, F., and R. Hunt
1947   *I Fought with Custer: The Story of Sergeant Windolph*. New York: Charles Scribner's Sons.

Huntington, F. C.
1959   Indian Survivor Doubted That Rain-in-the-Face Killed Custer. *Montana: The Magazine of Western History* 9(4):49.

Hurt, W. R., and W. E. Lass
1956   *Frontier Photographer: Stanley J. Morrow's Dakota Years*. Lincoln: University of South Dakota and University of Nebraska Press.

Kanipe, D.
1908   Letter, Kanipe to Walter Camp, August 4. Walter Camp Collection, Box 1, Folder 2, Brigham Young University, Provo, Utah.

Karl, D.
1990   *Glorious Defiance: Last Stands throughout History*. New York: Paragon Books.

Keegan, J.
1978   *The Face of Battle*. Guildford: Biddles.

Keegan, J., and R. Holmes
1985   *Soldiers*. London: Hannah Hamilton.

Keller, D.
1988   Myths of the Little Big Horn. Papers of the *Custer Battlefield Historical and Museum Association Symposium,* June 24, pp. 42–51, Custer Battlefield Historical and Museum Association, Crow Agency, Mont.

Kill Eagle
1876   Statement of Kill Eagle. Untitled article. *Army and Navy Journal* 14(10):149 (October 14).

King, W. K.
1981   Tombstones for Bluecoats: New Insights into the Custer Mystery. Unpublished MS (Cust 16901) on file, Custer Battlefield National Monument Research Files, Crow Agency, Mont.

Koury, M. J.
1968   *Diaries of the Little Big Horn.* Bellevue, Nebr.: Old Army Press.
1970   *Gibbon on the Sioux Campaign of 1876.* Bellevue, Nebr.: Old Army Press.
(ed.)

Kuhlman, C.
1940   *Custer and the Gall Saga.* Bellevue, Nebr.: Old Army Press.
1951   *Legend into History.* Harrisburg, Penn.: Old Army Press.

Langellier, K., H. Cox, and B. C. Pohanka (eds.)
1991   *Myles Keogh: The Life and Legend of an Irish Dragoon in the Seventh Cavalry.* El Segundo, Calif.: Upton and Sons.

Lewy, G.
1980   The American Experience in Vietnam. In *Combat Effectiveness: Cohesion, Stress, and the Volunteer Military,* ed. S. C. Sarkesian, 94–106. Beverly Hills, Calif.: Sage Publications.

Libby, O. G.
1973   *The Arikara Narrative of the Campaign against the Hostile Dakotas, June, 1876.* New York: Sol Lewis.

Liddic, B. R. (ed.)
1979   *I Buried Custer: The Diary of Pvt. Thomas W. Coleman, 7th U.S. Cavalry.* College Station, Tex.: Creative Publishing Company.

Lights
1909   Statement of Lights, Spring 1909. Walter Camp Collection, A312 C11735, Custer Battlefield National Monument Research Files, Crow Agency, Mont.

Little Buck Elk
1876   Statement of Little Buck Elk. Untitled article. *Army and Navy Journal* 14 (11):165 (October 21).

Lone Bear
1909   Statement of Lone Bear, January. Walter Camp Collection, A312 C11737, Custer Battlefield National Monument Research Files, Crow Agency, Mont.

Luce, E. S.
1943   Letter from Luce to Col. E. L. Nye, October 11. Research Correspondence File (1943), Custer Battlefield National Monument Research Files, Crow Agency, Mont.

McChristian, D. C.
1981   *An Army of Marksmen.* Ft. Collins, Colo.: Old Army Press.

McClernand, E. J.
1927   With the Indians and the Buffalo in Montana. *The Cavalry Journal* 36:7–54.
1969   *On Time for Disaster: The Rescue of Custer's Command.* Lincoln: University of Nebraska Press.

McCreight, M. I.
1936   *Chief Flying Hawk's Tales.* New York: Alliance Press.
1947   *Firewater and Forked Tongues: A Sioux Chief Interprets U.S. History.* Pasadena, Calif.: Trails End Publishing Company.

McDermott, J. D.
1978   *Forlorn Hope.* Boise: Idaho State Historical Society.

McLaughlin, J.
1989   *My Friend the Indian.* Lincoln: Bison Books, University of Nebraska Press.

MacMillan, T. B.
1876   Newspaper article. *Chicago Inter-Ocean,* June 24.

McMurray, K.
1991   Custer's Fateful Last Stand Still Cloaked in Mystery. *Northwest [Airlines] Compass Readings Magazine* 22(10):96–100.

MacNeil, R.
1987   The Indians Were Asleep in Their Tepees. *Research Review: The Journal of the Little Big Horn Associates,* n.s. 1(2):13–15, 22.

Magnussen, D. O.
1974   *Peter Thompson's Narrative of the Little Big Horn Campaign.* Glendale, Calif.: Arthur H. Clark Company.

Maguire, E.
1876a   Letter, Maguire to General A. A. Humphreys, July 2. In Tombstones for Bluecoats: New Insights into the Custer Mystery, by W. Kent King, 150–157. Unpublished MS on file, Custer Battlefield National Monument Research Files, Crow Agency, Mont.
1876b   Letter, Maguire to General A. A. Humphreys, July 10. In Tombstones for Bluecoats: New Insights into the Custer Mystery, by W. Kent King, 159–169. Unpublished MS on file, Custer Battlefield National Monument Research Files, Crow Agency, Mont.

Manion, J.
1984   Custer's Cooks and Maids. In *Custer and His Times: Book Two,* ed. J. M. Carroll, Jay Smith, and Nancy Allen, 151–206. Fort Worth, Tex.: Little Big Horn Associates.

Marquis, T. B.
1928   *Memoirs of a White Crow Indian (Thomas H. LeForge)*. Lincoln: University of Nebraska Press.
1931   *Wooden Leg: A Warrior Who Fought Custer*. Lincoln: University of Nebraska Press.
1933   Godfrey's Story Still Ranks as Best Account of Custer's Last Stand. *Billings Gazette,* August 13.
1967   *Custer on the Little Bighorn*. Lodi, Calif.: Dr. Marquis Custer Publications.
1975   *Custer, Cavalry, and Crows*. Fort Collins, Colo.: Old Army Press.
1976   *Keep the Last Bullet for Yourself: The True Story of Custer's Last Stand*. Algonac, Mich.: Reference Publications.

Marshall, S.L.A.
1972   *The Crimsoned Prairie*. New York: Charles Scribner's Sons.
1978   *Men against Fire*. Gloucester, Mass.: Peter Smith.

Masters, J. G.
1951   *Shadows Fall across the Little Horn: Custer's Last Stand*. Laramie: University of Wyoming Library.

Michaelis, O. E.
1876   Report to the Chief of Ordnance, October 3. Record Group 156, National Archives, Washington, D.C.

Miles, J. D.
1876   Typescript of Letter, Miles to Wm. Nicholson, Superintendent of Indian Affairs, Lawrence, Kansas, August 4. Walter S. Campbell Collection, Box 111, #5, Western History Collections, University of Oklahoma, Norman.

Miles, N. A.
1969   *Personal Recollections and Observations of General Nelson A. Miles*. New York: DeCapo Press.

Miller, D. H.
1957   *Custer's Fall: The Indian Side of the Story*. Lincoln: University of Nebraska Press.
1971   Echoes of the Little Bighorn. *American Heritage* 22(4):28–39.

Milligan, E. A.
1972   *High Noon on the Greasy Grass: The Story of the Little Bighorn by Indians Who Were There*. Bottineau, N.D.: Bottineau Courant Press.

Monaghan, J.
1959   *Custer: The Life of General George Armstrong Custer*. Lincoln: University of Nebraska Press.

Moore, M. B.
1987   It Was a Day of Bravery: Eyewitness Accounts of the Custer Fight. Unpublished MS in possession of the author.
1988   M. B. Moore to Richard A. Fox, March 29. Letter in possession of the author.
1989   Personal written communication to Richard A. Fox, undated. Materials in possession of the author.
1991   Personal communication, May 22.

Moore, M. B., and M. Donahue
1991   I Go with Custer and Will Be at the Death. *Greasy Grass* 7:22–32.

Neihardt, J. G.
1961   *Black Elk Speaks, Being the Life Story of a Holy Man of the Oglala Sioux.* Lincoln: University of Nebraska Press.

Nelson, C. L.
1969   The Custer Battalion at the Little Bighorn. Unpublished History Honors Thesis, Concordia College, Moorhead, Minn.

Nichols, R. H.
1983   *Reno Court of Inquiry.* Costa Mesa, Calif.: Privately published (in three
(ed.)   volumes; third volume publication date is 1984).
1984   Custer, the Final Hours: The Chronological Sequence of Events at the Battle of the Little Big Horn. Unpublished MS in possession of the author.

Noël Hume, I.
1969   *Historical Archaeology.* New York: Alfred A. Knopf.

Overfield, L. J.
1971   *The Little Big Horn, 1876: The Official Communications, Documents, and Reports.* Lincoln: University of Nebraska Press.

Pohanka, B.
n.d.   B. Pohanka to Richard A. Fox, Jr. Letter in possession of the author.
1988   B. Pohanka to Richard A. Fox, Jr., October 17. Letter in possession of the author.
1990   B. Pohanka to Richard A. Fox, Jr., August 27. Letter in possession of the author.

Post Returns
1877   Post Returns, Fort Robinson, April 1874–December 1884. Record Group 501, Roll 10, Microcopy 1028, Roll 617, National Archives, Washington, D.C.

Powell, P. J.
1969   *Sweet Medicine.* Norman: University of Oklahoma Press.
1981   *People of the Sacred Mountain: A History of the Northern Cheyenne Chiefs and Warrior Societies, 1830–1879, with an Epilogue, 1969–1974.* San Francisco: Harper and Row.

Quinn, J. G.
1876   Letter, Jonathan Quinn to Mrs. Maria Dreper, November 27. John S. Ogden Collection, ACC #331, Custer Battlefield National Monument Research Files, Crow Agency, Mont.

Rathje, W. L., and W. W. Hughes
1975   The Garbage Project as a Non-Reactive Approach: Garbage in . . . Garbage Out? In *Perspectives on Attitude Assessment: Surveys and Their Alternatives,* ed. H. W. Sinaiko and L. A. Broedling, 151–167. Washington, D.C.: Manpower Research and Advisory Services, Smithsonian Institution.

Red Horse
1916   The Battle on the Little Big Horn. *Teepee Book* 2(6):41–46.

Repass, C.
1985   *Custer for President*. Fort Collins, Colo.: Old Army Press.

Ricker, E. S.
1906a   Interview with Nick Buleau [Red Hawk's testimony], November 20. Ricker Collection, Series 2, Box 6, Reel 5, Tablet 29, Nebraska State Historical Society, Lincoln.
1906b   Interview with Respects Nothing, November 9. Ricker Collection, Series 2, Box 6, Reel 5, Tablet 29, Nebraska State Historical Society, Lincoln.
1906/   Interview with Iron Hawk, May 12, 1906 or 1907. Ricker Collection, Series 2,
1907   Box 6, Reel 5, Tablet 25, Nebraska State Historical Society, Lincoln.
1907   Interviews with Flying Hawk, March 8, and Standing Bear, March 12. Ricker Collection, Series 2, Box 5, Reel 3, Tablet 13, Nebraska State Historical Society, Lincoln.

Rickey, D.
1956   Interview with John Stands in Timber, August 8. Unpublished interview on file with Don Rickey and with author.
1963   *Forty Miles a Day on Beans and Hay: The Enlisted Soldier Fighting the Indian Wars*. Norman: University of Oklahoma Press.
1989   Letter plus notes and comments, D. Rickey to Richard A. Fox, Jr., April 27.
1990   Letter and map, D. Rickey to Richard A. Fox, Jr., February 24.

Robinson, D.
1929   Letter, Doane Robinson to Joe Eastwood, August 14. Doane Robinson Papers, Folder 27, 3359-B, South Dakota Historical Society, Pierre.

Robinson, W. W.
n.d.   Recollections of General W. W. Robinson, Jr., on Indian Prisoners of War. Unpublished MS, Walter Camp Collection, A312 C11937, Custer Battlefield National Monument Research Files, Crow Agency, Mont.

Roe, C. F.
1927   General Roe's Narrative. In *Custer's Last Battle,* ed. Robert Bruce, 8–18. New York: National Highway Association.

Rooney, J. M.
n.d.   Letter, J. M. Rooney to Walter Camp. Walter Camp Collection, BYU-195, Box 6, Folder 6, Brigham Young University, Provo, Utah.
1909   Letter, J. M. Rooney to Walter Camp, July 19. Walter Camp Collection, Box 7, Folder 5, Brigham Young University, Provo, Utah.

Ruehl, F. R.
1987   Indians Didn't Kill Custer's Men. *National Enquirer,* December 29.

Ryan, J. M.
1923   One of Custer's Sergeants Tells Story of Reno's Part in Fight on Little Big Horn. *Hardin (Mont.) Tribune,* June 22 (Supplement). (Also *Billings Gazette,* June 25, by same title.)

Sandoz, M.
   1942   *Crazy Horse: The Strange Man of the Oglalas*. Lincoln: University of Nebraska Press.

Schneider, G. A. (ed.)
   1977   *The Freeman Journal: The Infantry in the Sioux Campaign of 1876*. San Rafael, Calif.: Presidio Press.

Schuyler, R. L. (ed.)
   1978   *Historical Archaeology: A Guide to Substantive and Theoretical Contributions*. Farmingdale, N.Y.: Baywood Publishing Company.

Scott, D. D., and R. A. Fox, Jr.
   1987   *Archaeological Insights into the Custer Battle: An Assessment of the 1984 Field Season*. Norman: University of Oklahoma Press.

Scott, D. D., R. A. Fox, Jr., M. A. Connor, and D. Harmon
   1989   *Archaeological Perspectives on the Battle of the Little Bighorn*. Norman: University of Oklahoma Press.

Scott, H.
   1920   Interview with He Dog, Red Feather, and Whirling. Scott Collection, #4525, Box 4—Indian Wars, Smithsonian Institution, Washington, D.C.

Sills, J.
   1988   Were There Two Last Stands? Papers of the *Custer Battlefield Historical and Museum Association Symposium,* June 24, pp. 13–21, Custer Battlefield Historical and Museum Association, Crow Agency, Mont.

South, S.
   1977   *Method and Theory in Historical Archaeology*. New York: Academic Press.

Spencer, J. D.
   1983   George Armstrong Custer and the Battle of the Little Bighorn: Homicide or Mass Suicide? *Journal of Forensic Sciences* 28(3):756–761.

Stands in Timber, J., and M. Liberty
   1967   *Cheyenne Memories*. Lincoln: University of Nebraska Press.

Stewart, E. I.
   1952   The Reno Court of Inquiry. *The Montana Magazine of History* 2 (3):31–43.
   1954   I Rode with Custer. *Montana Magazine of History* 4(3):17–29.
   1955   *Custer's Luck*. Norman: University of Oklahoma Press.

Stewart, E. I., and J. R. Stewart (eds.)
   1957   *The Field Diary of Lt. Edward Settle Godfrey*. Portland, Oreg.: Champoeg Press.

Sweet, O. J.
1890   Official Report of O. J. Sweet. Non-Accession File (Burial and Re-burial Folder), Custer Battlefield National Monument Research Files, Crow Agency, Mont.
1912   Letter, O. J. Sweet to Walter Camp, November 24. Walter Camp Collection, A312 C11329, Custer Battlefield National Monument Research Files, Crow Agency, Mont.

Taunton, F. B.
1977   *"Sufficient Reason?": An Examination of Terry's Celebrated Order to Custer*. London: English Westerners' Special Publication No. 5, English Westerners' Society.
1986   *Custer's Field: A Scene of Sickening, Ghastly Horror*. London: Johnson-Taunton Military Press.

Taylor, W. O.
1948   *The Study of Archaeology*. Carbondale: Southern Illinois University Press.

Thomas, W. K.
1904   The Personal Story of Rain-in-the-Face. In *Indian Fights and Fighters*, by Cyrus Townsend Brady, 279–292. Lincoln: University of Nebraska Press.

Thompson, P.
n.d.a   Questionnaire, Walter Camp to P. Thompson. Hammer Collection, Box 2, Folder 9, Brigham Young University, Provo, Utah.
n.d.b   Questionnaire, Walter Camp to P. Thompson. Walter Camp Collection, A312 C11391, Custer Battlefield National Monument Research Files, Crow Agency, Mont.
1909   Letter, P. Thompson to Walter Camp, January 4. Walter Camp Collection, A312 C12470, Custer Battlefield National Monument Research Files, Crow Agency, Mont.
1914   Letter, P. Thompson to Walter Camp, March 16. Walter Camp Collection, A312 C12483, Custer Battlefield National Monument Research Files, Crow Agency, Mont.

Thralls, J. M.
1925   The Sioux War. *Kansas State Historical Collections* 16(1923–1925):573–576.

Tillett, L.
1976   *Wind on the Buffalo Grass*. New York: Thomas Y. Cromwell Company.

Two Eagles
1908   Statement of Two Eagles, December. Walter Camp Collection, A312 C11738, Custer Battlefield National Monument Research Files, Crow Agency, Mont.

Upton, E.
1874   *Cavalry Tactics, United States Army*. New York: D. Appleton and Company.

Upton, R.
1973   *Fort Custer on the Big Horn, 1877–1898*. Glendale, Calif.: Arthur H. Clark Company.

Urwin, G.J.W.
1990   *Custer Victorious: The Civil War Battles of General George Armstrong Custer.*
        Lincoln: University of Nebraska Press.

Utley, R. M.
1962   *Custer and the Great Controversy: The Origin and Development of a Legend.*
        Los Angeles: Westernlore Press.
1969   *Custer Battlefield National Monument, Montana.* Washington, D.C.: National
        Park Service.
1972   *The Reno Court of Inquiry: The Chicago Times Account.* Fort Collins, Colo.:
(ed.)   Old Army Press.
1973   *Frontier Regulars: The United States Army and the Indian, 1866–1891.*
        Lincoln: University of Nebraska Press.
1984   *The Indian Frontier of the American West, 1846–1890.* Albuquerque: Univer-
        sity of New Mexico Press.
1988a   *Cavalier in Buckskin.* Norman: University of Oklahoma Press.
1988b   *Custer Battlefield.* Washington, D.C.: Official National Park Handbook 132,
        National Park Service.

Van de Water, F. F.
1934   *Glory Hunter: A Life of General Custer.* Lincoln: University of Nebraska
        Press.

Vansina, J.
1985   *Oral Tradition as History.* Madison: University of Wisconsin Press.

Vaughn, J. W.
1961   The Mark Kellogg Story. *The Westerner/New York Posse Brand Book* 8(4):
        73–91.

Vestal, S. [Walter Stanley Campbell]
n.d.a   Interview with Mrs. One Bull. Walter S. Campbell Collection, Box 105,
        Notebook 41, Western History Collections, University of Oklahoma, Norman.
n.d.b   Interview with Two Moons. Walter S. Campbell Collection, Box 105,
        Notebook 15, Western History Collections, University of Oklahoma,
        Norman.
n.d.c   Interview with Waukutemonie; Interview with Moving Robe. Walter S.
        Campbell Collection, Box 111, Notebook 5, Western History Collections,
        University of Oklahoma, Norman.
n.d.d   Interview with White Bull. Walter S. Campbell Collection, Box 105,
        Notebook 23, Western History Collections, University of Oklahoma,
        Norman.
n.d.e   Interview with White Bull. Walter S. Campbell Collection, Box 105,
        Notebook 24, Western History Collections, University of Oklahoma,
        Norman.
n.d.f   Interview with Young Eagle. Walter S. Campbell Collection, Box 105,
        Notebook 32, Western History Collections, University of Oklahoma,
        Norman.
1932   *Sitting Bull: Champion of the Sioux.* Boston: Houghton Mifflin Company.
1957   The Man Who Killed Custer. *American Heritage* 8(2):5–9, 90–91.
1984   *Warpath: The True Story of the Fighting Sioux Told in a Biography of Chief
        White Bull.* Lincoln: Bison Books, University of Nebraska Press.

Wagner, G. D.
1973   *Old Neutriment*. New York: Sol Lewis.

Walker, J. E.
1966   *Campaigns of General Custer*. New York: Promontory Press.

Weibert, H.
1985   *Sixty-six Years in Custer's Shadow*. Billings, Mont.: Bannack Publishing Company.

Welch, A. B.
1915   Fort Abraham Lincoln Review. Unpublished MS, Welch Papers, Manuscript Collections #20602, State Historical Society of North Dakota, Bismarck.

Weller, J.
1966   *Weapons and Tactics: Hastings to Berlin*. London: Nicholas Vane.

Wells, W.
1987   Custer's Arrival Time at the River. Papers of the *Custer Battlefield Historical and Museum Association Symposium*, June 26, pp. 76–87, Custer Battlefield Historical and Museum Association, Crow Agency, Mont.
1988   The Fight on Calhoun Hill. Papers of the *Custer Battlefield Historical and Museum Association Symposium*, June 24, pp. 22–34, Custer Battlefield Historical and Museum Association, Crow Agency, Mont.
1989   Little Big Horn Notes: Stanley Vestal's Indian Insights. *Greasy Grass* 5:9–19.

Wertenbaker, T. J.
1954   The Archaeology of Colonial Williamsburg. In *Annual Report of the Smithsonian Institution for 1953*, pp. 447–454. Washington, D.C.: Government Printing Office.

Wesbrook, S. D.
1980   The Potential for Military Disintegration. In *Combat Effectiveness: Cohesion, Stress, and the Volunteer Military*, ed. S. C. Sarkesian, 244–278. Beverly Hills, Calif.: Sage Publications.

Willert, J.
1982   *Little Big Horn Diary: Chronicles of the 1876 Indian War*. La Mirada, Calif.: James Willert Publisher.

Young, T. C., Jr.
1988   Since Herodotus, Has History Been a Valid Concept? *American Antiquity* 53:7–12.

INDEX

Agincourt, battle of, 49
Allen, Dr. W. A., battlefield
    inspection of, 218, 250
American Horse: accounts of,
    366n.118, 371n.6; on last
    fighting, 216, 360n.115
Archaeography: as applied to
    Custer battle, 329–330;
    complements history,
    328; conditions needed
    in battlefield studies,
    338–339; and Custer
    mission objective, 333–
    334; in demonstrating
    limitations of fatalistic
    themes, 332; examples
    of, 329; future areas of
    study, 339–340; and his-
    torical documents versus
    artifacts, 334–336. *See
    also* Archaeology
Archaeology: contribution to
    history, 326–327; funda-
    mental tenet of, 5; goals
    of, 327–328. *See also*
    Archaeography
Army and Navy Journal edi-
    torials, 237, 238, 249

Baldwin, Capt. Frank, 353n.44
Barry, D. F., 164, 182; on du-
    ration of battle, 362n.4;
    photo by, 353n.44
Battalions, U.S. Army, 42–45.
    See also Custer battalion
Battlefield, definition of, 6
Battlefield archaeology: in
    analyzing battles, 9; in
    combat modeling, 10,
    94; contextual relation-
    ships in, 9, 39, 325; fire-
    arm analysis in, 53–58;
    on fire behavior, disin-
    tegration, 60–61; on

flow of battle, 59; In-
    dian material remains in,
    21; links oral and written
    accounts, 137–38; and
    prefatory causes, 229;
    prior studies using, 3–4;
    in providing, temporal,
    spatial, behavioral frame-
    work, 12; site taphonomy
    and, 127–29; and sta-
    bility/disintegration
    model, 39–40. *See also*
    Methodology
Beard, Dewey, accounts of,
    171, 287
Bear Lying Down, account
    of, 211
Benteen, Capt. Frederick:
    attempt to join Custer,
    29; battalion of, 296,
    305, 306, 312; as bat-
    talion commander, 25;
    and burials, 156–57; on
    cartridge cases, 158;
    criticizes Custer, 255;
    culpability of, in fatal-
    istic versions, 289; in
    1876 campaign, 25–30;
    on fatigue, 368n.46; on
    Indian strength, 255;
    orders of, 25, 307, 308,
    317; on panic, 229,
    363n.16; with Reno in
    hilltop fight, 28, 322,
    380n.7; scout to left of,
    25, 306–308
Bethune, Frank, on gray
    horses at Ford B,
    345n.21
Big Beaver, accounts of, 202,
    216, 356n.55, 359n.114,
    360n.116
Big Foot, in Cheyenne tradi-
    tion, 175

Bighead, Kate: accounts of,
    136, 147, 158, 199, 285,
    286; on C Company
    charge, 149–151; on
    infiltration, 147–148,
    199–200, 285; on Lame
    White Man assault,
    153–154
Black Hills (S.Dak., Wyo.),
    1874 7th Cavalry expe-
    dition to, 23–24
Black Kettle, 297
Bloody Knife: account of,
    233; death of, 269
Blummer, J. A., 359n.114,
    377n.89
Bobtail Horse, 189; at Ford
    B, 281, 369nn.29, 49;
    on village exodus,
    377n.92
Bourke, Lt. John, accounts
    of, 170, 213, 218
Bouyer, Mitch (scout): body
    of, 219; report to Custer,
    233
Bradley, Lt. James, finds Kel-
    logg, 180
Brave Wolf: accounts of, 142,
    167; on Ford B fighting,
    284
Bunching behavior, 47–49;
    in archaeology, 59;
    concept of, 47–49
Burdick, Usher, referencing
    left wing on Cemetery
    Ridge, 352n.20

Calf, at Ford B, 281
Calhoun, Lt. James: body of,
    145; as company com-
    mander, 141
Calhoun Coulee, location/
    topography of, 95
Calhoun Coulee episode,